Developing Citizens

A Comprehensive Introduction to Effective Citizenship Education in the Secondary School

Edited by **Tony Breslin** and **Barry Dufour**

Hodder Murray

www.hoddereducation.co.uk

Tony Breslin would like to dedicate this book to his fiancée, Ann Bowen, for her unflinching love, encouragement and toleration.

Barry Dufour would like to dedicate this book to his teenage son, Ben Fleming–Dufour, already developing as a good citizen.

Together, we would like to thank Terry Farrell and Denis Lawton for being inspirational coaches and mentors over many years.

Leading figures at the Citizenship Foundation and in the Association for Citizenship Teaching and the Association for the Teaching of the Social Sciences are among contributors to this text. The editors commend to readers the work of these organisations in their support for Citizenship Education and the broader social curriculum.

A proportion of the royalties from the sales of this book are being donated to the Citizenship Foundation so that they might continue their outstanding and groundbreaking work in this field.

The Publishers would like to thank the following for permission to reproduce copyright material: **pp. 134-141** © pfeg; **pp. 161, 162, 163, 164, 165, 166, 181, 182, 335, 336** Crown Copyright material is reproduced with permission of the controller of HMSO; **p. 337** *Teaching Citizenship* with permission of The Association for Citizenship Teaching (ACT); **p. 269** Healthy Schools Programme.

Orders: please contact Bookpoint Ltd, 130 Milton Park, Abingdon, Oxon OX14 4SB. Telephone: (44) 01235 827720. Fax: (44) 01235 400454. Lines are open 9.00–5.00, Monday to Saturday, with a 24-hour message answering service. Visit our website at www.hoddereducation.co.uk

First published in 2006 by
Hodder Murray, an imprint of Hodder Education,
a member of the Hodder Headline Group
338 Euston Road
London NW1 3BH

Impression number	6 5 4 3 2 1
Year	2010 2009 2008 2007 2006

Cover photos (front) © Tom Merton/Photodisc Red/Getty Images; (back) © Royalty-Free/Corbis
Typeset in 11 pt Perpetua by Phoenix Photosetting, Chatham, Kent
Printed in Malta

A catalogue record for this title is available from the British Library

ISBN-10: 0 340 92682 1
ISBN-13: 978 0340 926 826

ACKNOWLEDGEMENTS

We would like to thank all of the contributors to this book for their chapters and forbearance as it has developed and changed over a period of years. We hope that, overall, the final product does justice to their endeavours. We also thank those who have commented on plans and drafts or offered us advice along what has been a long but rewarding journey and the many friends from beyond our professional worlds who have both remained our inspiration and kept us "grounded".

We would also like to thank the many schools, colleges and organisations that have allowed us to include examples of their practice. The support and encouragement that we have received from our publishers Hodder Murray has been exceptional. We are especially grateful to Phillip Walters, Hodder Education's Managing Director, who saw the potential of our project and gave it his personal attention and to Jane Tyler, Victoria Taylor and Kate Harrison for their patient editing.

The trustees, staff and associates of the Citizenship Foundation, many of whom are contributors to this volume, deserve our sincere thanks for their co-operation and inspiration. Other organisations that have provided enthusiastic support include the Association for Citizenship Teaching (ACT) and the Association for the Teaching of the Social Sciences (ATSS) as have various members of the initial teacher trainers' network for Citizenship Education, citizED.

As well as his colleagues at the Foundation, Tony would like to thank those who have worked with him previously at Enfield School Improvement Service, at The School of St. David and St. Katharine in Haringey and at Langleybury School in Hertfordshire as well as the many students that he has worked with in both schools and at Weald College in Harrow. Special thanks are due to Terry Farrell, Ken Johnson, Mike Moores and Dave Wallace for "teaching him the ropes" as a teacher and to Denis Lawton and Paddy Walsh, the most inspiring and tolerant doctoral tutors in the business. He will now get on with the thesis!

Barry would like to thank those at Oxfam who assisted in the research for his chapters and his good friend and conscience, Doug Holly, for his invaluable support over background material and for generally being a sympathetic ear. Barry would also like to register his appreciation for the support and friendship he has experienced from the staff and his students at the School of Education at the University of Leicester, from the School of Sport and Exercise Sciences at Loughborough University and from colleagues and students in the Humanities Faculty at De Montfort University, Leicester. Finally, he'd like to thank KRCS Apple Centre in Leicester for their technical support.

Without support from all of the above, our task would have been more difficult and less rewarding.

Tony Breslin and Barry Dufour

CONTENTS

PART THREE
FOUNDATIONS FOR CITIZENSHIP
THE SOCIAL AND BUSINESS SCIENCES

PART FOUR
FOUNDATIONS FOR CITIZENSHIP
TECHNOLOGY, SCIENCE AND MATHEMATICS

PART FIVE
OBJECTIVES FOR CITIZENSHIP
CROSS-CURRICULAR THEMES, DIMENSIONS AND SKILLS

ENDORSEMENTS

The report that led to the citizenship order said: "We aim at no less than a change in the political culture of this country both nationally and locally: for people to think of themselves as active citizens, willing, able and equipped to have an influence in public life . . ." The challenge is being taken up. This book is a unique compendium of information and ideas that teachers will find of great help in this far from easy but overwhelmingly important task of education. This book will also tell members of the public what it is all about.

Professor Sir Bernard Crick
Formerly adviser on Citizenship to the DfEE and, subsequently, to the Home Office

This book gives an interesting outline of the historical development of the key themes within Citizenship and is bold enough to make predictions about future developments too. In doing so, it offers a valuable discussion of ethical issues and provokes a good deal of reflection. There is much for the experienced teacher of Citizenship, as well as those new to the area.

John Barter
Assistant Headteacher, Wrenn School and Executive Member, Association for the Teaching of the Social Sciences

Developing Citizens *arrives at a critical point in the evolution of the subject in schools. After a somewhat difficult gestation period, Citizenship is now beginning to gain credibility as a subject in its own right and as a key aspect in addressing community cohesion and engaging young people with the political system. In order for this upward curve to continue the rigor of the subject must be underpinned. This tome addresses this need, providing a series of papers that bring home to one and all the vitality of the subject and its critical nature. As a partner text to the recently published CPD Handbook,* Making Sense of Citizenship, *both for teachers and as a reader for those contemplating a PGCE in Citizenship or the CPD Certificate, there can be no better companion.*

Chris Waller
Professional Officer, Association for Citizenship Teaching

FOREWORD

I want to welcome and commend this book for painting a canvas of such breadth and depth. It deals equally comfortably with the history of Citizenship Education as with the current issues and tensions, such as the relationship between Citizenship in the curriculum and the whole school dimension. It brings together practitioners and thinkers from a whole variety of disciplines and backgrounds to address all the main questions and challenges in an honest and straightforward way.

Amongst many other topics, it considers problems like the shortage of trained, skilled teachers and how, realistically, to deliver Citizenship through other subjects. It examines the importance of the contribution of effective leadership and management to the implementation of a successful Citizenship policy, both within a school and in the school's relationship with the wider community. It is also brave enough to look at likely future developments and make recommendations.

I feel sure this book will be welcomed by a broad range of teachers, Citizenship coordinators, and advisers from inside and outside the formal education sector, looking as it does at the implications of Citizenship Education for the wider social education of young people. It puts the rationale for Citizenship Education firmly at the heart of the purpose of education as a whole, in its commitment to fostering critical thinking and questioning, whilst not losing sight of the greater need for inclusivity in a healthy, democratic society. Altogether, *Developing Citizens* represents an invaluable addition to the fund of knowledge and wisdom around Citizenship Education.

Jan Newton
Adviser on Citizenship Education to the Minister of State
Department for Education and Skills
London
March 2006

PREFACE

In 1973, Barry Dufour and I published *The New Social Studies: A Handbook for Teachers*. It was essentially a practical set of ideas and materials for teachers, although behind the practical suggestions lurked quite a lot of theory. We wrote it because we were both actively involved in the teaching of the kind of Social Studies that combined Humanities and Social Sciences. At that time there was no book available to help young teachers find their way through several complex and overlapping subjects and areas. Many teachers assured us that they found the book extremely useful but it has long been out of date and out of print. However, Tony Breslin and Barry Dufour have now produced an even better volume that takes as its focus the new Foundation Subject in the National Curriculum – Citizenship.

As someone who has been teaching and studying education policy for many years, I have no doubt in stating that Citizenship Education is the most important educational innovation in the last 50 years. One problem is, however, that we will need many more enthusiastic teachers to implement the new curriculum in a way that will excite young people. The advantage of this book is that the editors are too wise and experienced to try to provide one single curriculum blueprint for Citizenship Education. Instead, they offer a variety of curricular strategies that can be adapted to suit the strengths of particular schools and teachers. There is no one solution, but there is one prerequisite: a willingness to change or develop the ethos of the school in ways that will emphasise participation and involvement by the pupils themselves. This may be a tremendous challenge, but it can only be assisted by the approaches set out in this book.

With that goal in mind, the two editors, who share a perfect blend of practical experience and theoretical knowledge, have gathered together an excellent team of writers with a very wide range of expertise and from various subjects and perspectives. From what this team offers, any school should be able to plan its own school-based Citizenship curriculum, meeting all the requirements of the National Curriculum whilst designing a unique programme based on their own team of teachers and the particular characteristics of the school and its community. For the first time ever, it will be possible to design a worthwhile curriculum to answer the needs of young people growing up not only in an increasingly complex industrial democracy, but also in a world where problems of globalisation, poverty and environmental pollution are enormous.

This opportunity has been made possible by the introduction of Citizenship as a *compulsory* subject of the National Curriculum in secondary schools. But as both the editors emphasise in different ways, Citizenship Education is not just *another* subject, it has to be a different *kind* of subject.

The task is great, but this book will certainly help to provide many answers without limiting the creativity of teachers and pupils.

Professor Denis Lawton
Emeritus Professor of Education
Institute of Education, University of London,
May 2006

INTRODUCTION

The purpose of this book

The title of this book, *Developing Citizens*, is intended to be interpreted in two ways: *developing* as an adjective, describing school students who are growing and learning as citizens and who are *already* citizens under various laws and agreements, not least the United Nations Convention on the Rights of the Child. And *developing* as a verb, referring to the *active* responsibility of the school to enable, encourage and educate school students in Citizenship. Our book addresses both of these aspects making a clear case for the rights and responsibilities that school students do or should have conferred on them, while exploring how their Citizenship awareness can be developed by a plethora of strategies and approaches to teaching and learning across the curriculum and the broader school, outlined in these pages by more than 30 of the UK's leading specialists on Citizenship Education.

These specialists are teachers, academics, advisers and policy-makers, each commenting on a particular curriculum area or aspect of schooling, with the aim of exploring the best possible educational practices and opportunities provided by the landmark arrival of Citizenship as a National Curriculum subject. The contributors offer their expertise in illustrating how, for example, a Geographer, Religious Education teacher or Functional Skills specialist might contribute to a discrete Citizenship programme, a Citizenship-focused event, a Citizenship-related curriculum development, or a Citizenship team or department. Our claim – their claim – is not that English or History or Mathematics or Work-Related Learning or PSHE can do it all. The book is not a battle between the participants trying to 'claim' Citizenship for their subject; this is no time for a turf war over curriculum time and territory. Rather, we have asked our contributors to share what their expertise can bring to Citizenship's table, whatever the curriculum and pastoral structures in a given school.

Nor are we advocating a conventional cross-curricular model, the sort that often follows an audit in which most of the boxes are ticked but nobody has ownership of the final map. Rather, our contributors demonstrate, with concrete examples, how their subjects or aspects can be 'carriers' for the delivery or enhancement of particular elements of the Citizenship Programmes of Study. Indeed, we favour this notion of selecting a limited number of 'strong' or 'supporting' *carrier subjects*, probably aligned to a *core* Citizenship course, instead of a vague 'everywhere but nowhere' approach to cross-curricularity, as a framework for coherent, explicitly branded, whole school Citizenship Education.

The rise of Citizenship

Although we have always been enthusiastic and optimistic advocates of social education, the arrival of Citizenship, in the school curriculum and beyond, has sparked greater interest than either of us expected. Much of this is owed to the influence of Sir Bernard Crick and his colleagues and to organisations such as the Citizenship Foundation in their tireless lobbying for a wider political education in our schools as well as the leadership of particular politicians, notably David Blunkett as both Secretary of State for Education and Home Secretary, who have done much to sponsor Citizenship's rise. Indeed, commissioning Crick and his committee had been one of Blunkett's first acts after the election of the Labour government in 1997. But there is a broader, quasi-global dynamic at work. Whether the focus is on the lack of political interest apparently shown by the electorates of the mature democracies of the west, the needs of Citizenship educators in the emergent or pre-democracies of central and eastern Europe, the Middle East and parts of Africa, the issues of Citizenship as a status for asylum seekers and refugees and, indeed, for other immigrants or the broader swathe of social exclusion that sweeps the inner cities and rural outlands of the affluent world, Citizenship and Education *for* Citizenship are never far from the debate. And if Citizenship is not the term, then civic renewal, regeneration, participation or inclusion is. We accept and respect the academic distinctions between these concepts but we ought to acknowledge that these are shared agendas with different emphases, all with pertinence to the Citizenship classroom and beyond.

In this context, the recent interest in Citizenship and in Citizenship Education is long overdue. So often marginalised at the edges of tutor time or in under-resourced PHSE programmes or as Key Stage 4 options or in the friendly 'ghetto' of the A level sixth form curriculum, we believe that the subjects, themes and objectives of the social curriculum are centrally what school is about: preparing young people to be active, *effective*, informed citizens with all the skills and understandings that this involves: literacy, numeracy and much, *much* more. This book, conceived early in 1998, when Crick's committee first reported, and given impetus and urgency by the subsequent introduction of Citizenship to the National Curriculum at Key Stages 3 and 4 in September 2002, seeks to counter that long marginalisation of the social curriculum and the broader social aspect of schooling.

The book in outline

Against this background, we offer a comprehensive collection of chapters that seeks to address a wide range of specialist subjects and disciplines, cross-curricular areas and discourses, and approaches to schooling that individually or collectively play a part in the planned initiation, curricular provision and education of students in relation to the social world.

In *Part One,* we set out the context that Citizenship encountered when it joined the National Curriculum. We include a consideration of the history of the social curriculum and Citizenship in England and the state of provision in England on the eve of implementation in 2002 as set out in the baseline research carried out as part of the National Foundation for Educational Research (NFER) nine-year longitudinal study into Citizenship Education. The study, which is currently tracking a cohort of over 18,500 school students aged 11 to 18, is seeking to measure what impact the new Citizenship curriculum has on their knowledge, skills, attitudes and behaviour.

In *Parts Two, Three* and *Four*, we include chapters that address many of the curricular *foundations* on which Citizenship can build, in the arts and humanities, in the social and business sciences and in mathematics, science and technology. Each subject or area has something distinct to offer as a discipline, as do the teachers and subject leaders, as do those from other parts of the curriculum. Those subjects and areas that we have not had the space in these pages to address (especially music, PE and sport, and modern foreign languages) also have much to offer. Our suggestion is that schools select from this mix in light of their own curriculum model, community setting and staffing mix. On the one hand this is about assessing what different subjects might offer to Citizenship; on the other, it is more profoundly about unlocking the *existing* Citizenship expertise of the school's current teaching force. Given the issues of finding and facilitating access to Citizenship continuing professional development programmes and the relatively slow (but welcome) trickle of Citizenship PGCE students from the teacher training institutions, such an unlocking is no more than smart school management.

In *Part Five*, we look at some of the objectives of Citizenship: education for employability, sustainability, equality, engagement, participation and well-being; areas of learning that are less often organised on the traditional subject template but which are as vital as any subject element in the education of developing citizens. These chapters both underpin the rationale for Citizenship Education and extend it. Thus, their emphasis is, by definition, on the life and objectives of the wider school rather than the needs of any specific subject area.

Part Six explores a number of managerial and leadership strategies that pull together the various strands. Here, fundamental concerns such as the education and continuing professional development of teachers, team and department development, assessment and inspection are addressed. In addition, we have placed the chapters on PSHE and Religious, Moral and Spiritual Education in this section of the book because their contribution and overall planning by school senior managements is crucial for the substance and identity of Citizenship. There are strong grounds for arguing that these areas and this part of the curriculum map must show some obvious linkage, unity and clarity for both teachers and learners; only informed leadership can build such coherence.

Finally, in our *Conclusion*, we then make a series of recommendations based on our own analysis and that of our co-authors. In particular, we support the Citizenship Foundation's recent call for a National Strategy for Teaching and Learning in Citizenship in their April 2006 submission to the Education Select Committee.

Delivering Citizenship in schools: our analysis

Our position on the delivery of Citizenship in schools is based strongly on our personal and professional biographies. Both of us have experience as classroom teachers, as heads of department, as LEA advisers, and as examiners and inspectors. We also have close involvement with universities and with initial and continuing teacher education as well as experience in a range of subject associations and NGOs. We believe that the social curriculum, and notably Citizenship, needs expert and explicit delivery in clearly identified locations on the timetable and beyond *and* that it must pervade the life of the school; that the school must become *Citizenship-rich*. So as to crystallise this analysis for the reader at the outset, we have three central suggestions. We develop these as the book progresses and in the conclusion, but it is necessary to say a little about them now so as to 'frame' the chapters and sections that follow.

First, the emergent and maturing Citizenship agenda can be strengthened and informed by the subjects and cross-curricular areas featured here. It is for individual schools and their curriculum planners to decide what to draw on, how to blend it and how to position it in terms of any core Citizenship programme. In most curriculum frameworks, the traditional humanities subjects such as History and Geography will play some role as (probably 'strong') 'carriers' for Citizenship, as will PSHE and Religious Education. Especially at Key Stage 4, the various Social and Business Science subjects may also play a role (but their usual confinement to the option columns can be a drawback). So too should the perspectives offered by environmental, enterprise and global education, multicultural, anti-racist and human rights education, and the various strands of experience offered by the vocational curriculum and Work-Related Learning.

Second, we are as much concerned about the contribution of the teacher as their subject. Whatever inputs are selected from this menu, there is likely to be a far richer outcome if the skills and expertise of teachers from all of these areas are drawn upon, and in most schools, whatever the breadth of the curriculum model, this range of expertise and interest remains. We have already hinted at our scepticism around traditional cross-curricular curriculum audits. To reiterate a point made earlier, an audit of the abilities and expertise of the staffroom might be far more useful and might bring some surprise stars to the Citizenship party.

Third, and the early evidence from Ofsted, NFER, QCA and others supports this contention, some kind of *core* Citizenship programme, clearly branded as such, is likely to prove the most effective way of pulling these subjects, strands and (critically) teachers together. As a Cross-Curricular Theme, Citizenship was, from 1991, *less* than a subject. Now as a Foundation Subject of the National Curriculum we must consider it *more* than a subject; a new kind of subject if you will – never fully delivered in a single course or in 45 minute lessons, but these benchmarks of the 'subject' need to be there; for teacher, student, parent, governor and bursar alike.

Citizenship: a noble and necessary objective for schooling

The aim of Citizenship Education, however represented, should be to enable young people and adults to understand and make sense of their own lives and of local, national and global civic society. We cannot continue to bemoan apathy, political disaffection and community breakdown if we do not educate for effective participation in our communities and in our democracy. We need to raise our sights beyond the satisfaction of purely functional models of literacy to the aspiration of political literacy for all, a task that, as a society, we have left a little late. Building on Crick and the efforts of many teachers and educators who grapple daily with the same challenge, this book explores how schools and colleges can fulfill this noble objective. There is such a thing as society. We are duty bound to support and celebrate it and share in its renewal and, in such a project, Citizenship Education is vital.

This book goes to press after the aftermath of the 2005 General Election and the election of new leaders of the Conservative and Liberal Democratic parties. We trust that the third Labour government will do as much to *establish* Citizenship in the National Curriculum as the first and second did to *introduce* it. We also implore 'not-so-new' Labour to pay equal attention to the cross-curricular approach to joint PSHE and Citizenship provision taken in Wales, the global and education for mutual understanding perspectives brought to Citizenship Education in Northern Ireland and the model that places Citizenship at the heart of school strategic and development planning in Scotland. This is, ultimately, about outcomes not approaches and about what happens across the UK rather than just in England. We need to learn from experiences across these islands and beyond.

We trust also that the current government and the new party leaders will seek to rebuild the all-party consensus around Citizenship Education that Crick's first committee embodied. There were suggestions during the election campaign in 2005 that, had the Conservatives been elected, a review of the National Curriculum, led by the former Chief Inspector Chris Woodhead, would deliver the demise of Citizenship as an early outcome. Whatever the legitimate arguments about teacher workload and timetable over-crowding, that would have been a retrograde step. We recognise that matters such as the allocation of appropriate resources, initial and continuing teacher training and curriculum space pose real challenges for Citizenship Education – hence this book: education is for nothing if it is not *for* Citizenship, something that we trust David Cameron's *new Conservatism* will embrace and something we are pleased to see endorsed by the former Chief Inspector, David Bell.

We, all of the contributors featured here, are not just making an argument for a subject or course or qualification. We are arguing for a renewal and re-invigoration of schooling itself. It is for that reason that Denis Lawton, in the Preface to this volume, describes Citizenship Education as '. . . the most important educational innovation in the last 50 years' and Denis writes not as a New Labour spin-doctor but as one of the most consistently critical educational progressives over that period. Our political representatives serve us well when they argue about politics, not when they suggest that we should stay out of the debate. To contribute to the engagement of young people in politics, to promote legal and political literacy for all, to see active community engagement as the norm, to build a real understanding of rights and responsibilities, to defeat the corrosive evils of racism and youth disaffection is the vision of all of us in Citizenship Education. And for those who consider this a peripheral or unnecessary task, witness the enduring and apparently growing success of the BNP in some of our most disadvantaged areas, the involvement of young British born men in the London bombings and the emerging discussion about what it means to be British in the twenty-first century and how the current or a revised Citizenship curriculum might or should address these complex challenges of identity and cohesion. Indeed, we should take heart from the fact that the individual leading the review into the 'Britishness' issue is Keith Ajegbo, until recently headteacher at the genuinely "citizenship-rich" Deptford Green School. Let us continue to argue – teachers, school leaders, politicians, parents, young people – about how Citizenship Education is best done and what it might include rather than contest whether it should exist at all: *developing citizens* is, after all, the key task for all of us in education. As the title suggests, we intend that this book will enable you to do that job.

Tony Breslin and Barry Dufour
June 2006

PART ONE

CITIZENSHIP AND SOCIAL EDUCATION CONTEXTS, ISSUES AND REQUIREMENTS

1.1 The Fate and Fortunes of the Social Curriculum and the Evolution of Citizenship: A Historical Overview

1.2 Foundations and Baselines for Citizenship: The NFER Citizenship Education Longitudinal Study

1.3 Citizenship in the National Curriculum: Contexts, Requirements and Expectations

1.1 The Fate and Fortunes of the Social Curriculum and the Evolution of Citizenship: A Historical Overview

Barry Dufour

In Summer 2000, the third incarnation of the National Curriculum for England was published. At Key Stages 3 and 4, the revised curriculum included a new *compulsory* Foundation Subject – Citizenship – to be introduced to secondary schools in Autumn 2002 (DfEE/QCA, 1999). In the primary phase, Citizenship did not quite attain the same status but was implemented immediately as part of a joint non-statutory framework with Personal, Social and Health Education. The arrival of Citizenship as a 'proper' subject (rather than the 'everywhere but nowhere' Cross-Curricular Theme that it had been) was more of a landmark in curriculum and schooling than many could have imagined. Only those acquainted with the troubled history of Citizenship and the broader social studies in the UK would have been surprised. Only those familiar with the requirement for Citizenship Education (or something very similar) in most other countries of the western world would have seen it as long overdue. And only those aware of the challenging educational potential of the new Statutory Order would have been excited.

Moreover, though the approach was to be different in other parts of the UK, Citizenship was to be on the agenda too. Thus, in Wales, rather like the primary model in England, Citizenship and PSHE were to become part of a joint but *statutory* framework, often but not always delivered through a cross-curricular model. In Northern Ireland, the focus, much inspired by the ground-breaking work of the Education for Mutual Understanding (EMU) programme, Citizenship is emerging as having an especially global perspective. In Scotland, Citizenship has become not a curriculum subject but one of the key components of strategic whole school planning, such that it *has* to be one of the four elements in the Strategic Improvement Plan that each school is required to produce. Taken alongside the Republic of Ireland's statutory programme of 'Civic, Social and Political Education', arguably the trailblazer in all of this, we have for the first time five distinct projects across the UK and Ireland, all committed to the objectives of Citizenship Education and the broader social curriculum.

What might these projects learn from the past? The history of social education in the UK has been a story of successes and failures, of crests and dips on a rollercoaster of progress, with various educational, social and political pressures all exerting their influence along the way. Particular themes constantly re-emerge: matters relating to status, debates about 'subject' versus 'integrated' approaches, conceptual concerns, timetabling and assessment issues, the levels of official government support and the role of the subject associations, the LA advisory services and the schools themselves. This chapter attempts to summarise this history and offer some initial observations that might support the effective establishment of Citizenship today.

A brief history of the social curriculum: the nineteenth century to the 1960s

By the end of the nineteenth century, some Citizenship teaching was taking place, certainly in the elementary schools, but only where enlightened school boards and teachers believed in its value. As Heater has noted, there were even a few published school textbooks or 'primers' dealing with the constitution and government (Heater, 2001). However, when the subjects of History and Geography became established in the early twentieth century, as the key school subjects dealing with humanity and society, the existence of any direct civic education was dependent even more on the initiative of individual teachers who made a place for it. This situation of ambivalent status has been repeated many times over in the history of Citizenship and similar generic discourses in the school curriculum, and is again exercising curriculum researchers today.

In 1934, responding to the rise of totalitarian governments in mainland Europe, a group of academics, including some eminent social scientists from the London School of Economics and Political Science, set up the Association for Education in Citizenship to 'advance the study of and training in citizenship' in the belief that direct teaching about democracy in British schools would promote liberal values and act as a counter to sympathy for extreme right-wing ideas. Their view was that political and economic education, alongside History and Geography, could provide a better education for Citizenship than some of the other piecemeal attempts then current in some schools. But official government reports on schools and the curriculum, such as the Spens Report of 1938 (Spens, 1938) were not convinced that political discussion in the classroom was at all desirable.

Regardless of government support, the post-war years, especially until the early 1950s, witnessed the rise of a social studies movement in many of the secondary modern schools, which catered for the majority of pupils. Several handbooks appeared which outlined integrated courses often combining aspects of History and Geography with basic economic and citizenship themes. This experiment was short-lived for a number of reasons including opposition from Geography and History teachers because of the dilution of their subjects (boundary wars play an important part in the history of the social curriculum), because specialist teacher training was also lacking and because of the ill-defined and limitless content of social studies (Lawton and Dufour, 1973). Similar strains and challenges, not entirely absent from the pages of this volume, are also apparent today as Citizenship tries to establish its subject matter in schools.

However, the brief experiment of the 1940s and 1950s was followed by a more substantial attempt at innovation from the 1960s onwards, some aspects of which have continued to this day. A 'new social studies' movement arose which was influenced by three main factors; first, by the continuing search for a more relevant curriculum for the majority of school pupils that would better educate the worker-citizen (Crowther, 1959; Newsom, 1963) and, second, by the growing interest in teaching the social sciences in secondary schools partly influenced by widespread curriculum development in these approaches in the USA (Fenton, 1966; Lawton and Dufour, 1973) and partly by the growth of disciplines like Sociology in the universities.

Against this background, in the 1960s, a number of secondary schools including Kidbrooke School in South London and Cressex School in High Wycombe (where I created a Social Sciences faculty) developed and began teaching social science-influenced integrated courses. Alongside these programmes, Humanities courses, drawing on topic-based and enquiry-based teaching and learning, were also spreading, often incorporating aspects of History, Geography, Religious Education and English for younger secondary students and the investigation of major social issues for 14 to 16 year olds. These developments were given status, credibility and security by being underpinned by official curriculum projects and published resources. Alongside this, specialist Social Science subjects were expanding, with GCE and A Level courses in Sociology introduced to schools and colleges along with a professional subject association, the Association for the Teaching of the Social Sciences (ATSS), set up to support the new social studies and Sociology courses. The teaching of Politics and Economics in schools for 14 to 18 year olds also continued to expand (Lawton and Dufour, 1973; Crick and Porter, 1978), and Crick was a key mover in the establishment of the Politics Association.

None of these new subjects, and few of the courses, took the name 'Citizenship' but, taken together, all of these subjects and curricular areas contained elements which were, in effect, beginning to address the core concerns of Citizenship Education as defined in the National Curriculum of 2000. And some of the key 'movers and shakers' in today's Citizenship Education movement cut their teeth as students or educationalists during this period.

The 1970s and 1980s: subject expansion and the growth of the single-issue subjects and discourses

During the 1970s and 1980s, there was continuous expansion in the teaching of Sociology, Politics and Economics, with the later addition of Psychology for older pupils. Teaching about other cultures was also developing in many schools with extensive support from the Royal Anthropological Institute through its Teaching Resources Project although, with the exception of its inclusion as an element of the International Baccalaureate, Anthropology has never, to this day, achieved the status of an examination course at 14 to 16 or sixth form level (Street, 1982).

There had also been an increase in various humanities-based integrated courses throughout the secondary age range but the most dramatic growth was in the areas that we might define as single-issue subjects or discourses. I referred to them, in 1990, as a 'new social curriculum' (Dufour, 1990). These important areas included vocational education, personal and social education, health education, media education, peace education, gender education, multicultural and anti-racist education, development education, global education, environmental education, human rights education and, to a lesser degree, trade union education. With the lack of an official national curriculum, all of these areas could flourish in innovative schools and LEAs, taken up by forward-looking teachers who saw the need for them in terms of providing a worthwhile broader education and in response to changes in society. They rarely displaced the traditional school subjects but found space within subjects across the curriculum, in tutorial time and as special events within the schools. Most also benefited from a wide range of available teaching resources and from substantial teacher support networks in the form of associations or organisations (Dufour, 1990).

Many of these curricular areas were of course reflecting the campaigning themes of major social movements and single-issue pressure groups in the political and social spectrum beyond the school. These included the world-wide peace movement, the promotion of women's rights and equal opportunities, the anti-racist movement and multiculturalism, the human rights movement, the world development movement for greater economic justice for developing countries, and the environmental movement which was confronting global and ecological problems. Aspects of citizenship were at the heart of all of these movements and at the centre of their curriculum manifestations in the schools.

The impact of the National Curriculum from 1988 onwards

The 1988 Education Reform Act imposed a National Curriculum on England and Wales for the first time (HMSO, 1988). Other countries had long ago developed a national framework for their school curriculums. The Act specified ten Core and Foundation Subjects along with requirements for Religious Education and worship. The Act proposed a broad and balanced curriculum that:

a) promoted the spiritual, moral, cultural, mental and physical development of pupils at the school and of society;
b) prepared such pupils for the opportunities, responsibilities and experiences of adult life.

But the Act fell short of these grand intentions in many respects. Richard Aldrich suggests that the choice of subjects was little different from the school curriculum of 1904, certainly at the secondary level (Aldrich, 1996). The Act also failed to take advantage of new areas of social knowledge, even though, as outlined above, there had been major school developments in:

- the teaching of single social science subjects, such as Sociology, Economics and Government and Politics
- integrated or modular courses in Humanities, Social Studies and Business Studies
- thematic programmes that began to address single-issue areas such as development education, environmental education and global education

- vocational education, reflecting regular pronouncements from Labour and Conservative sources about the need for better work-related learning in schools.

The latter was especially, and famously, featured in Labour Prime Minister James Callaghan's 'Great Debate' speech at Ruskin College in 1976, and also in subsequent Conservative educational policy during the 1980s, notably in the form of the Technical and Vocational Education Initiative (TVEI). By 1988, the Conservatives were spending over £1 billion on this Initiative and related in-service training and yet vocational education as a major curriculum stream was entirely ignored by the Act.

As a result of all of this, the progress made in some of these areas either stalled or went into reverse. For example, History and Geography for 11 to 13 year olds had increasingly been delivered through an integrated or modular Humanities approach, sometimes including Religious Education and elements of English, and structured around topics, resource-based enquiry and active learning. But the nature of the new schemes of work in History and Geography required a substantial amount of content to be taught which left no time or space for anything else and also rendered it epistemologically and methodologically impossible for the two subjects to integrate: this latter problem was not entirely accidental and was reinforced at the highest levels[1]. As a result, these courses (and related PGCE provision) virtually disappeared at Key Stage 3. GCSE courses in Integrated Humanities also went into sharp decline as a result of the competition from the pre-eminent History and Geography programmes and the demands of a strictly subject-defined curriculum. However, as David Barrs notes in Chapter 2.4, a consequence of the security of tenure that the new National Curriculum offered Geography was a loss of innovation in Geography teaching. Likewise, writing from a History perspective, Kate Moorse notes in Chapter 2.5 how the shift from a concepts and issues based pedagogy resulted in the decline of many 'big ideas' at the heart of the progressive History teaching that bodies like the Schools Council History Project had done so much to promote. Social Studies teachers, many of whom had long argued for a broad, balanced curriculum for all, were not, then, the only losers. Single Social Science subjects at Key Stage 4 declined but were less affected post-16 where Sociology and Psychology both grew in popularity. These progressive disciplines seemed to offer an escape for A level students honed on Aldrich's pre-16 menu of 1904.

Quite apart from these specific problems, the National Curriculum in its entirety encountered intractable problems almost immediately on its implementation. The vast content mass of all the subjects along with the statutory guidance for each National Curriculum subject, quite apart from the non-statutory guidance, made it virtually impossible to teach in a 24 hour day. Widespread criticism quickly emerged from the teaching profession and from other expert educational opinion that the new curriculum was over-prescriptive, overloaded and could not be implemented in its then current form[2]. It seemed quite apt when a teacher, in an anonymous letter to *The Guardian* newspaper, described the first version of the National Curriculum as having been 'conceived by Kafka, designed by Dali and administered by Stalin'.

Between 1993 and 1995 the government responded to these criticisms by implementing the recommendations of its own Dearing Review to amend the requirements and reduce the content (Dearing, 1994). Thus 'Mark 2' of the National Curriculum was born and implemented in 1995. However, all of this confusion had serious and negative consequences for those areas, including Citizenship, which had followed the 1988 Act and been granted the designation 'cross-curricular'.

The strange case of the cross-curricular issues (1988–2000)

The first mention of Citizenship in relation to the National Curriculum, but not in a specific curricular sense, came in the *Consultation Document on the National Curriculum* (DES, 1987) which stated that successive Secretaries of State for Education had tried to find agreement on '. . . policies for the school curriculum which will develop the potential of all pupils and equip them for the responsibilities of citizenship and for the challenges of employment in tomorrow's world'.

This same document introduced the idea of 'themes', such as health education, which would be taught through the subjects, via a process of osmosis as we were later to discover. Two years later another document, *National Curriculum: From Policy to Practice* (DfEE, 1989) developed this notion further by proposing 'cross-curricular issues' that would infuse the Core and Foundation Subjects. Various 'issues' were noted including 'political and international understanding', 'economic awareness' and 'environmental education'. By 1990, the new National Curriculum Council began to publish a series of brief guidance booklets with *Curriculum Guidance 3: The Whole Curriculum* (NCC, 1990a) proposing 'cross-curricular elements' which would be divided into dimensions, skills and themes. One of the five themes was 'Education for Citizenship' as outlined in *Curriculum Guidance 8: Education for Citizenship* (NCC,1990b). With Citizenship set to arrive in schools as a Cross-Curricular Theme, several organisations emerged or regrouped to support this presumed growth. The most influential of these, the Citizenship Foundation, established in 1989, grew out of the Law in Education Project which had been set up by two teachers (Don Rowe and Tony Thorpe) and a lawyer (Andrew (now Lord) Phillips), five years earlier. The Centre for Citizenship Studies in Education was founded by Professor Ken Fogelman in 1991 at the School of Education at the University of Leicester, and the Institute of Citizenship, like the Foundation an independent NGO, was established in 1992 as a result of a Speakers Commission that had been established to address concerns around political disaffection, especially among the young.

This cross-curricular plan was seen by government advisers as a convenient device for making some provision in the school curriculum for aspects of personal, social, political and economic education that would otherwise find no place in an exclusively subject-based curriculum. Yet these same advisers, mandarins and politicians had only recently, during the latter half of the

1980s, willingly presided over the construction of this unadventurous, traditional and narrowly-conceived subject-oriented curriculum which was enshrined in law by the 1988 Education Reform Act.

As a result, from the beginning, there was considerable ambivalence, confusion and back-tracking at the highest levels of government and advisory bodies over the status of the cross-curricular elements. A fundamental flaw was that the 'elements' were not statutory, unlike the subjects which were defined by law and by the statutory guidance in each subject document. Furthermore, the detailed statutory Programmes of Study and Attainment Targets published in the early 1990s for each subject contained no references to cross-curricular elements; their status as a bolted-on afterthought confirmed.

As if inhabiting a different universe from the DES, which was responsible for the National Curriculum statutory guidance for the Core and Foundation Subjects, it was left to the National Curriculum Council to provide non-statutory guidance on the cross-curricular elements by way of its series of booklets. However, even this guidance was short-lived. When the NCC, to round off its individual booklets on each of the elements, produced a comprehensive guidance booklet on how all the elements could fit together and be implemented, thousands of copies were printed, never distributed and then pulped[3]. In addition, in a further twist of policy confusion and subterfuge, the new inspection agency, Ofsted (set up by the 1993 Education Act to inspect schools and, amongst other duties, to monitor and police the National Curriculum), drew up criteria and standards for the inspection of the cross-curricular elements which were to be issued as part of the inspection handbook for 1994. The section was written but never published[4].

In short, it seemed that, at the official level, the cross-curricular elements had been killed off, almost at birth. Official decisions had been taken, behind closed doors, without the education community being informed. It would appear that the DES and the NCC had accepted the fact of an overcrowded National Curriculum and that schools would not be able to tolerate further innovation. Indeed, much of the teaching profession was influenced by this official ambivalence that accorded a low status to the elements. And the non-statutory aspect was further compounded by the absence of the requirement to operate formal assessment procedures – which were integral to the subjects. Notwithstanding this, many LEAs produced their own guidance for schools on the implementation of the National Curriculum and the cross-curricular elements. Many saw the themes and dimensions as an important and integral part of providing a whole curriculum and entitlement to a broad and balanced education. And some schools also adopted the same view, making imaginative efforts to devise strategies and teaching schemes, albeit within the straitjacket of a subject-based and increasingly examination-driven curriculum. Making a reality of this vital programme for social education proved a real challenge. Although several models were proposed, the two main strategies were either permeation of the cross-curricular areas into subject teaching or separate provision through PSE (Personal and Social Education) slots in the timetable. Many schools used both but with varying success. It is therefore not surprising that a national school survey on the cross-curricular elements in the early

1990s indicated that the implementation had been variable, inconsistent and often unsatisfactory (Whitty et al., 1994).

The arrival of Citizenship in the National Curriculum: lessons from a troubled history

The Dearing Review of 1994 had suggested that following its proposed slimming down of the National Curriculum in 1995, there should be no further revisions to the National Curriculum until the year 2000 and while this briefly put the development of the social curriculum on hold, the election of the Labour Government in 1997 provided the key historically emblematic impetus for Citizenship in schools. As part of the planning for drawing up a new National Curriculum for 2000, the then Secretary of State for Education, David Blunkett, asked Bernard Crick, not only a long-term advocate for Citizenship in schools but also his one-time university tutor, to lead an advisory group, Education for Citizenship and the Teaching of Democracy in Schools. After much deliberation and extensive consultation in the education community[5], the group's Final Report was published in 1998 (QCA, 1998) with the recommendation that Citizenship should become a new subject in the new National Curriculum at Key Stages 3 and 4, as published in 2000 with implementation from Autumn 2002.

With this change in place, it would appear that one of the key obstacles to Citizenship Education over the last 100 years or more has been removed. It has shifted from the margins of schools, where it was taught by enthusiasts, to the core with the imprimatur of government support and enshrined in law as an official National Curriculum subject. But before the celebrations begin, we need to remind ourselves that it is not a traditional subject but, as Tony Breslin argues in these pages, a new *type* of subject and – in spite of much helpful guidance from the DfES and the QCA through Programmes of Study, illustrative schemes of work and exemplars – there are still fundamental problems to confront.

In terms of aims and objectives, the boundaries for classroom enquiry and student involvement in their schools, in their communities and in the wider world are still far from being explored. What was the view of the educational establishment when thousands of young school students felt it was their right and duty to withdraw from school in February 2003 to participate in the mass demonstration in London against the impending involvement of the UK government in a war on Iraq? Students and teachers still need to discover the potential and limits of their new freedoms, working as they do in institutions (secondary schools) that are not inherently participative or democratic. A key theme of many contributors to this text is that teaching democracy undemocratically is at best contradictory, at worst a non-starter; pedagogy matters but so does the structure of the school itself.

In this context, if Citizenship Education is to be effective, styles of teaching and learning must be reviewed and revised as necessary but at a pace that individual schools, departments and teachers are comfortable with. Crick foresaw this with his 'light touch' recommendations but, as we remark elsewhere, if *light* touch becomes *soft* touch then another opportunity for good quality social learning will have been lost. Citizenship Education has to be dynamic, active and engaging if it is to win the hearts and minds of teachers and students. The methods of assessment will also have to encapsulate this style and range of teaching and learning.

And quality of implementation continues to be a fundamental issue. While Citizenship has made an excellent start in many secondary schools since 2002, research by Ofsted and NFER, together with the anecdotal evidence of many of our contributors and their organisations, suggests that there is still much that is unsatisfactory (Ofsted, 2003; NFER/Kerr et al., 2004). We must be patient given the scale of the required change, but purposeful. It may be that only a higher profile in the timetable – with a dedicated and conventional subject slot for Citizenship – will begin to address the lukewarm and insufficient implementation in many schools. This would need to be allied with far more widespread in-service training on Citizenship. And partly to make room for a more extensive and enriched Citizenship Curriculum, a fourth edition of the entire National Curriculum may be due, as many educationists are arguing (*The Guardian*, 2003), in order to create a more flexible, relevant and engaging education.

School students are entitled to a high quality education in Citizenship, one which enables them to develop an understanding of central issues in human society and in their personal lives. Active participation in democratic schools and democratic society will further enhance their development as citizens. The full and effective implementation of the Citizenship Order in English schools will take time but there is already much enthusiasm for the new subject amongst educationists and students – the challenge will be to convert this into a universal endorsement and success.

REFERENCES

Aldrich, R. (1996) *Education for the Nation*. London: Cassell.

Crick, B. and Porter, A. (eds) (1978) *Politics of Education and Political Literacy*. London: Longman/Hansard.

Crowther (1959) *15–18, Report of the Central Advisory Council for Education (England)* – popularly known as the Crowther report. London: Her Majesty's Stationery Office.

Dearing, Sir R. (1994). *The National Curriculum and its Assessment* – popularly known as The Dearing Review. The School Curriculum and Assessment Authority: London. The review was compiled during 1993, published in early 1994 and acted on from September 1995.

DES (1987) *Consultation Document on the National Curriculum*. London: Department for Education and Science.

DfEE (1989) *The National Curriculum: From Policy to Practice*. London: Department for Education and Employment.

DfEE/QCA (1999) *Citizenship, The National Curriculum for England, Key Stages 3–4*. London: Department for Education and Employment and the Qualifications and Curriculum Authority.

Dufour, B. (ed.) (1990) *The New Social Curriculum: A Guide to Cross-Curricular Issues*. Cambridge: Cambridge University Press.

Fenton, E. (1966) *Teaching the New Social Studies in Secondary Schools*. USA: Holt, Rinehart and Winston.

Guardian, The (2003) *Revision Period* (from *The Guardian Education* supplement) 4 November. Consisted of an analysis and interviews with leading educational academics based on a conference at the Institute of Education, University of London entitled *Rethinking the School Curriculum: Values, Aims and Purposes*, a title shared with the book launched at the conference and edited by Professor John White.

Heater, D. (2001) 'Citizenship Education in England: Historical Features', *Teaching Citizenship*, Issue 2. London: Association for Citizenship Teaching.

HMSO (1988) Education Reform Act. London: Her Majesty's Stationery Office.

Lawton, D. and Dufour, B. (1973) *The New Social Studies*. London: Heinemann Educational Books.

NCC (1990a) *The Whole Curriculum (Curriculum Guidance 3)*. York: National Curriculum Council.

NCC (1990b) *Education for Citizenship (Curriculum Guidance 8)*. York: National Curriculum Council.

Newsom (1963) *Half Our Future* – popularly known as The Newsom Report. London: HMSO.

NFER/Kerr, D., Ireland, E., Lopes, J., Craig, R. with Cleaver, E. (2004) *Citizenship Education: Longitudinal Study: Second Annual Report: First Longitudinal Survey – Making Citizenship Education Real*. Nottingham: DfES Publications.

Ofsted (2003) *National Curriculum Citizenship: Planning and Implementation 2002/03*. London: Office for Standards in Education.

QCA (1998) *Education for Citizenship and the Teaching of Democracy in Schools: Final Report of the Advisory Group on Citizenship* – popularly known as The Crick Report. London: Qualifications and Curriculum Authority.

Spens Report (1938). *Report of the Consultative Committee on Secondary Education with special reference to Grammar Schools and Technical High Schools*. London: Ministry of Education.

Street, B. (1982) 'Social Anthropology in Schools: Teaching About Other Cultures', in B. Dufour (ed.) *New Movements in the Social Sciences and Humanities*. London: Maurice Temple Smith/Gower.

Whitty, G., Aggleton, P. and Rowe, G. (1994) 'Discourses in Cross-Curricular Contexts: Limits to Empowerment', *International Studies in Sociology of Education*, 4(1).

NOTES

1. In a confidential discussion with the individual concerned, I discovered that a member of the Geography subject working group was formally disciplined for attempting to make links with the History subject working group during the formulation of the National Curriculum.
2. Many books were published which were highly critical of the Conservative Government's policy on education and the National Curriculum. One, which brought together articles from academic commentators and government advisers and ex-officials responsible for key changes, was *Education Answers Back: Critical Responses to Government Policy*, edited by Clyde Chitty and Brian Simon, published by Lawrence and Wishart in 1993.
3. Information given to me in 1995 by someone who had been a very senior officer of the National Curriculum Council.
4. Information given to me in 1994 by a senior HMI.
5. Tony Breslin and myself established, with the support of Don Rowe at the Citizenship Foundation, an informal network called *Citizenship 2000*, composed of senior academics and subject association officers across the social education domain, who wrote and submitted a well-received and subsequently cited paper on Citizenship Education, drafted by former HMI Ian Shelton, to the Advisory Group, making a number of proposals including the need to avoid mistakes of the past and to give Citizenship full and equal legitimacy by making proper space in the overall school curriculum for the subject – we suggested 5% of timetable time, similar to that usually allocated to Religious Education. The paper is unpublished.

1.2 Foundations and Baselines for Citizenship: The NFER Citizenship Education Longitudinal Study

Elizabeth Cleaver, David Kerr and Eleanor Ireland

This chapter reports on the first year baseline findings of the Citizenship Education Longitudinal Study[1]. The National Foundation for Educational Research (NFER) has been commissioned by the Department for Education and Skills to carry out this groundbreaking nine year study which is tracking a cohort of over 18,500 young people who entered secondary school in 2002; a group which comprises some of the first students to have a continuous statutory entitlement to Citizenship Education in England from September 2002. The objective of the study is to provide:

> *. . . an assessment of the short-term and long-term effects of citizenship education on the knowledge, skills and attitudes and behaviour of pupils, and the creation of an informed evidence-based discussion of potential changes for the delivery of citizenship education to improve its effectiveness.* (Kerr et al., 2003)

The findings presented here result from a baseline survey, carried out as a pre-curser to, and first stage of, the substantive study, undertaken in the summer term of the academic year 2001–2 involving 7,500 students, 1,500 teachers and 318 schools in England and some reflections on nine case studies of schools involved in the implementation of Citizenship Education post-September 2002[2].

While the initial observations offered in this chapter are necessarily preliminary, their purpose remains important: they provide useful pre-compulsory baseline evidence of the extent to which Citizenship Education was already being taught, or under development, in schools, prior to its introduction as a statutory subject in September 2002 and it is now possible to begin the process of addressing the key research questions and aims of the substantive study. In short, these observations will take readers back to the context that National Curriculum Citizenship met at the time that it was introduced and thus facilitate some judgement, on the part of the individual reader, about the progress that has since been made.

The longitudinal study: scale and methodology

The ongoing substantive study uses a mixed methodology that gives a clue to its scale and comprises the following:

- Four cross-sectional surveys of students, schools and teachers, of which the baseline survey reported on here is the first. Student surveys (sent to one

tutor group in either Year 8, 10 or 12 in each participating school) were accompanied by questionnaires to school and college leaders and teachers in each participating school. Future surveys were undertaken in school years 2003–4, 2005–6 and will also be undertaken in 2007–8.
- A longitudinal tracking survey of a whole year group of students in a representative sample of 100 schools tracking the student cohort from Year 7 through Years 9, 11 and 13 (or equivalent when they are aged 18). Schools and teachers are also being asked to complete questionnaires each year up to Year 11 so that links can be made between pupils' experiences, skills, knowledge and attitudes and school characteristics and processes.
- 20 longitudinal school case studies. Ten schools were drawn from the schools participating in the baseline survey considered here. Ten were visited during the summer and autumn term of 2003. Ten further schools were drawn from the longitudinal sample population of schools. School visits include in-depth interviews with key personnel and student discussion groups. Each school will be revisited once every two years over the duration of the study.

Citizenship Education: the problem of definition

A necessary starting point for any baseline survey or substantive study is a consideration of the literature which addresses the concepts of Citizenship and Citizenship Education, such that we can be clearer about:

- how the terms are defined
- how these definitions influence approaches to policy and practice and
- how policy and practice can act to influence definitions of Citizenship and Citizenship Education.

The history of educating for citizenship in England has been well rehearsed. It is summarised in Barry Dufour's opening chapter in this collection, and will not be repeated at length here (see Batho, 1990; Brown, 1991; Davies, 1999; Heater, 1990, 2001; Kerr, 1999b, 1999c). One issue that has received considerable attention is the recognition that Citizenship and Citizenship Education are 'contested' concepts. Any definitions of Citizenship Education put forward are recognised as the by-product of a more wide-ranging debate about the changing nature of citizenship and its impact on the nature of modern society (see, for example, Scott and Lawson, 2001). This recognition is important precisely because it points towards the potential for an incoherent vision for, and varied practice in, the delivery of Citizenship Education to develop in English schools. Thus, despite the clear three strand definition of Citizenship Education put forward by Bernard Crick's advisory group (Crick, 1998) around political literacy, community involvement and social and moral responsibility, the literature suggests that there are still considerable questions to be addressed concerning its 'definition, purposes, and intended outcomes' (Pearce and Hallgarten, 2000) and whether it should be developed through existing curriculum subjects (see, for example, Arthur et al., 2001; Lambert and Machon, 2001; Moss, 2001) or independently.

As the Crick Report makes clear in its introduction, one of the challenges faced by the group was to find a working definition which blended the best of past approaches and existing definitions in a way that was acceptable to those from a variety of different backgrounds and political persuasions (Crick, 1998). The group was also influenced by the outcomes of England's involvement in the first phase of the IEA Civic Education Study which drew attention to the 'huge gaps that currently exist in the knowledge and research base which underpins this area in England' (Kerr, 1999c). In addition, it provided the group with details of definitions, models and approaches to Citizenship Education in other countries (Kerr, 1999a; Torney-Purta et al., 1999).

However, despite attempts to consider a range of definitions and evidence, current developments in Citizenship Education in England are not without their critics. These range from those who argue that Citizenship Education should not be part of the school curriculum (Tooley, 2000), and those who, while supportive in principle, have drawn attention to the deficiencies of the Crick Report in its handling of issues such as race (Hall, 2000) and gender (Arnot et al., 2000).

A number of common difficulties are therefore seen to underpin the development of Citizenship Education in the school curriculum and beyond. These include the need to: gain agreement on the conception or definition of Citizenship (McLaughlin, 2000); bridge the gap between policy intentions and actual practice; agree on the curriculum location for Citizenship (Frazer, 2000); achieve teacher ownership of the aims and teaching and learning approaches associated with Citizenship Education (McLaughlin, 2000); give teachers sufficient training and confidence to teach Citizenship Education through active approaches; gain agreement on how Citizenship Education should be assessed, reported and inspected; and help schools successfully to address the community involvement strand of Citizenship Education, in partnership with representatives from local communities.

Changing contexts for Citizenship Education: young people, community and home

A second key body of literature central to this research, drawn from the disciplines of sociology and politics, is that which debates the ways in which extended youth transitions to adulthood, prolonged periods of economic and domestic dependency and increased perceptions of risk may impact on young people's opportunities, desires and abilities to gain adult citizenship and to participate in traditional adult citizenship activities (including the embracing of adult social and moral responsibilities). In addition, there is a need to consider that literature which discusses the contemporary breakdown of 'traditional' forms of community life and indicates why traditional neighbourhood and community loyalties and networks may now be peripheral to the lives of young people in modern society. While not focusing upon Citizenship Education directly, this material has the capacity to provide some of the knowledge and understanding necessary to ensure the successful implementation of Citizenship Education in schools and to reveal potential ways of re-engaging young people with their local communities and local and national democratic processes.

Hackett (1997) argues that two of the traditional arenas for political socialisation – work and further or higher education – have radically changed for today's young people. While further and higher education attendance has increased, this has tended to be accompanied by part-time work and the accumulation of debt. This situation fosters a concentration on individual futures, leaving little room for collectivism and altruism. Moreover, longer periods of financial dependency and a reduction in opportunities to take part in political activities in the workplace means that the spaces that young people occupy offer few opportunities for exploring and fostering traditional politics.

Kimberlee (2002) takes this argument further, indicating that young people are not only delaying the assumption of a broad range of adult roles associated with adult citizenship, but also have less contact with the social environments in which such roles have traditionally been supported and developed (work, family, civic groups, the community etc.). He concludes that a broad range of youth-oriented identities are being created in other less traditional social sites (see also Heath and Cleaver, 2003; Hollands, 1995) and through artefacts such as clothing (see also Miles, 1998) where politics and political parties are largely absent.

Research also indicates that recognising that community and neighbourhood are contested concepts (Crow and Allan, 1994; Kenyon, 2000) may prove critical to the successful delivery of one of the three key recommendations for effective Citizenship Education (Crick, 1998): that students should learn about and become 'helpfully involved in the life and concerns of their communities'. Perhaps one of the most salient messages for the current study which emerges from this literature is that while neighbourhood and community for previous generations were associated with collective identities (local identity, i.e. where my neighbours and family belong, class and work identity, i.e. what my neighbours and family do), they are now increasingly associated with individual identities, i.e. as extensions of our homes (Forrest and Kearns, 2001). This provides one plausible explanation for young people's apparent disassociation from 'traditional' collective community involvement and neighbouring activities.

A further explanation for the apparent decline in community-based activities and support may lie in the fact that different groups can develop different 'time-geographies' and 'action-spaces' within a local area (Forrest and Kearns, 2001; Kenyon, 2000). Active community involvement and neighbouring may differ between different groups, and immediate next-door neighbours may know nothing about, or have little in common with, each other's work, workplaces, wider kinship groups or leisure activities.

In recognising the collapse of traditional support mechanisms and arenas of socialisation, this set of literature hints at the importance of understanding the changing nature of young peoples' out-of-school experiences if we are to revitalise and rebuild their social and moral responsibility to, and involvement in, traditional social situations and groupings. While the contingent and changing nature of family, work and community is now fully recognised in academic debates, this often lies in stark contrast to the idealised notions which have traditionally informed, and appear to continue to inform, policy and planning.

Contested citizenships and changing contexts: questions for our research

Given these lessons from these different bodies of literature, three key questions begin to arise, both for the baseline exercise and the substantive longitudinal study:

1 Recognising that Citizenship and Citizenship Education are contested concepts, is the confusion evident in the research literature on the meaning of Citizenship and Citizenship Education reflected in practice in schools?
2 How do young people understand and experience community and belonging both within and beyond school?
3 What implications do these initial findings have for schools endeavouring to implement Citizenship through the curriculum and Active Citizenship through involvement in school and wider local communities?

We will return to a consideration of these questions at the close of the chapter. First, we need to consider what the findings of our baseline and case study research say about the apparent place of Citizenship in the school curriculum at the time of the formal introduction of the subject to the National Curriculum in 2002 and the status of Active Citizenship opportunities within and beyond the school's boundaries at this point in time.

The place of Citizenship Education in the school curriculum

Survey data from our first cross-sectional survey (collected prior to the statutory introduction of Citizenship Education to the curriculum) suggests that existing approaches to Citizenship Education were varied.

Almost two-thirds (65 per cent) of school leaders surveyed stated they had an agreed strategy for teaching Citizenship Education. They claimed to take a whole school approach and felt they were already delivering some of the new requirements for Citizenship Education. This approach encompassed school ethos and values as well as teaching and learning approaches in the classroom. *Citizenship Education was most commonly taught, prior to September 2002, through Citizenship-related modules in PSHE in 90 per cent of schools*. In addition, three quarters of the schools in our sample stated that they took a *cross-curricular* approach to Citizenship, with Citizenship-related topics taught through Religious Education (RE), English, History and Geography, amongst other subjects. Over half of the schools (57 per cent) that responded additionally stated that Citizenship was taught through extra-curricular activities and one-off events: a mix of approaches that the editors of this collection are hardly complimentary about.

A variety of delivery plans for September 2002 onwards were found. Three quarters of the schools had already appointed a Coordinator for Citizenship Education. However, rather than teaching Citizenship in dedicated timeslots (as reported by 15 per cent of the schools), the majority of schools indicated that they planned to continue to use existing expertise to deliver the curriculum through a range of subjects.

Teachers reported that teacher-led approaches to Citizenship-related topics were more predominant in the classroom than participatory, active approaches. In addition they stated that they had little or no experience of assessing student outcomes in relation to Citizenship Education: just over four-fifths of teachers (83 per cent) said they did not assess students in Citizenship Education. Indeed, few schools reported that they had definite policies for recognising student achievement at the time of the survey (11 per cent at Key Stage 3 and eight per cent at Key Stage 4). However, three quarters of the sample stated that they planned to develop this in the future.

Survey responses revealed that while the majority of teachers claimed to understand the aims and purposes of Citizenship Education, many were unfamiliar with the new Citizenship Order (i.e. the National Curriculum requirements) and were uncertain about what they would be teaching in September 2002. Familiarity with the curriculum was largely found in responses to the school-level questionnaires (filled in by head teachers and other senior managers or Citizenship Coordinators). This confusion about Citizenship Education was reflected less in our case study responses, perhaps due to the fact that most case study schools had been teaching Citizenship Education for at least six months prior to interviews taking place.

However, when speaking of school staff not involved in the direct delivery of Citizenship, case study participants indicated that they were often hostile to, and dismissive of, Citizenship Education, viewing it as yet another initiative. In the words of the head of Year 10 in one case study school, 'the staff are not on side at all, they see it as a burden'. This general lack of support amongst school staff appeared to cause concern for those trying to champion the place of Citizenship Education on the timetable and was often attributed to a lack of understanding of Citizenship Education. Moreover, some disagreement as to the purposes and objectives of Citizenship Education was encountered in certain schools. In one school in particular, the Citizenship Coordinator's view of and vision for Citizenship Education as a subject was contrasted to that of the senior management team where Citizenship Education was viewed solely in terms of *Global* Citizenship (a focus which resonated with the specialist language college status of the school).

Unsurprisingly, when the above comments are taken into account, our survey found that the majority of teachers (71 per cent) had not received any training in relation to Citizenship Education. In order to develop a better understanding of Citizenship Education, teachers favoured greater training opportunities, particularly concerning subject knowledge (89 per cent) and teaching and learning approaches (65 per cent). The policy implications seem clear: CPD must be a firm priority, a point made by many other contributors to this volume.

The position of Active Citizenship within and beyond the school

Schools that responded to our survey stated that they provided many opportunities for students to be involved in *Active* Citizenship activities, such as school councils and clubs, both in and out of school. Moreover, school leaders stated that they were satisfied that the whole school was involved in discussion and decision-making about school matters. However, only just over half the teachers surveyed (57 per cent) subscribed to this view and less than a third of students (27 per cent) felt that they were consulted about school policies, findings that resonate with Hannam's claims in Chapter 5.7. Moreover, take-up rates of the activities provided for students were reported as low, with only ten per cent of students having participated in a school council, and only a third of students reporting that they had taken part in school council elections. Citizenship-related activities such as mock elections, environmental, political and human rights and debating clubs were also reported to have a particularly low up-take, with around five per cent of students involved in such activities.

Case study data suggests that despite a low take-up of opportunities to participate within the school, students felt strongly that they should be involved in the decision-making process. In the words of one Year 9 student: 'if there wasn't students there wouldn't be a school so we should have a say about what we want our school to be like'. Interestingly, however, a Year 9 student in another school was pragmatic about the level of involvement students could expect, stating that students' opinions should be listened to '. . . within reason. If they're good and they'll work . . . if they're feasible. You can't really let the pupils run the school'. In the main, students indicated that if they had a particular problem or issue that they wished to address they would take one of three routes in addition to or instead of using the school council: talking to their form tutor; going straight to the school head; or starting a petition.

And what of the school and student interface with the community beyond the school gates? Survey data reveal that the majority (95 per cent) of school leaders felt that there were good relationships between their school and the wider community. Almost three quarters (74 per cent) believed that students in their institutions were taught to contribute to solving problems in the community. However, case study responses suggest that while at the senior management level this view may be prevalent, students believed that they had little opportunity to participate within the wider community through the school and their sense of belonging to this community was limited. Where mentioned, students indicated that their contact with the local community through school tended to be limited to discrete events such as clearing a local woodland, visiting a local hospice or taking part in a musical event for old people, or associated with particular extra-curricular schemes such as the Duke of Edinburgh scheme. Crick's notion of Community Involvement seems to demand much more than this.

Factors affecting school approaches to Citizenship in the curriculum

Recognising the diversity of approaches taken to Citizenship Education, what factors appear to affect the model of provision that schools adopt? Initial reflection on the case study interviews suggests that the models of Citizenship curriculum provision that schools adopt may be affected by whether a school's ethos is narrowly results-oriented or supportive of a broader, more balanced education. Results-oriented schools appear more likely to adopt Citizenship as an examined subject and/or to view it as an added-value aspect of the less formal curriculum. The former strategy is used to give Citizenship status in the school, in teachers' and in students' and parents' eyes, while the latter strategy appears to stem from the wish for certain schools to help their exam-oriented students become more rounded individuals. In schools that support a broader, more balanced education, there appears less likelihood of the adoption of Citizenship as an examined subject. However, these schools may view it as adding value to their students' experiences, as the life skills that Citizenship can teach may prove more useful to certain students than traditional exam subjects. In the words of one assistant headteacher: 'You have to make sure you are providing opportunities for every single person with a whole range of abilities . . . clearly within that you could argue that Citizenship is an important part of it because you are preparing young people for work and life beyond school'. This was certainly supported by a group of students from the same school who intended to leave school at 16. When reflecting on the *utility* of Citizenship Education, they argued that Citizenship was better than other subjects as it taught them about real life issues: 'We talked about our past in History: what do you need that for?' But, as the editors argue, Citizenship as the preserve of the less successful or low-achieving brings problems of its own, not dissimilar to those long bemoaned by progressive advocates of vocational education and work-related learning.

In addition, the status that Citizenship Education receives in the school and the resources provided (staffing, time and money) appear to be affected by whether the delivery and organisation of Citizenship Education is driven by senior management or the Citizenship Coordinator. In general it appears that the higher the level of senior management support, the more developed Citizenship Education is within a school. For example, at one end of the scale, one case study school had full senior management support, to the point that all Key Stage 4 Citizenship Education modules were taught by members of the senior management team. In another school where the vision of the Citizenship Coordinator and senior manager appeared to be at odds, and a lack of communication had ensued, the status of Citizenship remained contested and little in terms of implementation was underway.

The school as a community

Turning to a consideration of *Active* Citizenship within schools, case study data lead us to suggest that, in many cases, low levels of involvement in school councils and school council elections may in part reflect a lack of interest in, as well as a lack of opportunity to take part in, and/or a lack of knowledge of, the school council system. When asked if they would like to be a member of the student council, or to run for election, students who took part in our case study interviews were unanimous in saying 'no'. In one school, Year 10 students argued that they would rather stay with their friends during their tutorial periods than attend school council with strangers. In a number of the schools we visited, student councils appeared to be in need of reorganisation and advertising. Furthermore, students appeared unsure as to how council members were elected or how often they met; indeed in some schools students were unclear as to who their student council representatives were.

Student enthusiasm for student councils appeared to be affected by two further factors. First, if students sensed that they lacked efficacy, they appeared to be less enthusiastic. In the words of one Year 10 student who discussed students' attempts to bring about a change in uniform: 'we tried but I got basically shouted at'. A Year 10 student in a different school had a similar comment to make: 'you can't [be heard in this school] because they don't listen to you . . . its what the teachers say and that's it'. Even in schools where students felt that they were listened to, and that their requests were taken seriously, students indicated that their voice had a low priority in the decision-making process. Second, enthusiasm for participation appeared to be adversely affected by a lack of feedback. Students revealed that they were often unsure whether their suggestions for change were effective or not: 'whether they listened to what we said, we don't know'.

The impracticality of taking part in after-school activities was highlighted by those students who travelled some distance to school and who were reliant on public or parental transport at the end of the day. The issue appeared to be further exacerbated in larger schools where a series of short staggered lunch breaks meant that not all students were available at the same time to take part in midday activities, and the time available was limited. As one Year 11 student stated: 'Normally we used to do things at lunchtimes but now its been shortened you can't . . . so there goes our activities . . . I would rather have a longer lunch and do more activities.'

In two case study schools, discussion ensued about whether a vertical 'house' system or a horizontal 'year' tutorial and pastoral system helped to create a greater sense of belonging to, and participation in, a school. One particular school had moved from a house system to a year system in recent years, while another was undergoing a change from a year system to a house system at the time of the case study visit. In both cases staff reflected on their feeling that the vertical 'house' system was more conducive to creating a sense of belonging and community; not least as friendly competition was more practicable between houses comprising year groups than between year groups per se.

When asked whether they felt a greater sense of affinity and belonging to their school or local communities, the students who took part in our case study interviews argued that school formed their main community base.

Certain factors were viewed as central to the formation and experience of community in school. First, students' sense of efficacy: the more students felt that they had a voice in their school the more they felt a sense of belonging and commitment to a school community. Second, students' resonance with the school ethos: for example those students who valued school and the qualifications it promoted appeared more likely to feel that they belonged to a school community than those who felt aliened by the educational system in general and the school specifically. For example, one student group indicated that they did not feel part of the school community as school was 'so boring' and at odds with their own life views and values. Finally, students' friendship groups: if students' key friendship groups were situated at school then they appeared more likely to associate with school as a community.

The school interface with the wider community

Case study data also indicates some of the factors may impact negatively upon the development of good relationships between the school and the local community. In particular, respondents indicated that wide ranging school catchment areas could limit the affinity that students felt to the community immediately surrounding the school. In addition, schools reported that they were often hard pressed to fit the range of activities and subjects necessary to fulfil their National Curriculum obligations into the school day. Extra-curricular activities such as community liaison were therefore often given a lower priority.

A general culture of hostility to young people was said to impact on students' and staff members' reluctance to interface with the local community. Respondents reported that bad behaviour of young people in the local community was often associated with school students. In turn, they believed that this affected the community's willingness to interface with the school and students alike. Students in particular stated that they felt alienated from the local community due to stereotypical images of local youths that were bandied about: 'they just think we're all vandals'.

Young people argued that the fact that their local communities did not cater for young people, providing no spaces which they could call their own, meant that they had little opportunity to take part in their neighbourhoods beyond becoming members of formal clubs such as the Girl Guides and sporting clubs. However, despite this disillusionment with their local areas, the majority of young people appeared to have a strong sense of duty to their local community. In particular students spoke of making sure they did not cause trouble for other people. Indeed, a degree of disgust was expressed by most students about the small minority of young people who vandalised their communities, thereby perpetuating the negative stereotypes of young people. Many of the young people we spoke to felt as uneasy as older age groups when passing groups of youths hanging around in the neighbourhood, and felt excluded from certain community spaces (such as youth clubs and recreation grounds) by a minority who caused trouble. For some students this lack of community space was further affected by the fact that the school facilities were not available to them, or to others, outside of school hours, and particularly during the holidays. Even one professed community school in the sample did not offer this facility.

The starting point for National Curriculum Citizenship: our conclusions

What can the analysis presented so far tell us in response to the three questions posed earlier in the chapter? First, in answer to the question: **is the confusion evident in the research literature on the meaning of Citizenship and Citizenship Education reflected in practice in schools?**, our data reveals that this may indeed be the case and that a number of key issues remain unresolved. In particular these include: agreement on the definition, aims and purposes of Citizenship Education, its location in the curriculum, how Citizenship Education should be assessed and how to develop and foster a community within school and relationships between schools and their local communities. Citizenship Education *is* implemented and understood in a variety of ways across the sample schools. Moreover, as staff members become more removed from the daily implementation of Citizenship Education, it appears that they become less familiar with the curriculum and more hostile to its implementation. *This lack of wider staff support was viewed as one of the main barriers to the successful implementation of Citizenship Education as a key curriculum subject in our case study schools.*

Second, **how do young people understand and experience community and belonging both within and beyond school?** Analysis reveals that students have varied experiences and views on community and participation within and beyond school. The evidence presented suggests that irrespective of the opportunities presented to students to experience Citizenship Education as a *curriculum* subject, and to become an active member of a school community, certain factors may act to frame the success of the approaches taken. In particular, student efficacy cannot simply be created but must be fostered, taking into account a series of factors such as students' cultural values and friendship groups and the local community's image of young people, alongside more structural factors such as a lack of available time, a lack of facilities for young people (including closure of school facilities out of hours). These factors, amongst others, may all act to influence students' sense of belonging to the school and their local community and their take-up of school-based and community-based activities.

Finally, **what implications do these initial findings have for schools endeavouring to implement Citizenship through the National Curriculum and Active Citizenship through involvement in the school and their wider local communities?** While we are quick to stress that the factors highlighted above are by no means the sole ones affecting the model of Citizenship delivery which develops within schools and/or students' understandings of, or attitudes towards, Active Citizenship, it is important to note that they point towards the need for future analysis to explore in greater detail the processes by which decision-making and resource allocation for Citizenship Education are driven within schools and the models of Citizenship Education which result from these processes. In addition, they indicate the need to address both the *in school* and *out of school* factors which may affect student participation in, and their sense of belonging to, the school community and the community beyond.

REFERENCES

Arnot, M., Araujo, H., Deliyanni-Kouimtzis, K., Ivinson, G. and Tome, A. (2000) 'The good citizen: cultural understandings of citizenship and gender amongst a new generation of teachers', in M. Leicester, C. Modgil and S. Modgil (eds) 'Education, Culture and Values. Volume 6' of *Politics, Education and Citizenship*. London: Falmer Press.

Arthur, J., Davies, I., Wrenn, A. and Kerr, D. (eds) (2001) *Citizenship Through Secondary History*. London: RoutledgeFalmer.

Batho, G. (1990) 'The history of the teaching of civics and citizenship in English schools', *The Curriculum Journal*, 1(1): 91–100.

Brown, C. (1991) 'Education for citizenship: old wine in new bottles?', *Citizenship*, 1(2): 6–9.

Crick Report, DfEE (1998) 'Advisory Group on Education and Citizenship and the Teaching of democracy in Schools' *Education for Citizenship and the Teaching of Democracy in Schools*. London: QCA.

Crow, G. and Allan, G. (1994) *Community Life: an Introduction to Local Social Relations*. Hemel Hempstead: Harvester Wheatsheaf.

Davies, L. (1999) 'Comparing definitions of democracy in education', *Compare*, 29(2): 127–40.

Forrest, R. and Kearns, A. (2001) 'Social cohesion, social capital and the neighbourhood', *Urban Studies*, 38(12): 2125–43.

Frazer, E. (2000) 'Citizenship education: anti-political culture and political education in Britain', *Political Studies*, 48: 88–103.

Hackett, C. (1997) 'Young people and political participation', in J. Roche and S. Tucker (eds) *Youth in Society: Contemporary Theory, Policy and Practice*. London: Sage and The Open University Press.

Hall, S. (2000) 'Multicultural citizens, monocultural citizenship?', in N. Pearce and J. Hallgarten (eds) *Tomorrow's Citizens. Critical Debates in Citizenship and Education*. London: Institute for Public Policy Research.

Heater, D. (1990) *Citizenship: the Civic Ideal in World History, Politics and Education*. Harlow: Longman.

Heater, D. (2001) *History of Citizenship*. Leicester: Allandale Online Publishing.

Heath, S. and Cleaver, E. (2003) *Young, Free and Single*. Basingstoke: Palgrave.

Hollands, R. (1995) *Friday Night, Saturday Night: Youth Cultural Identification in the Post-Industrial City*. Newcastle upon Tyne: University of Newcastle upon Tyne, Department of Social Policy.

Kenyon, E. (2000) 'Time, temporality and the dynamics of community', *Time and Society*, 9: 21–41.

Kerr, D., Cleaver, E., Ireland, E. and Blenkinsop, S. (2003) *Citizenship Education Longitudinal Study: First Cross-sectional Survey 2001–2002* (DfES Research Report 416). London: DfES Publications.

Kerr, D. (1999a) *Citizenship Education: an International Comparison (International Review of Curriculum and Assessment Frameworks Thematic Study 4)*. London: QCA.

Kerr, D. (1999b) 'Re-examining citizenship education in England', in J. Torney-Purta, J. Schwille and J-A. Amadeo (eds) *Civic Education Across Countries: Twenty-four National Case Studies from the IEA Civic Education Project*. Amsterdam, The Netherlands: The International Association for the Evaluation of Educational Achievement.[3]

Kerr, D. (1999c) *Re-examining Citizenship Education: the Case of England*. National Case Study for IEA Citizenship Education Study Phase 1. Slough: QCA/NFER.

Kimberlee, R. (2002) 'Why don't British young people vote at general elections', *Journal of Youth Studies*, 5: 85–98.

Lambert, D. and Machon, P. (eds) (2001) *Citizenship Through Secondary Geography*. London: RoutledgeFalmer.

McLaughlin, T.H. (2000) 'Citizenship education in England: Crick Report and beyond', *Journal of Philosophy of Education*, 34(4): 541–70.

Miles, S. (1998) *Consumerism as a Way of Life*. London: Sage.

Moss, J. (2001) *Citizenship Through Secondary English*. London: RoutledgeFalmer.

Pearce, N. and Hallgarten, J. (eds) (2000) *Tomorrow's Citizens: critical debates in citizenship and education*. London: Institute for Public Policy Research (IPPR).

Scott, D. and Lawson, H. (eds) (2001) *Citizenship Education and the Curriculum (International Perspectives on Curriculum Series: Vol 3)*. Westport, CT: Greenwood Publishing.

Tooley, J. (2000) *Reclaiming Education*. London: Cassell.

Torney-Purta, J., Schwille, J. and Amadeo, J-A. (eds) (1999) *Civic Education Across Countries: Twenty-four National Case Studies from the IEA Civic Education Project*. Amsterdam, The Netherlands: The International Association for the Evaluation of Educational Achievement.

NOTES

1 Some sections of this chapter have been previously published in the first year report on the Citizenship Education Longitudinal Study (see Kerr et al., 2003).

2 For further details about the Citizenship Educational Longitudinal Study, its design and latest reports and findings, see http://www.nfer.ac.uk/research-areas/citizenship/

3 The Study was known as the IEA Citizenship Education Study in England. It was felt that the term 'civic education' would be confusing for those schools, teachers and young people who participated, given the focus, at the time of the Study, of the Advisory Group's work on citizenship education.

FURTHER READING

Gearon, L. (2003) *How Do We Learn to Become Good Citizens? A Professional User Review of UK Research Undertaken for the British Educational Research Association*. Nottingham: BERA.

Kerr, D. and Cleaver, E. (2004) *Citizenship Education Longitudinal Study: Literature Review – Citizenship Education One Year On – What Does it Mean?: Emerging Definitions and Approaches in the First Year of National Curriculum Citizenship in England* (DfES Research Report 532). London: DfES.

Kerr, D., Cleaver, E., Ireland, E. and Blenkinsop, S. (2003) *Citizenship Education Longitudinal Study First Cross-Sectional Survey 2001–2002* (DfES Research Report 416). London: DfES.

Kerr, D., Lines, A., Blenkinsop, S. and Schagen, I. (2002) *England's Results from the IEA International Citizenship Education Study: What Citizenship and Education mean to 14 Year Olds* (DfES Research Brief 375). Available at http://www.nfer.ac.uk/research/down_pub.asp – accessed 29 November 2002.

Kerr, D., Ireland, E., Lopes, J. and Craig, R. with Cleaver, E. (2004) *Citizenship Education Longitudinal Study Second Annual Report, First Longitudinal Survey.* (DfES Research Report 531). Nottingham: DfES Publications.

Citizenship in the National Curriculum: Contexts, Requirements and Expectations

Ian Davies

The rise of the National Curriculum

It is important to understand the rationale behind the introduction and development of the original National Curriculum in order to grasp a sense of the curricular context that Citizenship Education is, today, a part of.

Traditionally the English education system has not been comfortable with strong regulation by central government. Well-known anecdotal evidence has at least one Labour Minister for Education in the 1940s proudly asserting that 'minister knows nowt about curriculum' (Chitty, 1989). The 'secret garden' of the curriculum was one that was not, officially, interfered with as individual teachers and schools were allowed to get on with the business of deciding what their students needed and implementing what they deemed appropriate. Of course, the existence of examination boards, the availability of commercially produced resources, the opportunities available in particular local areas and the time and commonsense philosophy of what needed to be done did not lead to unimpeded diversity. However, the 'triangle of tension' referred to by Briault (1976) was felt to be the best way of describing the tensions between central government, local government and schools, without any necessary dominance by one section of this educational community.

There was, nonetheless, some simple and good commonsense behind the development of the National Curriculum and, here, the key politician was Kenneth Baker. He outlined his reasons for the need to change during his speech to the North of England Education Conference on 6 January 1989, arguing that a *national* curriculum would:

- give a clear incentive for all schools to catch up with the best, and the best would be challenged to do even better
- provide teachers with detailed and precise objectives
- provide parents with clear, accurate information
- ensure continuity and progression from one year to another, from one school to another
- help teachers to concentrate on the task of getting the best possible results from each individual child.

However, three issues need to be highlighted in order to interpret this seemingly innocent picture. Each of these issues is directly relevant to the form of *negative* Citizenship Education that began to develop in the late 1980s and early 1990s.

Equality, economic performance and the moral maze: a context for effective Citizenship Education?

First, many felt aggrieved about the failure to address issues about equality. The National Curriculum seemed, in spite of Baker's apparent intentions, to be centrally concerned with the development of a test-driven and hierarchical system. Previously, there had been a positive concern that the diversity of practice that existed across the existing curricula prior to the National Curriculum acted against the needs of those who were not powerful. Now, many challenged the apparent imposition of the sort of *hegemonic* thinking that sociologists had long warned about. In short, it was suggested that the new arrangements, rather than offering an entitlement curriculum for all, represented a new and oppressive centralisation of practice, one model that claimed to fit all but *suited* few.

Second, it is important to note that these concerns about equality came to be congruent with issues about national economic performance. Barnett (1986) was an influential academic railing against the supposed other-worldliness of schools. Although his arguments seem generally not to be supported by evidence (Rubinstein, 1993), his influence is undeniable. By 1976, James Callaghan, in his famous speech at Ruskin College, was protesting about the inefficiency and ineffectiveness of schools, and during the 1980s the Technical and Vocational Education Initiative, which Linda Prince debates in Chapter 5.5, arguably in an echo of Ruskin, was established with the aim of making schools relate more directly to the 'real world' of work. This attitude has continued.

Third, there were what can broadly be described as moral and political imperatives to change the curriculum. If we were to believe (which I do not) that, due to the unprofessional influence of politically motivated teachers, 'there is no parent of school age children who does not have an educational horror story to tell' (as Baroness Warnock stated in her 1985 Dimbleby lecture) then something had to be done. The curriculum (and by implication, young people) had to be rescued from the hands of the exclusive and elitist 'educational establishment' who did not allow parents (or anyone else) to have any influence. As this 'establishment' principally consisted of Her Majesty's Inspectorate, Local Education Authorities and members of staff in university departments of education, radical action was seen to be necessary. Thus, a whole raft of educational reforms that challenged this establishment were introduced from the end of the 1980s, of which only the National Curriculum concerns us here. It is nevertheless important to see this particular initiative as part of a wider package: the formation of Ofsted, the launch of Grant Maintained Schools and City Technology Colleges, the devolution of budgetary control to schools (LMS) and, subsequently, league tables.

Education for Citizenship and the early days of the National Curriculum

In this context, the association of Citizenship Education, however marginalised, with the introduction of the National Curriculum proved problematic both for the curriculum radicals, with their concern to develop political literacy, and for practitioners. The reasons for the growth of interest in political education in the 1970s contrasted markedly with what began to be associated with *Citizenship* Education in the 1980s. Generally, a desire to democratise education and an acceptance that young people were surrounded by political messages (and had the capacity to understand them) was supplanted by the perceived need for volunteering by young people in a society with an ageing population, a rising crime rate and a shrinking welfare provision.

Although, for some, *Curriculum Guidance 8: Education for Citizenship* (NCC, 1990) was a document of permission which allowed professionals to get on with whatever they thought best, the now largely forgotten eight areas, the lack of assessment arrangements and the vague status of Education for Citizenship as a Cross-Curricular Theme, as Dufour has argued in the opening chapter, meant that this hastily put together, and in places incoherent, package was quickly neglected. Further, when placed in the context of a related initiative from the Speaker's Commission (HMSO, 1990) that stressed the primacy of the 'fourth dimension' (i.e. active volunteering by young people who had been enjoined to recognise their 'voluntary obligations' by the Home Secretary), there was great cause for worry.

In short, for many, it was unacceptable that this form of Citizenship Education was being promoted but a relief that it was given so little emphasis that it was never implemented. Whitty et al. (1994) described the disaster of Citizenship Education in the early 1990s, drawing attention to the absence of professional development programmes for teachers, low status in schools, inappropriate teaching styles and an absence of any clear notion of assessment or evaluation.

Citizenship Education: a reassessment and a 'proper' place in the National Curriculum

The key shift to something more positive occurred in 1997 with the appointment by David Blunkett (then Secretary of State for Education and Employment) of Professor Bernard Crick to chair a working group, with a range of memberships across the political spectrum, on Citizenship Education. This is not to suggest that the other essentially negative and intensely conservative motives referred to above had completely disappeared. Nevertheless, a desire to promote a communitarian vision, a genuine focus on political engagement and the positive influence of the European Union in relation to matters such as the implementation of the Human Rights Act gained a new recognition; certainly, a recognition that was largely absent from those Citizenship initiatives that had been prompted by previous governments.

As readers are aware, the Crick Report, *Education for Citizenship and the Teaching of Democracy in Schools* (DfEE/QCA, 1998), recommended a model of Citizenship that encompassed three strands: social and moral responsibility, community involvement and political literacy. The report was immediately accepted by the government and this document was then used as the basis on which to develop something that had a clearer educational focus, a statutory order for National Curriculum Citizenship based around three themes: areas of knowledge and understanding, skills of enquiry and communication, and skills for participation and responsible action. An associated Attainment Target was used to develop End of Key Stage Descriptors for the standards that students aged 14 and 16 should reach and a looser framework for work in primary schools was developed so that links appropriate to students' age could be made with PSHE and their broader personal and social development.

So, in August 2002, following a much longer lead-in time than had been granted for any other National Curriculum subject, Citizenship became a requirement and Foundation Subject of the National Curriculum in schools. Various government agencies have been proactive in supporting this new subject. Kerr (2003) has reviewed some of these support mechanisms. The Department for Education and Skills (formerly the Department for Education and Employment) has set up a Citizenship team which has sponsored the creation of classroom materials and helped to establish a subject association for teachers, the Association for Citizenship Teaching (ACT). The Training and Development Agency for Schools (TDA) has funded the citizED project (www.citized.info) that seeks to develop a forum for action among those who are responsible for newly established initial teacher education programmes, and a National Strategy for Teachers' Continuing Professional Development in Citizenship has been established. The Qualifications and Curriculum Authority (QCA) has produced a series of Schemes of Work for Key Stages 3 and 4 in order to assist teachers. Non-governmental organisations such as the Citizenship Foundation, the Institute for Citizenship and Community Service Volunteers and others have all been active in the creation of materials, and running workshops designed to support and explore the implementation of the National Curriculum.

While, of course, significant challenges remain, an approach to Citizenship Education that is fundamentally and pre-eminently about political literacy is now *formally* recognised within the statutory curriculum. Moreover, supported by a nine year longitudinal study, that is detailed by Elizabeth Cleaver and her colleagues at NFER in Chapter 1.2, and the sort of multi-agency interest set out here, Citizenship appears to have both a developing and progressive identity and a more plausible curriculum location than the notion of a Cross-Curricular Theme ever afforded it.

Nonetheless, a number of challenges remain in establishing Citizenship in the National Curriculum. Four issues, in particular, are pertinent, these being: the appropriateness of developing a National Curriculum subject called *Citizenship*; the nature of the Citizenship Education that is being promoted; status and staffing; and the nature of Citizenship's subject knowledge – how it can be identified, taught, learned and assessed.

National Curriculum Citizenship: a contradiction?

For those who originally championed the cause of equal access to knowledge as a means of ensuring common learning entitlements, the inclusion of

Citizenship Education in the National Curriculum is a welcome development. I would certainly wish to count myself as someone who supports that perspective. However, it is necessary to consider various other and less positive interpretations if we are to be able to reflect fully on the nature of Citizenship Education.

There have been some who have wished sensitive material, especially political matters, to be kept away from young people. Perhaps the most explicit (and worryingly naive or disingenuous) statement that reflected this point of view is that nothing but harm can result from the attempt to introduce pupils to material that is unsuitable for them (reported by Brennan, 1981, reflecting on reactions to previous initiatives related to Citizenship Education). Citizenship issues, some wrongly argue, are either too complex intellectually, too demanding emotionally or would leave young minds too obviously exposed to those who are driven by anti-democratic agendas. Is it acceptable, some ask, either for unscrupulous teachers to be given free rein to do what they like, or, perhaps even worse, to introduce some sort of state sanctioned programme in how to behave 'properly'?

These worries, although real and potentially serious, cannot be allowed to stand in the way of the development of an important area of study. To assert that young people should not be involved in Citizenship Education is simply implausible. Political issues always dominate (explicitly or implicitly) people's lives in schools, the workplace and elsewhere. It is essential that we do not succumb to the spurious attractions of a so-called 'neutral' education. Education, *pace* Freire, is *never* neutral. What we need to do is to ensure that learning takes place in such a way as to develop young people's understanding and capabilities for democratic action.

Currently in England, as the experience of the ill-fated Cross-Curricular Themes shows, nothing will actually happen unless a subject is accorded sufficient status: *everywhere*, as the editors of this text assert, is usually *nowhere*. The problem, then, is not whether Citizenship should be included as a National Curriculum subject (that much is obvious) but rather whether two other questions can be adequately addressed. That is, first whether the context of the National Curriculum (its origins and goals as described above) are congruent with the promotion of learning appropriate within a democracy and, second, the extent to which the precise version of Citizenship that has been included is itself appropriate. I am somewhat uncertain about my response to the first of these two issues but feel that enough has been said already in order to begin to answer positively and hopefully. My answer to the second of these matters is the key concern of the remainder of this chapter.

What sort of Citizenship Education has been included in the National Curriculum?

Crick (2000) has developed a specific rationale for National Curriculum Citizenship and some responses to his critics. A shrewd political operator with a dogged determination that has carried him through from his earlier attempts to develop political literacy in the 1970s, he has certainly achieved considerable success working with well-placed political supporters across the political spectrum (including Kenneth Baker, who was responsible for so much of the National Curriculum edifice). The subsequent cross-party support that, at least initially, greeted his committee's report meant that very little of the argument to 'keep politics out of schools' has been heard. However, Gamarnikow and Green (2000) outline the argument that has worried some left-leaning commentators and analysts, contending that Crick's model is a naively conservative one that 'reproduces a version of citizenship education unlikely to challenge the social mechanisms of inequality reproduction'.

This analysis seems to be the general position that a number of critics seek to give more precise expression to. Their point is that Crick's model of Citizenship is essentially supportive of the status quo: of existing inequalities of class, gender, race and so forth. Moreover, they see it as absolving government from the need to challenge these inequalities; civic activity, or active citizenship, will mediate tensions and moderate change. From this sort of position, Osler (2003), for example, seems to develop the above general argument into a blast against the Crick Report as 'an example of institutional racism'.

These criticisms are worrying. They are, however, perhaps to be expected. It is unlikely that an educational initiative alone will ever inspire a radical transformation of society and certainly any official reform of it is unlikely to promote or achieve such an objective. As much as we may hope for a genuinely pluralistic, participatory democracy, I am unaware of any example of a society that has secured this objective on a sustained and large-scale context merely through educational change. Although Crick is almost required to assert the need to 'transform the political culture of this country' (DfEE/QCA, 1998) in order for those in government and elsewhere, who like to think of themselves as well meaning liberals, to sign up to the cause, it is unlikely that the reality will reflect fully the highly charged rhetoric. Perhaps the best we can hope for is that a greater recognition of the structural conditions dominating education will help us to ameliorate the outcomes of which the critics warn.

Within that context it is politically necessary to recognise the good work that Crick has done, unrealistic to expect social revolution through the education system (however much we enjoy and feel emboldened by the rhetoric of the self proclaimed radicals) and important to listen – and respond – to critical perspectives. This is not meant as a plea for defeatism or conservatism: I am certainly not arguing for the preservation of the status quo. I am, however, suggesting that too much easy talk within seminars does not lead to very realistic, useful, political (and, as such, educational) action.

Life in schools: who teaches Citizenship Education?

It is too early yet to know the details concerning staffing arrangements in all schools. More will become clear during the completion of the various ongoing evaluation projects (such as the National Foundation for Educational Research's longitudinal study) and, possibly, the work of Ofsted. It is, however, already clear that Crick has warned against too strong an emphasis on a perspective that sees Citizenship Education merely as a 'rebadging' of existing programmes in Personal, Social and Health Education.

> *To put it gently, schools will be in difficulty, in terms of assessment, examination (for instance through the GCSE Short Courses in Citizenship Studies) and inspection if headteachers, and senior and middle managers, whether by misunderstanding, inertia or desperation amid so many other demands, take a line of least resistance and think that PSHE, with a wee bit of padding and pulling, can do the trick.* (Crick, 2000)

The complementariness and distinctiveness of PSHE and Citizenship are clear and important, as Jan Campbell and Liz Craft establish in Chapter 6.2. But, there are early signs (Ofsted, 2002; Halpern et al., 2002) that there is uncertainty in too many settings. Citizenship Education is seen both as the whole purpose of the school and as a low status matter that is best dealt with by everybody generally and nobody specifically. The neglect of political issues and the emphasis on interpersonal relationships, warnings about health (mainly smoking, drugs and sex) and practical guidance on how to complete application forms for jobs and entry into further and higher education is of great concern but it is not, of itself, Citizenship Education.

It is, of course, little surprise that this may be happening. The subject is new, there was a need to avoid too great a prescription if one was to allow both the necessary freedom for teachers to develop it in their own way, and for the needs of different groups of pupils, and, by so doing, the proper recognition of teachers' professional status. It also helped enormously when arguing for the new subject to be accepted if it was seen both as something that could practically be achieved (i.e. little additional work would be required) and that it could be interpreted generously. Crick's 'strong bare bones' of a curriculum outline was necessary for Citizenship Education because of its very nature, essential if it was to gain curriculum access and risky in the extreme when used in the context of a teaching force that has been battered by years of attack on their independence. The absence of any real force of qualified teachers (only 150–250 Citizenship PGCE students qualified in each academic year during 2001–5) is an obvious fact in the development of any new subject but a frighteningly dramatic indication of the challenge still to be met. Perhaps one way in which the National Curriculum can be implemented successfully is by continuing to be positive (negative attitudes now would serve only those who would wish to see a return to a very different form of Citizenship Education) and by searching for intelligent practical classroom and school-based approaches to CPD. Here, the recently launched National CPD Strategy is a welcome move.

Doing Citizenship: teaching, learning and assessing

Throughout most discussions about Citizenship Education pedagogical issues highlight the real heart of good work. In the growth of a new subject the philosophers are vitally important but only when we go beyond their rhetoric will we show that Citizenship has achieved maturity. This means that we have consciously to develop a clearer understanding of subject knowledge, teaching methods and assessment strategies. Together with others, I have elsewhere (e.g. Davies and Thorpe, 2003) developed arguments (illustrated by practical curriculum resources) relating to what can be discussed as the procedural concepts of Citizenship. It is not enough for us to be concerned about mere subject matter as defined by one constitutional framework or one set of issues that are somehow deemed to be more important than others. Rather we have to focus on the business of *doing* Citizenship. This means in essence three things. First, we need to identify the substantive concepts that most concern us about Citizenship, concepts that are likely to include power, justice, legitimacy and so on. Those concepts do more than specify what content needs to be learned; instead they provide a framework for *thinking* about Citizenship.

Second, we need to identify more clearly the nature of the procedural concepts associated with Citizenship. That is, we should be able to be clear about what people need to do when they are studying Citizenship. In the field of history education, where some work has already been done on procedural concepts, it is recognised that evidence, change, cause and empathy are things that learners have to come to terms with. It is not enough to know about History, students must know how to study *historically*. We need to identify, as concepts, things (such as, perhaps, participation and inclusion) that students can both think about and practise.

Third, the process of that form of study will require a number of issues to be explored. We already know from a variety of studies (e.g. Hahn, 1998) that classroom climate is a vital ingredient of success when people are being educated about political matters. That climate will extend within and across classrooms and into the whole school context. We need to consider, in other words, the significance of an appropriate context for what people can do as they relate to each other through clear understanding and purposeful action. The very useful work in history education is valuable, though, only to a certain extent. The nature of Citizenship Education requires action and not just quiet individual reflection. In many History classrooms the purposes of study relate to the learners and the academic discipline (and indirectly to the wider society); in Citizenship the purposes relate to the discipline of Citizenship, the learners and the society within which they live (in the school and elsewhere). This essential *action* dimension can be developed when the substantive and the procedural concepts are linked by means of an appropriate pedagogy in which classroom climate is an essential factor.

Finally, assessment, as Tony Breslin argues in Chapter 6.5, will always be a key consideration in this discussion. It will be a vital part of decision-making about what will be taught and how it will be developed. It is likely that we will be able to develop sensible forms of understanding of good and less good activity in relation to Citizenship, collaborative means of communicating those analyses (self-evaluation as well as others) and a link to future teaching. This is very clearly not an argument for the establishment of the sort of mechanistic National Curriculum levels that reward some and punish others but rather for an evaluative framework to be more clearly developed that relates to what, pedagogically, we feel to be useful citizenship education. This is not then an argument to abandon the National Curriculum but rather for more work to be done so that we can develop our understanding of the essential nature and processes of Citizenship Education itself.

'Two cheers for democracy' and some urgent action

The needs of education for *effective* Citizenship and the nature of our National Curriculum make two uneasy partners. However, I wish to argue that inclusion of Citizenship Education within the National Curriculum is cause for some celebration. E.M. Forster once wrote a piece entitled 'two cheers for democracy' and it is perhaps this cautious, reserved, wary but positive approach which I wish to convey. The need for those who care about the further development of democracy is to work positively with young people so that constructive and critical political perspectives are developed. The framework of the National Curriculum provides a positive opportunity but, given our tradition of unsuccessful action, some urgent action is required to put flesh on that skeleton.

REFERENCES

Barnett, C. (1986) *The Audit of War: The Illusion and Reality of Britain as a Great Nation*. London: Macmillan.

Brennan, T. (1981) *Political Education and Democracy*. Cambridge: Cambridge University Press.

Briault, E. (1976) 'A Distributed System of Educational Administration: an international viewpoint', *International Review of Education*, 22(4): 429–39.

Chitty, C. (1989) *Towards a New Education System: The Victory of the New Right?* Lewes: The Falmer Press.

Crick, B. (2000) *Essays on Citizenship*. London: Continuum.

Davies, I. and Thorpe, T. (2003) 'Thinking and Acting as Citizens', in A. Ross and C. Roland-Lévy (eds) *Political Education in Europe*. Stoke on Trent: Trentham.

Department for Education and Employment/QCA (1998) *Education for Citizenship and the Teaching of Democracy in Schools. Final Report of the Advisory Group on Citizenship*. (The Crick Report). London: DfEE/QCA.

Gamarnikow, E. and Green, A. (2000) 'Citizenship, Education and Social Capital', in D. Lawton, J. Cairns and R. Gardner (eds) *Education for Citizenship*. London: Continuum.

Hahn, C. (1998) *Becoming Political*. London: SUNY.

Halpern, D., John, P. and Morris, Z. (2002) 'Before the Citizenship Order: a survey of citizenship education practice in England', *Journal of Education Policy*, 17(2): 217–28.

HMSO (1990) *Encouraging Citizenship*. London: HMSO.

Kerr, D. (2003) *Developing Citizenship Education in England: Results from the IEA Civic Education Project*. Paper presented at the American Education Research Association conference, Chicago.

NCC (National Curriculum Council) (1990) *Education for Citizenship*. (*Curriculum Guidance 8*). York: NCC.

Ofsted (2002) *Citizenship: Survey Report: Preparation for the Introduction of Citizenship in Secondary Schools 2001/2. HMI 730*. London: Office of Her Majesty's Inspectorate of Schools.

Osler, A. (2003) 'The Crick Report and the Future of Multiethnic Britain', in L. Gearon (ed.) *Learning to Teach Citizenship Education in the Secondary School*. London: RoutledgeFalmer.
Rubinstein, D. (1993) *Culture, Capitalism and Decline in Britain 1750–1990*. London: Routledge.
Whitty, G., Rowe, G. and Appleton, P. (1994) 'Subjects and themes in the secondary school curriculum', *Research Papers in Education*, 9(2): 159–81.

FURTHER READING

Hahn, C.L. (1998) *Becoming Political: Comparative Perspectives on Citizenship Education*. Albany: State University of New York Press (SUNY).
Heater, D. (1999) *What is Citizenship?* Cambridge: Polity Press.
Lockyer, A., Crick, B. and Annette, J. (2003) *Education for Democratic Citizenship*. Aldershot: Ashgate.
Potter, J. (2002) *Active Citizenship in Schools: a good practice guide to developing a whole school policy.* London: Kogan Page.

PART TWO

FOUNDATIONS FOR CITIZENSHIP THE ARTS AND HUMANITIES

From Art and Design to Citizenship: The Role of Built Environment Education

Lesley Burgess and Catherine Williamson

Distant others dictating directions?

The National Curriculum Art and Design Order (QCA, 1999; DfEE, 2000a) can be recognised as a deliberately flexible framework. It is predicated on the importance of developing *creativity*, *imagination,* and knowledge and understanding of *cultural heritage*, and accommodates different approaches to teaching these difficult-to-define concepts. However, this flexibility is both its weakness and its strength. For some Art and Design teachers the National Curriculum rubberstamps an orthodox approach that privileges practical work informed by a patriarchal, high art canon; a practice that continues to be rewarded with good grades in examinations, – negating any reasons for revision or reconceptualisation. Yet, for others, the National Curriculum champions change, encourages inclusivity and promotes partnership; allowing for the developing professional knowledge of teachers and the contemporary concerns of young people to drive and direct curriculum content. At one extreme, Art and Design is considered uniquely creative, an autonomous realm divorced from other forms of social and cultural production. At the other, it is seen to engage critically with contentious issues and difficult debates making an important contribution to pupils' understanding of what it means to be a citizen in a postmodern society.

Nailing the jelly to the wall

Art has always been a slippery subject, difficult to define succinctly since it can be seen to extend across the fine art, craft and design continuum and include all aspects of visual and material culture, both past and present. This breadth belies the general perception of Art and Design in mainstream education as a practical subject preoccupied with direct observation, self-expression, and the acquisition of technical skills; a counterpoint to the logocentric curriculum. It is true that Art and Design teachers sometimes feel that constricting timetables and limited finances trap them in their classrooms where they repeatedly ricochet against the walls unable to resolve conflicting priorities or make connections with outside agencies. They are also aware that pressures to accord with objective standards of practice can result in teaching becoming an unreflective technical process. Therefore, it is of no surprise that teachers are sometimes tempted to be territorial and reinforce subject boundaries rather than risk diluting existing provision by layering it with new, cross-curricular initiatives. However, any perception of Art and Design as orthodox and insular is a limiting stereotype and one that needs to be challenged. It fails to recognise Art and Design's contribution to the *critical* as well as the *creative* curriculum or to acknowledge that many teachers are keen to exploit productive tensions between heritage culture and contemporary practice and are excited by the possibilities of creative partnerships.

In this chapter, we aim to show how, despite limitations and temptations, Art and Design teachers (and their pupils) can become agents of change, making significant contributions not just to the developing Art and Design curriculum but also to pertinent whole school issues and debates – in this instance Citizenship and the built environment.

Art and Citizenship

Art and Design contributes to Citizenship through helping pupils to:

- recognise how artists, craftspeople and designers have responded to issues, problems and events in contemporary and past times
- express their own ideas, beliefs and values through creative work and
- negotiate, make decisions and take responsibility in collaborative projects that explore the role and function of Art and Design in the school, locality and wider world.

Source: *Citizenship through Art and Design at Key Stage 3* (DfEE/QCA, 2000b).

Beyond the QCA statements little has been written about the contribution of Art and Design to Citizenship Education in secondary schools. Notable exceptions are chapters by Smith (2004) and Hickman (2003). Smith insists that it is 'difficult to convey the form, nature and benefits of the higher order values, practices, skills and outcomes implicit within the best educational encounters' *in* the Arts (2004: 33). He points out that aspects of Citizenship are integral to such encounters. In contrast, Hickman focuses on learning *through* Art and Design when he suggests that, to educate young people as citizens who can make a meaningful contribution to society, we should recognise that 'meaningful contribution' can, and should, include activities that challenge authority and provoke dissent. He claims:

> *One potent myth of modernism is the personification of the artist as transgressor and outsider. Therefore many, perhaps even most, western artists are not known for their socially responsible behaviour. It could be said, however, that they have made useful contributions to society because of their willingness to transgress social mores and engage with the politics of dissent.* (2003: 85)

Hickman describes how Art and Design has the potential to challenge, but also to perpetuate, racial and cultural stereotyping. He points out that although much contemporary art is concerned with social commentary, schools have perceived its introduction into the secondary curriculum as too radical, prompting cries for a return to traditional art skills. Importantly, he recognises that a 'certain tension is all for the good – resisting the status quo, challenging orthodoxies and rule breaking are essential attributes of meaningful Art and Design activities and, one would hope, of a healthy society' (ibid: 89).

Clearly, there are different ways in which teachers can involve young people in 'values' education and differing views on how this can be achieved (Addison and Dash, 2000). The built environment project outlined below provides one example of how Art and Design can make a 'meaningful contribution' to Citizenship. It involves participants in designing and making plans and models of spaces and places in response to given scenarios, while at the same time challenging them to reconsider taken-for-granted beliefs about identity, belonging and rights. It privileges the critical without denying the importance of praxis. Learning is simultaneously practical and dialogic.

Art and built environment education

> *The built environment has an important role to play in school education; in drawing together different fields of learning, and fundamental skills that include visual literacy; and in preparing children to participate in the shaping of their surroundings. It is an ideal subject for demonstrating the importance in education of interdisciplinary work, since in reality fields are seldom entirely segregated. It is a valuable educational resource, through which to encourage a literate and informed populace, needed for its maintenance and regeneration.* (Diamond Report, 1996: 24)

The relationship between children and their urban environment is highlighted by Goodman (1960), who questions whether the modern city, as a human institution, adopts a helping mode towards its young citizens, or whether, due to concealed technology, family mobility, loss of country, loss of neighbourhood tradition, and the eating up of play spaces, it can no longer accommodate young people's needs. In 1976 the built environment gained attention as a resource for Art and Design education through the Front Door project, part of *Design in General Education,* a research project at the Royal College of Art. It stressed the need for a critical and analytical approach. Baynes claims it called into question a curriculum 'made up of benign problems' where the ethic of the classroom was to know the answer, an approach that gave young people 'a lot of practice in absorbing knowledge, little in reasoning or decision making' (in Adams and Ward, 1983: 25). In response Adams calls for a balanced view, expressing a concern that learning which emphasises socio-economic and political aspects often neglects the subjective view and individual response. They quote Raban to reinforce this perception: 'The city as we know it, the soft city of illusion, myth and nightmare is as real as the hard city one can find on maps, in statistics, monographs, on urban sociology and architecture' (ibid: 20). They suggest that Art and Design is one of the few places in the curriculum where this balance can be fulfilled.

Recently, the role of built environment education has again become high profile with the launch of the Commission for Architecture and the Built Environment's (CABE) Education Foundation (October 2003). Its remit is 'to ensure greater public understanding of the importance of quality urban design through increasing access to opportunities for learning about and through the built environment' (CABE, see www.cabe-education.org.uk). Ben Spencer, Head of Education, argues that:

> *The primary reference point for the built environment in terms of Art and Design is quite simply the stuff that is out there. Teachers need to start with the familiar, explore the variations, the surprises, the oddities, and challenge people to question 'why is it like that?'* (Spencer, December 2003)

Researching the role of the built environment and Citizenship

In 2002 a questionnaire of 70 partnership secondary schools carried out through the PGCE Art and Design course at the Institute of Education, University of London identified that although the built environment is recognised as a valuable resource and one that is central to pupils' lived experience, it remains under-used and under-explored. This questionnaire was part of a research project (funded by Business Links Units through the Higher Education Funding Council) to identify the existing and potential role of the built environment in Art and Design education. The research was prompted, at least in part, by the MacPherson Report (1999) which, following the death of Stephen Lawrence, encouraged teachers to look again at race relations and recognise how they are influenced by urban cultural dynamics, including the physical and social environment.

Buckingham (2000: vii) suggests that 'young people today are postmodern citizens – cynical, distracted, no longer possessed of the civic virtues and responsibilities of older generations'. He claims that this is a response to their own powerlessness, their exclusion from the discourses and the decision-making process. Similarly, Wilkins' research (1999) reveals that young people's definition of the role of the 'good citizen' is restricted to minimal public duties and the defence of private property. Freire (1999) insists that the problem lies in the fact that students have not sufficiently developed habits of critical dialogue, that their discussions lack the rigor of reflection: reflection on how attitudes and values are formed and how they might be reformed. He suggests this is the reason why there is often an imbalance between chronological age and 'epistemological curiosity'. He claims, 'in many cases, epistemological curiosity remains truncated, giving rise to students who are intellectually immature' (1999: 53).

Wilkins also argues that Citizenship Education, reluctantly delivered by teachers lacking personal knowledge, skills, confidence and a positive enthusiasm for the subject, will undoubtedly fail, as many attempts to introduce these vital issues into the curriculum have done before (Wilkins, 2004: 26). His research identifies how student teachers' initial, positive attitude towards Citizenship Education is undermined by their own lack of civic awareness, which in turn impacts on their confidence to teach the subject. The questionnaire completed by the Institute of Education's PGCE Art and Design students and their subject mentors in partnership schools, confirms that, although there are examples of exemplary practice, many feel insecure about how to *critically* investigate such issues through built environment or Citizenship Education. Clearly, the opportunity to address this in Initial Teacher Education (ITE) needs to be exploited.

Agents of change?

> *PGCE students form the bridge between classroom pragmatism and the 'not yet possible'.* (Addison and Burgess, 2003: 163)

The PGCE course at the Institute of Education is based on a well-developed model of partnership with London schools and enjoys a reputation for curriculum innovation and change. Trainee teachers bring a range of expertise, backgrounds and previous professional training that can feed and sustain the debate and create a fascinating critical dynamic. Initial Teacher Education is recognised as a crucial point at which to encourage new teachers to develop their subject knowledge and explore topical issues. Increasingly, beginning teachers are starting to resist existing orthodoxies, exploit creative partnerships and develop expertise in critical and contextual studies including skills in discourse analysis. This is informed by wider debates in education, for example, Creativity (NACCCE, 1999), and new initiatives in the art world including the reconceptualisation of 'socially engaged' art practice promoted by the Arts Council England (Interrupt 2003/4 www.interrupt-symposium.org/) and the launch of the Platform website in November 2004 (www.platform.org.uk).

As noted, the Institute of Education's research confirms that a lack of subject knowledge and understanding militates against sustained involvement in such issues; it also identifies the need for professional partnerships to support curriculum development and locate relevant resources. In order to address these needs the Institute of Education invited interested organisations to collaborate with them and develop a learning resource to introduce built environment issues and civic awareness into the Art and Design curriculum. The Prince's Foundation recognised the potential synergy afforded by collaboration and agreed to support a pilot project. As the project developed it became clear that many of the issues raised were also pertinent to Citizenship Education.

Place Making: linking the art of building to the making of community

> *Design is not only knowing about the future; it is about imagining it, shaping it and bringing it about. This needs to be emphasised and made real in learning.* (Baynes cited in Diamond, 1996: 8)

Place Making is the result of a creative partnership between the Institute of Education and the Prince's Foundation that draws on the Foundation's experience of delivering professional education in the field of architecture and the built environment. Its aim is to generate inquiry into the components that make up a place and to initiate a participatory learning process that develops an awareness of, and consideration for, individual and collective needs within a community. It provides a framework within which to explore the basic principles of Citizenship in relation to the processes through which communities evolve.

Underpinning the project is the belief that the built environment concerns everyone and that the quality of this environment has a direct influence upon the quality of people's lives. How it is made, looks and functions is continually evolving. Its development is influenced by a diversity of people and agendas: historical, cultural, economic, political and environmental. As simple settlements have evolved into large bustling cities, the tasks and decision-making processes of Place Making have become assigned to planning bodies, architects and engineers. Design and construction processes have become more complex and are increasingly driven by commercial viability; consequently, there are fewer opportunities for public involvement, consultation and debate.

> *Too often people feel they have no contribution to make to their built environment, they feel no connection with it, as they have no part in building it.* (Bolgar, Director of Architecture & Design, The Prince's Foundation, 2003)

The Place Making 'experience' covers all aspects of creating a community; from understanding the need for basic shelter, exploring how structures are modified for functional and aesthetic reasons, to designing a settlement with consideration to the local environment and people's social and cultural needs. A participatory problem-solving approach, generated by a series of scenarios and challenges, looks at how the built environment evolves over time and investigates how it reflects and affects a community's quality of life.

Outline: mapping the content

At the start of the project each participant is given an image of an uninhabited and undeveloped environment. As the project progresses they discover that they are not living in isolation but share the same location with others and, still later, that these shared locations constitute an island. They have to consider the climate, physical features and available materials as they create in the first instance their personal shelter and, subsequently, a settlement. Simple frame structures made by each participant are clad and decorated to create a personalised shelter. The scenarios and processes involved in creating these shelters are designed to nurture a sense of identity and establish a sense of ownership. Understanding is developed through reflection on how decoration can signify personal and cultural identity. Using examples of buildings from different historical, social and cultural contexts, participants are encouraged to investigate how buildings and public spaces can record and reflect the status and preoccupations of their owners and makers. Having determined the function of their shelter, each participant negotiates the role and position of it within the settlement. As the project develops participants move from individual to collective concerns and therefore have to consider and discuss increasingly complex issues. The focus moves from a preoccupation with personal survival strategies towards consideration of how different cultural, economic, religious, social and political values can influence the way communities evolve. Throughout, key issues are introduced by the teacher to promote discussion, provoke enquiry, and link the activities to students' lives. Speculative debate, a key feature of the project, encourages high order thinking skills and stimulates the need to know.

> *Does somebody have to be in charge? Who makes the rules? Why can't we share responsibility? What happens if I don't want to be a part of this so-called community?* (Questions from a group of Art and Design students)

> *They recognised that form and decoration could signify exclusivity as well as inclusivity . . . It took them a while to realise why you couldn't put the public toilets upstream of the fish farm . . . Where to position the church and the mosque provoked a lively debate.* (Their Art teacher)

Developing a discursive environment

> *Dialogue as a process of learning and knowing must always involve a political project with the objective of dismantling oppressive structures and mechanisms prevalent in society . . . Critical educators should avoid at all costs the blind embracing of approaches that pay lipservice to democracy and should always be open to multiple and varied approaches that will enhance the possibility for epistemological curiosity with the object of knowledge.* (Macedo in conversation with Freire, 1999: 53)

The role of the teacher in this process is significant. Since the introduction of National Curriculum Art in 1992, which emphasised the need for knowledge and understanding to inform making, Art and Design teachers have become progressively more skilful as critical educators, engaging students in the interpretation and analysis of visual and material culture through classroom dialogue (Addison and Burgess, 2005). Drawing on the different methods employed by art historians, cultural critics and gallery educators, they are able to move beyond formal analysis to discourse analysis. Developing a discursive environment can be one of the hardest tasks for teachers, especially in subjects that, until recently, have concentrated on practice rather than theory. However, there needs to be a unity between the two. As Freire (1999: 51) points out, in order to achieve this unity one must have 'epistemological curiosity', a curiosity that investigates the nature of knowledge, its foundations, scope and validity: one that is not always present in dialogue. By staging scenarios and encouraging critical reflection and dialogue, the Place

Making project goes some way towards achieving this unity and curiosity. It encourages a shift from cynical disengagement to *critical citizenry* using Art and Design as an interlocutor (Rogoff, 2000) as well as an object of study.

Future action

> *Knowledge territorialisation needs to be avoided in favour of some new object of knowledge in which a semblance of parity and reciprocity might take place between the constitutive components of study and through which a form of cultural politics could emerge from the work rather than be imposed on its materials.* (Rogoff, 2000: 8)

Having established an understanding of 'community' (alongside an understanding of architecture and critical aesthetics), the Place Making project went on to encourage students to think about how and why they could establish relationships with 'outsiders'. For example, how to design bridges to link with other islands, whether or not to develop advertising to promote trading and tourism and if, and why, it might be necessary to control and monitor access. Border-crossing, although one of the most overused metaphors in educational theory, is significant here, not just in the context of the project but also more widely in Initial Teacher Education, where collaboration between subjects at Key Stage 3 and Key Stage 4 to address whole school issues remains limited.

David Lambert, Director of the Geographical Association, poses the question, 'Do geographers read landscapes differently to artists?' (2003). Exploiting synergies between Art and Design and Geography to develop Citizenship Education through the built environment is one obvious way forward. Recent developments in the Art and Design curriculum to include a critical understanding of contemporary visual and material culture are mirrored in Geography education with its increased emphasis on cultural geography and enquiry-based learning. The responsibility of Initial Teacher Education providers is to identify common pedagogic links and demonstrate how core skills and subject knowledge can be incorporated in new or unfamiliar ways. Teachers need to perceive themselves as agents of change and foster the political skills and advocacy required to make new things happen beyond a set of perceived boundaries or constraints. They also need to consider whether their aims can be best achieved independently or collaboratively, not only with outside agencies, but across subject boundaries too. This will enable educators to address global and local Citizenship rather than resort to a traditional and historical data-bound perspective. Place Making sits within a pedagogic framework that promotes epistemological curiosity, creative enquiry, experiential learning and the notion of audience as community. Using scenarios to help young people reconstruct the past in order to deconstruct the present and envisage the future can encourage them to be agents of change too. It involves them in communities of learning and in a dialogue about what critical citizenry might mean.

As indicated through the Place Making project, Art and Design teachers, especially those new to the profession, are rapidly developing the pedagogic skills and subject knowledge necessary to make a significant contribution to Citizenship Education, one that goes beyond mere reproduction of any status quo.

> *Teachers must join their students in exploring all possible paths, including what may appear to be dead ends, if better paths into the future are to be found. It is amazing how often a 'safe' path becomes a blind alley and an unlikely overgrown trail leads to a previously unknown highway.* (Romey and Elberty Jnr., 1984: 315)

REFERENCES

Adams, E. and Ward, C. (1983) *Art and the Built Environment*. Essex: Longman.

Addison, N. and Burgess, L. (2003) 'Challenging orthodoxies through partnerships: PGCE students as agents of change, in N. Addison and L. Burgess (eds) *Issues in Art and Design Education*. London: RoutledgeFalmer.

Addison, N. and Burgess, L. (2005) 'The Friendly Interventionists: reflections on the relationship between critical practice and artists/teachers in secondary school', in D. Atkinson and P. Dash (eds) *Social and Critical Practices in Art Education*. London: Trentham Books.

Addison, N. and Dash, P. (2000) 'Values in Art and Design Education', in N. Addison and L. Burgess (eds) *Learning to Teach Art and Design in the Secondary School*. London: RoutledgeFalmer.

Bolgar, B. (2003) (Director of Architecture and Design, The Prince's Foundation) quoted in *Place Making: Linking the art of building to the making of community*. Project Report funded by the Prince's Foundation.

Buckingham, D. (2000) *The Making of Citizens*. London: Routledge.

DfEE (2000a) *National Curriculum Order for Art and Design*. London: QCA for DfEE.

DfEE/QCA (2000b) *Citizenship through Art and Design at Key Stage 3*. London: QCA for DfEE.

Diamond, R. (1996) *The Built Environment and the National Curriculum*. London: The Arts Council of England.

Freire, P. and Macedo, D.P. (1999) 'Pedagogy, Culture, Language and Race: A Dialogue', in J. Leach and B. Moon (eds) *Learners and Pedagogy*. Milton Keynes: Open University Press.

Goodman (1960) quoted in C. Ward (1979) *The Child in the City*. London: Penguin.

Hickman, R. (2003) 'The role of art and design in Citizenship Education', in N. Addison and L. Burgess (eds) *Issues in Art and Design Education*. London: RoutledgeFalmer.

Lambert, D. (2003) 'A burden on the memory or a light in the mind?', *Teaching Geography*, 28(1).

MacPherson, W. (1999) *The Stephen Lawrence Inquiry: Report of an Inquiry*. London: HMSO.

NACCCE (1999) *Report for the National Advisory Committee on Creative and Cultural Education – All Our Futures: Creativity, Culture and Education*. London: DfEE.

QCA (1999) *The National Curriculum for England – Art and Design*. London: QCA.

Rogoff, I. (2000) *Terra Infirma: geography's visual culture*. London: Routledge.

Romey and Elberty Jnr. (1984) quoted in D. Lambert and D. Balderstone (2000) *Learning to Teach Geography in the Secondary School*. London: RoutledgeFalmer.

Smith, F. (2004) 'The contribution of the Arts to values education and citizenship', in R. Bailey (ed.) *Teaching Values and Citizenship across the Curriculum*. London: RoutledgeFalmer.

Spencer, B. from an interview by C. Williamson, 6 December 2003.

Wilkins, C. (1999) 'Making Good Citizens: the social and political attitudes of PGCE students', *Oxford Review of Education*, 25 (1 and 2): 217–30.

Wilkins, C. (2004) 'Citizenship Education', in R. Bailey (ed.) *Teaching Values and Citizenship Across the Curriculum*. London: RoutledgeFalmer.

Drama and the Citizenship Curriculum: Engagement and Enquiry as a Creative Process

Jennifer Foreman

Can teaching Citizenship within Drama benefit both subjects? The abstract phrases and intellectual concepts of the Citizenship Programmes of Study make it seem unlikely that Citizenship could work within Drama, a subject alive with immediate concrete experience. For example, we are told that pupils should be taught about 'the key characteristics of parliament and other forms of government' and 'the electoral system and the importance of voting'. These elements of democratic society hold profound importance for us but they are likely to seem as dry as dust to the average teenager. However, if teachers can use Drama to breathe life into these issues then it is possible to imagine the two subjects working in partnership. In this chapter, and focusing in particular on Key Stage 3, I will outline how we deliver key aspects of the Citizenship Programme of Study through a Drama based Scheme of Work at the school where I work, Newland School for Girls in Hull. First, though, it is necessary to explore the arguments for such a collaboration a little further.

How Drama benefits Citizenship

The experiential nature of educational Drama can animate Citizenship issues. For example, in role-play based on Orwellian reality pupils might 'become' a family living in a police state where Big Brother watches every move and where members of the family can be taken away and never seen again. Re-enactment of the pain of the 'Disappeared' in Argentina brings home the fact that this happens in today's world. Emotional involvement in situations arising in a society which is totally undemocratic enables a young person to reflect on how such oppression would affect their lives. The teacher might take this further by encouraging pupils to reflect on the connection between personal liberty and government. Once pupils start to think more deeply they suddenly realise that the freedom of speech we take for granted is only possible because we have a democratic form of government. The next step is for them to explore the intellectual questions. What is democracy? How have our democratic rights come into existence? How can we protect them? Dramatic engagement has provided the starting point for further enquiry.

How Citizenship themes benefit Drama

If Drama can benefit Citizenship then what can Citizenship do for Drama?

When writing Citizenship into our Drama Scheme of Work I used 'real' issues taken from contemporary events, historical sources, literature and film. This gave substance to the social and moral themes already covered. Topics such as human rights, law and forms of government are highly important and, when embodied in concrete examples, they can make Drama lessons more challenging and interesting. Nor need the impact of such Drama lessons stop the moment young people leave the classroom. Pupils can be motivated to raise funds and support charities. They can start to think about the way they can improve how things are in their school through participating in school councils or pupil campaigns.

Teaching, learning and thinking in Drama and Citizenship

Each subject has much to gain from the other when it comes to teaching and learning. The use of empathy, so relevant to Citizenship, is a hallmark of successful Drama teaching. Sensing what other people are feeling is a skill relevant across subjects but in the Drama space we concentrate on a pupil's ability to 'act out' this feeling to bring topics 'alive'. To encourage teenagers to identify strongly with characters, to 'feel' what others feel is an important aim for much of our teaching. It is vital that learning develops the teenager's emotional intelligence. Through 'teacher in role', 'thought tracking', 'hot seating' and other techniques, Drama teachers promote reflection and judgement. Group work involves negotiation, conflict resolution and leadership skills. Successful group work does not simply 'happen' when we ask pupils to get into groups. Each member of the group has to have a function – as scribe, narrator or actor. We know that some pupils will attempt to subvert the learning process but if we talk openly about this the others can have the confidence through peer pressure to turn the situation round.

The current interest in 'Philosophy for Children' (or 'P4C') whereby the intention is to create a climate of open questioning or 'a community of enquiry', as set out in Will Ord's chapter – Chapter 2.7 – and described in greater detail in Cleghorn's *Thinking Through Philosophy* (2002), is an important development and should enhance the role of Drama skills in general teaching practice. The current focus on teaching and learning in the government's Key Stage 3 strategy has (among other things) underpinned the importance of thinking skills and enquiry which should be part of a good Citizenship-and-Drama lesson.

The drawbacks of teaching Citizenship within Drama

Losing sight of the purpose of activity is only one risk where joint delivery is concerned. In Citizenship-and-Drama classes, as in any other area of curriculum practice, it is vitally important for teachers to critically assess the learning that is going on in the lesson. Teachers need to set clear objectives and use strategies for learning (such as the Key Stage 3 strategy). Even then a combined approach can bring difficulties, especially for the status and integrity of Drama itself. There is a danger that the Citizenship element may overwhelm the Drama element because of a lack of understanding of Drama techniques *and* because of the content load that Citizenship appears to bring. An immediate concern, and this has been especially evident in the primary sector, is the danger of Drama being squeezed out by other initiatives. A recent report from the National Foundation for Educational Research records that a survey of 1,700 headteachers and teachers found that in their schools 'Drama was taught separately in fewer than half' (NFER, 2003).

But despite the danger that linking Drama with Citizenship might privilege Citizenship over Drama, the two subjects can benefit each other. However, for this to happen there has to be an explicit commitment to, and understanding of, *both* subjects from the headteacher and the leadership team.

Assessing provision for Citizenship

Once the link between Citizenship and Drama has been made, and the decision to establish some identified joint delivery taken, it is essential to document the elements of Citizenship already covered within the school. Ways to do this are set out in the *Teacher's Guide and Exemplar Scheme of Work for Citizenship at Key Stage 3* (DfES, 2001). First of all conduct an audit (carried out by one or more of the leadership team) of Citizenship related work in all subjects including PSHE and the pastoral system. As well as classroom practice, this should take into account the school's annual programme of events, such as fundraising, visits, Duke of Edinburgh or ASDAN Awards programmes, school productions, sports events, activities weeks and all extra curricular work. To this are added the school's links with parents and the community as well as partnerships with schools, colleges and other organisations. The structures by which the school responds to pupils' views (for example through a school council) are also important.

Evidence from the audit that we conducted at Newland School for Girls showed that the *values* of Citizenship, as identified in the DfES guidance, did permeate the school. We deliver Citizenship through whole-school activities and there are opportunities to deliver strands of Citizenship in all curriculum subjects. However, and this is critical, the word 'Citizenship' was not part of our everyday vocabulary and, to be honest, we did not fully understand what was meant by this new subject. Herein lay the rationale for positioning and identifying Citizenship within key schemes of work and here the school's Drama programme had much to offer.

To ensure the success of Drama within Citizenship (and vice versa), an effective scheme of work is essential. This should set targets, outline clear objectives and cover the National Curriculum requirements. It should show progression and differentiation and must also be open to development and change. Teachers need the framework of a good scheme but it must not be a straitjacket – teenagers differ from each other and each class is different. It is impossible to cater for all eventualities in a written scheme and teachers must adapt methods and content to suit their classes or court disaster. An approach to professional development which involves peer observations and resource development as well as responding to current research is essential, if we are to develop as teachers.

Citizenship through Drama: an example of a Key Stage 3 Scheme of Work

The Key Stage 3 Citizenship and Creative Arts programme which we have set up at Newland School for Girls is organised so that each year-group has six units of work per year. Each unit runs for approximately six weeks and there are two lessons per week. At least three of the units for each year-group have Citizenship themes. I will describe a unit from each year-group to illustrate how Drama and Citizenship work together.

Year 7: The *Lord of the Flies*

In Year 7 one unit is based on Peter Brook's film of the novel *Lord of the Flies* by William Golding. The film is black and white but this is not usually a hurdle because it is so well edited that pupils can appreciate how the dramatic content is enhanced by the black and white photography. Pupils imagine they are stranded on an island, then using mime and working in small groups they 'build a fire', 'find shelter' and act out island life. Each group then decides on the skills needed for a good leader. These are then made the subject of a whole-class discussion. The objective is to use open questioning to explore 'Why do we need leaders?' 'What are the possible styles of leadership?' 'Why do we have government?' 'What forms do governments take?' Pupils vote for their chosen style of leader, devising short improvisations. After watching the scenes we compare the different leadership styles and their effects on the island society.

A main objective is to explore the basic rules governing orderly meetings or assemblies. Issues, such as food-gathering or ways of escaping from the island, are discussed and votes taken. Awareness is raised of speaking skills, negotiation skills and how to vote. Pupils are involved in individual, pair and small group work. They start to learn about the dynamics of groups, how to reason and how to resolve conflicts. As citizens of the island they share roles and responsibilities for 'their' area and draw up a charter of 'Rights and Responsibilities'. The leaders try out their skills of persuasion. Two assignments of homework are set. One is to learn a list of spellings and meanings of words such as: 'democracy', 'parliament', 'government' and 'citizenship'. The second is an extended piece of writing or a writing frame (depending on ability) about, for example, 'Our Island and Our Rules'. The reasons why the social order on the island in the film collapses are explored.

Year 8: Rights, Responsibilities and Refugees

The introductory unit for Year 8 is 'Human Rights, Responsibilities and Refugees'. Complicated emotional questions surrounding ordinary people who become refugees are tackled at 'one remove' through role-play. Some pupils are prejudiced when discussing refugees or asylum-seekers and this creates a volatile teaching situation. Many teachers will avoid the issue because it is too difficult to handle. Drama enables pupils to 'act out' a refugee story and other pupils find it easier to challenge a character with prejudiced views because they are talking about the character and not their classmates. Dramatic role-play offers an excellent opportunity for pupils to take an objective view of issues.

Using 'real life' refugee stories is a way of introducing pupils to the role of voluntary organisations such as Save the Children and the Red Cross. For homework pupils research these on the internet and use the information to develop role-play and hot-seating exercises in lessons. Here we are sowing the seeds of future involvement in community projects and laying the early foundations for future careers.

Year 9: Personal Finance Education

In Year 9 we have a unit on personal money management. We imagine a family where a teenager has run up a huge telephone bill, or an older sister is addicted to buying from a catalogue. Pupils suggest their own ideas and we discuss attitudes towards money, savings, debt and credit. We encourage a climate of trust in the lesson so that sensitive issues can be discussed if pupils wish. Homework covers subject-specific language and information-gathering on topics such as 'how credit works'. In the future we could explore the global economy, fair trade, taxation and public services. Our Year 9 unit starts from the pupils' own personal experience and enables them to act out teenage roles, something that, unsurprisingly, has great appeal to this age group.

This unit involves making film shorts around the money-management theme, using iBook laptops and digital cameras. The pupils 'become' film production groups for a soap opera. Each member of the group has a role such as camera-person, director, actor, image-maker and so on. The learning process is structured and moves from mind map to story line to camera angles and story-board through to filming and editing. Work in groups, the use of equipment and the sharing of responsibilities are higher level skills. Not every group is successful and this is also a valuable experience! Successful teams become independent learners, evaluating their films and moving on to explore other genres and other money matters. The advantage of building up a stock of films is that they can be shown to next year's class to inspire them to think of ways to build on the success of those who went before.

Additional Themes for Key Stage 3

Additional themes for Key Stage 3 include 'children at war', 'image and message in the media', 'why we need laws and legal systems', and 'anti-racism and anti-discrimination'. Drama and Citizenship working together can be a powerful force to teach children how to be critically alert and more aware of democratic values. Teaching methods which impart the skills of independent learning mean that pupils are not only on their way to becoming informed citizens but are learning strategies for dealing with whatever the future may hold for them.

Drama based cross-curricular Citizenship Days

As the editors of this volume underline, Citizenship activities and events also have much to offer and can support key aspects of curriculum delivery. In Year 7 we run a 'Democracy Day' during which pupils hold elections, put questions to candidates (at first the candidates were teachers but now we have a school council and the candidates are the pupils) and learn how to vote. In the first year I arranged this with staff from the Hull Guildhall and we held the candidate speeches in the City Council Chamber. This was the first time pupils had any notion of what the City Council was, or where it was.

In Year 9 we devote a day to Amnesty International. Pupils show plays, read poems and devise dances on themes based on human rights. We write letters in support of a political prisoner as advised by the Amnesty urgent action campaign. Pupils take this very seriously and we keep them informed by means of pupil bulletins and a termly newsletter if someone is released.

From apathy to engagement: aspirations and strategies

Instead of bemoaning the fact that young people know very little about parliament and are apathetic about the prospect of voting, we need to find ways to engage them emotionally, intellectually and spiritually in learning about Citizenship and democratic values. We need to learn more about how to open up questions for our pupils and appeal to their natural curiosity while not allowing the disaffected minority to keep the rest back. We need to develop our skills and learn alongside our pupils how to become informed, responsible citizens with a desire to play a positive and active role in the theatre of life. Figure 1 provides some pointers as to how this might be done.

Figure 1
Strategies for building effective school-based Citizenship

- Assess the whole school provision for citizenship.
- Start with issues that pupils can easily identify with.
- Develop Drama teaching and learning skills to include new thinking.
- Let the pupils know what you are doing and why you are doing it.
- Find ways to promote Drama and Citizenship through cross-curricular days.
- Run whole staff training on Citizenship across the curriculum and within Drama so that everyone can learn from these developments.
- Ask if and how children are learning and don't presume to know.
- Strive to create a 'community of enquiry' where pupils and teachers learn together.

REFERENCES

Cleghorn, P. (2002) *Thinking Through Philosophy*. Educational Printing Services.

DfES (2001) *Teacher's Guide and Exemplar Scheme of Work for Citizenship at Key Stage 3*. London: DfES.

NFER (2003) *Academic Digest 3.10*. June. National Foundation for Educational Research.

FURTHER READING

Cleghorn, P. (2002) *Thinking Through Philosophy*. Educational Printing Services.

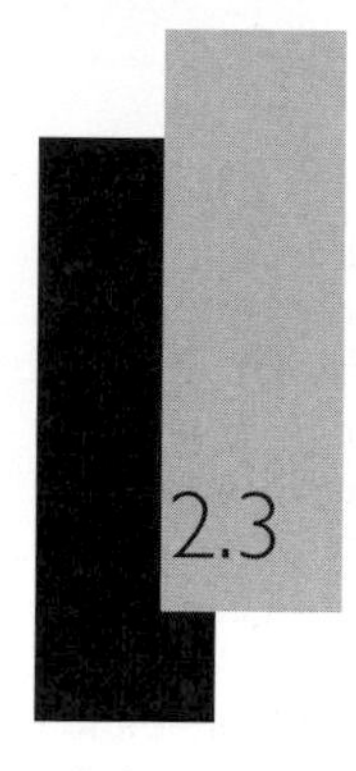

Not 'whether' but 'how soon'!: English and the Citizenship Curriculum

Michael Callanan

The teacher of English: a typical biography

I am a child of '88. When Roger Knight interviewed me at Leicester University School of Education in 1987, I told him I wanted to radicalise pupils; not quite to make revolutionaries of them but to show them how to recognise the ideology present everywhere in culture, to resist indoctrination by mass media and to question conventional wisdom. The following year I had become an apparatchik of Conservative Party policy, delivering the National Curriculum, whose English component might not unfairly be described – in spite of all its strengths – as Thatcher's attempt to subdue the radicals in education, substituting a blend of technocracy and patriotism where free thought had (at least in pockets) been the flavour of the previous 20 years[1].

The present administration has improved matters a little for what I still think of as the 'progressive' English teacher. The 'list of major writers published before 1914' (DfEE/QCA, 1999: 36) has become less prescriptive, allowing us to exercise a smidgeon more judgement. But fundamentally we are in the same position as in 1988. The literacy strategy addresses genuine matters of children's learning but its basis in a list of skills – however important those skills – is potentially reductive and dully transactional. The tweaking of GCSE English and English Literature examinations has barely changed the content and delivery of Key Stage 4 since the abolition of 100% coursework; modularisation will presumably stoke further the system's fiery obsession with assessment.

It is tempting, in this light, to greet the Citizenship curriculum with scepticism or disdain. Another half-baked government initiative, we suspect, designed to paper over the cracks in the educational property it gladly inherited: controlling, centralising and saddening for the liberal arts teacher.

I take the opposite view. I am not putting a brave face on it when I say Citizenship may be the most fruitful opportunity for the English department and teacher since 1988, especially if that teacher feels that the National Curriculum and the examination system often contrive to deflect us from our main goals[2]. Where the English curriculum busies itself with Shakespeare and spelling so that *Daily Mail* readers don't lose sleep, Citizenship articulates for young people a vision of who they are and might be. An overstatement, I admit: the Citizenship curriculum is vague and untried; the good English teacher has always encouraged the independent, questioning mind, whatever the limitations imposed. But perhaps the greatest risk in implementing the development lies in our own reactions as teachers; for the English teacher there is so great an affinity between what the profession professes and the aims of the Citizenship curriculum that we may think 'we're doing that already' and carry on regardless. This would be a grave error of self-knowledge: at present, most of us often deliver aspects of that curriculum but if the last 15 years have taught us anything it is that we usually teach better inside a structure[3]. If we believe in the values of Citizenship – and I believe most of us do – then we must integrate it systematically into our practice.

This is the right moment too for the English Department to assume a key cross-school role. In the absence of many Citizenship experts, the English Department may be a school's most important force for determining how the subject can be taught.

English, Citizenship and the curriculum

The logical place to begin – and end – is the curriculum itself, with a view to seeing how we can best combine the two disciplines[4]. Of course there are links proposed in the National Curriculum between Citizenship and English which are telling – and curious. What could make more sense than using strand En3/1i–1o, 'writing to persuade and to analyse', to deliver Citizenship's 'skills of enquiry and communication'?

The links also make perfect sense for the two other attainment targets, En1 and En2, but the omissions here are at least as significant as the suggestions. The links for En1 'Speaking and Listening' (1a–1e) concern how pupils learn to structure, vary and enrich their talk. With their reference to 'markers . . . illustrations, evidence . . . rhetorical devices . . . visual aids [and] technical vocabulary' these dimensions of En1 are clearly about 'performance' speech – whole class talks, prepared presentations, formal debates.

Reading is linked to citizenship learning in a similarly limited manner, in En2/4a–4c: pupils here learn to select from and evaluate texts and to sift fact from opinion; all specifically in 'information texts' (DfEE/QCA, 1999: 35).

So what do the proposed links prompt English teachers to do? They invite (a) the evaluation of gobbets of factual writing (perhaps about Citizenship), detecting when they are biased, before (b) coaching children for class talks somewhat akin to (c) the argumentative essays they will then write. It would be highly regrettable if the strengths of English teachers and the opportunities afforded them by the progressive humanities agenda of the Citizenship curriculum were to be clouded by enacting an unimaginative, even banal, ABC of socio-political engagement. Why be literal when we can be literary?

Listening and speaking

Performative speech is an important aspect of citizenship. Every school benefits from a debating society, a space where young people can express independent views in a fluent, organised and formalised fashion, a place that echoes that 'Other Place' so that young people can imagine themselves into parliament and broader democratic processes. Everyone needs to imagine, to practise, before taking part in the real thing. Boys who may have less interest in extended written work often excel in the demands of debate. And if the Mother of Parliaments may seem like a yoo-hah boys' club at times, it is surely through debating that those oddly ritualised but oh-so-important arguments about – what? – our Health Service, our environment, our peace-or-war – will come to be meaningful for our youth. This is especially true for those who may think it's 'not for the likes of us' – the poor, girls, children from ethnic minorities. The basis for a healthy culture of debate in a school is established especially in English lessons, where the conventions of debating should be taught and practised[5]. And few of us as teachers do not benefit from the reminder to maximise talk by the maximum number of pupils, when research continues to remind us that we teachers still talk too much[6].

Nonetheless, speaking and listening for Citizenship ought not to be primarily about performance. It is perhaps ironic that one of the major alternatives is to be found in the 'Drama' section of En1 which has pupils 'use a variety of dramatic techniques to explore ideas [and] issues . . .' (DfEE/QCA, 1999: 32). Yes, Citizenship must be analytical and opinionated but it must just as surely be exploratory; pupils learn to hold and defend views but ideas must first be found, arrived at, by exploration. What ideas? What issues? All of us who have delivered Drama lessons at secondary school are familiar with that sinking feeling when another group of girls caution their peers about unwanted pregnancy while a gang of teenage warriors brings a drive-by shooting to a swift if noisy conclusion. But the great strength of drama is that it allows imaginative and collaborative energies to be focused on issues too complex for a sound-bite or a fact sheet. Truth is many-sided; no one has perfect knowledge. Crucially, Drama allows children to understand how we misunderstand each other all the time. Acknowledgement of our limited comprehension of what it is to belong to another race, sex, economic zone, religion, historical moment . . . is the beginning of our understanding of others. Drama is treated more fully in Chapter 2.2.

The 'Group discussion and interaction' section of En1 (DfEE/QCA, 1999: 31–32) explicitly invites pupils to enact in classroom talk the habits of Drama. They are required to 'take different views into account and modify their own views in the light of what others say' (En1/3b: ibid: 31). 'Modification' of viewpoint is a demanding business: what if you're simply right and the rest of your group is wrong? To many of us, not just pupils, 'modification' feels like 'capitulation' so we refuse to budge an inch; for others, having an independent thought can seem too much like hard work, when others with stronger feelings or louder voices will do it for them. And our political culture – which regards any change of policy as a damaging admission of failure – does not provide the ideal model.

For this generation – perhaps the most personally assertive and party-politically-disengaged since the inception of mass education – no skill could be more critical. Of course, the teacher establishes the tone (respectful of others, willing to take turns) which underpins fruitful discussion. And then structure is crucial. One useful technique is a simple note-taking exercise. Before the discussion, each individual notes briefly 'What I think now' about the issue, alone and in silence, preferably. At the end, the exercise is repeated under the heading 'How my view has changed, if at all'. Crucially, students' ideas must be allowed to remain unchanged; this permission will lay the groundwork for characters who resist plurality to allow their views to change on future occasions.

Standard English

One distinct sense in which the National Curriculum models its ideal citizen lies in its preference for Standard English, the 'dominant' or 'prestige' national dialect; pupils are to 'use spoken standard English fluently in different contexts' (En1/1f: DfEE/QCA, 1999: 31). For pupils whose families speak something approximating to the standard (something as broad as standard English is itself only ever approximate) this will be unproblematic. And as our typical citizen has become wealthier, longer educated and more likely to listen to the television than a neighbour, more of us are using standard forms habitually. However, a significant proportion of Britain's pupils come from homes where the standard is not usually employed – typically working-class homes or those in the farther flung regions. The asymmetry between the language felt to be 'proper' to the family and community on the one hand, and that being promoted as 'correct' or at least 'preferred' by the school, at times leads to tensions between home and school and for some children these tensions lead to an identity crisis.

The solution lies not in a rejection of the teaching of Standard English; it is a matter of entitlement that all our pupils shall acquire the prestige dialect so that they can take part in public processes on an equal footing – at least grammatically speaking – with their peers. However, it would be a sad omission to teach the standard without teaching *about* the standard. Our pupils must learn of the socio-historical chance that has led to the preference of one dialect over all others (and, arguably, its subsequently developed capacity for dealing with greater conceptual complexity)[7]. The point here of historicising knowledge about language variation is a profound one. Yes, our pupils should understand 'the importance of standard English as the language of public communication' (DfEE/QCA, 1999: 32) but should not come to believe that it is the 'correct' or 'only appropriate' dialect of English. Having learnt the benefits of the ability to deploy the Standard, our pupils should learn to respect the rich heritage of language variation in this country, just as they should learn of our richly diverse ethnicities.

Reading

Question: What is the English department's most important material resource?
Answer: Its whole-class sets of readers.
Question: How does the English department teacher deliver Citizenship?
Answer: Through its whole-class sets of readers.

The links suggested between Citizenship and English might make the pedestrian proposal of reading 'information texts' but the National Curriculum races away with the awareness that young people are more likely to derive new ideas, and more sophisticated ways of thinking about them, from literary texts, particularly fiction: of the five pupil quotations which head the Citizenship Curriculum (DfEE/QCA, 2000: 182), two of them are explicitly literary. This comes as no surprise. Not only are many of the books beautifully written, and imaginative, but they rely on that universal for human interest: narrative. And the stories they tell, of individuals and their relations with one another and broader communities, are ideal for fostering the 'informed, thoughtful, responsible' citizen, one who will 'play an effective role in society' (ibid: 183).

When Barrie Day wrote in the Autumn 2003 edition of the NUT supplement 'Teacher to Teacher' (Centurion Press, London) that he 'sniffed the death of the English . . . which helped pupils to be uplifted, to take flight and skim the stars' (p. 5), owing to the literacy framework which he had himself piloted, it was the attempt to teach a class reader – 'Louis Sachar's stunning novel *Holes*' (p. 4) – which confirmed his worst fears. 'The pupils were dazed, bored and confused . . . ripping apart good texts with the aim of spotting subordinate clauses and connectives.' (p. 4). He is right to fear the ruin of our best resource in excellent novels like *Holes.* Set in a prison camp for teenage boys, it explores ideas of justice and responsibility and above all the making of one's own fate. Mr Day would probably agree that government initiatives which stretch the remit of English teaching are not all bad, despite his reservations about the framework. *Holes* is not only inspiring but also makes an ideal vehicle for Citizenship teaching.

Goodnight Mister Tom

But if I had to save one class reader from the sinking ship of the stock cupboard, it would be Michelle Magorian's *Goodnight Mister Tom* (1981). Not because it is now available in an excellent pupil's hardback edition nor for the passable, award-winning TV adaptation with John Thaw in the title role (1998, Carlton). And not because NATE (the National Association for the Teaching of English) publishes a Framework-style scheme of work on it that encourages a healthy variety of group-reading strategies. I would save it because, of all the books I have taught at KS3, it is the most moving and characterful novel, with appeal to both boys and girls[8], as well as the full breadth of reading abilities. Lucky, then, that it is such a rich source for delivery of the Citizenship curriculum.

The plot concerns an ageing widower who grudgingly accepts an undernourished evacuee into his country home in 1939. Their mutual affection grows quickly as the boy – Will – overcomes years of neglect, learning to read and make friends for the first time and to nurture a talent for art. When the boy is summoned home by his increasingly insane mother to help care for an illegitimate child, Mister Tom saves the day, rescuing the boy to a better life.

The teaching advice that follows will surprise few; indeed, given its familiar and class-bound nature, the ideas may disappoint[9]. But we need not discover a new pedagogy to deliver Citizenship in English. Merely by tweaking our present practice, we can teach almost all of its knowledge and understanding through a single reader. So the ideas below form no more than a set of suggestions of how to do what we do best, but wearing a citizen's cap. And not a single dry-as-a-bone worksheet in sight.

1a. The justice system/human rights and responsibilities. A role-play in groups: a tribunal into Will's future, after Tom has 'kidnapped' him from sedation in hospital. Preparing roles based on fictional characters rather than institutional roles (described, say, in prompt cards designed for Citizenship lessons) means that children have already entered imaginatively into the processes at work. Prepared talks encourage less confident pupils to participate; prepared questions will allow the least confident to be heard.

1b. Different (regional) identities/mutual respect. Scanning the text for examples of Tom's non-specific 'country' dialect will generate useful English language distinctions between the phonetic rendering of pronunciation or accent (as in 'mebbe' for 'maybe') and Tom's idiom or grammar (as in 'You'll be wanting breakfast, like'). A citizenship-informed lesson would not only validate Tom's dialect as, in a neutral sense, an effective form of communication but would help learners see that Tom's human warmth and wisdom – his identity even – are caught up with his characteristic use of language. Further, pupils can compare the similarly sympathetic portraits of the Scots soldier who befriends Will and the Londoners who assist Tom in his desperate search.

1c/1d/1e. Government. Set in the early years of the second world war, *Goodnight Mister Tom* offers ideal opportunities to compare 'Then and Now': the controlling and centralised government at war with, perhaps, our present government. This is an opportunity for research: pupils would make a list in class of features of the 1940 government expressed in everyday life (built up largely through incidental detail in the novel). Homework might be to fill in a side-by-side list about each government, using either research or an (informal) interview with an adult.

Likewise, class discussion might cover the tensions of electoral democracy when a country goes to war. Using news articles or TV reports about the recent mass demonstrations against war, and statistics about varying patterns of support for British involvement in the gulf conflicts, would help young citizens understand the limits of public influence in democratic nations. Beginning (or better, ending) debates with (secret) ballots stimulates the sense of group decision-making.

Such work would lead naturally into a consideration of *1h. Significance of the media*. The image in the novel of a small community gathering around a wireless in the church hall to hear Chamberlain's declaration of war would prompt assessments of contemporary mass media. Pupils might identify sources of news information about international events, and develop their critical sense by exploring the strengths and limitations of different electronic media (TV/radio/internet) and their institutions (BBC, independent, foreign broadcasters; public vs commercial companies; news vs documentaries or dramas). When pupils report the events of

1939–40, utilising contemporary media, their social significance will be highlighted.

A study of the film adaptation would raise fruitful questions about how (commercial) TV 'constructs' the past differently from the novel and how such dramas come to be produced, advertised and sold.

1i. The world as a global community. The UN is, of course, one outcome of World War II. Having read the novel, which ends – nostalgically, one could argue – looking forward to a brighter day, students might debate whether that day has come. They might use the model of the character Carrie. She has to fight – as a girl – to receive the secondary education she deserves and yearns for. Pupils can write a letter to Carrie from themselves in the present, telling her in which ways her 'future' fulfilled its promise and the ways in which it has disappointed.

Whichever of the above tasks a young reader undertakes, she will surely take from this novel a sense of Tom and Will as model citizens – and not in the ironic sense of civil conformity. Tom shows children that a stranger does not have to mean 'danger'; he cares for Will because he is needed. Will, rather closer in age to the readers, is seen growing up to take part in family and community.

Endnote

It is easy to mock the idea of teaching children how to be citizens, to laugh at lessons in how to be good. But it is not much harder for teachers of English to inspire our pupils: to look critically at the world, to recognise what is valuable in it and to play their part. We may have come a long way from selecting the best literature for the moral improvement of the young but there is still no better place than a good book to start making a change[10].

REFERENCES

Andrews, R. (1995) *Teaching and Learning Argument*. London: Cassell.

Andrews, R. (2001) *Teaching and Learning English*. London: Continuum.

Brindley, S. (1994) *Teaching English*. Buckingham: Open University Press.

Cox, B. (1989) *English for Ages 5–16*. London: DfES.

DfEE/QCA (1999) *The National Curriculum for England: English*. London: QCA.

DfEE/QCA (2000) *The National Curriculum for England: Citizenship*. London: QCA.

Furlong, T. and Ogborn, J. (1995) *The English Department*. London: The English and Media Centre.

Goodwyn, A. (1992) *English Teaching and Media Education*. Buckingham: Open University Press.

Magorian, M. (1981) *Goodnight Mister Tom*. London: Puffin.

Moss, J: 'Citizenship Education: what's in it for English?' in the Spring 2000 English update of the *Times Educational Supplement*.

Perera, K. (1994) 'Standard English: the debate', in S. Brindley *Teaching English*. Buckingham: Open University Press.

Protherough, R. and King, P. (1995) *The Challenge of English in the National Curriculum*. London: Routledge.

Sachar, L. (2000) *Holes*. London: Bloomsbury.

West, A. 'The centrality of literature', in Brindley (1994) *Teaching English*. Buckingham: Open University Press.

NOTES

1 Brian Cox's (1989) delineation of English teachers' different 'views' of themselves is insightful – as is Andrews' (2001: 6) additional category.
2 See Moss, J: 'Citizenship Education: what's in it for English?' in the Spring 2000 English update of the *Times Educational Supplement* for a 10-point proposal of the benefits to English of Citizenship.
3 Protherough and King (1995) point out that, while many practitioners object to the content or implementation of the National Curriculum, few object to it in principle.
4 Furlong and Ogborn (1995) give sound advice on flexible curriculum planning.
5 See Andrews (1995).
6 See Andrews (2001), especially 'Classroom talk'.
7 For a fair and fuller consideration of Standard English, see Perera in Brindley (1994: 79–90).
8 For research on how girls specifically benefit from a specifically critical reading of a class reader, see Brindley's work on *The Turbulent Term of Tyke Tiler* in Brindley (1994: 237–45).
9 Andrew Goodwyn (1992) has good ideas for use of other media, while defending a cultural heritage.
10 Alastair West (1994) casts a sceptical eye on the educational benefits claimed for literature but remains useful here in his emphasis on the pupil's own production of meaning in a range of context-driven readings.

FURTHER READING

Brindle, K. (2000) *GCSE English Frames: Genre*. Dunstable: Folens.
Curtis, D. (1993) *Teaching Secondary English*. Buckingham: Open University Press.
Magorian, M. (1981) *Goodnight Mister Tom*. London: Puffin.
Nield, J. (2000) *GCSE English Frames: Style and Purpose*. Dunstable: Folens.

2.4 Geography and Citizenship: Opportunities for Participation

David Barrs

Geography is a subject that develops knowledge and understanding about the human condition within environmental contexts, both physical and human. It brings a spatial dimension to this understanding and draws its case-work from largely contemporary contexts. From this understanding it seeks to predict patterns and trends. As well as a school subject it also contributes to the development of social policy. If prediction comes from understanding then it is possible to develop policy that counters injustice, protects the environment and secures a better future for citizens around the world. It is a central argument of this chapter that Geography has a responsibility to engage with Citizenship in pursuit of this very rationale. Similarly, Citizenship without Geography is likely to be impoverished and, conceivably, might at least appear to be narrowly national.

Geography: a recent history

As a subject, Geography has had a challenging journey over recent decades. In 1991 the Geography Statutory Order was published and the subject became established alongside others as a compulsory component of education for children aged 5–16. Its future seemed secure. However, this was at the expense of the innovation which had characterised the development of Geography throughout the 1970s and 1980s. Geography teachers and academic geographers had collaborated throughout the period and their efforts were supported by the Geographical Association and curriculum development agencies such as the Schools Council. Teachers had a certain freedom to innovate and to tackle contemporary issues. There was a sense of independence and, some would argue, an autonomous professionalism. As with other subjects, the government was rarely involved in questions of what to teach and how to teach it.

With the arrival of the National Curriculum this changed. The *security of tenure* which compulsory status afforded replaced the climate of development and innovation that had seen school Geography rise in popularity. On the one hand, GCSE syllabuses bore testimony to the developments of earlier years and enabled the subject community to feel that they still had influence. On the other hand, statutory subject orders began to standardise the Geography curriculum and this was defined in very utilitarian terms. Information was promoted at the expense of understanding or engagement with topical issues. Geographical enquiry and issues-based approaches were virtually ignored and, with this, much of the skills-based orientation of the subject was put on hold.

The rigidity and over-prescription of the earlier National Curriculum was weakened with the revision of the subject order in the 1990s, but teachers were reluctant to take advantage of this because of the agenda of accountability that had emerged not just with the introduction of the National Curriculum itself but with the arrival of Ofsted, the publication of school examination results and, later, performance management. Resources, particularly textbooks, had been designed with the National Curriculum in mind and few seemed to be prepared to risk challenging the orthodoxy that had emerged with that National Curriculum. And, of course, those emerging as Newly Qualified Teachers from PGCE programmes, whatever the sterling efforts of their tutors, entered a profession and, increasingly, a subject culture which was, albeit reluctantly, conformist at heart and shorn of the spirit of innovation and curriculum development of the 1970s and 1980s. If the action plan for Geography, launched in March 2006, a two year programme of DfES funded activity to enhance teaching and learning in Geography and *begins* to address these realities, it will have achieved much.

Citizenship and the renewal of Geography

This recent history goes some way to explain a climate in which Geography teachers can seem reluctant to innovate and to embrace the potential that new developments such as Citizenship and ICT offer. As the editors of this collection note, one downside of Crick's 'light touch' approach to Citizenship is that it presumes that a perspective of innovation and curriculum development remains at the heart of the profession. The reality is that the various top-down changes introduced in the late 1980s – whatever the need for them at that time and the benefits that they may have brought – impacted more on this innovative spirit than perhaps on anything else. A key purpose of this chapter is to present Citizenship as an exciting new opportunity and context for the teaching of Geography, one which can spur again the innovation and breadth of thinking that spurs the best Geography teaching: a chance to connect the subject to peoples' lives in a genuinely meaningful way as well as a chance to apply geographical thinking to contemporary social issues once more.

Despite (or because of) the challenges of its recent history, Geography has developed and maintained a strong subject community. Although I write with a certain bias, I would contend that the Geographical Association is one of the most successful and enterprising of the subject associations with a long history of curriculum development (Grimwade et al., 2000). Alongside ICT, Key Skills, the Key Stage 3 Strategy and the primary literacy and numeracy strategies, Citizenship offers a real opportunity for Geography's renewal. Moreover, further opportunities for exploiting Citizenship–Geography links have come with the recent launch of a new category of Specialist School – Humanities Colleges. Through this conduit schools may opt to pair English, Geography or History with each other or with Citizenship or Religious Education.

The framework for this chapter is rooted in the National Curriculum Programmes of Study for both Geography and Citizenship. As a carrier subject, to use the editors' term, and possibly within the context of a broader cross-curricular approach, Geography can make a distinctive contribution to progression in Citizenship. And it can do so while addressing the needs of its own Programme of Study. Table 1 sets out *some* of the key connections and cross-currents between the Key Stage 3 Citizenship and Geography Programmes of Study.

Table 1: Subject similarities
Citizenship and Geography Programmes of Study at Key Stage 3

Citizenship **DfEE and QCA (1999a)**	**Geography** **DfEE and QCA (1999b)**
Knowledge and understanding about becoming informed citizens	**Knowledge and understanding of places**
Pupils should be taught about: **a** *the legal and human rights and responsibilities underpinning society and the work of community-based national and international voluntary groups* **i** *the world as a global community, and the political, economic, environmental and social implications of this, and the role of the European Union, the Commonwealth and the United Nations*	*Pupils should be taught:* **3b** *to describe the national, international and global contexts of places studies* **3d** *to explain how and why changes happen in places, and the issues that arise from these changes* **3e** *to explain how places are interdependent and to explore the idea of global citizenship*
Developing skills of enquiry and communication:	**Geographical enquiry and skills**
Pupils should be taught to: **2a** *think about topical political, spiritual, moral, social and cultural issues, problems and events by analysing information and its sources, including ICT based sources* **2b** *justify orally and in writing a personal opinion about such issues, problems or events* **2c** *contribute to group and exploratory class discussions, and take part in debates*	*In undertaking geographical enquiry, pupils should be taught to:* **1b** *suggest appropriate sequences of investigation (for example, gathering views and factual evidence about a local issue and using them to reach a conclusion)* **1e** *appreciate how people's values and attitudes, including their own, affect contemporary social, environmental, economic and political issues, and to clarify and develop their own values and attitudes about such issues* **1f** *communicate in ways appropriate to the task and audience*

While, though, the attempt here is to examine the means by which Citizenship can enrich the teaching of Geography and thereby support geographers in achieving the high standards that are expected of them, the reader should not conclude that the delivery of Citizenship through other subjects is sufficient in itself. As the other contributors to this volume make clear, Citizenship, like Geography and other subjects in the National Curriculum, has its own Programme of Study, one that requires significant knowledge and experience on the part of the teacher. An effective Citizenship programme is likely, therefore, to include discrete time allocated to it *and* some form of cross-curricular or 'carrier' delivery.

From Key Stage 3 Geography to Key Stage 4 Citizenship

A key difference between the Key Stage 3 and Key Stage 4 Programmes of Study for Citizenship is a specific reference at Key Stage 4 to the wider issues and challenges of global interdependence and responsibility, including sustainable development and Local Agenda 21. This mirrors Geography's focus at Key Stage 3 as set out in Table 2, which also makes some other links, notably around the socio-economic base shared by Citizenship and social and economic Geography. The bigger point, though, is that Key Stage 3 Geography can lay a key foundation stone for Citizenship at Key Stage 4. In so doing, it contributes to the development of students' socio-economic and political awareness and to their broader Education for Sustainable Development (ESD), itself now seen as a key aspect of a broad, balanced education.

Table 2: Subject similarities
The Geography Programme of Study at Key Stage 3 and Key Stage 4 Citizenship

Citizenship **DfEE and QCA (1999a)**	**Geography** **DfEE and QCA (1999b)**
Key Stage 4	**Key Stage 3**
Knowledge and understanding about becoming informed citizens	**Knowledge and understanding of environmental change and sustainable development**
Pupils should be taught about: **1e** *how the economy functions, including the role of business and financial services* **1f** *the opportunities for individuals and voluntary groups to bring about social change locally, nationally, in Europe and internationally* **1i** *the United Kingdom's relations in Europe, including the European Union, and relations with the Commonwealth and the United Nations* **1j** *the wider issues and challenges of global interdependence and responsibility, including sustainable development and Local Agenda 21*	*Pupils should be taught to:* **5a** *describe and explain environmental change and recognise different ways of managing it* **5b** *explore the idea of sustainable development and recognise its implications for people, places and environments and for their own lives*
Developing skills of enquiry and communication:	**Breadth of study**
Pupils should be taught to: **2a** *research a topical political, spiritual, moral, social or cultural issue, problem or event by analysing information from different sources, including ICT based sources* **2b** *express, justify orally and in writing a personal opinion about such issues, problems or events* **2c** *contribute to group and exploratory class discussions, and take part in formal debates*	*Through the study of two countries, pupils should be taught the knowledge, skills and understanding relating to:* **6f** *population distribution and change* **6h** *the changing distribution of economic activity and its impact* **6i** *development* **6j** *environmental issues* **6k** *resource issues*

Table 3 illustrates how one school (Hassenbrook School, Thurrock) is using the Geography and Citizenship Programmes of Study in a complementary way while maintaining a clear identity for Geography department based Citizenship provision.

Table 3: From Programmes of Study to classroom practice
Delivering Citizenship through using Geography as a 'carrier subject'

CASE STUDY
Hassenbrook School, Thurrock

Students are able to experience learning in Citizenship through Geography in each of the three strands of the Citizenship curriculum.

Knowledge and understanding about becoming informed citizens

Here the students:

- study population change and distribution using an interactive study 'Six Billion Human Beings' (http://www-popexpo.ined.fr/english.html), which uses maps and gives an insight into demography and different cultures;
- study the European Union through preparation for and participation in a debate that explores the principles behind EU funding and Britain's role as a net donor;
- explore interdependence through a study of the relationship between Brazil and France;
- address Education for Sustainable Development through a local environmental study exploring the concept 'local actions mean global effects';
- explore the world as a global community through a study of the globalised nature of the oil industry and a related study of international treaties.

Developing skills of enquiry and communication

In developing the skills of enquiry and communication, the key activity is a role-play based on the *favelas* of Rio de Janeiro. This places the students in the role of a migrating Brazilian family who have to find a *favela* on their first night in the city. Peer-to-peer communication is important. The pupils empathise with the families during reflective discussion at the end of the role-play.

Developing the skills of participation and responsible action

These skills are developed through:

- sponsoring a ten-acre area in the Ecuadorean rainforest and the writing of letters to children in an Ecuadorean village that has been visited by one of the teachers at the school;
- studying a 'Geography through football' unit which explores the relationship between More Economically Developed Countries (MEDCs) and Less Economically Developed Countries (LEDCs) and involves writing to MPs about the exploitation of child labour in the making of footballs;

- participating in the school's Environment Club which works with the Geography Department to carry out an Environmental Quality Assessment of the School as the basis of a piece of coursework;
- the discussion of students' responsibilities with regard to litter and noise pollution and a consideration of the conclusions reached in light of the views of students at another school who have done a similar piece of work.

Further details are available from Huw Llewellyn who is Head of Geography and Citizenship Coordinator at the school

'Global' Citizenship, Agenda 21 and Education for Sustainable Development

In 1992 the United Nations convened a summit of Member States in Rio de Janeiro in Brazil. It came to be known as the Earth Summit. Agenda 21 was the programme of action that was agreed by those present. Part of this programme was to develop sustainability principles at the local level which in turn led to the development of Local Agenda 21. Doorstep paper collections and the growth of civic amenity points are evidence of local authorities adopting Local Agenda 21 policies. The environmental issues that underpin Agenda 21 are not only central to 1j of the Citizenship Programme of Study at Key Stage 4, and to 5a and 5b of the Geography Programme of Study at Key Stage 3, but are also common to most GCSE Geography specifications and provide a further opportunity for geographers to deliver lessons or units of work with learning objectives that cover the needs of both subjects within Geography or for geographers to make a key input to discrete Citizenship programmes or activities around this theme.

The United Nations, itself, also provides a context for joint Citizenship and Geography lessons, as well as opportunities for active Citizenship, with a global theme. Aside from the work of the Security Council, the work of the UN is little understood, yet it touches on most aspects of our daily lives. A former Secretary-General, U Thant from Burma, once explained the work of the UN as that of the 4 Ds – development, demography, disarmament and dialogue. That was in the 1960s. More recently others would summarise the work of this international body as being concerned primarily with sustainable development, conflict resolution and human rights. One can discern a strong overlap between these references both with the schemes of work that prevail in most Geography departments and the essence of Citizenship Education itself.

Additionally, the UN provides a range of opportunities for developing the skills of enquiry and communication as well as the skills of participation and responsible action. Almost any topic can be dealt with in the context of a UN working group, conference or committee with groups of students representing countries and constructing arguments from the point of view of that country (see Table 4). Students can also be deployed to act as reporters,

and elsewhere) and those rooted in the wider school and local community. In terms of their own skills and knowledge, geographers and Geography departments clearly have as much to contribute to the latter as the former.

The global dimension: opportunity and obligation

The tradition of Personal and Social Education in the modern comprehensive school, the statutory position of Religious Studies and the social dimension to many National Curriculum subjects have ensured some *coverage* of local, national and international issues: the drugs trade, world debt, migration, pollution, racism, unemployment, HIV/Aids and the arms trade. Many of these issues are well *covered* in various parts of the school curriculum, including Geography, albeit without the kind of social scientific rigour that the editors of this volume argue for.

Perhaps because of this, we are not so good at developing a 'can-do' attitude in terms of what can be done by way of addressing these issues. The role of international organisations; the meaning of treaties and international law; the importance of consensus in the absence of a world police force, army or legal system – these are complex ideas removed from our day-to-day existence in a wealthy, stable and industrialised UK. Teachers are not confident in tackling the controversial issues that emerge when they move from *coverage* to *policy*. Professional development audits of Citizenship skills often demonstrate that teachers do not feel confident about their knowledge and understanding of the United Nations, the Commonwealth and the European Union. This insecurity around global issues ought to be both opportunity and obligation. If it is not addressed, the danger is that schools will educate generations of xenophobic cynics rather than informed, healthily sceptical global citizens who are confident about their own cultures as well as their ability to move between other cultures both locally and abroad. In short, at present too many of our students can analyse the problems but are not equipped to engage with, or argue for, the solutions.

Many, if not most, single-issue pressure groups are dealing with issues that are essentially international in nature and they propose a policy perspective. Voluntary groups such as Friends of the Earth and Greenpeace with regard to the environment, Amnesty in respect of human rights and the Campaign against the Arms Trade are locally and nationally organised (and accessible) but internationally concerned. Environmental issues are not exclusively matters of national sovereignty or national Citizenship. Therefore, the solution lies in collaboration between states and understanding between peoples: a genuinely global Citizenship. This is a classic example of the importance of *acting locally but thinking globally* – a good strap-line for a dynamic Geography department which is determined to seize the opportunity afforded by the Citizenship agenda.

REFERENCES

DfEE (1998) *Education for Citizenship and the Teaching of Democracy in Schools: Final Report of the Advisory Group on Citizenship*, 22 September 1998. Suffolk: QCA Publications.

DfEE/FEFC (2000) *Citizenship for 16–19 Year Olds in Education and Training: Report of the Advisory Group to the Secretary of State for Education and Employment*. Coventry: Further Education Funding Council.

DfEE/QCA (1999a) *National Curriculum: Citizenship*. London: DfEE/QCA.

DfEE/QCA (1999b) *National Curriculum: Geography*. London: DfEE/QCA.

Grimwade K., Reid, A. and Thompson, L. (2000) *Geography and the New Agenda: Secondary*. Sheffield: Geographical Association.

Home Office (2003) *The New and the Old: the report of the 'Life in the United Kingdom' Advisory Group*. Croydon: Home Office Social Policy Unit.

The author would like to acknowledge the useful comments made on this chapter by David Lambert, Chief Executive of the Geographical Association.

Citizenship and History: An Easy Alliance?

Kate Moorse

Ironically, History frequently suffers from the glib assumption that History and Citizenship are largely synonymous and that because certain bodies of content are 'covered' in History which touch on allied knowledge and shared concepts, that somehow, a conceptual framework and appropriate and relevant knowledge will transfer in young people's consciousness – almost by osmosis. In such instances, it is highly probable that both subjects suffer through no explicit connections being made at all.

It is clearly true that much of the knowledge and understanding involved in History is central to a solid understanding and appreciation of Citizenship but, on its own, History cannot lay claim to a monopoly of those things which go to make up the Citizenship that is defined by the statutory order. Much of what historical education does well in the hands of the accomplished teacher is to teach and practise skills of critical evaluation, argument and enquiry that are eminently transferable. They have a core purpose in History and with a well-selected knowledge base they are what gives History its relevance to, and preparation for, adult life. So too in Citizenship, but the History teacher must become a teacher of Citizenship, explicitly deploying such skills within the context of the Citizenship Programme of Study.

Citizenship, as defined in the statutory order, comprises more than a body of knowledge and set of skills. It is predicated on a set of values and attitudes which are in sympathy with those enshrined in liberal democracy and which also support political, religious and ideological pluralism within contemporary society. The revised (National) Curriculum of 2000 finally sought to identify and make explicit those values and attitudes that underpin what this society chooses to teach its youth. In both cases, it should be remembered that the statutory order is only the *minimum* entitlement and that schools are at liberty to include additional material and experiences and to adopt their preferred pedagogies. It is also the case that Citizenship as a National Curriculum subject at Key Stages 3 and 4 is still 'young' and developing. Nor will the teaching of History stand still and so it will be a long time before the possibilities of either subject (or both in combination) is exhausted.

Doing both subjects justice

Each of the subjects in the National Curriculum carries a DfES 'importance' statement (QCA/DfEE, 1999) that seeks to make explicit what is distinctive about the contribution that their study should make to the formation of the individual. A comparison of these 'importance' statements for History and Citizenship (see Figure 1) is a useful exercise to undertake and a good place to start in assessing what, realistically, can be claimed for History's potential contribution to Citizenship.

Figure 1

'Importance Statements' in History and Citizenship

The importance of History

History fires pupils' curiosity about the past in Britain and the wider world. Pupils consider how *the past influences the present, what past societies were like, how these societies organised their politics, and what beliefs and cultures influenced people's actions.* As they do this, pupils develop a chronological framework for their knowledge of significant events and people. They see *the diversity of human experience,* and understand more about *themselves as individuals and members of society.* What they learn can influence their *decisions about personal choices, attitudes and values.* In History, pupils *find evidence, weigh it up and reach their own conclusions. To do this they need to be able to research, sift through evidence, and argue for their point of view – skills that are prized in adult life.*

The importance of Citizenship

Citizenship gives pupils the knowledge, skills and understanding *to play an effective role in society at local, national and international levels.* It helps them to become *informed, thoughtful and responsible citizens who are aware of their duties and rights.* It promotes their spiritual, moral, social and cultural development, making them more self-confident and responsible in and beyond the classroom. It encourages the pupils to play a helpful part in the life of their schools, neighbourhoods, communities and the wider world. It also *teaches them about our economy and democratic institutions and values;* encourages respect for different national, *religious and ethnic identities;* and develops pupils' *ability to reflect on issues and take part in discussions.*

The convergence of the distinctiveness and importance of both subjects is striking but it can also be deceptive. A major, but easily overlooked, plank of the Citizenship order is the expectation that young people will *experience* and come to appreciate the importance of *engagement* and *participation* in activities that arise from within the school and local community. The need for such activity means that it cannot simply be 'bolted on' or confined to the edges of the History programme, to PSHE or to any other area of the curriculum. Thus, the schemes of work for any subject aiming to contribute to, or act as a carrier for, the delivery of Citizenship should include opportunities for such activity. This participative focus is intended to enable the young person to operate effectively in the adult world and requires the teacher to pay attention to matters of teaching and learning, to think laterally about ways in which an ethos of participation can be engendered and when it is appropriate to take a position on a given issue.

The expectation that individuals and groups have responsibilities as well as rights and the capacity to make a difference is central to this brand of 'community-active' Citizenship. The responsibility of individual subjects, therefore, lies in furnishing young citizens with the knowledge and understanding across the curriculum that causes them to become 'informed' and, therefore, most likely to act in the community's 'best interests'. Central to this is a rigorous training in the interrogation and evaluation of evidence together with the development of an appreciation of, and respect for, different points of view; skills and dispositions at the heart of the historian's craft. The need is for curriculum opportunities that encourage and enable young people to appreciate the complexity of cause and effect, the rich diversity of perspectives on any given issue and the possibilities for purposeful engagement. And History can offer much here.

Planning for the needs of the two subjects in tandem on whatever scale requires the teacher of History to don Citizenship spectacles and to have a broad view of what each subject comprises and, here, CPD provision in aspects of the Citizenship curriculum, especially the active dimension, is likely to be important. It would be disingenuous, though, to insist that every time that it arises, the Citizenship weighting should match that of the History weighting. On occasions, the Citizenship emphasis in the 'History' lesson or module will need to be pre-eminent, but, as David Barrs points out in Chapter 2.4, when discussing the position of Geography in relation to Citizenship, the foremost responsibility of the subject specialist is to ensure the effective, successful delivery of *their* subject. More often than not, the Citizenship component will arise in a defined and specific context and serve to explore a given historical or Citizenship concept or issue.

Teaching through concepts is important. Post National Curriculum, it may be argued that less has come to hinge on these big ideas, both within subjects and across the curriculum as a whole, but they retain a central place in History, as they do in Citizenship. In this context, it is perhaps worth remembering that the structure of, and the rationale for, the Schools' History Project (originally the Schools' Council History Project) (1978) consciously sought to make History *relevant* to pupils' lives and contained a range of learning *experiences*. Such a principle is central to today's Citizenship curriculum.

Thus, for the History curriculum planner, a practical starting point would be to annotate the Citizenship order with the potential for addressing its aspects in the department's schemes of work. The History Programme of Study (QCA/DfEE, 1999) is more flexible since 2000 and, in any case, the programmes of study have always set out a minimum entitlement for schools to customise to suit their own circumstances. Recent guidance from the QCA (QCA/DfES, 2001) suggests ways in which schools can map and audit such opportunities together with a range of exemplar units illustrating Citizenship through other subjects.

The central role of enquiry

On a day-to-day basis, everything we do in History should be instilling in young people a sense of value for (historical) evidence and a respect for truth, whilst realising that the latter may be elusive and relative if, nevertheless, a desirable goal. By engendering a sense of the worth of enquiry as well as the skills by which to undertake an enquiry, we are equipping young people both with a powerful tool for future use and also with a set of spectacles which discourages them from taking all that confronts them at face value. By requiring young people, from time to time, to position themselves in a given debate, issue or enquiry, we encourage the evaluation and marshalling of evidence to support a point of view and an appreciation of the value of living according to a chosen set of values: objectives that ought to be at the heart of any Citizenship programme.

Thus, during the course of Key Stage 3, the last Key Stage when all are required to study History, there should be an opportunity for students to investigate a contemporary issue or event within its historical context. This enables the learner to engage with the media and with a range of other sources and to address political, social, cultural and economic contexts both contemporaneously and in the past. The focus of the enquiry may be an international conflict or development such as a country realising its independence; it may be a civil conflict or trade or industrial dispute; it may be an issue within the local area such as the merits of widening a road or building a mental health facility. The opportunities for developing political, economic or other literacies, whilst in the context of an open-ended enquiry, cannot be fully planned for as they are not entirely predictable. Nevertheless, they should be anticipated by the teacher and there are clearly ways in which the teacher's strategic intervention can cause students to trip over such matters.

The QCA Scheme of Work for Citizenship at Key Stage 3 (QCA/DfES, 2001) carries two examples that support teachers in such an approach and which fit easily within the History stable. Unit 11 (Why is it so difficult to keep peace in the world today?) provides one possible way of setting up an enquiry into a conflict with a particularly historical bias (it sits alongside similar units addressing similar issues from both geographical and religious education standpoints). It is outlined outside of any defined content (although it is exemplified through conflict in the Balkans in the 'points to note' section) but the activities described are easily adaptable to any number of contexts.

In the accompanying Teachers' Guide, teachers are offered a generic template through which to approach a topical issue of any sort (Appendix 8: Planning an enquiry into a topical issue in Citizenship). Again, the emphasis is on the types of key questions to raise and a set of learning and enquiry processes which can be experienced. In both cases, the integrity of both Citizenship and History is facilitated through the planning process although it will be up to the teacher to push home the learning points for both subjects at strategic points in the enquiry process, requiring two sets of spectacles to be used. In both instances, an assumption is built in that participating in such enquiries is likely to develop in young people a commitment to the object of that enquiry and a desire to follow events related to that object as time passes. It is suggested that here are opportunities for delegating or assuming responsibility on behalf of others, of collaboration and representation in the many ways in which a teaching group might continue to monitor a situation and communicate subsequent developments whilst its members are occupied on another area of study.

Although appropriate as a study at any Key Stage, such an enquiry could be usefully undertaken at the end of the World Study after 1900 and/or at the close of Key Stage 3. It provides a context within which pupils can apply with autonomy the skills and understandings acquired over the course of the Key Stage (and before, in the primary school). As a result, such an enquiry provides a valuable assessment opportunity for both subjects. This approach to contemporary enquiry will be very familiar to History teachers with experience of the Schools History Project Modern World Study as originally conceived and has relevance for any twentieth-century GCSE history syllabus.

Citizenship and the 'stuff' of History

To reiterate, the most straightforward context for teachers and students of History to explore Citizenship issues, apply Citizenship understanding and practise Citizenship skills is where the content relates directly to both subjects; where the 'stuff' of the subjects collides. The obvious example (and one explored through the QCA modelled 'hybrid' unit in their Scheme of Work – Unit 12) is the struggle to extend the franchise in England, initially to wider cohorts of men and subsequently to women. The winning of the vote by the various constituencies, the class and cultural interests that came into play all provide potential for understanding processes and appreciating the significance of such struggles to democratise society, both by those before us and also by groups around the world today.

The understandings derived by historical studies such as these are valuable – even indispensable – but without actively relating such matters to the present day, the potential for Citizenship Education will not be fully exploited or fulfilled. For instance, knowledge of the English and British journey towards a universal franchise goes a long way to explain the British 'take' on democracy, but the question as to whether this is how it is also viewed in the US, the nascent countries of the old eastern block, South Africa, Iraq or Iran needs to be raised or contrived by the teacher.

Indeed, there is scope to move beyond the status quo in this country and interrogate the question 'what do we mean by a democratic society?' and/or 'is the model promoted by the west to emergent democracies either the most appropriate or the most desirable?' Furthermore, an important teaching point for both subjects is the role of histories in determining ideological and cultural standpoints and the importance of suspending judgements as individuals in the absence of adequate knowledge. This may follow on naturally but cannot be taken for granted. Thus, the curriculum planning that takes place needs to make such issues explicit, enabling the individual teacher to find their most preferred way to make connections and comparisons and facilitating distinct and visible links with other subjects in the curriculum and the various strands of school and community life. In this context, actual 'electoral' activity within the school (holding a 'mock' election, establishing a school council, reviewing the process through which the school's governing body has emerged) and the local community (perhaps through engagement in the National Youth Parliament or a local youth forum) provides a further opportunity to consolidate such learning: democracy as taught, as done, as done in the school, and as done in the local community. The point is that the stuff of History and Citizenship, both in the classroom and beyond, is common, even if the focus differs. The trick is to position the learning in History (which may be primarily around the British experience), the learning around the international dimension (which may take place in History, Geography or English) and the learning as experienced (which may be delivered through curriculum enhancement activities supported through a core Citizenship programme) within a coherent whole. The outcome is clear: Citizenship Education supporting the achievement of the objectives of the History curriculum and History teacher; History and History teachers making a clear and explicit contribution to the school's Citizenship programme.

Live issues and the locality

In the setting of the immediate locality there are plenty of opportunities to bring History and Citizenship together in this way, as the following case studies demonstrate.

CASE STUDY 1

Engaging with a community

One school spotted the potential in investigating the role of a local regiment in World War I both for addressing issues about conflict in general as well as the Great War and also for uncovering local and family histories. The active decision to go out to the community and seek those members with direct experience of the regiment either through memories or through family stories and to draw on those people as sources of evidence is in itself encouraging a participatory approach and developing a sense of community. Extending the focus of the study to an out-of-hours History club has led to the setting up of a website for use by the community and interested parties further-a-field. (Members of the local community are also invited to contribute material to the website, which is proving to be a successful initiative). Similarly, taking mixed age and family groups to the battlefields at Ypres has generated extensive and diverse discussions and enabled pupils to make tangible connections and to gain profound insights into the experience of war and its impact on individuals, families and successive generations. Subsequent studies of more recent and contemporaneous conflicts are rendered more meaningful for pupils with the backdrop that their study of World War I has provided.

CASE STUDY 2

The potential of Heritage Education

A local campaign to save an historical domestic building from property developers and to persuade an eminent national heritage organisation to invest in its restoration has provided schools and the community with a set of experiences on which to draw for lessons on pressure group politics. The history of the house in question has provided such fascinating detective work and has provoked such interest in the local and national press that a body of ready-made resources now exists to support an active enquiry into what was, in effect, a model for active citizenship.

In local schools, History, Citizenship and various curriculum enrichment and extra-curricular activities came together to make, or rather to enable students to make, powerful arguments for the survival of this local resource. Issues of power and interest were prevalent and opportunities for participation extensive. Those involved could see that they had made a difference. Historical enquiry through the investigation of a contemporary community issue had produced real Citizenship learning.

Furthermore, the story to be uncovered by successive cohorts of pupils is that of a highly successful pressure group which succeeded in its goal to save the property but it also follows through into the decisions that were subsequently made over the way the building should be restored and interpreted and, indeed, to the way in which it needs subsequently to be managed into the twenty-first century.

At any time, in a locality, planning debates will be in progress. They may not be as significant or substantial as the one described above but there is bound to be one with interesting historical ramifications. Using this as a way of exploring the planning process and structures of local government makes a modest but significant contribution to active, effective Citizenship Education; if pressure groups are involved, this adds another dimension. At the same time, this type of study delivers a local dimension to the History Programme of Study at Key Stage 3 that is still under-represented in many schemes of work. The relationship of the built environment to the community, as Lesley Burgess and Catherine Williamson explore in detail in Chapter 2.1, has to be an important issue for both subjects. It is currently underplayed in most school curricula and something worthy of exploration and consideration. For example, what would be lost to the community if *X* was demolished to make way for *Y*? Who would be affected? What do we/I think? What responsibility do we/I have to those who lived and worked here in the past? What function/role does our heritage have in today's world? And whose heritage are we conserving? What conflicts of interest are there to resolve? The Building Exploratory in Hackney, East London and other similar resources support schools in providing excellent Citizenship experiences of this sort for their pupils.

CASE STUDY 3

Exploiting the locality's potential

In another example of drawing on the local community, the origins and history of a large derelict building that had long been a feature of the local area again provided a starting point for historical enquiry and Citizenship learning. In exploring their interest in the building, students learned about the philanthropic and religious values of the Victorian period, values which had led one man to build a modestly priced hotel for the men who had come to East London to build the docks, warehouses and housing in the nineteenth century. From a position of no knowledge of the building's provenance, the group (and the teacher) discovered the detail of 100 years of its history and that of the surrounding area through the study of a wide range of source material.

Amongst other things, their investigations showed that the building had become a hostel for homeless men in the twentieth century and that George Orwell had stayed there, under cover, when researching his classic novel *Down and out in Paris and London*. They learnt something of Orwell's politics and motivation, something of the society in which he lived and the issues current at the time. They learnt that the building had continued as a hostel until relatively recently so that it still represented a landmark or base for many of the East End's homeless today – particularly the older population with longstanding memories.

Interviews with representatives from Shelter and the *Big Issue*, together with a focus on poetry presented through the *Big Issue*, led to a wide discussion of the issues surrounding homelessness and society's attitudes towards it historically and today. This led to a scrutiny of students' own attitudes and the language they used to describe the phenomenon. The group made a conscious decision to avoid pejorative terms in the future and censored their peers if they heard inappropriate language or sentiments. This class, too, used the pastoral system and assembly time to communicate the findings of their study to other students in the school. In due course, and largely as a result of the interest shown by the school in the building, letters appeared in the local newspaper about the future of the building and/or the valuable site it occupies. Reporters wrote about the building's history but got their facts wrong (from the students' informed position as 'experts'). Students spontaneously took up the challenge; wrote to the paper to put right the facts (correcting detail about the builder of the hotel and providing biographical information about George Orwell's sojourn there); they entered the debate about the role the building had played in the local community over time and commented on its architectural merit as well as the health and safety issues the building presented through having been allowed to fall into disrepair and dereliction (there have been a number of accidents through some of the original occupants returning to seek shelter, managing to get in only to meet unsafe floors and ceilings, rats and other vermin).

Arguably this unit delivered on a number of fronts. Delivered within the context of an (integrated) Humanities context, there was, from the outset, a clear Citizenship agenda incorporated into the planning. It is true that some of the outcomes could not have been planned for but the teacher's ability to spot the opportunities and to adopt the appropriate 'spectacles' enabled the pupils to engage as autonomous enquirers and to make decisions for themselves, taking ownership of their new-found knowledge and to deploy it to 'make a difference': Active, and increasingly informed, Citizenship but starting from the exploration of a historical source in the local community. And, given that the local student population was in excess of 90 per cent Bangladeshi in family origin and that they were working in English as an additional language, the learning had a particular pertinence. The literacy work that this enquiry afforded caused pupils to employ a range of genres and strategies in their writing and led the students and their teacher to a consideration of cultural expectations over the role of the 'home' and the 'family' in the lives of the students and their communities and in the lives of the homeless about which they were learning.

CASE STUDY 4

Exploring individual and group contributions to the community

There is mileage, here, for a school to forge links with its local history society/ies. One such organisation took up the issue of parks and green spaces with a view to surveying the existing provision and the state of repair of the established parks and the potential there may be to extend provision through the annexing of derelict land. Local school students carried out the research, which involved the consideration of health and safety issues and local governance, as well as researching the origins and constitutions of the parks and open spaces dating from Victorian and even earlier times. Traditions of philanthropy, understandings and beliefs about disease, health and recreation from the past, set into relief those things which we take for granted today and which lie at the heart of values and attitudes which underpin many of our institutions. Again, historical enquiry, through local community engagement, producing real Citizenship learning and developing real Citizenship skills.

CASE STUDY 5

Exploring individual and group contributions to the community

Assessing the role of an individual in a significant historical event or development within the context of other causal factors has long been a feature of the study of History. It was once used as an assessment criterion for examinations and coursework at 16+. Within the history of the local area will be personalities responsible for bringing about change or contributing to developments elsewhere. Finding out about people's lives, their motivation, the influences upon them, their social background and their historical context, as well as their achievements, offers mileage for Citizenship as well as shedding life on an important aspect of History.

An oral history initiative in one London borough brought to the fore an individual who had lived a significant part of his life as a community activist and was representative of the Afro-Caribbean community within the borough. He had come to the UK in 1948. The individual concerned is now a prominent local businessman, who established the Afro-Caribbean Association, founded the local Community Relations Council in 1975, and successfully campaigned for the local council to fund its work and appoint a paid director. More recently he had set up the Black Business Association, to support young Black people starting up their own businesses. From his testimony, an educational resource pack was formulated for use by local schools.

By using this example the History unit was given a local dimension, while being flexible enough to enable students to extend their understanding of History at national and international levels, by focusing on events during his life in the UK and in Jamaica, his country of birth. There was also an opportunity for students to judge the significance of individuals in history. Opportunities for delivering the framework for Citizenship were another strong element. Through such an approach, students learn about the work of pressure groups and how they can influence local and national governments. They are asked to consider how individuals, through their work and actions, alone and with others, can make a difference and are subsequently encouraged to communicate their opinions through a variety of methods.

The ability of History to illustrate and explore multiple identities of citizens

An important feature of Citizenship Education today must be to affirm the importance of personal identity and to establish the expectation that each one of us is likely to assume a number of different identities across a lifetime and that we are likely to carry more than one at any one time. An understanding of the ingredients that go to make up a national, social, cultural or religious identity and the way that events or historical figures can come to be reported through the years can help offset the sort of myths and 'received wisdoms' often used to justify prejudice and hostility, not least around the current moral panic about asylum seekers and refugees.

The History teacher is in a privileged position to deliver a History education which seeks to recognise 'the subtleties and contradictions which work behind the myths with which we often live' (Slater, 1992) whilst rehearsing arguments and supporting students in challenging stereotypes and interrogating evidence. Using festivals and anniversaries to question what they represent for a given group of people signals the significance of shared values and understandings. For example, 1989 was an important date for French consciousness and that of French speaking peoples throughout the world, marking as it did the 200th anniversary of the revolution, as was 1988 for Australia.

One school has developed a study that started with an historical enquiry into the Ukraine under Stalin in the 1930s and continued with a consideration of the period under Nazi occupation. Moving from a study of totalitarianism in its various guises, pupils then studied the testimony of Ukrainian refugees arriving and living in the UK after World War II. Examining the experiences at a distance permitted the appreciation of both diverse experiences and, perhaps more significantly, diverse personal responses which quickly extended to parallels drawn with experiences and feelings of refugee and asylum-seeking class-mates joining the school today. The impact on pupils' attitudes and behaviour provided a focus for reflection and affirmation of values to be shared by the school community as a whole. Much of this unit of study took place through the medium of discussion and the outcomes were communicated within the school community using assemblies and tutor periods.

Considering what events or memories might have meant for the various groups involved at the time, and for their descendants or counterparts today, develops a degree of empathy and a prism through which to view such markers. Anniversaries can be particularly poignant, and provoke strong feelings, for groups within the British Isles, be these minority groups throughout the UK or the distinct communities in Northern Ireland. Rather than seeing such things as simply nationalist or partisan, the teacher of History is in a position to place them in a context and begin a fuller exploration. From a Citizenship dimension, this helps to develop an open-mindedness in pupils which teachers of Religious Education have so long striven to do through religious festivals. Moreover, it explodes a real and pertinent issue around the terms 'citizen' and 'citizenship' which the editors of this volume rightly identify as a key concern, not just for polemicists but for classroom practitioners.

A 'thinking frame' for Citizenship

Finally, to return to the key Citizenship-related concepts and their place in the teaching and study of History. Many of these are central to any study of the past but the school as a whole should be encouraged to plan for their access by students. This is particularly important because not all will study History beyond the age of 14, a reality that places both enormous pressure and enormous responsibility on the History Curriculum at Key Stage 3. Although the Citizenship-related concepts of monarchy, government, democracy, autocracy, totalitarianism, diversity, gender and so forth are likely to resonate through many if not all of the units studied at Key Stage 3, the time available to do justice to each and every one on each occasion is necessarily limited. Their treatment therefore does need to be explicitly planned for. And issues of continuity and progression need to inform the curriculum thinking both within the subject, and within and across the curriculum more widely. Here, Citizenship has an important role to play.

One mechanism is to devise a set of key questions which become increasingly explicit to students in undertaking their enquiries and which sit alongside context specific questions. Such questions should be seen as central or universal questions which can be adapted to a given historical context but through which pupils can build a developing understanding of how ideas, institutions and practices have evolved and to imbue a sense of the process of change.

As readers will be aware, when the National Curriculum first came into existence, there was a set of non-statutory Cross-Curricular Themes, of which Citizenship was one. At that time, and in response to the structure of that curriculum, a whole-curriculum initiative took place, focused on the Centre for Cross-Curricular Themes at Goldsmiths College (Inman and Buck, 1995; Buck et al., 1994). The ten (subsequently 11) central questions devised at that time may be viewed as just one example of the types of question which could be used when planning to ensure that History and other Humanities subjects convey a broad Citizenship perspective. Citizenship, the Foundation Subject introduced as part of the revised National Curriculum of 2000, draws in aspects of many of those original themes. Those questions were, and I would contend might remain as follows:

- What is the nature of our rights and responsibilities in everyday life?
- On what bases do people influence and control others?
- What is the balance between individual freedom and constraints necessary for co-operative living?
- In what ways do people organise, manage and control their relationships?
- In what ways are people different and with what consequences?
- How do people learn the requirements of a particular culture?
- What constitutes a community, how are communities organised?
- In what ways are the welfare of individuals and societies maintained?
- On what basis do people make decisions when faced with particular choices?
- What is our relationship to the physical world and to non-human species?
- In what ways have people sought to explain the universe and to give meaning to their lives?

Whilst such questions will need 'domesticating' within a given subject context – for instance, in the case of History, for different historical contexts or periods – and for different groups of pupils, at the very least they provide the basis for a common 'thinking frame' for the subject teacher engaged in the delivery of Citizenship, either within 'their' subject or as part of a multi- and interdisciplinary Citizenship team. It is not far to travel to think how such a set of questions might translate into historical periods, distant in time and place, and only a little further still to think of ways in which students may be enabled to make links with, and across, the present.

REFERENCES

Buck, M., Inman, S. and Moorse, K. (1994) *Historical Association Occasional Paper 10: Educating the Whole Child – cross-curricular themes within the history curriculum.* London: Historical Association.

Inman, S. and Buck, M. (1995) 'Setting a Framework for Personal Development' and 'Citizenship Education – more than a forgotten cross-curricular theme?', in S. Inman and M. Buck (eds) *Adding Value: Schools' Responsibility for Pupils' Personal Development.* London: Trentham.

QCA/DfEE (1999) *The National Curriculum Handbook for Secondary Teachers in England (Key Stages 3 and 4).* London: QCA.

QCA/DfES (2001) *Citizenship – A Scheme of Work for Key Stage 3.* London: QCA.

Schools History Project (1978) *A New Look at History.* London: Holmes Macdougall.

Slater, J. (1992) in P. Lee, J. Slater, P. Walsh, J. White and D. Shemlit, *The Aims of School History: The National Curriculum and Beyond,* The London File. London: Tufnell Press.

FURTHER READING

Arthur, J., Davies, I., Wrenn, A., Haydn, T. and Kerr, D. (2001) *Citizenship Through Secondary History.* London: RoutledgeFalmer.

Inman, S. and Buck, M. (eds) (1995) *Adding Value: Schools' Responsibility for Pupils' Personal Development.* London: Trentham.

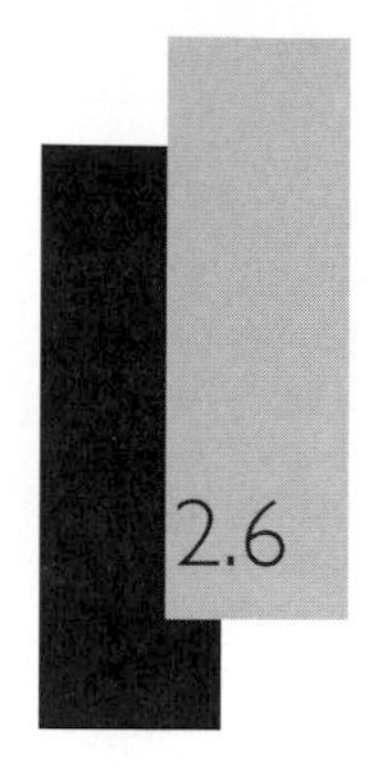

Citizenship and the Humanities: Bridging the Boundaries

Deirdre Smith

In the *National Curriculum Handbook for Secondary School Teachers in England, Key Stages 3 and 4* (DfEE/QCA, 1999), the importance of the new statutory Foundation Subject of Citizenship is defined in a comprehensive paragraph, as follows:

> *Citizenship gives pupils the knowledge, skills and understanding to play an effective role in society at local, national and international levels. It helps them to become informed, thoughtful and responsible citizens who are aware of their duties and rights. It promotes their spiritual, moral, social and cultural development, making them more self-confident and responsible both in and beyond the classroom. It encourages pupils to play a helpful part in the life of their schools, neighbourhoods, communities and the wider world. It also teaches them about our economy and democratic institutions and values; encourages respect for different national, religious and ethnic identities; and develops pupils' ability to reflect on issues and take part in discussions.* (DfEE/QCA, 1999)

Substitute the word *Humanities* for Citizenship in the paragraph above and the definition remains every bit as appropriate. The concerns of Citizenship are at the heart of Humanities teaching and learning. The Citizenship order has many references to the Humanities subjects as curriculum areas that can deliver Citizenship. The Humanities subjects with their emphasis on enquiry have the right methodology to ensure active teaching and learning in Citizenship.

Background: Humanities before the National Curriculum

Prior to 1988 and the introduction of the National Curriculum, the humanities area of the curriculum had seen much innovation and a great variety of interpretation in different schools. The Humanities Association, then known as the *Integrated* Humanities Association, worked closely with the agents of change, through conferences, the association's journal and newsletters, and through campaigns and action with governmental and non-governmental organisations to promote and enhance a Humanities Curriculum that sought to:

- encourage an understanding and respect for the individual, other people and different cultures

- encourage a critical examination of a wide range of social, economic and political issues
- provide opportunities to interpret and respond to local, national and global events.

A significant number of secondary schools developed integrated approaches to the Humanities Curriculum area in both Key Stages, to provide vibrant courses of relevance, excitement and active involvement in the community and, almost without exception, schools provided a Humanities entitlement at Key Stage 4, although this varied in form. In some schools it was a choice of humanities subjects: Geography, History, Social Science, Sociology, RE or Economics, while in others, particularly in London and Leicestershire, Integrated Humanities courses were provided as part of the core curriculum and four Integrated Humanities syllabuses were developed at GCSE level. These encompassed the broad aims for Humanities education above. From their inception in the late 1970s through to the beginning of the 1990s the appeal of these syllabuses and the take-up by schools steadily increased.

Retrenchment: the arrival of the National Curriculum

The introduction of the National Curriculum saw many schools reappraising their curriculum philosophy. For a short time it looked as though History, Geography and Religious Education (which had been alone in always having compulsory status as a school subject) would be part of an entitlement curriculum for 14–16 year olds, and teachers of History and Geography rejoiced as it seemed their subjects were to receive enhanced status. The optimism was short lived, as the government recalculated and decided that pupils' entitlement should be reduced to *either* History *or* Geography. The question of 'what to do about Social Science, Economics, not to mention Integrated Studies, Integrated Humanities, Environmental Education or World Studies which may also be represented on the school timetable' was considered and teachers of these disciplines felt isolated and threatened as their subjects were removed from the curriculum altogether in many schools (Gill, 1990), although some remained as Key Stage 4 options in a small number.

At Key Stage 3 the Humanities Curriculum was also narrowed as the prescriptive and over-crowded National Curriculum orders for History and Geography with their multiple layers of Statements of Attainment were implemented in ways which left little space for the key values of Humanities education and rendered it well nigh impossible even to integrate History and Geography.

The Dearing Review (1994) failed to bring either new ideas or rationality to the curriculum debate because the central aim was to trim the National Curriculum to manageable proportions. Steve Johnson, President of the Humanities Association at the time, used the analogy of musical chairs, stating that, 'at Key Stage 4, a further chair was removed, and when the music stopped, it was the turn of History and Geography teachers to feel isolated and threatened (Johnson, 1994)'. There was to be no statutory requirement for pupils to study either subject at Key Stage 4. Of those subjects usually associated with the humanities, only Religious Education remained an entitlement for all 14–16 year olds. Meanwhile, the Cross-Curricular Themes, including Citizenship, key elements of the broad and balanced curriculum promised by the 1988 Education Act, were receiving less and less attention and had been virtually ignored by Dearing.

By the mid-1990s 'the centralisation of power in education together with an erosion of the relative wealth and status of teachers' left many Humanities practitioners feeling marginalised and impotent (Hargreaves, 1994). In 1994 the Humanities Association called upon Humanities teachers to 'adopt a proactive role by leading the debate on the knowledge, understanding and skills young people will require in the new post-modern, post industrial world' reminding them that their aim 'is not only to help pupils understand their social world but also to encourage them to develop the skills and ambition to change it' (Johnson, 1994).

The Humanities Association guidance on the Humanities Curriculum outlined a series of aims (similar to those that underpin the present-day Citizenship order), concepts (such as freedom, democracy, sustainable development), skills (such as the ability to recognise the validity of different points of view) and key experiences (such as planned community action). The Association called for a 'New Humanities' appropriate for the twenty-first century which would promote a more holistic understanding of the social and physical world (Johnson, 1994) and, resultantly, a new generation of Humanities syllabuses was developed at GCSE which sought to provide ways of recognising pupils' achievement in Humanities education.

From Humanities to Citizenship

The three key elements that are central to Crick's reports (DfES/QCA, 1998; DfEE/FEFC, 2000; Home Office, 2003) and underpin both the new curriculum requirements and the broader Citizenship agenda – Political Literacy, Social and Moral Responsibility, and Community involvement – and the associated Programme of Study, bear a close correlation to the aims, skills and experiences set out for Humanities education during the 1990s and to those present in the resultant GCSE Humanities syllabuses (or specifications as they had by then become). The specifications, prepared for first examination in 2001, also articulated the major contribution they could make to providing accreditation for much of the Citizenship Programme of Study at Key Stage 4. Little wonder, then, that the debate on the National Curriculum and the advent of Citizenship as a new Foundation Subject and entitlement for all pupils aged 11–16 was broadly welcomed by the Humanities Association in 1999. As Dave Walker, Chair of the Association at that stage, wrote:

> *Citizenship is clearly a major part of the new agenda . . . and is at the heart of an agenda of social inclusion. Its concerns are involving children and schools in decision-making. It is about raising questions, enquiry and finding out answers. Citizenship is about active learning and empowerment. It is about the central*

> *concerns of the Humanities . . . The Humanities Association intends to make citizenship a major area for development for the start of the new millennium. We will define our aims in relation to Citizenship. We will produce advice about curriculum organization for Citizenship and we will support the development of strategies and approaches to Citizenship. The concepts and perspectives that are the Humanities are at the centre of a curriculum for social inclusion.* (Walker, 1999).

It was within this context that the Association called for making the start of the new millennium the start of a new Humanities at the very heart of the new curriculum (Walker, 1999). Thus, 'Bridging the Boundaries', as the subtitle of this chapter puts it, has formed a major part of the work of the Humanities Association and Humanities practitioners over recent years. The close links between the Humanities and Citizenship agendas have been developed, honed and promoted through conferences and publications, through working with DfES and QCA, and with the various Citizenship and Development Education agencies and NGOs and through ongoing work around the 2001 Humanities GCSE specifications launched by AQA, OCR and WJEC. At LEA level, as Figure 1 reveals, interesting work on the promotion of the common objectives, interests and values that span Citizenship and the Humanities was also underway.

Figure 1
Bridging the boundaries between Citizenship and Humanities Education

CASE STUDY

Making Implicit Citizenship Explicit through Humanities, Wirral LEA (2001)

Quick off the mark: a response to Crick's interim report

The interim report of the Citizenship and Education for Democracy Working Group looked to 'an order which would provide Citizenship through history, geography and English' (DfEE/QCA, 1998). Although this was not the final outcome in the Statutory Order; and was indeed not practicable since History and Geography were not compulsory subjects at Key Stage 4, this proposal provided an important and exciting starting point for curriculum development in Citizenship in many Wirral schools and prompted the Humanities Inspection and Advisory Team to set up its own working group of teachers of Humanities, History, Geography, RE and the Social Sciences, to consider ways in which Citizenship might be taught and learned through their subjects.

What's in a name?

Since Citizenship was to be a subject, with its own clear identity, we realised that, in any provision of Citizenship through other subjects, the three key elements of the new Citizenship curriculum would need to be clearly identified and overtly taught and so the project adopted the title: Making Implicit Citizenship Explicit through Humanities. A group of enthusiastic and committed teachers, including two who later became Wirral's two Advanced Skills Teachers for Citizenship, came together to take forward what was embraced as an exciting curriculum development and instituted or generated:

- a series of regular meetings to discuss methodology and available resources;
- an audit of the curriculum, completed by all participating teachers at both key stages, that led to the generation of plans showing actual and possible Humanities and Citizenship links;
- a programme of 'Sharing good practice in the Humanities and Citizenship' sessions held termly, where teachers held demonstration lessons, engaged the participants actively in these lessons, and shared their planning;
- the staging of the first of an ongoing series of Wirral Citizenship Conferences, held in the Council Chamber in 2000, which showcased best practice from a range of local schools and organisations and was attended by a range of Citizenship agencies;
- the production of Humanities schemes of work and unit and lesson plans that identified clearly Humanities, History, Geography and Social Science objectives alongside those for Citizenship objectives;
- the identification of key issues, notably around assessment, recording and reporting and the development of a 'Wirral Model' for assessment, recording and reporting in citizenship.

From the audits, and the related work of the group, it was clear that a significant proportion of the Citizenship order could be delivered through the Humanities and that a Humanities approach was clearly appropriate as long as the delivery of National Curriculum Citizenship was made explicit within this.

Recent national developments that consolidate the links between Humanities and Citizenship

The 2003 Ofsted report, *National Curriculum Citizenship: Planning and Implementation*, states: 'A wide range of curriculum models has been used for Citizenship. In the majority of cases Citizenship has been set within existing Personal, Social and Health Education (PSHE) programmes. Generally this arrangement is proving unsatisfactory' (Ofsted, 2003). This is hardly surprising since QCA's Initial Guidance in Citizenship stated:

> *Different forms of curriculum provision can be made for citizenship:*
> - *Discrete citizenship provision with separate curriculum time.*
> - *Teaching citizenship within and through other subjects.*
> - *Citizenship events, activities, tutorial work.*
>
> *A combination of these is needed in a whole-school approach.* (QCA, 2000)

From the perspective of the Humanities Association, and notwithstanding the points made by Jan Campbell and Liz Craft in Chapter 6.2, placing Citizenship *solely* within the remit of PSHE has meant that the characteristics of the Humanities dimension have been lost or, at best, diminished, a dimension that the Humanities Association gives renewed emphasis to in its recent exhortations:

> *The humanities dimension and humanities approaches provide a means of involving students in the exploration of contemporary issues important to human kind through which they can apply their direct experience of the world around them and extend their understanding of it in local, national and global contexts. It engages students in active enquiry about people and their interaction with their environment from the cultural, economic, environmental, historical, spatial, moral, political, religious, spiritual, moral and social perspective.* (Humanities Association, 2003)

Ofsted has also expressed concerns that, in cross-curricular and PSHE based approaches, many school pupils are not aware that they are studying Citizenship. Thus, there is a need for schools to:

> *. . . review their existing planned implementation of citizenship, and to ensure that they have put in place a broad, coherent and progressive curriculum with scope for work in depth.* (Ofsted, 2003)

This situation had shown no significant improvement by 2005. As David Bell, the former Chief Inspector of Schools, commented in his address in Liverpool:

> *One of the difficulties associated with the place of citizenship in the curriculum has been the assumption in many secondary schools that its natural home is as part of the Personal, Social and Health Education programme where it is taught alongside issues such as sex and relationship education, personal finance and healthy eating. This is often due to a misunderstanding or misreading of the national curriculum, or because it is within these programmes that space for teaching new material can most easily be found. Yet while many schools have made a link between citizenship and personal education, they have not exploited the obvious links between citizenship and the humanities. Yet humanities subjects provide opportunities to develop the curriculum in a way that is economical of time and makes sense to pupils.* (Bell, 2005)

He offers several examples of ways in which teaching and learning in the Humanities can make a substantial contribution to the Citizenship Curriculum overall.

The critical point about the Wirral case study cited in Figure 1 is that it delivers significant elements of Citizenship *explicitly* within the context of the Humanities. Clearly identified objectives explicitly drawn from the Citizenship Programmes of Study and linked formative and end of Key Stage assessment, and reporting strategies provide one route to meeting the type of concerns expressed by Ofsted. The Wirral model also exemplifies ways in which teaching elements of Citizenship through the Humanities, especially at Key Stage 3, can bridge boundaries and provide a broad, coherent, progressive, active and worthwhile curriculum in both Citizenship and Humanities.

The position is less simple at Key Stage 4 with the tendency of schools to 'crowd' the curriculum with GCSE dominated courses, the subsequent and often exclusive focus on GCSE achievement and the absence of a Humanities entitlement (in the sense that the requirement is for one aspect of the Humanities to be available to all pupils through the option process rather than for it, necessarily, to be studied). In this context, the proposals from Tomlinson (DfES, 2003, Tomlinson, 2005) for 14–19 provision that retain at least a tentative place (or perhaps 'space') for Citizenship in the core programme are to be welcomed. The requirement that pupils should learn about Citizenship at least up to the age of 16 may prove the means of ensuring the sustainability of a Humanities approach.

Accrediting Citizenship and the Humanities at Key Stage 4

There are now valuable opportunities for accrediting both the Humanities and Citizenship at Key Stage 4. Here, one approach is, of course, to adopt one of the three GCSE short courses in Citizenship Studies, possibly as part of a joint programme also offering a short course in RE, an approach that has a clear role for the Humanities specialist and one outlined in more detail by Tony Breslin elsewhere in this volume.

Some schools (see Figure 2), however, have moved to placing GCSE Humanities in the core curriculum at Key Stage 4, thereby providing GCSE accreditation in the Humanities and meeting significant elements of the Citizenship order at Key Stage 4. This establishes Humanities as, in the terminology of this text's editors, the *carrier* subject (Case study A). The WJEC (Welsh Joint Education Committee) Double Humanities model learns from longstanding practice in GCSE Science and provides a framework that is both innovative and flexible, allowing schools to offer '. . . two GCSEs in Humanities for the price of one' (Lewis, 2001). Although in Wales Citizenship is not a statutory requirement (but rather an element of the PSHE framework as set out early in Part One of this volume) the WJEC GCSE Humanities specification has a strong Citizenship focus and, for this reason, has been adopted by one Wirral school and others beyond the Welsh border to provide not only two Humanities GCSEs but clear accreditation for aspects of the Citizenship order (Case study B).

Figure 2

Practical examples of innovative, accredited Citizenship Education through GCSE Humanities

CASE STUDY A

The AQA Humanities Specification

The John Hanson Community School, Hampshire, has a long tradition of excellent and innovative practice in the Humanities, in Citizenship and in peer education.

The Head of Humanities is also Chief Examiner for the AQA Humanities GCSE and at John Hanson a significant proportion of the school's Citizenship programme at Key Stage 4 is taught through utilising Humanities as a 'carrier' subject and gains accreditation through the GCSE.

The school's 'Children's Rights Peer Education Project' won a national award, the Foreign and Commonwealth Office Award for Education in Human Rights, as well as contributing to the school receiving the prestigious British Council's 'International School Award'.

Students are trained in experiential teaching techniques and teach their peers. Teachers work together and are extending its scope to include lower school and primary school students. (Waller, 2003)

In summer 2005 a long awaited and comprehensive textbook to support the AQA Humanities specification was co-edited by the head of Humanities at John Hanson School and published by Hodder Murray (Waller et al., 2005).

CASE STUDY B

The WJEC Humanities GCSE Specification

Park High School in Birkenhead has developed a curriculum at Key Stage 4 using the Welsh Joint Education Committee (WJEC) Humanities GCSE to provide accreditation for pupils in Humanities, in another Humanities subject, and for significant elements of the Citizenship programme of study. The role of Head of Humanities is combined with that of Citizenship Coordinator.

Funding for 'Gifted and Talented Pupils' under the 'Excellence in Cities' initiative has enabled a day trip to the Anne Frank House in Amsterdam and has generated high quality pupils' writing and drama which was presented at Wirral's Commemoration of National Holocaust Memorial Day, 28 January 2004, work that underpinned progress towards the GCSEs and coverage of the Citizenship requirements.

Changing curriculums, specialist schools and the subject specialism agenda

Humanities-informed approaches to Citizenship and its accreditation, at both Key Stage 3 and Key Stage 4, are likely to grow further through the focus on teaching and learning in the Key Stage 3 Strategy, the post-Tomlinson 14–19 initiative, the expansion of the specialist schools programme to include the Humanities and the current focus on the importance of subject specialism.

Matters of accreditation have already been addressed in this chapter and elsewhere in this text. The extension of specialist status (at last) provides an opportunity for schools to specialise in the Humanities through a combination of discrete and integrated programmes. Thus, the Humanities Specialist Colleges programme enables schools to develop curricular models based around a combination of two of the following teaching areas: History, Geography, English, Humanities, Citizenship or RE. In November 2005, Humanities was the Specialist Schools Trust's fastest increasing second specialism. As such, this *demands* that there is the sort of bridge between Citizenship and the Humanities (or rather Citizenship and the *other* Humanities) set out in this chapter.

The emerging focus around subject specialism is perhaps more double edged. The specialism push can, at one level, be a threat to *integrated* approaches but, nonetheless, the importance that it accords to the work of subject associations in supporting curriculum development and improving teaching and learning is long overdue and has been welcomed by both the Humanities Association and the Association for Citizenship Teaching. As such, it promises to ensure a practitioner role in future developments in both the Humanities and Citizenship areas. We must ensure the promise is kept; we ignore the resultant opportunity at our peril.

REFERENCES

Bell, D. (2005) 'Citizenship through participation and responsible action', speech to CSVs Barclay's New Futures Conference, 15 November 2005, London: Ofsted.

Dearing, R. (1994) *The National Curriculum and Its Assessment, Final Report*. London: School Curriculum and Assessment Authority.

DfEE/FEFC (2000) *Citizenship for 16–19 Year Olds in Education and Training: Report of the Advisory Group to the Secretary of State for Education and Employment*. Coventry: Further Education Funding Council.

DfEE/QCA (1998) *Education for Citizenship and the Teaching of Democracy in Schools: Final Report of the Advisory Group on Citizenship Education*. London: QCA.

DfEE/QCA (1999) *The National Curriculum*. London: DfEE.

DfEE/QCA (1999) *The National Curriculum Handbook for Secondary School Teachers in England*. London: QCA.

DfES (2003) *14–19: Opportunity and Excellence*. London: DfES.

Gill, B. (1990) 'Clarity Begins at Home', *Humanities Resource,* 4(1). Cheshire: Humanities Association.

Hargreaves, A. (1994) *Changing Teachers, Changing Times*. London: Cassell.

Citizenship Education, therefore, seeks to empower young people for reasons that are fundamental to peace and democracy in our collective future; to encourage people to be active citizens rather than passive subjects. But what kind of education is most appropriate for achieving these goals?

Thoughtful dialogue as an essential Citizenship skill

Clearly, young people need more than information if they are to engage with their communities in thoughtful, realistic and beneficial ways. They need to:

- communicate well with each other
- think critically, independently and fairly
- be genuinely motivated to participate
- appreciate how their own lives relate to larger communities
- learn how to put collective plans into action
- reflect on and learn from their participation
- be given the freedom and trust to take responsibility.

In short, they need opportunities to learn Citizenship skills and dispositions, as well as information. *What good is 'Citizenship knowledge' without the wisdom to use it well?*

The Citizenship National Curriculum and Programmes of Study recognise the need for these essential skills. Section 2 (Skills of Enquiry and Communication) and Section 3 (Skills of Participation and Responsible Action) specifically require young people to learn how to think, communicate and act well in communal contexts.

So how can teachers encourage their pupils to develop the skills of enquiry, communication and participation, particularly when timetables are so full already? The *Philosophy for Children* (or 'P4C') approach to teaching and learning has much to offer in this area. P4C is:

- appropriate for all ages and abilities
- applicable across the curriculum, in all subject areas
- based on the use of a communal dialogue (or 'enquiry') as the central means of learning
- focused on the *processes* of teaching and learning, not just the content
- a 'democratic form of education' where children have the opportunity to direct more of their own learning
- skills based, can accelerate learning, and improve behaviour; it therefore does not detract from the long-term demands of examination specifications or programmes of study but, indeed, supports these.

Essentially Philosophy for Children provides teachers with an extremely flexible framework within which pupils can develop their thinking and communication skills through guided dialogue. The value of this 'guided dialogue' has been clearly recognised by Professor Sir Bernard Crick in the context of values education:

> *. . . children learn responsibility best and gain a sense of moral values by discussing with good guidance from the earliest age real and controversial issues. Talk, discussion and debate are the bases of social responsibility and intercourse and the grounding and the practice of active citizenship.* (Crick, *RE Today*, Spring 2000)

Why might dialogue be so important in Citizenship Education?

Democracy. First of all, democracy relies on good communication; 'rule by the people' requires the people to express, listen, reflect and respond to each other. As John Dewey argues in 'Democracy and Education' (1916), democracy should not be viewed as simply a 'form of government', but more as a 'mode of associated living, of conjoint communicated experience'. It is the means through which we respond to and create change in the world. Consequently – and as Dewey concludes – education should emphasise community, communication, intelligent enquiry, and a reconstructive attitude as the best way to serve its citizens, and democracy.

Complexity. Second, Citizenship Education involves many complex and controversial issues and concepts where different perspectives need to be appreciated. For example, 'freedom' is an extremely important concept in the context of Citizenship, and yet it is very difficult to define. How would the Dalai Lama, George Bush, or an Iraqi define it? How do their definitions affect their ideas and actions? Thoughtfully guided dialogue offers a natural way for pupils to challenge, deepen and corroborate their understanding of complex concepts in a working context.

Dispositions. Third, dialogue is a participative activity that is hallmarked by a sense of collaboration and mutual progression. It is not a chat or series of vaguely related comments, constantly mediated by an authority figure (the teacher). With good facilitation, young people can use dialogue both to deepen their understanding of factual content and to develop their community skills and attitudes through, and with, each other. It allows the emotions, as well as the intellect, to be employed and explored. Citizenship dispositions (empathy, tolerance, respect, or open-mindedness, for example) can therefore be embraced and evolved along with the factual content.

Values. Values taught 'directly' (of the 'don't tell lies!' variety) often have little lasting impact:

> *I don't believe that values can be taught – taught directly that is. They must arise from actual or imagined experience if they are to have meaning; or else they are but a set of rules to learn by rote . . . Moral values must surely arise from experience if they are to enter into a person's character so that they as if instinctively influence behaviour.* (Crick: Address on 'Value' for the Gordon Cook Foundation, Glasgow, 1998)

If children are to develop their own sense of values and apply them to their actions in and out of school, they need the chance to explore and challenge them with others through dialogue, allowing their values to 'arise from experience'.

Controversial Issues. Teachers can fear discussing certain issues in class because they are controversial or sensitive areas. However, it might be argued that much of this tension does not arise from the issue itself, but from the discursive classroom context. For example, if the teacher is viewed as an 'ultimate authority' on the issues, if class members have not learned to distinguish 'arguing against the point' and 'arguing against the person', or if discussions are perceived as being 'won or lost' rather than 'helping everyone understand more deeply, if differently', then tension will naturally arise. However, open enquiry and dialogue – properly understood by all – can allow these tensions to be addressed and diffused directly rather than lie ignored or explode uncontrollably. Indeed, good dialogue and negotiated ground rules are the only real way of dealing with controversial or sensitive issues. The only practical alternative is to ignore the problem, and often to our peril.

Dialogue, then – far from being mere conversation – is a powerful and egalitarian approach to exploring Citizenship. Furthermore, it does not rely on limited academic criteria for success such as writing well or reading a lot. Everyone, of any ability or age, can be fully included.

Introducing Philosophy for Children (P4C)

The Philosophy for Children (P4C) approach has specialised in this area of thinking/enquiry/communication skills for 30 years, and it is now practised in over 40 countries. It can be used with children of all ages, all abilities and in any subject due to its skills-based approach to education. It is particularly relevant in the field of Citizenship because the actual process of learning is democratically guided both by the teacher (or 'facilitator') and the class (or 'community of enquiry'). Here are a few of the key principles of P4C:

- P4C is pupil-centred, and focuses on the skills of enquiry, participation and communication (skills of philosophising).
- The teacher adopts a role of 'facilitator', helping children to sharpen their thinking skills and dispositions, and enquire into a question communally.
- The class becomes a 'community of enquiry' where each participant aims to help the community understand a focal question more deeply.
- Reflective time is given to both the content of an enquiry, but also to the processes of learning through which a deeper understanding of an issue has occurred. Rather than 'give them a fish', it teaches pupils to 'fish for themselves'.
- Discussion must be distinguished from talking; enquiry into a particular question should be hallmarked by a sense of progression, each opinion building on those expressed beforehand.

The basic model for a P4C enquiry

A P4C enquiry offers a skeletal seven-step structure for discussion to help participants build their thinking and communication skills. Here is the basic model:

1 *Stimulus and reflection:* A thought-provoking and relevant stimulus is given to the pupils (e.g. a newspaper article on war). They have a few minutes of private reflection time in silence, and jot down anything that it makes them think about (memories, feelings, ideas etc.).
2 *Sharing reflections:* In small groups (of four or five), pupils listen to each other's reflections in turn, practising their expression and listening skills. They also get to appreciate that the same stimulus (and, by association, any experience in life) can generate very different responses in people.
3 *Question negotiation:* Pupils then create a thoughtful and philosophical question that arises from their reflections through negotiation. What made them curious? What would they like to investigate further?
4 *Sharing questions:* The group questions (e.g. When is war worth it? Are wars necessary? etc.) are displayed on the board for all to see.
5 *Voting:* Pupils vote – as individuals – for which question they would most like to discuss as a community of enquiry. The agenda is driven by their curiosity and interest, giving them a sense of ownership and responsibility in their own education.
6 *Enquiry:* Participants sit in a circle (where possible!), and the enquiry begins, guided by the teacher ('facilitator'). Analytical vocabulary can be introduced here (Assumptions in the question? Definitions? Interpretations?) as well as tactics for enquiring into the question. The enquiry aims to deepen understanding about the question, building on shared opinions, rather than reach a definitive answer.
7 *Reflection:* The enquiry ends by reflecting on both the content and the *process* of the enquiry. Content reflections consider progress made with regard to the question itself (in this case 'war'). Process reflections focus on the way in which progress was made. What was helpful in the way we addressed the question? What would help us improve our next enquiry?

These seven steps do not have to happen as a whole sequence, and there are innumerable ways in which the facilitator may vary each step to emphasise certain skills or concepts with the community. For example, if the facilitator wants to improve participants' listening skills – a 'process' objective – he or she might pause after Sharing Reflections (Step 2), and ask each participant to consider who in their group listened to them best, and give reasons for their view (body language, non-interruption, eye contact etc.). Alternatively, the facilitator might want participants to consider the concept of 'war' – a 'content' objective – and therefore guide the discussion towards definitions or interpretations of words in the elected question. The basic model therefore offers enormous flexibility, allowing teachers to develop the skills or understanding according to the needs of their particular pupils.

During the enquiry, pupils may be encouraged to reflect, express, create questions, communicate coherently, challenge ideas, seek clarifications, consider assumptions/definitions, think about other views, listen, analyse/synthesise alternative views etc. It's worth noting that this isn't a 'debate' or a 'class chat' – the community of enquiry is working *together* to understand something more deeply and ensure that there is structured *progression*. It doesn't stop people disagreeing if they wish, but it does prevent 'forced side-taking' or an unnatural adoption of black/white attitudes in issues that are often grey areas! Here, Figure 1 is instructive of the potential of the P4C model with a group of Year 7 pupils.

Figure 1
Case study: Can children be philosophical?

A sample of philosophical questions raised by a Year 7 Community of Enquiry (in a mixed ability, non-selective comprehensive) using a picture stimulus produced a fascinating outcome. The picture contained images that raised questions about power, appearances, conflict and authority; all Citizenship themes!

- 'Is appearance everything?'
- 'What is normal?'
- 'When should you give up?'
- 'Does size matter?'
- 'Should you base personality on appearance?'
- 'What is the point of fighting a battle you know you can't win?'
- 'Should you look up or down on your enemies?'
- 'Is any obstacle too big to overcome?'
- 'Can man move mountains?'

Thinking skills and dispositions in P4C

Thinking skills have gained much greater recognition in recent years as a means to accelerate learning, improve behaviour and self-awareness, and extend communication abilities both orally and in writing. In the P4C context, thinking skills are summarised as the '4 Cs':

1 *Critical thinking:* the ability to provide and evaluate reasons for opinions. 'Arguing with a point, not a person'.
2 *Collaborative thinking:* the ability to discover, contribute and build ideas with others.
3 *Creative thinking:* the ability to use a variety of thinking approaches (lateral thinking, imagining other perspectives etc.).
4 *Caring thinking:* the ability to recognise the role of emotions in an enquiry (empathy, sensitive phrasing etc.).

Again, the P4C enquiry model offers teachers a structure in which these specific skills can be evolved in a natural context. One enquiry, for example, might include a focus on 'giving good reasons for opinions', and the reflections at the end of the enquiry might ask participants to identify whether good reasons were used or not.

'But we don't have time for this!'

It might be argued that demands on the school timetable do not allow for luxurious lessons on thinking skills, open enquiries, or asking too many questions. As an ex-Head of RE, a school governor and an Assistant Head of Sixth Form, I can fully appreciate this reaction! However, there are two key reasons against this view:

- First, research has repeatedly shown – here and abroad – that pupils who enquire in some lessons tend to be more motivated, understand their subjects more, and retain information for longer periods than those who learn by rote. Furthermore, both behaviour and academic achievement tend to be improved across the ability range. Taking time to advance these skills, alongside the required 'content lessons', actually accelerates pupils' learning progress across the curriculum and for their future years at school and beyond.
- Second, it is difficult to imagine that the objectives of Citizenship are going to be reached if these skills are ignored in favour of didactically delivered content. Can you imagine a 'good citizen' who cannot listen well, cannot behave reasonably in an argument, or is incapable of independent thought? What, indeed, will the future be like if these skills and dispositions are ignored in favour of content or 'information driven' targets?

Here, Citizenship and Philosophy for Children approaches share a common problem, one that the editors of this text restate at every opportunity, that they are somehow a distraction from the 'real stuff' of schooling (literacy and numeracy) and from the quest to raise standards. Nothing could be further from the truth. Rather, Philosophy for Children strategies, Citizenship Education and, indeed, other approaches that concentrate as much on the *how* of learning as the *what* of learning, as Derry Hannam has shown (Hannam, 2002), can have a profoundly positive and more inclusive impact on achievement itself. Little surprise then that the Case Study below is drawn from a school that is participating in the Campaign for Learning's 'Learning to Learn' programme and where, therefore, P4C is central to effective learning, and hence achievement, itself.

CASE STUDY
Kingsbrook School, Milton Keynes

Kingsbrook School has been developing P4C for the last three years as part of the Northamptonshire Raising Standards Partnership (RSP) 'Learning to Learn' project. Teachers at the school have been using EBLO funding to trial P4C approaches at the school in a number of ways:

- whole staff and specialist group training in P4C;
- implementation of P4C through a variety of subject lessons, including English, RE, Art, Geography, History, Technology and ASDAN;

- Year 10 tutors are trialling six Citizenship modules using a community of enquiry approach. It is intended that the work will also be extended post-16;
- A 'Philosophy Lunch Club' has been established, with regular sessions run by the students. Issues raised and discussed have ranged from homophobia to racism both in and beyond school.

Celia James, Deputy Head and the Raising Standards Project Manager at Kingsbrook, reports that:

> *The various formal evaluations of the Kingsbrook students' experience of P4C activity so far have been most encouraging. They seem to value the work for a range of reasons. The community of enquiry is a multi-faceted process. For some participants it provided a confidence boost, 'It helped me realise I can talk and say my views instead of everyone doing it for me'. Others appreciated the way that the dialogue was conducted in a circle because 'it's better than talking with tables in front of us'. 'We all had a chance to say our own points – it wasn't just who the teacher picked.' 'Everyone listens and it's really quiet.' There is a general consensus that P4C is 'a really good way of learning because it really makes you think' and 'it would be good if all lessons were like it.'*

P4C: Some practical tips and starting points

Teachers can improve their students' skills of enquiry and communication by:

- having visual reminders of the Citizenship skills required, perhaps created by the community itself (symbols, words or phrases on posters etc.?)
- seating everyone so that everyone feels included and equal, and in contact with each other (eye contact? spacing?)
- giving participants specific roles and responsibilities; share authority (a scribe to chart 'community ideas' on the board during an enquiry, for example?)
- encouraging participants to communicate among themselves, and not 'through the teacher' all the time (might the teacher avoid eye contact sometimes?)
- identifying one or two aims that might be emphasised by you in the enquiry; for example, 'looking for good reasons for shared opinions' (helpful in evaluation/assessment)
- modelling specific terms that will develop their philosophical vocabulary (assumption, interpretation, definition, counter example etc.)
- leaving time, however short the lesson, to reflect on the progress the community has made, both in terms of content, and the process through which deeper understanding of an issue was achieved ('learning to learn')
- employing different group sizing to focus/broaden the learning community at particular times

- encouraging pupils to build on the ideas of their peers: is progress being made through the dialogue? (Here, asking pupils to start their contribution with 'I agree/disagree with [pupil's name] because . . .' can be most effective.)
- being imaginative with stimuli used for discussion, thus appealing to visually, kinaesthetically, aurally and intellectually stimulated pupils rather than any one group
- asking pupils to keep a 'Book of Our Enquiries', a 'Thought Wall' display space, or individual 'Thought Diaries' as a record and reference.

Senior managers can support this process through facilitating the training of a cluster of staff in P4C techniques, before cascading these skills through the school's INSET programme and signalling their importance in the School Improvement Plan and in Performance Management Targets. Indeed, they might go further by having the sort of whole school policy set out in Figure 2, thereby underlining the importance of P4C approaches to the ethos of the school and its approach to learning.

Through such a policy, all involved in the teaching process are encouraged to develop the 4 Cs of P4C (*critical*, *creative*, *caring* and *collaborative* thinking) – and not just in the Philosophy for/with Children sessions but across and outside the curriculum, for example in Citizenship related pursuits and initiatives such as school councils, mock elections and so forth.

Figure 2
Exemplar: a sample P4C whole school policy

PHILOSOPHY FOR CHILDREN (P4C) AT THIS SCHOOL – THE PRINCIPLES

Within this school, we acknowledge:

1. that every person's **experience** is unique, and so are their **interests**
2. accordingly, that formal as well as informal time should be created for individuals to **raise questions** that help them to **make sense** of their experience and curriculum, and to **share and pursue** their interests
3. that children need support in **formulating** such questions
4. that this requires teachers themselves to focus on **listening** to children, as well as to introduce and model the **language and discipline of philosophical enquiry**
5. that the language and discipline of enquiry can often be learnt best in the course of **whole-group discussion** (because)
6. there is a special value in learning **with** others (in a Community of Enquiry) and in learning from others.

PHILOSOPHY FOR CHILDREN AT THIS SCHOOL – THE PRACTICE

We have at least one teacher trained to SAPERE Level 1 (see P4C entry in Organisations and Websites on page 356) in philosophical enquiry who is committed to developing a Community of Enquiry within their class, with the following as basic aims and practices:

7. Periodically, the children sit in a **circle** (or horseshoe – so that they can see each other) and enquire into questions that **they themselves have created** from a shared story or stimulus.
8. In such circles, everyone is given an **equal opportunity** to contribute to the choice, as well as creation, of questions and to the enquiry itself (e.g. by voting, turntaking, etc.).
9. Two clear aims of Philosophy for Children are to develop **understanding** and **good judgement** through critical examination of *meanings* of words, *facts* of the matter, personal *feelings*, *views* and *values*, etc.
10. Another clear aim is to build a sense of **community**, though proper respect is paid to **differences** of interpretations, beliefs, feelings, views and values (e.g. wrong to 'put down', right to 'pass', etc.).
11. Children are encouraged to develop virtues of thinking, such as **reasonableness**, **open-mindedness** and **patience** (e.g. by calling for reasons, celebrating changes of mind, not interrupting).
12. Both the individual and the community benefit from regular pauses for **silent reflection** ('thinking time'), which may lead to better discussion, and to resolute or **creative activity** beyond the enquiry.

P4C in summary

P4C requires teacher training to be carried out most effectively. However, it may be worth picking a picture or other stimulus and experimenting with the basic P4C structure to get a glimpse of what might be involved.

If children are to grow up as 'good' (i.e. effective) citizens then, at the very least, they need the skills to engage meaningfully with their own thoughts and those of others. Only then can we put trust into the actions that follow. P4C offers a way in which these skills can be developed across the curriculum without cost to syllabus content or examination success; indeed, it can improve pupils' learning *and* their behaviour.

REFERENCES

Dewey, J. (1916) 'Democracy and Education', in J.A. Boydston (ed.) (1980) *John Dewey: The Middle Works, Volume 9*. Illinois: Southern Illinois University Press.

DfEE/QCA (1998) *Education for Citizenship and the Teaching of Democracy in Schools: Final Report of the Advisory Group on Citizenship*. London: QCA.

Hannam, D. (2002) *CSV Reports on the Impact of Citizenship in Schools*. London: Community Service Volunteers (CSV).

FURTHER READING

Cam, P. (1993, 1994, 1997) *Thinking Stories* (Volumes 1, 2 and 3). Australia: Hale & Iremonger.

Cam, P. (1995) *Thinking Together – Philosophical Inquiry for the Classroom*. An excellent and brief introduction to Philosophy for Children. Australia: Hale & Iremonger.

Fisher, R. (1998) *Teaching Thinking: Philosophical Enquiry in the Classroom*. London: Cassell.

Haynes, Joanna (2001) *Children as Philosophers*. London: RoutledgeFalmer Education. 'P4C' in the primary school context.

Huddleston, T. and Rowe, D. (2001) *Good Thinking – Education for Citizenship and Moral Responsibility* (Volumes 1–3 for pupils). London: Evans Brothers and Citizenship Foundation. A range of practical activities for learners at Key Stages 3, 4 and 5.

Lipman, M. (1991) *Thinking in Education*. Cambridge University Press. (Matthew Lipman is the founder of Philosophy for Children.)

Lipman, M., Sharp, A. and Oscanyan, F. (1980) *Philosophy in the Classroom*. Temple University Press.

Ord, W. and Jenkins, J. (2002) *Themes in RE* (Book 3), and the associated *Teacher Resource File*. London: Heinemann. (This brings together RE, Citizenship and Thinking Skills resources for pupils in KS3.)

PART THREE

FOUNDATIONS FOR CITIZENSHIP
THE SOCIAL AND BUSINESS SCIENCES

Developing Economic Citizens: Business, Enterprise and Economics for All

Jenny Wales

The economic dimension to political understanding and participation

The introduction of Citizenship offers the opportunity for a great leap forward for Economics and Business Education. Every student in a secondary school in the UK is now entitled to curriculum time devoted to discovering 'how the economy functions' (QCA, 2001). Until 2002, students could leave school with no concept of the connections and trade-offs in the economic world they were entering. Increasingly, young people are asked to make complex economic decisions with little or no preparation. At every election, people are encouraged to cast a vote but on what basis? Many of the subtle distinctions between the policies of the political parties are *essentially* economic but how can a voter be expected to evaluate the alternatives if no one has helped them to understand these connections and trade-offs? Indeed, might the apparent apathy and disaffection claimed of (in particular) young voters be attributed to a lack of economic awareness; for without this awareness many policy options are likely to appear indecipherable and irrelevant.

The drawback is that many teachers are afraid of attempting to unpick this section of the Citizenship orders. Awarding bodies have attempted to ignore it, books quietly forget about it and non-specialist teachers try to avoid it. Excuses are legion but are often based on a lack of knowledge and fear.

Why is the way the economy works considered to be such a mystery? The young child tugging the parent's arm in a shop trying to persuade that parent to buy them an ice cream and a packet of crisps is an unwitting economic citizen. A year or two later, armed with pocket money, they start to allocate their resources and their economic citizenship grows. All economics really does at this level is to put some jargon in place of ordinary words and make connections to show consequences. Once these connections are made, it is relatively straightforward to work out the outcomes of some 'what if?' questions. But often we don't get beyond the jargon or make the connections; take taxation: it should not be hard to grasp that we need to pay taxes if we want the government to provide healthcare, education, transport and all those other services that we so much want. Unfortunately, as Figure 1 shows, there is evidence that many potential voters just don't understand this simple relationship (Davies et al., 2002). The table shows the responses on the taxation–public spending question of over a thousand students of above average ability between the ages of 15 and 17.

Figure 1
Opinions on government expenditure and taxation

	The government should spend:	**Agree**
a	more money to provide better services for all	93%
b	less money and the people should pay more	8%
c	less money	13%
	Everybody should:	
d	pay less tax	74%
e	pay more tax	3%

Of this survey group, 72 per cent thought that they did not pay taxes at all. They were unaware that all consumers pay VAT on many of their purchases. There is also evidence to show that economic understanding does not improve with age. Research reveals that adults hold similarly inconsistent views on the relationship between taxation and government spending (Furnham and Lewis, 1986). It has also been demonstrated that some adults justify this view with a belief that government spending is wasteful so cuts can be made with no loss of provision – a view, of course, sometimes encouraged by opposition politicians of all persuasions (Williamson and Wearing, 1996).

Addressing the mysteries of Economics through National Curriculum Citizenship

One solution to this deficit in economic understanding is to turn to a teacher from an Economics or Business Studies background to draw out the simple concepts that underpin the ideas that are key to the development of *Economic* Citizenship. In this context, teachers of Business Studies or Economics have a key role to play in Citizenship teams and they can also contribute to many other sections of the orders. The rights and responsibilities of consumers, employers and employees form a part of all GCSE Business Studies courses and Business Studies teachers are often used to teaching them in the active, investigative manner which is appropriate for the Citizenship classroom. The economic aspects of the United Kingdom's position in Europe, including its relationship with the European Union, is covered in a practical way in most Economics courses. Students can therefore move beyond the rather dry account of European political institutions, which tends to be the focus in most general Citizenship textbooks. The challenges of global interdependence and responsibility, including sustainable development and Local Agenda 21, feature in many Business Studies and Economics specifications, often within sections on trade and ethical responsibility. Again, experience in teaching these courses should be utilised within the planning and delivery of Citizenship programmes.

Economics and Business Studies specialists can also contribute to other areas closely related to Citizenship, not least the recently launched provisions for Enterprise Education or the aspects of Personal Finance Education that Linda Thomas considers in Chapter 3.4. Finally, Business Studies teachers, in particular, are some of the most enthusiastic users of ICT in schools and are therefore well equipped to deal with the range of electronic and net-based resources that can sometimes baffle other Citizenship teachers.

Developing the skills of Economic Citizenship in the classroom

Business Studies and Economics contribute not only to the content of the Citizenship Order – the 'knowledge and understanding' aspect of the curriculum. They also address the skills that are central to the National Curriculum Citizenship Programmes of Study: skills of 'enquiry and communication' and skills of 'participation and responsible action'. Such skills are an essential ingredient of good Economics and Business Studies education; have long featured in progressive Economic and Industrial Understanding programmes; and match closely those regularly demonstrated in the Business Studies or Economics classroom. In such a setting, researching and evaluating current issues is a core activity and, as all GCSE Business Studies and Economics courses include evidence-based assessment, teachers constantly ask students to interpret data and raise questions about its validity. This is a key to the kind of *effective* and critical Citizenship proposed by the editors of this volume.

Like Economics and Business Studies, Citizenship is not a subject that usually has 'right' answers (although it might seek to develop desirable approaches and 'good thinking', to use the title of one established set of Citizenship resources (Huddleston and Rowe, 2000)). Thus, students have to learn to deal with their own and other people's perspectives and teachers need to deal with controversial issues, including those on which they may have a personal position. As Jan Campbell, Don Rowe, John Keast and other contributors to this collection note, many teachers shy away from dealing with controversial issues because they feel insecure. As disciplines, Business Studies and Economics are full of uncertainty and alternative perspectives and teachers in these areas learn to deal with this as a matter of course. Trade-offs, often with an ethical dimension, are at the core of decision-making and the allocation of resources, and students are encouraged to learn to evaluate the alternatives. Again, the place of the Business Studies and Economics teachers in the Citizenship team is vital.

Utilising the skills of the Business Studies or Economics teacher to teach controversial issues in the Citizenship classroom

The 'stakeholder' model has a lot to offer Citizenship as a strategy for dealing with controversial or contentious issues. In the Business Studies classroom it is used as a method of evaluating business activity from the perspectives of different groups who are affected by the actions of a business. This takes place on different scales and can be applicable to different sorts of organisations:

- If the school decides that students can run a tuck shop selling snacks and sweets, who will be affected?
- If a supermarket chain wants to build a new store in the local area, who will be affected?
- If a chocolate bar maker decides to buy its raw materials from the cheapest supplier rather than a fair trade supplier, who will be affected?

From activities such as these, students learn to develop arguments to support different perspectives. It's often not as clear-cut as the initial question might suggest. Might a tuck shop put the dinner ladies out of work? If the chocolate bar manufacturer doesn't cut its costs, it may lose out to the competition and close down so people are made redundant. As the discussion grows so does the range of stakeholders (or affected citizens), the range of perspectives and the range of issues for consideration.

Being able to put yourself in someone else's shoes is a very sophisticated activity. Students are asked to 'use their imagination to consider other people's experiences and be able to think about, express, explain and critically evaluate views that are not their own' (DfES, 2000). This is no mean feat. It goes well beyond the achievements of much of the adult population. It needs to be experienced initially in a secure environment in which no one's sensitivities are threatened. Unless this is achieved, students may reject strategies that use the stakeholder approach to achieve this objective in future.

Role-play is a technique often used to help students understand stakeholders' perspectives in the Business Studies or Economics classroom because it provides just such a safe environment. In the Citizenship classroom it can also help students to develop greater confidence as well as a deeper understanding of the material.

Ofsted (2002) advises inspectors to look for:

- an up-to-date knowledge and enthusiasm for the subject, engaging pupils in discussion of issues which they see will affect their lives, building towards the knowledge, skills and understanding associated with becoming an informed and active citizen
- encouragement of pupils to think about controversial issues with sensitivity and objectivity and to challenge in appropriate ways.

In some Citizenship classrooms, complex issues may be dealt with in such a superficial manner that students are unable to draw the critical conclusions that are implicit in Citizenship and that Ofsted is seeking. Indeed, some would contend that this has too often been the case in conventional, tutor delivered PSHE programmes. It is not the result of deliberate intent but the unwitting outcome of circumstances. Often resources use sophisticated terminology that is not fully understood by non-expert teachers. Materials can also be presented from one point of view, according to their provenance. Again, this may not be recognised by non-specialists. The guidance of a specialist teacher, such as somebody from a Business Studies or Economics background, means that key points can be identified and superficiality can be avoided.

Classroom strategies don't have to be complex to achieve critical thinking. They just need to help students to realise that there is often no simple answer. *President for a Day*[1], an ICT based simulation often used in both Geography and Economics classrooms, guides students to this sort of conclusion. The activity is extremely valuable and effective. However, if it is used in its entirety, it offers conclusions that can lead students to a particular point of view before they have had the opportunity to consider the issues for themselves. The solution is to stop before the end of the simulation and encourage students to come to their own conclusions and then review the opinions of the Tear Fund, which has produced it. A subject expert from Economics, Geography or Sociology is more likely to recognise this.

While working with resources like *President for a Day*, lessons can be structured so students are asked to 'express, justify and defend orally or in writing' their own opinion as well as 'contributing to group and exploratory class discussions'. As a result, they learn that the tabloid newspaper approach – the making of vociferous, unsupported statements – is not an adequate response.

The Citizenship-friendly teaching strategies of Business Studies and Economics

The nature of Business Studies and Economics can lead to active, investigative classrooms, which help students to develop the full range of Citizenship skills. The frequent use of role-play, discussion, group work and research on current issues give students opportunities to practise their skills on material that contributes to the programme of study.

In the context of the Business Studies or Economics classroom, it is important that students are made aware of the Citizenship aspects of the work. Thus, Ofsted inspectors are advised to ask students: 'How do teachers make it clear to you when you are studying something about Citizenship, even when the lesson is also about other subjects or topics?' (Ofsted, 2002).

Topics such as taxation, government spending, inflation and unemployment should therefore be dealt with in this broader context. Students often find it hard to transfer ideas from one classroom to another so it is important to have a strategy for recording Citizenship experiences when they are being gathered from across the curriculum.

Unfortunately, as Economics is available to few students at Key Stage 4 and Business Studies is not a compulsory subject at Key Stage 4, it cannot be assumed that the Citizenship experience they provide will be available to every student. Strategies therefore have to be in place to manage the missing economic element in so many Citizenship programmes. It may be that the best option is to take a fourfold approach:

- Include the Business Studies or Economics specialist as a key member of the Citizenship team.

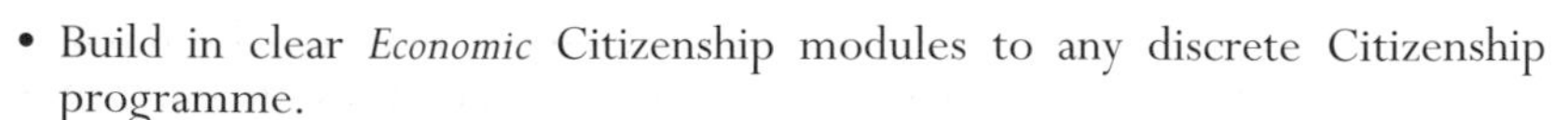

- Build in clear *Economic* Citizenship modules to any discrete Citizenship programme.
- Ensure that optional Business Studies and Economics courses take account of this discrete core programme and build on it.
- Use the emergence of Enterprise Education, now a statutory requirement at Key Stage 4, and the push towards Personal Finance Education as an opportunity to further develop the economic dimension to Citizenship learning.

Integrated or 'off timetable' days, Enterprise Education and Citizenship

Off timetable days provide an opportunity for students to experience Enterprise Education in the context of a coherent Citizenship programme, a strategy strongly advocated in the recommendations with which the editors close this text. Enterprise or trading based days have a long tradition in some schools and are often led by Economics or Business Studies specialists.

Thus, a year group might spend a day involved in activities like *The Trading Game*[2] which develops understanding of the working of the market and how things can go wrong. Such activities can be organised within the school. Alternatively, such a day might involve a series of activities in which students have opportunities to work on their Citizenship skills in the context of the Economics and Business Studies linked sections of the Citizenship Programme of Study. A range of activities has the advantage of meeting several aspects of the Order. It may also allow organisation on the basis of smaller more manageable groups in which students feel more at ease when it comes to expressing opinions and concerns. However, debriefing after the day is critical if students are going to translate their experiences into a deeper understanding in a wider context. Business Studies or Economics teachers ought to be involved in this debriefing in order to help students to develop their thinking and consolidate their learning.

Integrated days can also be used to give a taster for Key Stage 4 options. Business Studies teachers sometimes complain that the Geographers and Historians persuade students to take their courses because they have access to them at Key Stage 3. An integrated day, delivered as part of the Citizenship Curriculum, planned to be both fun and informative, can give Business Studies and Economics teachers the opportunity to demonstrate their wares to Key Stage 3 students. This win–win scenario can be a useful strategy to encourage such teachers to contribute to the Key Stage 3 programme. Some organisations[3] will put on these kinds of events for a school, thus removing some of the planning burden and increasing the novelty of the occasion. Here, an approach to the local Education–Business Partnership can be an excellent starting point.

Making the most of Business Studies and Economics teachers in the delivery of Citizenship

Many Business Studies and Economics teachers are fully committed to examination classes and have little time for other activities. They have always been in short supply, so it is important to use them effectively. The teacher who is an enthusiast for Citizenship will always find a way to become involved but it remains important to devise strategies to make the most of their limited time. Figure 2 outlines a range of ways in which their talents might be drawn on.

Figure 2
Strategies for involving Business Studies and Economics specialists

Discrete Citizenship Programmes
Business Studies and Economics teachers who are Citizenship enthusiasts can make an invaluable contribution in those schools that have some form of discrete programme, as promoted by the editors of this collection. They can provide guidance on developing schemes of work and on the use of resources, they can help others to develop appropriate teaching strategies and they can, of course, contribute to delivery.

Carousel or Modular Models
In many schools, non-specialists, often tutors, teach Citizenship and may lack both the expertise and enthusiasm to do so. One way of maximising the opportunities that this system offers is to arrange a carousel or modular programme within which tutors 'specialise'. This allows them to develop or carry out activities within their expertise including the economic domain. If timetabling permits, students can move round a group of tutors for different parts of the Programme of Study. Whatever the circumstances, the skills of the Business Studies or Economics teacher can be used to the full.

Through CPD
If the Business Studies or Economics teacher does not have time to participate in teaching Citizenship, they may be able to provide guidance to others, perhaps by leading a CPD session at a training day. Help from an expert can make others more confident in their approach. Putting teachers into the student's position by carrying out the activities is often more engaging than just talking about them. It also allows issues to arise naturally as people relax and are happier to admit the gaps in their knowledge. It is not just Citizenship students who fail to recognise that there is more than one perspective on an issue! Working through the activities that form the scheme of work, explaining issues and discussing the potential outcomes of a debriefing session will enhance the experience for both teachers and students. Although activities usually come with teacher guidance, there is nothing like a face-to-face session to explain and reassure people. Some published materials in the field use terminology that non-expert teachers may not understand and on occasion can even be inaccurate. Working with an expert can clarify matters.

Supporting Business Studies and Economics teachers in the delivery of Citizenship

Whatever role the Business Studies or Economics teacher plays in the delivery of Citizenship, they need support. Teaching Citizenship is different from teaching GCSE Business Studies or Economics and certainly different from delivering AS and A2 examination courses, the fare of many such specialists. Experts and enthusiasts almost always want to impart a thorough grounding in *their* subject to their students. In Citizenship, it is important to learn to be selective in drawing on one's 'home' subject. Even where the Business Studies or Economics specialist is playing only a supporting role, the teacher has two particular needs:

- Training in order to understand the context in which they are working. The depth of study is critical because students will be overwhelmed if they are expected to deal with unnecessary technical complexity within a Citizenship framework. Supply and demand, yes; drawing complex economic diagrams, no.
- Time to carry out whatever role they have been asked to fulfil effectively – this is essential, whether they are guiding others or directly involved themselves.

Supporting Citizenship: the practicalities and rationale

In a team, the sharing of expertise is critical. A Business Studies or Economics teacher can be used to guide others in working with the knowledge required as well as developing appropriate teaching strategies because they have experience of both. If directly involved, they will be able to influence the shape and structure of the course. Whatever the role, the Business Studies or Economics expert can help to make sure that Citizenship really works. Here it is important to:

- check the schemes of work to ensure that they are coherent in terms of subject development and provide students with the opportunity to draw conclusions for themselves
- check resources to ensure that they are accurate and up to date. Business and the economy move very fast and the context for activities therefore needs to take this into account. At Key Stage 4 and post-16, these subjects generally attract students because they deal in familiar and current contexts and Citizenship needs to build on this
- check that staff understand and can use other Citizenship resources (i.e. those not from their stable) effectively
- be a willing friend when people need help.

It's in the interest of Economics and Business Studies as subjects to make their contribution to the broader Citizenship programme engaging and exciting. After all, through both Citizenship and Enterprise Education, we have, for the first time, an entitlement to Business and Economic Education for all. We ought to make the most of it.

REFERENCES

Davies, P., Howie, H., Mangan, J. and Telhaj, S. (2002) 'Economic Aspects of Citizenship Education: An Investigation of Student Understanding', *The Curriculum Journal*, 13(2): 227–49.

DfES (2000) *National Curriculum, Citizenship*. London: DfES.
Furnham, A. and Lewis, B. (1986) *The Economic Mind*. Hemel Hempstead: Harvester Wheatsheaf.
Huddleston, T. and Rowe, D. (2000) *Good Thinking* (Volumes 1, 2 and 3). London: Citizenship Foundation.
Ofsted (2002) *Inspecting Citizenship*. London: Office for Standards in Education.
QCA (2001) *Citizenship: A Programme of Study for Key Stage 4*. London: QCA.
Williamson, M.R. and Wearing, A.J. (1996) 'Lay People's Cognitive Models of the Economy', *Journal of Economic Psychology*, 17(1): 3–38.

NOTES

1. *President for a Day* is available from Tear Fund.
2. *The Trading Game* is available from Christian Aid.
3. Young Enterprise and Just Business provide such details and contact details are provided in the Organisations and Websites section on page 352. Young Enterprise has long been the leading organisation in promoting mini-enterprise based activities in schools including a long established national competition and provides CPD for teachers and schools in this area.

FURTHER READING

Davies, P. 'Contributing to Citizenship Education by Improving the Quality of Students' Arguments', *Teaching Business and Economics,* 8(1).
Davies, P. (2002) 'Principals or Agents? Developing Citizenship through Business, Economics and Financial Education', *Journal for Social Sciences and their Didactics* 2002–1.
Wales, J. (2002) *A Citizen's Guide to the Economy.* London: Heinemann.
Wales, J. and Clarke, P. (2004) *Learning Citizenship: A Practical Guide to Teaching Strategies in the Secondary School*. London: RoutledgeFalmer.

Learning about the Law: Education for Legal Awareness

Tony Thorpe

Ignorance of the law

The case for helping young people understand more about the law seems clear. Laws are an important means through which power is exercised and the actions of individuals and organisations controlled. They affect people of all ages, and impinge on all aspects of daily life. They provide protection for people when they are vulnerable, and offer a means of resolving disputes. It therefore seems important – from both an individual and societal perspective – that these processes and rules are widely understood. In this respect, law-related education becomes an entitlement. 'It is a fundamental requisite of the rule of law that the law should be made known. The individual must be able to know of his legal rights and obligations' (Mr Justice Burton)[1].

In reality, however, there is evidence of considerable public uncertainty and ignorance about certain aspects of the law – amongst all groups of people, including the young. There is frequently an inability to distinguish between civil and criminal law; people are often uncertain, misinformed or unaware about the law covering routine aspects of their lives; and many fail to recognise the legal element in a particular situation. This almost always works to their detriment, either as a victim or perpetrator.

Some writers have looked at the need for legal understanding in relation to the provision of medical care – which treats ailments *and* works to prevent sickness and disease. By analogy, understanding the law enables people to make sense of and deal with everyday law-related problems, *and* helps them to recognise in advance the law-related nature of certain situations, thereby reducing unnecessary conflict and the need for recourse to lawyers and the courts.

Legal understanding also contributes to social cohesion. Familiarity with the law and possession of the skills and confidence to access legal information reduces individuals' feelings of alienation from the law and has the potential to create greater engagement with organisations within the community. Understanding the law is an important aspect of community involvement.

Law in schools

GCSE and A level Law courses have been taught for many years in schools and colleges throughout England and Wales. However, these courses tend to be academic in nature and to reach a relatively small and narrow section of the student population.

Aside from these, law-related issues have, in general, been covered rather thinly in the curriculum. Prior to the establishment of Citizenship as a National Curriculum subject, their representation was probably strongest in the Social Studies and Integrated Humanities courses offered in many secondary schools throughout the 1970s and 1980s. These courses commonly provided a six-week unit on 'law and order' – concentrating mainly on the nature and causes of crime and the treatment of offenders.

This *criminological* perspective towards law was almost certainly a reaction to contemporary concerns about law and order and also a reflection of the increasing number of Sociology and Social Science graduates who were then entering the teaching profession. It also illustrated a prevailing view – still strong today – that law and crime are almost synonymous.

The main strength of this approach was that it tried to provide students with some understanding of the complex, socially derived, nature of crime – and, in doing this, discouraged swift, uninformed judgements. It was strong on the social causes and impact of crime, but offered little understanding about the nature or content of the law itself. Although students were able to understand a little more about recidivism or the underlying causes of delinquency, they were unlikely to know anything about their own legal position were they to be stopped by the police that evening after school.

In an attempt to remedy this situation and to promote the development of legal awareness in schools, the Law Society in 1984 funded a five-year *Law in Education Project*. This produced and disseminated a range of law-related materials specifically written for use with 14–16 year old students by teachers without any legal training and with a focus on both criminal and civil law[2]. The project evolved in 1989 into the Citizenship Foundation, now widely seen as the leading and most influential independent educational charity in the Citizenship Education field. One outcome of the Foundation's work is the *Young Citizen's Passport* – a pocket guide to the law for 14–19 year olds that is now about to go into its 11th edition and of which over one million copies have thus far been distributed (Citizenship Foundation, 2006a). The passport has inspired a range of related materials including a similar guide for young asylum seekers and refugees (Citizenship Foundation, 2006b), elements of a Home Office guide for those working on the new education programmes for newcomers to Britain (Home Office, 2004) and a website targeted at young offenders and those at risk of offending – *Rizer* (Galleries of Justice, 2004).

By the early 1990s, Citizenship Education had been identified as a Cross-Curricular Theme (NCC, 1990), and – under the Education Reform Act 1988 – technically, part of the whole curriculum. However, the subject did not have National Curriculum status and therefore rarely a separate or identifiable slot on the timetable. The promotion of legal awareness relied very much on the enthusiasm and initiative of individual teachers. But with the heavy workload of incorporating the other curriculum changes required, schools and teachers gave law-related education an understandably low priority.

Significant changes however took place in 1998, with the publication of the final report of the government's advisory group on citizenship, chaired by Professor Bernard Crick (DfEE, 1998). The key citizenship concepts identified in this document, such as fairness, justice, the rule of law, freedom, rights, and responsibilities, were all closely linked to law, as were many of the 'essential elements' of knowledge and understanding. When Citizenship Education became part of the National Curriculum in August 2002 (DfEE, 2000), major sections of the Programme of Study – in terms of knowledge, skills and understanding – contained significant law-related components.

Challenges

The inclusion of Citizenship Education as part of the National Curriculum provided, for the first time, an opportunity for the development of legal awareness and understanding of all young people in England and Wales. In the remainder of this chapter I would like to discuss briefly a number of further questions surrounding the teaching of law-related education within this context.

A 'light touch'?

During 2002, in the months immediately preceding and following the introduction of Citizenship Education as a National Curriculum subject, advisory staff from DfES and QCA reminded (and reassured) secondary school teachers that a 'light touch' had been used in prescribing the subject's content. By this they were referring both to the very general way in which the content of the Citizenship Curriculum is described and to the associated expectation that schools were *expected* to mould their own Citizenship programmes such that these met the distinct needs of the students that they taught and the communities which they served.

One reading of the early evidence from the ongoing NFER Longitudinal Study into the process and impact of the introduction of Citizenship to the National Curriculum led by David Kerr and his team (and discussed in Chapter 1.2) is that the 'light touch' approach has allowed some schools off the hook in making the appropriate structural preparations for Citizenship in terms of curriculum provision, departmental support and staff development.

Deciding what to teach

The topics listed in the Programme of Study that are most closely connected with the law include (for Key Stage 3) legal rights and responsibilities, basic aspects of the criminal justice system, *and* the role of the European Union. In Key Stage 4, rights and responsibilities of consumers, employers and employees, the operation of the civil justice system, *and* the role of the government and courts in shaping the law are also added.

And, the above notwithstanding, this reveals the great strength of the 'light touch': that it is *not* overly prescriptive. It avoids burdening schools with a detailed and complex syllabus and recognises that few schools have staff (at least in the short term) with the specialist expertise to teach all the areas that might be identified in a more comprehensive list. It also takes into account the dynamic nature of Citizenship Education with a content that is constantly changing.

Of course, the weakness, however, is the very general nature of the references – particularly with respect to *legal rights and responsibilities*. Which rights and responsibilities do teachers include? There are so many to draw from. Although there is clearly some merit in this non-prescriptive approach, there is a tendency for teachers to limit their attention to criminal (as opposed to civil) law and to thereby perpetuate a limited view of the law. A predominant focus on criminal law in the curriculum raises the question of whether this is the best use of available time (an important factor in Citizenship Education) given that for most people, for most of the time, it is civil law that has the greater impact on their lives.

A further consequence of presenting *legal rights and responsibilities* as a single heading is the implication that they form a distinct area within Citizenship Education, and are therefore to be covered as a separate topic. In fact, the very opposite is true. Legal rights and responsibilities permeate and enhance almost all aspects of Citizenship.

Deciding what to choose within the law-related area is a complex task. Quite often, to minimise uncertainty (and work), we are all reluctant to jettison existing topics that function well. Some questions that might help the selection process are as follows:

- What topics link to young people's sphere of experience, current concerns and needs?
- On what topics would students welcome clarification?
- What will the student personally gain from engaging in learning about a particular topic? (The concern here is that an appropriate agenda – one relevant to the student – is being followed).
- What different and enriching ways of learning does this topic offer?
- What Citizenship issues does this topic raise?
- How might the proposed topics be grouped and ordered to ensure clarity and development – for students *and* teachers?

Expert knowledge

Few teachers have any kind of training or background in the law, and research indicates that the legal aspects of Citizenship Education are amongst the areas in which teachers have least confidence in their ability. Unfortunately, there is no immediate remedy to this problem – but it *is* possible to adopt certain measures that are, over time, likely to develop a teacher's confidence and competence in handling the law.

The first of these – as the editors of this collection and many other contributors stress again and again – is through the creation of a specialist Citizenship team, whose members' principal commitment is to teaching *Citizenship* Education. This gives teachers complete responsibility for preparing and delivering materials, and therefore greater opportunities to refine and develop their skills. It will, in the longer term, almost inevitably, improve their understanding of the subject matter and therefore their teaching.

The second concerns the role that the teacher chooses to adopt in class. Few Citizenship teachers, even those with specialist qualifications, are likely to have a detailed knowledge of *all* issues that might be covered. The very broad nature of Citizenship Education tends to militate against this. Even lawyers lack certainty in commenting on some of the law-related issues raised in Citizenship lessons.

In view of this, the only viable alternative seems to be to adopt an enquiry-based approach to working in the classroom, in which the teacher fosters a critical, explicit examination of the issue, identifies the key questions, and then takes responsibility (ideally with students) to investigate further and find the required answers.

A third route is to build up a network of links with professionals who can bring their specialist knowledge and experience to support the teaching and learning of law-related issues. Organisations and individuals able to help in this way include the police, magistrates, the Citizens Advice Bureau, local trading standards offices and trade unions. The Citizenship Foundation also runs a scheme in London linking or 'twinning' solicitors with a small number of schools that it is seeking to make available nationally and for which it has produced a supporting pack (Citizenship Foundation, 2005).

Interest and accessibility

A popular perception of law is of a dry and complex subject, using language and terminology not immediately accessible to the layperson. In some respects this view is entirely accurate, but the most pressing problem for Citizenship teachers is not the technical language used in contracts and deeds, but how to ensure that students develop the knowledge and understanding of the legal areas specified in the Programme of Study.

In one sense, the most obvious route is simply to convey the information directly to students – by word of mouth, on screen, or on paper. All teachers, however, know of the limitations of this approach and of the general need to engage students in some kind of activity through which learning may take place.

One very practical way in which this can be done in law-related education is through mock trials or tribunals. These may take the form of conducting a complete case or of recreating particular stages of trial or tribunal – such as questioning and cross-examining witnesses, listening to evidence, reaching a verdict, or deciding on a sentence or levels of compensation.

On a larger scale, the Citizenship Foundation, in partnership with the Bar Council and Magistrates' Association, run two large annual mock trial competitions open to schools from all parts of the United Kingdom[3]. Mock trial events[4] are also organised by the National Centre for Citizenship and the Law at their base, the excellent *Galleries of Justice*, in Nottingham, and through local initiatives of the Magistrates' Association (notably through the Magistrates in the Community programme), the police and local courts.

At a more general level, however, teachers need to find ways of *routinely* engaging students in discussion and work on law-related issues, and here it may be helpful to refer to the underlying concepts of Citizenship Education, already cited above. Rights, responsibility, justice, fairness and the rule of law are all essential components. They are also concepts that engage us at a moral and emotive level. My view of rights, responsibility, and fairness will be different in *some* way from yours. We will also have different emotional reactions to situations or issues – such as racial discrimination or environmental protection – that are based on these concepts.

The moral dimension

Another way of illustrating the same point is through the notion of *social and moral responsibility* – one of the three strands of Citizenship Education identified in the *Final Report of the Advisory Group on Citizenship* (DfEE, 1998). It is the *moral* aspect of responsibility that is particularly important in a Citizenship teaching context because it is this that provides the basis for debate between students, and contributes to defining a particular topic as a *Citizenship* issue.

In selecting topics for study, teachers therefore need to access the moral and emotional elements of the subject, *not* to teach right from wrong but to maximise chances of student involvement and give students the thinking skills to come to their own conclusions. In a law-related context this will determine the choice of case study used for discussion or analysis, and the way in which a particular topic might be approached. For example, a preamble to work on juries and the Crown Court might take the form of a dilemma faced by someone who is called up for jury service but is uncertain (or unwilling) to attend. In deciding whether this person should or should not take on this responsibility, students are, *at the same time*, learning about the purpose, function and nature of a jury.

Case studies for discussion or mock trial benefit from a similar *moral* element – and one that, in particular, is contestable. A case where one person or organisation is *clearly* in the right or wrong is less likely to generate debate than one where the arguments are balanced on both sides. Cases involving competing human rights are interesting in this respect, where students try to determine which right should predominate and, again, useful resource materials exist (e.g. Huddleston and Rowe, 2000).

Conclusion: the importance of representing the law

A number of years ago I ran a workshop with teachers using materials designed to help students understand more about the subject of child employment. Currently, in England and Wales, the part-time employment of children below the age of 16 is largely controlled through local by-laws, but in many parts of the country these laws are not widely adhered to. In the discussion that followed the exercise, one teacher said he would be very unlikely to teach the topic because it reflected so badly on the law. He felt that the failings of law were not something that should be brought to his students' attention.

The teacher's comment raises an interesting dilemma about the way in which Law should be represented in Citizenship Education. Is it appropriate for the law to be seen to be failing or to have other shortcomings? Should teachers present a positive, enabling view of the law? The answer, I would suggest, to both questions is 'yes', but perhaps with certain provisos. Probably few Citizenship teachers want their students to accept the status quo (and therefore the law) in an uncritical fashion, but most, if not all, would urge their students to remain within the law, following democratic procedures for change. Most Citizenship teachers would also like to remove some of the mental obstacles that students might have about the law – by reducing their alienation from the law and increasing their confidence to gain access to it. However, many people who find themselves involved in some kind of legal process, vis-à-vis divorce, unfair dismissal or a claim for compensation, frequently comment on the problematic nature of the judicial process. For Citizenship teachers, it is a very difficult balance to represent the law accurately, one that is likely to be thrown into even sharper focus now that the joint proposal from three leading organisations to develop a broader Public Legal Education strategy has been accepted by the Secretary of State for Constitutional Affairs[5], a proposal that promises to ultimately bring law-related education to a much broader audience.

Another question that it is interesting to ask is whether there are any areas of law that it is not appropriate to discuss? If there are, what are they and why? *Some* teachers at certain faith schools are reluctant to give students (in Years 10, 11, 12 or 13) details of the law relating to contraception or abortion. Other teachers are concerned that teaching about the law contributes to what they believe is a worryingly litigious society. How should we respond to these concerns? Are there any areas of the law that students should remain ignorant of? Are there any circumstances in which teachers should withhold information about a student's legal rights?

I think the general answer to all these questions has to be 'no'. There *may* be circumstances, for teaching purposes, when it is better to delay tackling certain law-related issues until students have reached the appropriate stage of intellectual or moral development. It may also be wise to delay discussion of a topic that is particularly sensitive to members of the group, or if the time available does not allow the teacher to provide a full and adequate explanation. Otherwise, there does not seem to be a case for withholding information about the law – information which, arguably, all have a right and responsibility to acquire.

REFERENCES

Citizenship Foundation (2005) *Lawyers in Schools: a twinning programme resource pack to support teaching about the law as part of the Citizenship curriculum*. London: Citizenship Foundation.

Citizenship Foundation (2006a) *Young Citizen's Passport: your guide to the law in England and Wales*. London: Hodder Murray.

Thorpe, T. and Jarvis, R. (2006b) A *Guide to the Law in England and Wales for Young Asylum Seekers and Refugees*. London: Citizenship Foundation.

DfEE (1998) *Education for Citizenship and the Teaching of Democracy in Schools: Final Report of the Advisory Group on Citizenship*. London: DfEE.

DfEE (2000) *Citizenship: National Curriculum*. London: DfEE.
Galleries of Justice (2004) *Rizer:* www.rizer.co.uk. Nottingham: Galleries of Justice.
Home Office (2004) *Life in the United Kingdom: a journey to citizenship*. London: The Stationery Office.
Huddleston, T. and Rowe, D. (2000) *Good Thinking* (Volumes 1, 2 and 3). London: Evans Brothers/Citizenship Foundation.
NCC (1990) *Curriculum Guidance 8: Education for Citizenship*. York: National Curriculum Council.

NOTES

1 From a judgement given by Mr Justice Burton in the case of Salih and Rahmani v Home Secretary (2003).

2 Now published in two volumes under the title *Your Rights and Responsibilities* by Don Rowe and Tony Thorpe, published by Evans Brothers in partnership with the Citizenship Foundation, ISBN 0-237-52310-8.

3 The Citizenship Foundation runs the Bar National Mock Trial Competition (aimed at Key Stages 4 and '5') in partnership with the Bar Council and the Magistrates Court Mock Trial Competition (aimed at Key Stage 3, notably Years 8 and 9) in partnership with the Magistrates' Association and the Department for Constitutional Affairs.

4 Mock trials used in the Citizenship Foundation's mock trial competitions and an accompanying video are now available from the Citizenship Foundation.

5 Advice Now, the Legal Action Group and the Citizenship Foundation jointly published a discussion paper, *Towards a Public Legal Education Strategy*, early in 2005. Resultantly, as this book goes to press in early 2006, the Department for Constitutional Affairs has announced the launch of the Public Legal Education and Advisory Support (PLEAS) Taskforce. Against this background, the questions raised in this chapter may have pertinence far beyond the secondary school Citizenship curriculum, notably in the fields of further and adult education and, possibly, in work-based learning.

3.3 From Media Studies for Some to Media Literacy for All: Towards a New Citizenship?

Stuart Price

Media Education and Citizenship

This chapter advocates the use of Media Education in order to develop a critical model of Citizenship, a project which is markedly different both from the agendas advanced by official agencies[1] and from the commercial imperative which lies behind the promotion of 'corporate citizenship'. The general position taken in this chapter is based on my experience as a teacher of Media Studies, beginning in London comprehensive schools (1982–89), and continuing as a lecturer in further and then subsequently in higher education.

In the course of the argument, attention is drawn to the current practices of media departments in two Leicestershire schools[2], as a way of understanding the challenges created by the growth of media studies as a distinct subject within the Humanities curriculum. This growth is considerable; Wreake Valley College, one of my examples, teaches as many as 120 students over its two-year 'A' level course together with ten groups of students (30 in each group) at GCSE, despite its status as an option (in competition therefore with other choices). Rawlins School, where media courses are also popular, has over 100 students studying media production, 200 in each of its GCSE groups, 35 in film and 40 in communication studies.

Media Education, Citizenship and Critical Analysis

In the British context, calls for the cultivation of good citizenship will always encounter obstacles, a series of practical and conceptual impediments that threaten to impose serious constraints on the development of any educational project. The causes of this difficulty are identified below, but should not obstruct the urgent need to strengthen the role of Media Education.

At present, this field of teaching and learning offers an expanding operational base within which a great variety of activities known collectively as 'media studies' take place. Practical production, 'skills' training, and introductions to new media, exist alongside older traditions which remain preoccupied with television and film. The awarding bodies that organise the field at both 'A' level and GCSE (OCR and AQA) provide guidance and resources for students. Yet within this broad domain at least one activity presents an exceptional opportunity for the exercise of an enlivened critical practice and thus the growth of 'more democratic and inclusive approaches to education'[3].

The current to which I refer emerges from various forms of *critical* textual analysis, where 'text' is understood as any 'meaningful cultural form' (Thompson, 1995) rather than written or printed material alone. Texts may therefore include advertisements, newspaper articles, websites, television programmes and so on. The traditions that contribute to the type of enquiry suggested here include social semiotics, critical linguistics, studies of rhetoric and the general term which may justifiably be used for all these approaches – critical discourse analysis[4]. Critical discourse analysis investigates the context in which media messages are produced. So, for example, studies of media texts that take the *form* of newspaper articles, will always display certain characteristics, whatever their specific content.

In the case of content itself, a very simple method can be taught to students, one which identifies the distinction between *references* which texts make to a world we know and understand, and the sometimes questionable *propositions* built on these references. It is the difference, for instance, between a statement that cannot be denied, such as 'World Trade Centre Destroyed', and the more developed and controversial concepts, like 'We Are All Americans Now', which accompany them.

Text and society

As part of a strategy for encouraging the development of active and 'empowered' citizens[5] (Huddleston, 2004), the adoption of any type of textual studies may at first seem a retrograde step. The rise of new media technologies and the increasing sophistication of student projects might suggest that the simple work of 'de-coding' texts has become superfluous. It is, however, precisely the development of complex forms of representation that increase the need for an educated awareness of structure. Structure here is not just the 'shape' of the material under study, but also its 'place' in the wider social and political environment. In fact, it could be argued that the organisation of 'advanced' societies depends upon the circulation of broad types or genres of text[6]. Text remains, therefore, the 'presiding unit of pedagogy and of academic criticism' (Brooker, 1999).

As two of my colleagues teaching in schools have argued, 'students must be able to *read* the media critically' (Warner and Carter-Bland, interview 2004[7]). This suggests a continued need for theories of *literacy*, provided these are understood within the context of the production and circulation of public meanings drawn from a range of symbolic resources (language, image, design, generic form, intertextual reference, etc.).

Such an approach has little in common with perspectives which simply advocate routine participation in public life through the 'use of the modern media' (Buckingham, 2003). The danger with the latter is conformism and passivity; students might simply be trained to recognise the broad outline of processes and institutions which they are not ultimately required to understand as *hierarchies of power*. In Buckingham's view, media literacy 'involves a form of critical thinking which is essential to informed citizenship' (2004).

The growth of a highly polemical public environment, in which a number of powerful social actors (politicians, advertisers, private companies, etc.) vie for the attention of students, provides more evidence of the need for this kind of critical awareness[8]. Yet this should not conceal a fundamental and rather prosaic reason for the universal scrutiny of textual material. It is the ready availability of electronic and printed matter which makes close study of advertisements, programmes, articles, websites, films, etc., a natural activity in an environment characterised by unlimited resources[9].

Sometimes condemned as encouraging speculation, the importance of teaching a critical method which is relevant to pupils' needs, lies in the democratic possibilities of the procedure; the production by students of 'subjective' readings is actually an essential contribution to the validity of interpretation. If texts are repositories of meaning, the full implications of which can only be understood within a cultural context, then the experience of students represents an essential part of this environment and should contribute to the authenticity of explanation. This should develop into an approach, the 'theoretical' aspects of which can find expression in practical activity. In line with this precept, media teachers at Rawlins School maintain that 'students should be encouraged to research media conventions' before producing their own work, which may then in turn be examined to investigate how far it has challenged mainstream representations. To take another example, pupils at Wreake Valley might study *Saving Private Ryan*, but would gain perspective on such material by comparing it with contemporary British documentaries[10].

A return to a critical language

In general, then, this chapter argues for a return to those more radical attitudes revealed in the once widespread use of critical terms, many of which seem to have disappeared. An obvious example would be *sexism*, which established its presence in everyday speech. Employed prominently throughout the 1980s in education, it also became one of a number of important categories for semiological analysis, contrasting favourably with the rather muted discussion we have these days of *gender roles* and *identities*. The concept of sexism was, however, soon mocked and, eventually, condemned as evidence of a fussy 'political correctness'; such an attack was designed to undermine its effectiveness as one element of a vibrant social critique. As scholars like Williamson recognise, 'we have deprived ourselves of the language' necessary to construct progressive positions from which to make attacks on social inequality and injustice. The disappearance of the category sexism has helped, in Williamson's opinion, to obscure its continued persistence as a feature of lived experience. Since 'the reality . . . is still with us', she argues, 'it is time to resuscitate the term and renew the critique' (Williamson, 'Sexism with an alibi', *The Guardian*, 31 May 2003). This observation could be extended and applied to those forms of critical enquiry that Media Education should encourage, and leads to the next part of the discussion – the relationship between language use and democracy.

Language, Citizenship and democracy

This chapter began by mentioning the existence of restrictions that limit the effective 'delivery' of Citizenship as an educational programme. It is now possible to expand on this issue; the first question relates to the mood which prevails within education itself. There is certainly, in some institutions, considerable wariness amongst teachers and students, who feel that the introduction of a new goal for study represents yet another imposition from above.

Here we encounter a significant difficulty in constructing a meaningful programme of Citizenship: the contradiction between encouraging the exercise of rights, and the source of the policy itself. In a political system which makes a show of advocating democracy, but which seems more enthusiastic about the process of *governance*, linguistic appeals to students can appear as much a *disciplinary* address[11] as an attempt to establish progressive attitudes to public life. In this case, New Labour's adherence to certain values can be found within the language chosen in official documentation, policy updates, speeches and other interventions in the public domain. My argument here is that the exercise of authority and the imposition of values which do not originate in schools themselves, is partially revealed in the way that government sources frame important announcements, guidelines and instructions. So, once again, we might recognise the practical worth of discourse analysis. In the case of government pronouncements, it is their *rhetorical* quality which is immediately apparent.

Rights and responsibilities?

One instance of this rhetorical approach is the very first item in the National Curriculum on Citizenship, which argues that pupils should learn about 'the legal and human rights and responsibilities underpinning society' (www.nc.uk.net). This places one very familiar phrase ('human rights') in a context that limits the usual range of its articulation. The clumsy combination of 'legal' and 'rights and responsibilities' is typical of what I have called the disciplinary character of New Labour utterances, yet the principle of analysis used here is based, quite simply, on recognising what should be the absolute *independence* of one particular *unit of meaning*. In other words, the term *human rights* represents a clear *reference* to an ideal which stands over and above questions of legality and responsible behaviour. As a concept, 'human rights' is meant to indicate an inviolable condition; it carries an essential resonance which the document tries to compromise. It is the awkwardness of attaching extraneous categories to a free-standing notion which should alert the analyst to authoritarian interference. The discourse analysis recommended in this chapter should therefore (if the 'project' of Citizenship Education is to be taken seriously) be applied to the very documents which produce it discursively. As Dillon argues (1995) 'language affords us the means of evaluating the world' and thus of acting successfully within it.

This brings us to the next point: in order to achieve this success, a place or location must be available which can allow the strengthening of an autonomous perspective. So far as possible, then, an *independent* field or discipline must exist, a locus of values and beliefs capable of generating the critical perspective so vital if we are sincere about building genuinely democratic attitudes. Media Education might, almost by accident, have provided the ground for an energetic challenge to what might otherwise prove a questionable consensus.

The reason for its comparative freedom of manoeuvre lies in its original exclusion from the National Curriculum. What Buckingham calls the 'dramatic increase in centralized control' (Buckingham, 2003) represented by the 1988 Education Act, certainly reduced the power of media as a mainstream pursuit, because it subsumed its study within English. At the time, many media teachers in schools agreed with Len Masterman's defence of a distinct subject and despaired at his opponents' attempt to relegate Media Studies to a subordinate status[12] as though it represented a service industry for other more academic endeavours[13]). Yet, the advantage of such an exclusion from the ranks of the respectable is, according to some current practitioners, freedom from intrusive inspection and the consequent opportunity to 'pursue other agendas' (Warner and Carter-Bland, interview 2004).

Corporate Citizenship, 'Agenda-setting' and media literacy

The restrictions placed on the development of Citizenship in general must also be seen within the context of a society in which many people are becoming increasingly disengaged from formal civic structures. Part of the cause of this disenchantment may be historical, in the sense that continued allegiance to a constitutional monarchy is bound to exert a powerful influence on public consciousness, not least because many public institutions derive their formal authority from the Crown. At first sight, this may seem to be irrelevant to a relatively fresh enterprise, one that seeks to encourage the growth of an active consciousness amongst school students and young people in general. The legacy of the past, however, needs to be addressed because, as Coleman argues, 'historically the British were subjects and that status needed little elaboration' (Axford and Huggins, 2001)[14].

In present circumstances, however, further exploration of this issue has become a matter of urgency, especially when we realise that 'traditional' rights are not only part of the fabric of ordinary existence, but seem to exercise renewed appeal when governments make authoritarian interventions in public life. Interference with the supposed independence of the judiciary or attacks on established institutions such as the House of Lords may then be represented as an affront to 'liberty' in general, reinforcing the apparent value of magisterial authority as a bastion against the growth of a doctrinaire modernity[15].

Whatever the cause of an increasingly dysfunctional citizenship, individuals have certainly become alienated from traditional political expression. In the meantime, their political and corporate masters invoke the spectre of globalisation in order to establish the need for flexibility in the labour market and for low wages.

This strategy is intimately linked to New Labour's declared belief in the importance of education. When Labour politicians evoke the term, they seem actually to mean a competence-based curriculum in which the creation of Citizenship is necessary for social cohesion. The exhortation to become 'flexible' represents a managerial edict, essentially a *directive* in the guise of an emancipatory goal; the worker or consumer may be seen as malleable, but the condition of citizenship demands instead a series of established rights which cannot be watered down or bartered away.

At the same time, the growth of 'corporate citizenship' (or, as it is sometimes termed, corporate social responsibility or CSR), in which private companies are expected to demonstrate a commitment to worthy but politically innocuous projects (planting trees, helping communities, contributing to the arts), means, above all, an increase in the use of *public relations* and an obsession with *reputation management*. Most political and commercial organisations strive to create an 'authorised' version of their social character, one which is often at variance with their day-to-day practices.

It may seem odd, within Media Education programmes, to emphasise the study of the social practices of powerful groups besides the media themselves; yet those teachers and academics familiar with the development of 'media-centric' theories may realise how important it is to resolve this issue. Most critical standpoints within Media Studies at least begin with the assumption that the study of media forms and texts requires a certain vigilance. This is sometimes because media organisations are thought to represent the 'cultural' wing of political authority, or because they supposedly fail to present a reliable account of lived experience.

Such critiques are limited in scope, in that they over-emphasise the subservience of media institutions, presenting them as tools of repression or as a distortion of 'objective' reality. The strength of CDA[16] as an analytical tool (and therefore as an essential component of 'media literacy') lies first in its commitment to long-established principles of rational enquiry. The central hypothesis it follows is that all texts are composed of cultural references that can be noted and analysed. The next issue, therefore, concerns the use of *literacy* as a practice that refers to, but does not equate with, the ability to read and write.

As Friere shows in the case of parallel examples like 'political literacy', the noun itself 'appears metaphorically' (Freire, 1985) and is employed in many contexts to indicate a 'specialised' form of interpretation (Lankshear and Knobel, 2003). The suggestion here is that a certain method is required, or at least an insight into rules and practices which animate particular disciplines. The metaphorical use of the term 'literacy' betrays therefore a certain polemical quality (Buckingham, 2003), one which can imply either an attempt to bolster the status of a particular subject (particularly so with regard to

Media Studies) or which indicates a demand for a critical or sceptical approach to media output in general.

The latter is often linked to the idea that the media are responsible for offering some consistent ideological perspective, and that there is therefore an urgent requirement to train students in techniques which enable them to avoid the pitfalls of indoctrination (Lankshear and Knobel, 2003). 'Agenda-setting' in its established sense, therefore, is the notion that the media, as an instrumental force, decide which issues are worthy of public attention, or which should achieve special prominence. This position is held throughout the subject and is strongly represented in various dictionaries and textbooks.

'Agenda-setting' and Media Studies

So, for example, the correlation of public agendas and media content was asserted by McCombs and Shaw in 1972 (in Lenart, 1994; and Manning, 2001), and again by Watson and Hill, who argued that the media 'set the order of importance of current issues' (Watson and Hill, 1989). Gill and Adams also mention 'the ways in which the media decide which information and which issues are most important for the public' (Gill and Adams, 1992), while O'Sullivan and his co-authors describe agenda-setting as the process through which the media 'wittingly or unwittingly structure public debate and awareness' (O'Sullivan, 1994).

If, however, we are compelled to move away from this model it must be to gain a sharper critical insight, not to collapse the entire position into simple ideas of audience flexibility or resilience. A departure from the traditional template of 'agenda-setting' need not result in scrapping the entire concept, but might suggest looking a little further afield for evidence of competing centres of power and influence. When students are, for instance, required to 'appreciate the important role and responsibility of the media in presenting information to the public' (from National Curriculum in Action[17]), then it is vital that they should understand the larger political context in which this takes place.

It seems that the growth of an industrialised social order in which new 'mechanisms of social cohesion' must be sought in mass media forms (Robins and Webster, 1999) has led to the assumption that mediated communication *itself* has become a dominant cultural force, a perception which provides in turn a rationale for theories of both domination and resistance (Hall, 1980). This chapter has been more concerned to emphasise the ways in which a number of other 'issue proponents' (Dearing and Rogers, 1996) present content to its audiences. This moves away from a 'media-centric' position to one which recognises the activities of other centres of authority, and identifies in particular the growing collusion, institutional and linguistic, between political and commercial powers. Unless brought into the equation, such tendencies will negate Key Stage 4's emphasis on the importance of students playing an active part in democratic and electoral processes. Part of the problem may lie in the loose way in which 'democracy' is used, to refer both to democracy as a system of government (a social institution based on the formal mechanics of representation), and also to an ideal embodied within the concept, a governing principle which can be applied to every aspect of public conduct; in other words, a principle of fair representation in all walks of life. This ideal cannot be expunged from the everyday use of 'democracy' in its contemporary bureaucratic form but, once again, the assimilation of terms into larger concepts should be the starting point for analysis.

This chapter argues that the importance of *media* texts lies not in their ability to reinforce the hierarchical divisions of a social system through hegemonic address (Tuchman, 1974; Hall, 1980; Bennett et al., 1986), nor in their supposed role as a disguise for the real conditions of power, but with regard to two related functions. The first, indicated above, is their regular and thus expected appearance within a wider institutional and discursive framework. The second is the *transformative* capacity they represent: the way the media generate new forms of meaning based upon established sources[18]. In this sense, the production of media texts based upon critical depictions of social life, may ensure continuity between classroom analysis and practical exploration of media genres.

Media Studies and the defence of democratic rights

Contemporary Media Studies, exactly because it has so often been attacked as inconsequential or frivolous (and thus sometimes excluded from the realm of respectable academic enquiry), owes nothing to those elements within the educational establishment which still think it useful only for practical instruction or a muted form of civic education[19]. It has the opportunity therefore to build on quite radical foundations, concerning itself not so much with a body of knowledge but with a conceptual field[20]. Furthermore, Media Studies has now at its disposal a variety of analytical techniques which go beyond the semiological conventions once used to interrogate the imagery produced in film and advertising, new approaches which are also more sophisticated than those which concentrated on the ideological bias supposedly characteristic of news messages. Discourse analysis, in particular, has provided new directions for a reconfigured study of media, one which examines the production of meaning in relation to the terms, references, propositions and themes which are circulated in public debate. In one sense, this means returning to a larger sense of public communication and a study of the public sphere and its 'electronic' equivalent, and refusing to be drawn into the uncritical replication of professional practices, which sometimes represents little more than the production of the 'flexible' labour mentioned above.

The opening paragraphs of this chapter drew attention to the problems inherent in making appeals for the reconstruction of Citizenship and must ultimately recognise that we inhabit an era in which the 'space' available for such endeavours has been dominated by neo-liberal conceptions of public conduct. The reappearance of neo-liberal principles, with their emphasis on the 'responsibility' of citizens who are at the same time asked to be 'flexible' workers and 'discerning' consumers, finds its origin in the transnational character of capital and the increasing instability of 'free' markets and the type of employment they are able to provide. This explains the salience of, on the one hand, those forms of 'directive' address (the production of persuasive messages) which characterise political interventions in a period of declining civic engagement, and on the other rather idealised references to forms of 'global' citizenship, dependent on the supposed benevolence of corporate power and drawing heavily upon a rhetorical appeal to responsible behaviour. It is this change of emphasis that threatens to obscure the urgent need to maintain and defend democratic rights in their unadulterated form.

REFERENCES

Atkinson, M. (1984) *Our Masters' Voices*. London: Methuen.

Axford, B. and Huggins, R. (2001) *New Media and Politics*. Thousand Oaks, London, Delhi: Sage.

Barker, M. (1989) *Comics*. Manchester: Manchester University Press.

Bennett, A., Mercer, P. and Woollacott, J. (1986) *Popular Culture and Social Relations*. Milton Keynes: Open University Press.

Brooker, P. (1999) *A Concise Glossary of Cultural Theory* London and New York: Arnold.

Buckingham, D. (2003) *Media Education*. London: Polity Press.

Buckingham, D. (2004) 'Survival skills', article in *The Guardian,* 27 July.

Dearing, J.W. and Rogers, E.M. (1996) *Agenda-Setting*. Thousand Oaks, London, New Delhi: Sage.

Dillon, M.C. (1995) *Semiological Reductionism*. New York: State University of New York Press.

Fairclough, N. (1995a) *Critical Discourse Analaysis*. London and New York: Longman.

Fairclough, N. (1995b) *Media Discourse*. London and New York: Arnold.

Freire, P. (1985) *The Politics of Education*. New York, Westport, London: Bergin & Garvey.

Gill, D. and Adams, B. (1992) *ABC of Communications Studies*. Cheltenham: Nelson Thornes.

Hall, S. (ed.) (1980) *Culture, Media, Language: Working Papers in Cultural Studies, 1972–1979*. London: Hutchinson/Centre for Cultural Studies.

Heater, D. (1999) *What is Citizenship?* Cambridge: Polity Press.

Hodge, R. and Kress, G. (1988) *Social Semiotics*. Cambridge: Polity Press.

Huddleston, T. (2004) *Citizenship and Society*. London: Citizenship Foundation.

Kress, G. and van Leeuwen, T. (2001) *Multimodal Discourse*. London and New York: Arnold.

Lankshear, C. and Knobel, M. (2003) *New Literacies*. Milton Keynes: Open University Press.

Lenart, S. (1994) *Shaping Political Attitudes*. Thousand Oaks, London, New Delhi: Sage.

Manning, P. (2001) *News and News Sources*. London: Sage.

Mattelart, A. (1991) *Advertising International*. London and New York: Routledge.

O'Sullivan, T., Hartley, J., Saunders, D., Montgomery, M. and Fiske, J. (1994) *Key Concepts in Communication and Cultural Studies*. London: Routledge.

Price, S. (2003) 'Competing Discourses on the Web? Diversity, Anarchy and Corporate Address', in *Diversity or Anarchy?* Luton: University of Luton Press.

Robins, K. and Webster, F. (1999) *Times of the Technoculture*. London: Routledge.

Thompson, J.B. (1995) *The Media and Modernity*. Cambridge: Polity Press.

Tuchman, G. (1974) *The TV Establishment: Programming for Power and Profit*. Englewood Cliffs, New Jersey: Prentice Hall.

Watson, J. and Hill, A. (1989) *A Dictionary of Communication and Media Studies*. London: Arnold.

Williamson, J. (2003) 'Sexism with an alibi', article in *The Guardian*, 31 May.

NOTES

1. Some progressive views have been expressed, however, by Government ministers: Tessa Jowell noted that 'decoding our media will be as important to our lives as citizens as understanding great literature is to our cultural lives' (cited in Buckingham's 2004 *Guardian* article, 'Survival skills').
2. My thanks to Victoria Carter-Bland and Mark Warner of Rawlins School, Leicester and to Darren Lisserman of Wreake Valley College, Syston, Leicestershire.
3. From Leicester University's Centre for Citizenship Studies in Education (www.le.ac.uk/education/centres/citizenship, 19 February 2003).
4. For various models of critical analysis, see Atkinson (1984), Fairclough (1995a and 1995b), Hodge and Kress (1988) and Kress and van Leeuwen (2001).
5. Note here Ted Huddleston's work at the Citizenship Foundation (2004).
6. A view of communication not just as the sending of messages, but 'as a system of thought and power and as a mode of government' (Mattelart, 1991: x).
7. Teachers at Rawlins School, Leicester; interview, 30 April 2004. Victoria Carter-Bland is Head of Media and Mark Warner is Advanced Skills Teacher in Media.
8. This is addressed in more detail further in the chapter.
9. The prevalence of texts within lessons, seminars and lectures also attests to the continuing existence of a tradition of enquiry inherited in part from literary criticism.
10. Interview with Darren Lisserman, teacher of Media Studies at Wreake Valley College, Leicester (July 2004).
11. Address here is understood as 'the construction of a message which attempts to animate some aspect of a recipient's subjectivity' (Price, 2003: 286).
12. I worked during this period as a teacher of English and Media Studies in a series of comprehensive schools (one in the London Borough of Merton and two within the eventually defunct Inner London Education Authority).
13. Media students could at least be relied upon to record the school play; Buckingham recognises this tendency to regard those taking the subject as 'academic underachievers' (Buckingham, 2003: 88).
14. This statement may need to be treated with a little caution, since the growth of industrial cities and the reform of local government in the nineteenth century gave rise to a 'vigorous municipal citizenship' (Heater, 1999: 133).
15. In which for example individual subjects have recourse to 'law and justice with mercy' (website of the British Monarchy, www.royal.gov.uk).
16. The usual 'shorthand' for Critical Discourse Analysis.
17. See www.ncaction.org.uk/subjects/citizen/progress
18. The concept of transformation appears in Barker (1989: 127) as the way in which structures (textual forms) mould individual items of content, and consequently generate particular meanings.
19. Formal structures, such as the National Curriculum, for example.
20. What Buckingham calls 'conceptual understandings' (Buckingham, 2003: 53).

FURTHER READING

Buckingham, D. (2003) *Media Education*. London: Polity Press.
Price, S. (1998) (2nd edn) *Media Studies*. London: Longman.

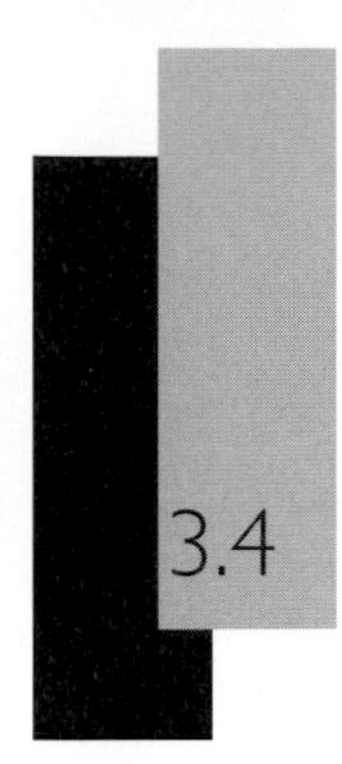

Citizenship and Financial Literacy: The Role of Personal Finance Education

Professor Linda Thomas

Financial literacy in a complex world

The citizens of tomorrow will have to deal with financial circumstances that are very different from those faced by their parents and grandparents (FSA, 2003). If current trends continue, responsibilities and risks that are at present borne by the Government and employers are likely to be transferred to individuals. In future, citizens will need to plan for retirement incomes, protect against the risk of losing homes and jobs and fund social and long-term care. To meet these core welfare needs they will need to use capital markets and buy financial services products rather than relying on the state or their employer.

These markets are highly complex. Making a choice between the huge variety of products on offer in any one field (for example, pension schemes or life assurance policies) is often very difficult for individuals, according to widespread personal anecdote and to recent American research (Iyengar et al., 2003). Furthermore, some providers behave in an unprincipled manner, for example by pushing credit to vulnerable individuals (Mayo and Mullen, 2003). This does little to restore consumer confidence in markets and activities that are seen as volatile and prey to financial scandals. In this context the role of Personal Finance Education (PFE) within the Citizenship curriculum is a crucial one. It should help young people to put money in its place early on, to acquire a critical understanding of present trends and to gain sufficient competence and confidence to engage with and have some control over financial markets that will otherwise dictate their lives. Within Citizenship, PFE is not only about understanding *better* but also about understanding *differently*. It is therefore both an opportunity and a challenge for schools and teachers.

How are schools responding to the opportunity presented by National Curriculum Citizenship?

The decision to confer statutory designation on Citizenship at Key Stages 3 and 4 in the National Curriculum is affecting schools' curricular choice in terms of the provision of PFE. This is shown by the results of a survey of secondary schools conducted as one element of an evaluation of PFEG's[1] *Excellence and Access* project[2] (Thomas, 2004). Some 150 schools were asked to select the curriculum strategy used to provide PFE. Table 1 in Figure 1 shows that in those schools where personal finance was taught before the introduction of Citizenship, it was likely to be taught either as an identified issue within a small range of subjects or integrated within the same range of subjects.

Table 2 in Figure 1 shows that once they became aware of the Citizenship requirement, the same schools reported moves towards whole school and specific-issue approaches that, in most cases, were direct reflections of their decisions with regard to the place of Citizenship within the curriculum.

Figure 1

Personal Finance Education (PFE) before and after the introduction of National Curriculum Citizenship

Table 1: Pre-Citizenship Curricular Organisation in Project Schools

Curricular organisation	%
Whole school approach	2
Specific issue within Mathematics, Business Studies and Personal/Social/Life Skills	28
Integrated within Mathematics, Business Studies and Personal/Social/Life Skills	32
Other	8
Not taught	30

Table 2: Post-Citizenship Curricular Organisation in Project Schools

Curricular organisation	%
Whole school approach through Citizenship	23
Specific issue within PSHE/Citizenship	62
Specific issue within Performing Arts and Mathematics	6
Integrated within Personal/Social/Life Skills and ICT	9

Source: *Excellence and Access Project Evaluation* (Thomas, 2004)

In the past, despite protestations about its importance from headteachers and teachers, PFE has had to compete for teachers' time and resources with a range of other pressures stemming from a very strong national agenda and the emphasis on accountability and league tables. The introduction of Citizenship as a statutory element in the National Curriculum now seems to be sufficiently attractive to persuade schools and teachers to respond positively to the opportunities for personal finance education contained therein.

What kinds of problems are encountered as schools respond to these opportunities?

The experience of PFEG's *Excellence and Access* project suggests that schools face particular problems as they respond to the challenge of providing PFE within Citizenship.

Young people's knowledge base

1,660 pupils from 20 secondary schools selected through stratified random sampling completed a questionnaire assessing their levels of confidence on a range of financial knowledge (Thomas, 2004). Questions were of the form 'How much do you know about the taxes people pay?' Pupils were asked to respond by means of the following scale.

A Lot 5 4 3 2 1 *Nothing At All*

A substantial percentage of pupils claimed not to know much (scores of 1 or 2) about financial matters. 60–80 per cent claimed ignorance on four items (taxes, company finance, loans/overdrafts/mortgages and interest rates), 40–60 per cent on another four items (exchange rates, current/savings accounts, bank statements and wages/pensions) and 33 per cent on one item (cheques and credit and debit cards). The percentages for those students claiming confidence in their knowledge of the formal vocabulary of financial capability (scoring 4 or 5) were correspondingly low (see Figure 2).

Figure 2
Student confidence in financial matters

Student items	% of students claiming confidence in their knowledge of financial terms (scoring 4 or 5)
Cheques	29
Current/savings account	29
Bank statements	29
Wages	27
Exchange rates	26
Taxation	26
Interest rates	16
Overdrafts etc.	18
Roles of financial institutions	12

Source: *Excellence and Access Project Evaluation* (Thomas, 2004)

On the other hand when pupils were asked to talk about their practical knowledge of personal finance, and to share their financial experiences, they were vocal and animated. They avoided the use of formal vocabulary and invariably responded by referring to their involvement in the day-by-day financial activities and discussions of family and friends and to television adverts and programmes (Figure 3 provides transcripts of interviews with different groups of pupils).

Figure 3
Personal finance: what the pupils say

Interviewer	If you're thinking of the job you want to do one day, are you thinking 'I want to do that because it pays well' or is it more because you enjoy doing it or what else?
Pupil 1	Because I enjoy doing it.
Pupil 2	I'd rather do a job I enjoy doing.
Pupil 3	My Dad doesn't like his job very much but he has to stay with it.
Pupil 1	It can be really bad if you're stuck with a job you don't want to do.
. . .	
Interviewer	When you go abroad and you need to exchange foreign currency, how do you feel about that, do you think that's pretty easy or is it complicated?
Pupil i	My Dad gets a little card with the exchange rate on it and then he gives it to Thomas Cook and he hands them so much money and says 'I want that in euros' and they just give it to us, it's easy.
Pupil ii	Is it all in the euro?
Pupil i	Not all of it, not if you travel outside of Europe.
Pupil iii	It's made it much easier with the euro.
Pupil ii	I reckon if we went to euros it would probably be more simple.
. . .	
Interviewer	How did you learn all these things?
Pupil a	The news.
Pupil b	Your parents, they usually have to work them out.
Pupil c	They're always going on about bills, VAT and that.
Pupil d	My Mum's always nagging my Dad to do the accounts, the taxes.
. . .	
Interviewer	Are there different kinds of mortgages or are they all the same, more or less?
Pupil	I saw on the telly the other day that if you share a house and one person dies and the other person keeps the house. I think there are different types.

Source: *Excellence and Access Project Evaluation* (Thomas, 2004)

Pupils were heavily influenced by these encounters with financial activities and discussions. They learned from them and they became the basis of very secure knowledge, values and belief systems (as Figure 4 illustrates).

Figure 4
Pupil perspectives on taxes, debt and mortgages

Pupils were asked about taxes:

Pupil 1	If you are on income support or family tax credit or something like that, you don't have to pay them and they fund things like the government and the hospitals.
Pupil 2	I just know that you have to pay them. I think it's a bit tight really. Like you've earned the money and then they just take it off you again.
Interviewer	What about paying for hospitals and things that we all need?
Pupil 2	They don't pay for things like for us, they do pay for hospitals.
Interviewer	And schools? What more could benefit us than schools?
Pupil 2	They benefit us in some ways like; there's other ways that they don't benefit us. They waste it, they get some people off the streets. You won't stop that though, it's people's decision if they want to become homeless, most of the time anyway, so it's just a bit stupid. But I think what they should do, my idea, they should have like a little card and you tick everything that's relevant to you and they could check up. Like if you have children then you should pay for their stuff but you shouldn't have to pay for stuff like homeless people and stuff like that because that just isn't your problem. It's good to help but . . .
Pupil 1	I think it should be your choice if you want to help but you're not given the choice.
Pupil 2	Yes, which isn't very fair.

Pupils were asked what they thought about when they heard the word debt:

Pupil i	You've spent more than you've got.
Pupil ii	You're owing the bank.
Pupil iii	Some people if they gamble they get into really big debt and then they have to try and pay it off and they can't.
Pupil ii	And then they go to a gambling thing and try and win money and they use more money and get a bigger debt.

Another group of pupils were asked what mortgages were for:

Pupil a	You can only use a mortgage for a house I would say.
Pupil b	Because we're trying to buy a house.
Pupil c	To buy a house and important things.
Pupil b	Yes, a house is really important, especially if you've got a family or something like that and you've got to look after them.
Interviewer	So would you consider renting?
Pupil b	Well yes.
Pupil c	You could rent.
Pupil b	If you rent and then decide to move then you don't get any of the money back that you've paid on it.

Pupil a	But if you rent and you've lived there for ages, then you're paying more than it's worth, you could have bought it originally.
Pupil c	And with the rent the owner they can, they have more control over you. They can tell you if they want you to move out and things like that.

Source: *Excellence and Access Project Evaluation* (Thomas, 2004)

What the *Excellence and Access* project clearly shows is that pupils lack confidence in their knowledge of financial matters. Their financial experiences outside school are also very powerful and the folklore that develops is bolstered by the activities and discussions of family and friends. These are problems that must be solved if pupils are to develop a deeper understanding of the nature of the financial system and its impact on individuals. Pupil knowledge needs to be consolidated beyond the personal anecdote; it needs securing through some form of formal curriculum provision.

Teachers' confidence

Seventy-two teachers from a sample of *Excellence and Access* project schools completed questionnaire items assessing their level of confidence in their personal finance knowledge, skills and understanding.

Two thirds felt confident in their ability to support the development of pupils' knowledge and skills in the areas of personal budgeting/expenditure and methods of payment. At least one third felt confident in their ability to support work on exchange rates, financial institutions and global financial impact. Less than a third felt confident in the area of taxation (as noted in Figure 5).

Figure 5
Personal finance: how teachers feel

Teachers were asked to use the following scale to rate their confidence and skills in supporting personal finance education in a range of contexts. The results are presented as percentages.

Low 1 2 3 4 5 High

Question	1 & 2	3	4 & 5
Management of personal expenditure, short and long run	8	25	67
Different methods of payment e.g. cheques, credit cards	8	28	64
Fluctuating exchange rates	34	32	34
Local and national taxation	40	30	30
Roles of financial institutions	38	26	36
Impact on individual of local, national, global finance	31	30	39

Source: *Excellence and Access Project Evaluation* (Thomas, 2004)

There is a danger that teachers' lack of confidence and experience in the area of personal finance education will encourage them to adopt a content-based approach to the design of learning experiences where the first words to appear are about content. 'Let's do something on debt', 'Let's do something on banking' or 'Let's do something on credit cards'. In these circumstances it would be very difficult for teachers to set sufficiently challenging work for pupils, to maintain good classroom practice and to promote pupil learning through engagement.

Is it possible to solve these problems?

The formal evaluation of PFEG's *Excellence and Access* project shows that it is an effective starting-point for those schools wishing to provide PFE within Citizenship.

Providing varied learning experiences for pupils

The project shows that it is possible to improve pupils' financial awareness. It does not impose a uniform set of activities on pupils. It does not tell them the information they require or give the right answers. Instead, it encourages pupils to *engage* with the different experiences and perspectives of other pupils, teachers and representatives of financial institutions. By doing so pupils learn to challenge what are sometimes unhelpful and restrictive conditioning and folklore. And through engaging with the experiences and perspectives of others they are undertaking the very stuff of good *Citizenship* Education itself.

Sometimes putting matters into a local or personal context helps to get pupils excited (see the first case study account in Figure 6). In the second case study account, the teacher's use of her own practical experience is highly effective.

Figure 6

PFE as engagement with the experiences and perspectives of others

CASE STUDY A

Because we were using IT we were able to use the internet to look at the City Council's website to look at how they spend their income and how they generate their income. The class looked at huge amounts of money that they've never really perceived existed before. They'd only been dealing with something like the £3 that we'd asked them to pay for the trip and then we were looking at £22m projects, or the £35m being spent on a Leisure complex, just getting to grips with the enormity of that. And we looked at election promises, because we had an election coming up two weeks into the project and we looked at what the Labour Party was going to promise. They'll put more policemen on the street, well, how much was that going to cost? What part of the budget would that be? And then we had the election and they are looking at whether those promises, those pledges in terms of financial promises are now being implemented.

CASE STUDY B

They go on about gearboxes exploding because I was driving to work one day last November and my gearbox exploded and I've got a 4 by 4 so it's like two gearboxes. I had to have a hire car for two weeks which cost £400 and the cost of the gearbox is £1600 so that's nearly two grand. I put it on the credit card because it was an emergency but I didn't have that sort of money just floating around doing nothing and you pay more interest on a credit card so it costs you more for that money. So what I did at Christmas was to go out and get a bank loan and paid the credit card off with the bank loan because that was a lower interest rate and then just recently I re-mortgaged which is even lower and I paid the bank loan off. If you are able to use practical examples, they loved the one about the gearboxes, none of them have forgotten that.

Source: *Excellence and Access Project Evaluation* (Thomas, 2004)

Developing teacher confidence

Excellence and Access project teachers are overwhelmingly positive about the project's potential and their role within it, with 86 per cent expecting it to improve the teaching and learning of personal finance and 93 per cent expecting it to play an important part in increasing pupils' skills. They report their own developing confidence and financial awareness, their appreciation of project materials and their ability to use them interchangeably (as evidenced in Figure 7).

Figure 7
Building teacher confidence in PFE through Excellence and Access

'As a teacher you are becoming more financially aware and you're transmitting that. It's empowering.'

'There was a very nice wall chart showing the euro and the different countries that have accepted the euro and I use that now in my language lessons, so that was good.'

'I did have a sort of project similar to this in the spring term of Year 11 that was just worksheets and boring rubbish like that. It just came from textbooks and this has been a development of that work that has been very positive because it means that now I've got something that is a lot better so it's been positive in that respect.'

Source: *Excellence and Access Project Evaluation* (Thomas, 2004)

Personal Finance Education for all

The *Excellence and Access* project is also helping schools to provide finance education for all pupils by introducing inclusive and culturally diverse programmes.

One teacher described it as an eye-opener when pupils in a special school made unexpectedly big improvements. She was realistic about the possibilities of engaging her pupils in PFE. She acknowledged that they were unlikely to be financially independent of their families or to be able to get a loan or buy a car. Nevertheless she wanted to provide them with enriching experiences of using money for shopping and of budgeting their pocket money.

Other teachers also feel that the work is very successful, they enjoy it, it works well with pupils and staff, they want to repeat it in future years and they believe they are moving on (see the two case study accounts in Figure 8).

Figure 8

Diversity, inclusion and Personal Finance Education

CASE STUDY C

We have a large ethnic minority group of pupils who are Muslims and they have issues with finance in terms of mortgages, which they're not allowed in their traditional form, so that throws up other issues such as the fact that a lot of our pupils live in extended families in a house and again that's got its own finance issues. So we have had to concentrate on those things in putting the programme together. Our adviser has mentioned and I know the woman at the Building Society that is setting up packages for Muslim mortgages and they seem to know quite a lot about it. It would be nice to get someone in from there to help with that.

CASE STUDY D

We have within the school (a behaviour referral unit) a programme for youngsters who are in mainstream schools who are in danger of being excluded and we take them for a short period of time . . . we monitor, observe and advise the student and the school. The idea is that the student goes back to school and re-engages. They are the only youngsters in the school who have had any input and its purpose was to trial out the resources . . . I'm quite comfortable with the resources we've got . . . and I think it will broaden their horizons; they will certainly have a better understanding on how to manage money. I think they'll also have a better understanding and knowledge of the taxation system and why you pay tax . . . we're now trying to build in the ethical aspects like fair trade and globalisation.

Source: *Excellence and Access Project Evaluation* (Thomas, 2004)

PFE through Citizenship: the lessons from *Excellence and Access*

Citizenship implies a commitment to social ideals and the fostering of a sense of communal responsibility that transcends individual self-interest. In this context PFE can make a contribution by increasing young people's understanding of the nuts and bolts of social existence, tempering what could be naive, uninformed, sometimes over-idealistic views with some hard-nosed appreciation of the economic constraints within which all societies operate. But its purpose must be to ensure that young people have sufficient confidence and competence to make their own judgements about matters that are at the very heart of the concept of Citizenship – the relationship between individual rights and social responsibility, freedom and licence, equity and exploitation.

This is a challenging agenda for pupils, teachers and schools but PFEG's *Excellence and Access* project has demonstrated that considerable progress can be made. It offers the following advice to those schools and teachers wishing to explore the provision of PFE within Citizenship:

- In designing learning experiences for pupils, it is important to focus on what young people recognise as the kind of relevant, realistic and practical problem-solving situations that they already encounter outside school. In these situations formal content matter acquires meaning.
- The provision of support in the form of materials and collaborative networks is more effective if teachers recognise and use the design and teaching of Personal Finance Education programmes as an opportunity to learn and extend their own knowledge and confidence.

REFERENCES

FSA (2003) *Towards a national strategy for financial capability.* London: Financial Services Authority.

Iyengar, S.S., Jiang, W. and Huberman, G. (2003) *How much choice is too much? Pension Research Council Working Paper 2003–10*. University of Pennsylvania, USA. Available at http://prc.wharton.upenn.edu/prc/prc.html

Mayo, E. and Mullen, I. (2003) 'Plastic fantastic? Take Two'. Article in *The Guardian*, 20 December, London, UK.

Thomas, L. (2004) *Excellence and Access Project Evaluation*. London: PFEG.

NOTES

1 PFEG is an education charity whose mission is for all young people to leave school with the confidence, skills and knowledge they need in financial matters so that they can participate fully in society. For more information visit the PFEG website at http://www.pfeg.org

2 The four-year *Excellence and Access* project was launched in 2001 to increase teacher skills and confidence in providing personal finance education. For resources and case studies visit the PFEG website at http://www.pfeg.org

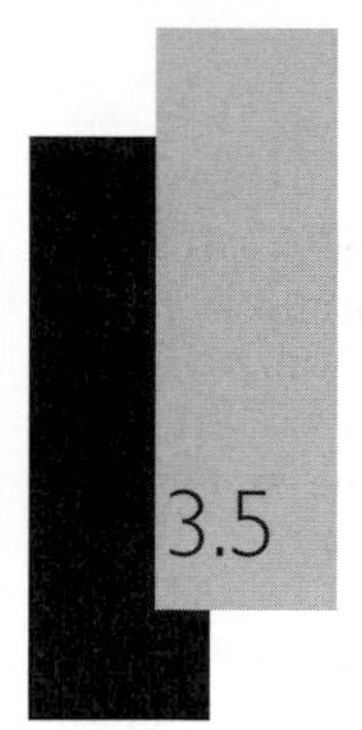

3.5 From Political Education to Political Literacy: Equipping Young People for Life in a More Genuine Democracy

Ted Huddleston

The emergence of 'political literacy'

The emergence of the term 'political literacy' in the early 1970s signified a new departure in the teaching of politics in English schools. Until then, very little explicit work in political education had been undertaken in schools in the UK. Any political education that did take place was, largely, either aimed at elite students and based around the acquisition of information useful in preparation for high-status professions, or seen as a means of inculcating in the children of the working classes the virtues of patriotism, humility, service and political deference (Batho, 1990).

In contrast, the term 'political literacy' suggested a way of teaching politics that was neither instrumental nor class-based. That is to say, that existed primarily for reasons other than the realisation of a preconceived political objective, and to which all young citizens were entitled, regardless of their background or career prospects. It represented a form of teaching and learning that had as its ultimate goal the creation of a new generation of citizens, critically aware, potentially active, and equipped to play their part in a society that was more genuinely democratic (Davies et al., 1999).

For a while, during the 1980s and 1990s, ideas of political literacy were sidelined in favour of, among other things, single issue-based forms of education, such as environmental education, peace education, and development education (Davies et al., 1999). It was not until the report of the Crick committee in 1998 that political literacy began to take on serious educational significance as a curriculum area in its own right. The Crick report described political literacy as one of three essential 'strands' of Citizenship Education – along with 'social and moral responsibility' and 'community-based learning' – and as an integral element in the creation of a 'citizen democracy' (QCA, 1998).

Disconcertingly, when Citizenship became a National Curriculum subject in 2002, no mention was made of political literacy as such. The term does not occur in the statutory Order for Citizenship. Nor does it occur in the guidance documents that accompany it. Political literacy is *implied* in the sorts of knowledge, understanding and skills specified for teaching and in the exemplar schemes of work, but precisely what it is intended to consist of – above and beyond the rather loose collection of generalised learning outcomes set out in official documents – is not made clear.

So what actually does political literacy mean in this context? What are its aims? What is its content? How is it learned, and what does this imply for practice in schools?

Let us begin with the basics. Any idea of political literacy depends, in the first instance, upon what we mean by 'politics'. Now, politics can be defined in many different ways. In its most general sense, it is:

> *. . . the process by which a group of people with different opinions or interests reaches collective decisions about the way their life together should be organised.*

It is a process that involves persuasion and negotiation, and some kind of mechanism for reaching a final decision, such as voting. It also involves power and authority, and an element of coercion – if only to ensure that collective decisions are made binding on the group as a whole. On this definition, any social institution – the church, the football club, even the family – has its own 'politics'.

When it comes to National Curriculum Citizenship, however, we are not so much concerned with politics in this general sense, as with politics as it relates to the *citizens* of a state, i.e., with what it is to be a citizen of a state, and the rights and responsibilities of citizens of a state to each other and to citizens of other states.

More particularly, we are concerned with what it is be a citizen of a *democratic* state. Different types of political system require a different type of citizen. The rights and responsibilities of individuals living as free and equal citizens in a democratic society differ significantly from those of citizens living, say, under a totalitarian regime.

Citizenship in a democratic society

Given that the sort of political literacy with which we are concerned here has, as its primary focus, the actions of citizens of a democracy, the question arises: what distinguishes the actions of citizens of a democracy from those of citizens living under other types of political system? In other words, what are the distinctive features of political participation in a democratic society?

Democracy is a complex concept. At its heart lies the notion of political equality, and political equality is capable of practical expression in a range of different ways. Democracy is not just about majority rule: resolving disagreements over public policy by putting them to a vote – one person, one vote – in which the greatest number prevails. It is also about public deliberation. It involves dialogue and debate – not simply between parliamentary representatives in Westminster, but between ordinary citizens wherever they might be. Moreover, although voting and public deliberation are important forms of democratic participation, they are not the only ones. Individual or group citizen action – locally, national or internationally – can be a form of democratic participation in its own right.

The basic elements of political literacy

So what are the different types of skill, knowledge and understanding that citizens need in order to be able to participate fully in the political life of this sort of society?

At least three sorts of competency seem to be required:

- *Factual knowledge* about the institutions and processes of government and how they work – locally, nationally and internationally
- *Practical skills* of research, analysis, communication and action
- *Conceptual understanding* of political ideas and arguments and how they relate to current issues and debates.

How do these different sorts of competency relate to each other? To begin with, it helps to see them as essentially inter-related rather than as completely distinct. Without the capacity for action, political knowledge is merely a collection of inert facts. Ideas and arguments are ineffectual unless they are grounded in knowledge of actual political situations. Political action uninformed by ideas and arguments is mindless activism.

Broad and balanced provision

This suggests that not only should all three of these areas of learning receive adequate coverage in school, but also that political literacy teaching should not be restricted to one type of learning process. In fact, given the different sorts of learning implied, no form of provision is likely to be effective that does not make use of the whole range of learning opportunities available in a secondary school, from formal classroom work to special events, visits, student councils and community involvement – down to the structures and relationships that characterise the school's ethos.

It also suggests that, where possible, teaching aimed at the different areas of learning should overlap in practice. This is not to say that a particular area of learning should not have greater priority on occasions, however. Certain contexts are more conducive to particular kinds of learning than others. It is likely, for example, that the classroom makes the most effective venue for conceptual learning, and community-based projects for practical skills learning.

Schools do not have a surfeit of time for Citizenship Education, let alone for political literacy. The important thing, therefore, is to try to achieve broad and balanced provision in whatever time is available. This sort of 'mixed economy' is *not* always being achieved at the moment, however, as is evident in the emergence of *two contrasting tendencies* in current practice. Each derives from an overly narrow conception of what political literacy teaching involves.

The 'civics' approach

The 'civics' approach places factual knowledge – about local and central government, the European Union and so on – and the transmission of factual knowledge from teacher to student firmly at the centre of political literacy teaching. It tends to conceive political literacy as an academic, classroom activity, and operates on a theoretical, 'textbook' model of how political institutions and processes work.

This sort of approach harks back to traditional forms of teaching. It leaves little room for students to reflect upon or develop their own political beliefs and values; to cultivate the skills and virtues of democratic debate; or to learn about the sorts of practical strategy that make for effective action in the political world as it actually exists. Quite the opposite, in fact: on account of being grounded in the political *status quo*, it tends to discourage rather than encourage critical argument and debate, or any form of active political involvement beyond, perhaps, voting in elections.

The 'experiential' approach

In contrast, the focus of interest of the 'experiential' approach lies not within the classroom, but within the larger community – in and beyond the school. It emphasises politics as practice and learning through active participation in *real* political processes. It proceeds from the belief that students need to experience politics directly, not just be taught about it, and owes much to the 'youth-led' model of social action common in informal education. A central feature of this approach is the progressive involvement of the young people in taking personal responsibility for their activities, for their learning, for themselves and for each other.

While there is much to be said for learning from actual involvement and for students taking more responsibility – as well as for the high levels of student motivation that can be stimulated through personal involvement – this sort of approach has a number of limitations.

First, there are practical and ethical restrictions on the sorts of real political experience that schools can provide for students. At a practical level, what is provided is left to the mercy of arbitrary events and what students happen to be interested in at the time. This makes planning for a broad and balanced curriculum difficult, if not nigh on impossible. At an ethical level, schools simply cannot provide students with direct personal experience of involvement in forms of political action like civil disobedience or 'playing the race card' – even though a grasp of the issues surrounding forms of action like these could be thought of as an important element in political education. Second, there is a danger of unwitting bias creeping into the teaching process through the predominance of 'populist' causes likely to be adopted by students. There is little opportunity for students to grasp, or even take seriously, less popular or minority causes and forms of opinion. Third, there is more to political literacy than being an effective campaigner. Democratic politics is as much about beliefs and values as it is about practical strategy. It is to do with, among other things, fairness, social justice and the common good, not just getting what you want for yourself.

Conceptual understanding: the missing link?

Factual knowledge and practical skills are necessary, but not sufficient elements in political literacy. What is also needed is some measure of *conceptual* knowledge – that is, the capacity to grasp and apply political concepts (Crick, 2000).

Concepts are not true or false, but the means by which we make sense of the world. They make thought and communication possible. The more developed or sophisticated our conceptual knowledge the more developed and sophisticated our thought and communication can be.

This is as true of the political world as it is of any area of human interest and understanding. It is through political concepts that we make sense of the political world and our actions in it – our understanding of what political institutions and processes are and why they exist, our awareness of ourselves as citizens, and our ability to recognise political situations and discuss them with others. They make it possible for us to develop a vision of how society should be and reflect upon our motives for wishing to change, or maintain existing arrangements.

Teaching and learning directed towards improving conceptual understanding is an essential element in political literacy. It informs the factual and the practical, and links them together into a unified and distinctive process. It is not so much an 'approach' to, or a 'model' of, political literacy as such, but a means of generating a way of teaching political literacy that is broad, balanced and coherent – able to provide young citizens with the requisite skills, knowledge and understanding needed for them to be able to participate fully in political life.

This implies a special role for conceptual learning in curriculum planning – in several ways. First, it implies that political concepts can provide criteria – though not the only criteria – for selecting and structuring the content of political literacy teaching. Concepts can be represented and grasped at various levels of sophistication, e.g. what students are capable of understanding by 'democracy' at Key Stage 4 may be qualitatively different from that at Key Stage 3. This allows for a certain amount of continuity and progression to be built into schemes of work for different age groups. Second, it implies that a certain amount of discrete lesson time should be set aside for learning activities that have a specific focus on developing students' conceptual understanding – more of this later. Third, it implies that, where possible, critical reflection of a conceptual nature should be built into learning activities that would otherwise be predominantly facts- or skills-based. An example of this might be the building of regular debriefing sessions into a community-based project, providing opportunities for reflection upon the sorts of beliefs and values involved, moral issues raised, and so on.

Identifying political concepts

The problem at the moment, as any analysis of currently available teaching resources for Citizenship will show, is that, for a number of reasons, this aspect of political literacy is often sadly lacking in practice. With very few exceptions[1], little time or thought has been devoted to what the teaching of conceptual knowledge should involve in schools or how it might be taught most effectively.

So where do we start? The first task is to identify the sorts of concept that are most relevant to political literacy – at least, to political literacy as we have outlined it here. That is to say, concepts without which democratic thought and communication would not be possible. Unfortunately, it is just not practicable to produce an exhaustive list. There is no end to the number of concepts available; nor is there a 'correct' list just awaiting identification. However, some political concepts are clearly more significant than others and would appear on any reasonable list. These are the ones that should concern us in schools.

A useful distinction can be made between 'procedural' and 'substantive' concepts. Procedural concepts are value-free. They are the fundamental ideas by which thought or communication of any political colour is structured and made possible. Important examples are:

- Power
- Authority
- Government
- Citizenship
- State
- Representation
- Ideology.

In contrast, substantive concepts embody political *values*. They are the means by which *particular* political opinion or argument is developed and expressed. Substantive political concepts can be grouped into general categories, such as 'virtues', 'ideals', 'systems', 'ideologies'. Important examples of these are:

Virtues	**Ideals**	**Systems**	**Ideologies**
Tolerance	Justice	Democracy	Liberalism
Fairness	Freedom	Monarchy	Conservatism
Openness	Equality	Dictatorship	Socialism
Respect	Solidarity	Theocracy	Fascism

Teaching political concepts

Once the concepts to be taught have been established, the next task is to find methods of presenting them that are interesting and accessible to school students. Direct teaching is unlikely to be effective. It is also, largely, inappropriate. Concept learning is more than the memorising of dictionary definitions. It is about broadening and deepening the ability to *use* concepts. It is not as though students do not already have some basic understanding of many political concepts, e.g. 'freedom', 'fairness', 'equality'. What political literacy is about is helping students to develop a more wide-ranging and sophisticated understanding of the political concepts they are already familiar with, as well as introducing them to ones they have not yet come across.

Political literacy is also about learning that many political concepts – in particular, substantive ones – are contentious, and interpreted differently by different people. This is because substantive political concepts have no 'true' meaning as such. What, for example, is true 'equality'? Is it equality of opportunity? Or equality of outcome? Or some other form of equality? Everything depends upon the context and the value-system of the person using the term.

Involving students in argument and debate

So how are political concepts to be taught? Given that what we are concerned with is improving students' usage of political concepts, the most appropriate way would seem to be providing students with opportunities to practise using political concepts themselves – by involving them in actual political argument and debate.

Debate is only possible where there is something to debate, of course. A good place to start, therefore, is with political *problems*: contentious issues on which students can take sides. Any political problem will do, but to provide a coherent programme of discussion work of this kind, a range of political problems will be needed. The best way to select these is to look to the perennial sorts of problems that tend to characterise life in a democracy, e.g. What are the rights and responsibilities of citizens? How much should we be dependent on the state for welfare? How far should tolerance go?

Problems of this nature are more easily assimilated when presented in concrete contexts. So instead of attempting to involve students directly in an abstract discussion of, say, the limits of tolerance, it is more effective to invite them to explore the problem more obliquely through the medium of an imaginary scenario, newspaper account, dialogue, letter, story, or the like. Students can be encouraged to identify and reflect upon the political concepts concerned through group problem-solving and discussion activities. Learning generated in the context of a particular context, real or imaginary, can then be applied to a range of other political situations.

The most natural location for this sort of guided discussion work is the classroom. For a practical example of such a lesson, see Case Study 1. However, as has been intimated above, there are plenty of opportunities for introducing argument and debate into learning activities predominantly concerned with other forms of political literacy learning – in particular, factual and skills learning. For an example of this, see Case Study 2. It is, after all is said done, in the integration of these different forms of learning – conceptual, factual and practical – that political literacy comes to life and begins to give students the feeling that they genuinely are citizens of a democratic society.

CASE STUDY 1

A lesson exploring different forms and functions of government

Students are given a scenario about an imaginary country that until recently has been controlled by foreign invaders. Having regained charge of the country, tribal elders meet to decide how it should now be ruled. Students are allocated roles in the meeting and asked to develop and defend arguments for one of four different options for government – namely, (1) continuing to cede power to the warlord who united the people and overthrew the invaders; (2) bringing back the former king from exile; (3) returning to religious control as in bygone times; (4) electing representatives to a parliament. These arguments are then put to the class as a whole and a vote taken. In the process, key political concepts are made explicit and explored, e.g. dictatorship, monarchy, theocracy, democracy – and important underlying questions discussed, e.g. What is the fairest form of government? What are the functions of government? Finally, students research the characteristic forms of government currently in place in different parts of the world, and reflect upon the views they have developed in the context of actual political situations, e.g. rule by constitutional monarchy in the UK.

(Huddleston, 2004)

CASE STUDY 2

A mock election with a more genuine element of political debate

Instead of asking volunteer students to role-play an election campaign (the usual practice in mock elections held in schools), invite the local MP and local representatives of political parties into school to campaign against each other in school for the votes of the student body. Set up the process as it would take place in a real local or general election – with numbered ballot papers, ballot boxes and voting booths. By introducing real politicians and providing opportunities for student interaction with them in hustings, it is possible to introduce an element of more genuine political debate than the relatively uninformed and stilted debate that can currently tend to characterise mock elections in school.

REFERENCES

Batho, G. (1990) 'The History of the Teaching of Civics and Citizenship in English Schools', *The Curriculum Journal,* 1(1).

Crick, B. (2000) *Essays on Citizenship*. London: Continuum.

Davies, I., Gregory, I. and Riley, S.C. (1999) *Good Citizenship and Educational Provision*. London: Falmer Press.

Huddleston, T. (2004) *Citizens and Society: Political Literacy Teacher Resource Pack*. London: Citizenship Foundation/Hodder and Stoughton.

QCA (1998) *Education for Citizenship and the Teaching of Democracy in Schools*. London: QCA.

NOTE

1 Exceptions are to be found in work of the Citizenship Foundation's Political Literacy Project (see Huddleston, 2004), and, more generally, materials from the Philosophy for Children (P4C) movement, as outlined in Will Ord's chapter – Chapter 2.7.

FURTHER READING

Crick, B. and Porter A. (1978) *Political Education and Political Literacy*. London: Longman.

Davies, I., Hogarth, S., Huddleston, T. and Rowe, D. (2002) 'Political Literacy: An Essential Part of Citizenship Education', *The School Field,* 13(3), Autumn. Ljubljana: The Slovene Society of Researchers in the School Field and the Educational Research Institute.

Douglas, A. (2003) 'Educating for change in political culture?', *Teaching Citizenship*, Issue 5, Spring.

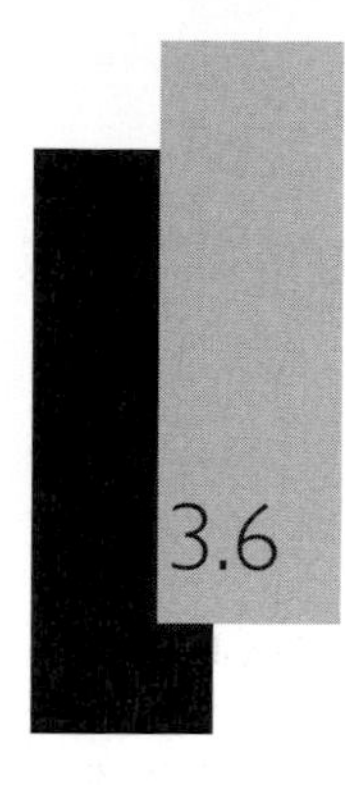

Sociology and Citizenship: Laying the Foundations of the Social Curriculum

3.6

Mike Moores

Underpinning Citizenship: the need for a *sociological* approach

> *The study of Sociology is of essential importance for anyone who would regard themselves as an informed citizen in today's world. In identifying both the continuity and the diversity of human experience, Sociology teaches us sympathy for the cultures of others at the same time as it helps us better understand the institutions of our own society. No field is more demanding than Sociology, yet none at the same time is so able to change and deepen our view of ourselves. Studying Sociology should not be merely a neutral process of learning, but one which unsettles pre-existing assumptions, challenging our prejudices and preconceptions.* (Giddens, 1986).

In this chapter I want to explore some aspects of the claims made by Anthony Giddens in the above statement, with a view to arguing that Sociology, as an academic, but also potentially life-changing discipline, is *uniquely* placed to service and underpin the Citizenship Curriculum in schools and colleges. Compared to many other disciplines, Sociology offers countless opportunities to involve young people in the processes of *thinking* about the society in which they live, their role in it, and their relationship with other citizens. Sociology also offers young people the stimulus to *act* in their communities in an enlightened and tolerant manner. It follows that any citizenship course *not* firmly rooted in and informed by Sociology will be impoverished in all respects.

I want to begin by suggesting that what might be termed 'essential Sociology' gives the discipline a 'head start' over many other fields of study – the intellectual base of Sociology is, unavoidably, deeply concerned with Citizenship issues. I then want to examine the specifications in Citizenship Studies currently on offer from awarding bodies, with the purpose of pointing out the high level of Sociological content (especially conceptually) therein. Finally, I want to suggest how Sociology can service the different types of curricular and CPD provision that educational managers and leaders might decide to institute for Citizenship.

Essential Sociology and Citizenship – just what is the connection?

Like other social sciences, Sociology really first saw the light of day in the mid-late 1800s as European nations industrialised and urbanised at a revolutionary rate. Writers such as Karl Marx, Emile Durkheim and Max Weber were the key analysts of this period, attempting to document and make sense of the new forms of social arrangements taking shape. These writers, who came to be known as the 'founding fathers' of Sociology, were aware that the drift from rural to urban settlements at that time would generate new types of communities, new forms of consciousness and identity, and new issues relating to social cohesion. Durkheim, in particular, was concerned that *social solidarity* in a newly-modernising and industrialising society could be endangered because people's roles were becoming more specialised, differentiated and contractually-based. In a period of rapid social change there was always the possibility of *anomie* – a state of normlessness in which individuals become confused or uncertain about their attachment to the group and the values of that group. At worst, in a rapidly changing society in which individualism was rampant, anomie would result in people putting self-interest before shared norms. Obligations and responsibilities towards others would be weakened. For Durkheim, the key question was this:

> *If we follow no rule except that of a clear self-interest . . . how should we acquire a taste for any disinterestedness, or selflessness or sacrifice?* (Durkheim, 1947).

So here we have one of the early sociologists, writing well over a century ago, asking questions about *belonging to communities*, questions about *rights and responsibilities towards others*, and, crucially, questions about *active citizenship and how it might reinforce social solidarity.* And all of this against a backdrop of the mass migration of social groups, increasingly diverse populations, and the potential for social conflict. The similarities between the context in which Durkheim was writing and the historical moment we find ourselves in are astounding. In our post-September 11th world – where the UK has seen riots in northern towns with significant Asian-origin populations, where the government is making plans for US-style nationality/citizenship procedures, and where asylum-seekers provide the tabloids with endless opportunities for stories about the nation being 'swamped' by new groups – the *key* issues are still surely sociological and, at the same time, *citizenship* issues. And it was not just Durkheim who was writing about citizenship issues (though, at the time they might not have been seen as such, or termed as such). Weber's interest in power and authority structures as they took new shape in modernity, Marx's outrage at the alienating processes and structures of capitalism, and Toennies' work on *Gemeinschaft* and *Gesellschaft* – all of these examples demonstrate that, from its very beginnings, sociologists have been absorbed by issues relating to political awareness, participation and community outcomes. What is striking, of course, is that these are *still* absolutely 'live' issues for sociologists and students of Citizenship alike. The links between the two fields of study have always been, and remain, immensely powerful.

If we now look at the key themes which might be said to underpin Sociology we can see a further demonstration of the idea that the intellectual base of the discipline is unavoidably linked with Citizenship issues. Here I want to consider four key sociological themes in particular. These fundamentally engage with issues of Citizenship and are set out in Figure 1.

Figure 1
Four themes central to both Sociology and Citizenship

1	Avoiding ethnocentric attitudes
2	Understanding the importance of the nature/nurture debate
3	Understanding the tension in social life between free will and determinism
4	Striving for objectivity

The theme of *avoiding ethnocentric attitudes* is central to sociological thinking. The idea that cultural practices can be systematically ranked on a continuum that runs from 'acceptable' to 'unacceptable' is, in itself, unacceptable to sociologists (especially when the practices judged to be 'unacceptable' happen to take place in 'exotic' or minority cultures). Instead, sociologists would insist that cultural practices have integrity within their own culture, reflect long-standing norms, and are functional for that culture. To take an example, arranged marriages within Asian communities generate significant resistance from many whose experience is more likely to be of 'romantic love' marriages. Ethnocentric attitudes – believing that the cultural practices of *your* culture are superior to those of any other culture – need to be neutralised if a truly social scientific approach to the analysis of social behaviour is to prevail. The same is true for the study of Citizenship – if students are to develop a genuinely tolerant attitude towards their fellow citizens in a culturally diverse society, then ethnocentric attitudes need to be identified and suspended. A respectful understanding of other groups' death rituals, marriage ceremonies, naming systems, etc. is crucial. Thus, Citizenship learning needs to embrace this sociological key theme.

The *nature/nurture* debate is another key theme in Sociology, and the nurture viewpoint is the one, clearly, which Sociology promotes. We are what we are, largely speaking, as a result of environmental and social, rather than biological and genetic factors, insists the sociologist. This philosophical standpoint clearly has relevance in the field of Citizenship. If we examine the position of women in society, or the positions of some ethnic minorities, we will see structured disadvantage. We will note similar social inequalities relating to social class and disability. Citizenship students, along with Sociology students, need to wrestle with the notion that 'our genes are not our destiny'. This contention, of course, carries with it huge implications for social change, the life-chances of individuals from relatively disadvantaged social groups, and social policy. In the UK there has been a series of debates recently about the allocation of Higher Education places. One aspect of this debate has been about whether or not it is legitimate to *positively discriminate* in favour of those applicants who come from social groups traditionally under-represented in post-18 education. What should government policy be on this matter? Quotas for students from these groups? Entry to university for these students with lower grades than the grades asked for from students with more advantaged backgrounds? Whatever the policy measures adopted, we can clearly see the notion that social factors, not biological characteristics, shape life-chances – a key idea which arises time and time again in Sociology and which should also figure largely in the study of Citizenship.

The third key theme in Sociology is the *free will/determinism* debate. This controversy runs through many disciplines and it should, ideally, be the basis for a lot of classroom discussion in Citizenship Education. The debate deals with the tension in social life that stems from the fact that we are both created by, but also create, social structures. Put another way, it examines the idea that our actions *can* shape our destiny, and that of others, but that social structures and expectations will often limit our choices and actions. In other words, our lives might often be determined by social forces rather than by our free will. If we take the examples of the recent World Trade Organisation/globalisation protests, or protests about road-building schemes, or individuals from deprived backgrounds rising up society's class and status 'ladder' to reach high positions in politics or business or public life, we can see how this debate is central to social life. And in a Citizenship context, it connects with many young people's desire for social justice at a personal level and a more just world at a global level. In the 1960s, young people wanted to 'change the world'. Today's teenagers often voice a more modest desire – to 'make a difference', but no matter how ambitious a young person might be, this key theme encourages students to think about becoming politically active (while remaining aware of the institutional resistance to such participation). Political elites don't have to have it their way all the time!

The final key theme I want to deal with is *striving for objectivity*. Sociologists from different branches of the discipline disagree about how realisable a goal objectivity is, but none denies that it is important. In many respects it is self-explanatory – in Sociology and in the study of Citizenship the controversial issues will be flying 'fast and furious' around the classroom. Genetically-modified crops, designer babies, third world poverty, nuclear weapons, domestic violence, institutionalised racism, the glass ceiling, ageism, the police and ethnic minorities – the list goes on, but this list reflects the world we live in. Tabloid-style views are easy to come by, but those based on a cool appraisal of evidence, a willingness tirelessly to seek out a wide range of views on both sides of the debate, and a sensitive ultimate judgement are of a totally different order. Teachers of Sociology have worked at these skills themselves for many years and have tried to pass them on to their students. Citizenship teachers will need to develop the same skills.

So, as far as the links between the two fields of study go, there can be no doubt that 'thinking sociologically' and 'thinking citizenship' share two obsessions – the need to understand the human and social processes that characterise our society and also the desire to develop the communal tools to change society for the better.

Citizenship specifications – what level of sociological content? (and vice versa)

In this section I want to point to the shared conceptual base of National Curriculum Citizenship and that found in the established Sociology and Social Science specifications.

All of these courses are underpinned, it might be argued, by a *particular* concept which has dominated both academic social science and social policy debates since the end of World War II – meritocracy. This concept is, of course, highly controversial in academic circles, and there are those who are sceptical about how achievable a meritocracy is, those who remain unconvinced about its desirability, and those, such as Michael Young, who question whether a society which *was* a meritocracy would actually be a more harmonious one (Young, 1961). In the public and policy arenas, though, the desire to equalise opportunities for all social groups has gained wide-spread support, and this is reflected in both sets of specifications. Students following both courses will study how specific social groups' life-chances are limited, and also how this reflects an inefficient use of a society's human capital. Equal opportunities and the legal system, differential benefit from and access to the welfare state, poverty and deprivation, differential levels of success in the education system; this is just a selection of the meritocracy-related issues featuring in both Sociology and Citizenship courses. In our increasingly culturally-diverse and complex society, issues relating to social class, gender, ethnicity, age, disability and sexual orientation promise to become more, not less, significant. Sociologically informed Citizenship courses will allow students to discuss the ways in which we might become a more just society.

And there are other issues and concepts which figure significantly in both fields of study. Culture and identity is a good example. Global issues is another. Social policy is a further example. The list of shared concepts is, in fact, huge, and reflects the duty of those involved in both Sociology and Citizenship Education to help students in their urgent need to make sense of the pressing issues of the day.

Perhaps the most obvious area of overlap in conceptual terms, though, is in the study of political systems and political behaviour. Students following both Sociology and Citizenship courses need to know, understand, apply and evaluate concepts such as democracy, the state, government, power, political parties, political participation, pressure groups and globalisation. They also have to be able to write effectively about a set of 'isms' such as capitalism, communism, totalitarianism, and so on.

So, much of the common 'content' of the two courses reflects the need for young people to become comfortable with the idea that political understanding is a pre-requisite for being an active citizen. In more general terms, though, the two fields of study attempt to make sense of society through a common set of concepts.

Citizenship Education – roles for the Sociology teacher

It should be clear from the above that Sociology specifications on their own are a sound basis for delivering large segments of any Citizenship Education programme in the sense that a Sociology or Social Science specification can provide a 'carrier' course for National Curriculum Citizenship. This has a particular pertinence given the apparent reluctance of some teachers and schools to opt for formal examination courses in Citizenship (i.e. Citizenship *Studies*) itself. In schools where students opt for Sociology courses at Key Stages 4 and 5, or where Sociology or Social Science is part of an entitlement core, this can be seen as one way of enhancing or delivering, in particular, the Political Literacy strand of the Citizenship curriculum. Sociologists can also contribute to 'carousel' systems of delivery, perhaps offering short modules on topics such as cultural diversity, new and older diaspora, or crime and punishment. This latter approach, of course, has the advantage of reaching all students in a year group, not just those who opt for Sociology or Social Science.

But the sociologist is valuable beyond the particular constraints of any Citizenship 'lesson' and, as the editors of this collection underline, Citizenship obviously needs such lessons but *cannot* be delivered *solely* within them. In this respect a further, vital way in which a sociologist might contribute to this wider Citizenship provision is by organising or advising on the planning of Citizenship events. Sociology teachers usually have contacts with agencies and organisations in the wider community and these groups will often be able to provide guest speakers on topics related to Citizenship issues. Matters such as religious and ethnic diversity, the role of the police officer in the community, and the workings of local civic institutions, to name but a few, are all realistic themes for speakers to address and this form of provision itself links with the Community Involvement strand in Citizenship Education, alerting students to a range of local activities they might become involved in.

Sociology teachers are also adept at leading research-based work. They might, for example, support students involved in a survey and observation exercise that seeks to evaluate the degree to which their school meets the needs of children with special learning needs. Another manifestation of this form of activity would be for students to carry out a study of the degree to which their school reflects the multicultural nature of the local community. These sort of activities link with the Social and Moral Responsibility strand in Citizenship Education as they clearly encourage students to think about the rights and responsibilities of *all* groups of learners in schools. In order to make judgements and decisions about matters such as, say, equal opportunities in their school, students need to be able to gather, analyse and evaluate evidence on this matter. Such research has long been the bedrock of coursework in Sociology specifications at various levels and, thus, sociologists are ideally placed to develop these skills in students.

In short, the Sociology teacher is extremely well-equipped to teach the knowledge of the Citizenship Curriculum and the associated Citizenship *skills*: ways of thinking about society, approaches to research and the gathering of evidence, the confidence to engage in the process of active citizenship, in the school, the local community or beyond.

Turning to practicalities – unearthing the hidden sociologists

I have stressed throughout just how important it is that Sociology teachers play a central role in the delivery of Citizenship Education in schools if the Citizenship agenda is to be as effective as it can be, and everything that I have written so far should lead education managers to appreciate this. If your school does not employ a sociologist, employ one! The likelihood, though, is that you already do. You might find that your PSHE coordinator has a Sociology background, or your Careers coordinator, or your Work Experience coordinator, or members of your GNVQ team. Sociology teachers were obliged to seek out 'new pastures' with the advent of the original National Curriculum in the late 1980s which saw many schools cut out Sociology and Social Science from their curriculum offer. Search them out, welcome them back from Further Education or seek out newly qualified teachers with a Social Science background. A specific recommendation of the Crick reports on both National Curriculum and 16–19 provision (DfEE/QCA, 1998; DfEE/FEFC, 2000) was that the teaching profession should again welcome teachers from such backgrounds, and the new PGCE programmes devoted to supporting the Citizenship curriculum are already attracting such applicants.

And there are other reasons why you simply have to involve sociologists in your Citizenship team. If we consider the points set out in Figure 2, it should be clear that sociologists have a great deal to offer colleagues not just as team members or leaders but in the provision of in-house training sessions. Unearthing and then drawing on the expertise of the 'hidden sociologist' on your staff (or within your LEA) is one route to effective CPD that may be much more effective than simply buying in a consultant who will be elsewhere in the country the following day.

Figure 2

Five reasons why Sociology specialists should contribute to the delivery of Citizenship in schools

1. Teaching controversial issues is the very essence of Sociology teaching – it is what sociologists do in their lessons.
2. Sociology teachers have a considerable knowledge of the concepts that are central to Citizenship lessons – because Sociology and Citizenship share common stands in their conceptual bases.
3. Sociologists are adept at teaching students how to identify and research social issues.
4. Sociologists generally teach in a 'democratic', discursive way, developing discussion and debating skills in students.
5. Sociologists tend to have good links with agencies in the wider community and are therefore central to a school's attempt to break down school–community barriers.

Given these points, it would seem logical, therefore, that sociologists should take a lead or key role in CPD activities for the Citizenship Team in schools.

In fact sociological approaches to teaching styles, student involvement in school decision-making processes and student involvement in the wider community tie in with what Titus Alexander calls 'Citizenship Schools' – schools which have changed their ethos and become more open, democratic and willing to see students as potential leaders and decision-makers, rather than 'deficit-units' which have to be filled with facts and drilled into conformity (Alexander, 2001). A more inclusive form of schooling is on the horizon and, in our post-September 11th world, it is sorely needed.

REFERENCES

Alexander, T. (2001) *Citizenship Schools*. London: Campaign for Learning.

DfEE/QCA (1998) *Education for Citizenship and the Teaching of Democracy in Schools*. London: QCA.

Durkheim, E. (1947) *The Division of Labour in Society*. New York: The Free Press.

DfEE/FEFC (2000) *Citizenship for 16–19 Year Olds in Education and Training*. Coventry: FEFC.

Giddens, A. (1986) 'Preface', in M. Joseph, *Sociology for Everyone*. Cambridge: Polity Press.

Young, M. (1961) *The Rise of the Meritocracy*. Harmondsworth: Penguin.

PART FOUR

FOUNDATIONS FOR CITIZENSHIP TECHNOLOGY, SCIENCE AND MATHEMATICS

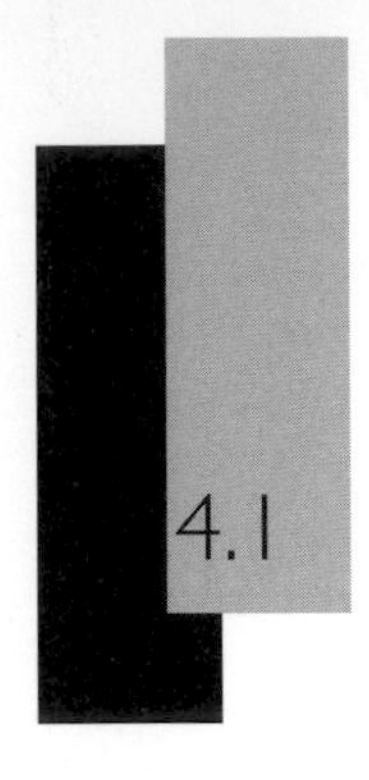

Information, Communication and Learning Technologies: Equipping the Digital Citizen

Tony Lawson

The swift development of Information Technology (IT) and its transformation through Information and Communication Technology (ICT) into Information Learning Technologies (ILTs) have enormous consequences for schools and colleges in the twenty-first century. The citizen of the twenty-first century will need to be able to access and deploy the facilities available through ICT in order to play a full part in the social, economic, cultural and political life of society. To be a citizen will be to be a digital citizen.

The development of Information Technology in schools

The introduction of IT into schools can be divided into roughly three stages. From around 1980, the focus of introducing IT into schools was the technology itself, with limited numbers of computers, often located in specific departments. Training for teachers was largely restricted to instructions on how to handle the software and hardware, underpinned by the assumption that this would promote the integration of IT into subject areas. The result was that deployment of IT was narrow and haphazard, with some students having little access to computer facilities during the course of their education. In the second stage, from about 1990, the emphasis moved to pedagogical and curriculum concerns, as teachers sought to find best practice in their use of ICT and deploy computers in ways that were educationally efficient. From around the turn of the century, a third focus developed in examining the social and institutional factors that impinge upon the use of ICT and ILTs in schools (see Somekh, 2000). It is in this latter stage that the Citizenship dimension of ICT emerges.

The role of ICT in schools

ICT occupies a contradictory position in the school curriculum that parallels the situation of Citizenship Studies, in that it is potentially both a discrete subject of the National Curriculum and a facility that can be employed in all curriculum areas. The problem in attempting to deliver both is that there is a limit to the number of computers and areas in which they are kept, as well as issues concerned with the networks and bandwidth needed to service competing demands on the systems. ICT as a distinct subject is concerned with the acquisition of skills and knowledge about computer applications, but has a wider role in promoting:

- the pupils' spiritual, moral, social and cultural development
- key skills such as communications and working with others
- thinking skills, enterprise skills and education for sustainable development.

(DfEE/QCA, 1999: 8–9).

With the introduction of Citizenship Education into the curriculum, the role of ICT in promoting Citizenship should be added to this list. However, the contradictory position of ICT in schools has practical consequences for schools as they struggle to juggle the competing and escalating demands of ICT teachers, other subject teachers and the pupils themselves for computer time:

> *The bottle neck is the kids' demands for ICT. We no longer have the infrastructure (or bandwidth) that can cope with this demand. We cannot see this as being alleviated.* (ICT Coordinator, Sedgewick Secondary School. Quoted in Comber et al., 2002 – Strand 3 of *ImpaCT2*)

The importance of ICT in education

If the twenty-first century is the Age of Information, then, as conceptions of labour move from manual to knowledge work, the ability to manipulate information and communicate effectively with others will become central characteristics of the successful worker. As information goes global, knowledge is no longer restricted to the classroom or is any longer certain. The twenty-first century citizen will therefore need to develop new interpretation and evaluation skills and problem-solving capacities if they are to respond effectively to a complex changing social world. Moreover, the potential of ICT to transform the nature of the relationship between teacher and learner is immense, as it has the capacity to undermine the traditional role of the teacher as the imparter of knowledge to the student. However, as schools approach the Information Age, they face a number of issues relating to the Citizenship agenda and ICT.

The digital divide

This refers to differential access to computer facilities and the information-rich internet by social groups (see DfEE, 2000). Initial interest in this area focused on the gender dimension, as female students seemed less interested than males in applications such as spreadsheets and databases, and when female students did express enthusiasm for computers, they tended to be marginalised, as the male students dominated the scarce resources in schools. However, as more machines and greater bandwidth allowed much wider access and as new applications such as communications technologies (most notably e-mail and the internet) became the focus of learning activities, this division has diminished.

commensurate with the resources available and with an eye to developments in this area. Second, they need to have in place programmes that address the social, political and economic dimensions of ILTs and not just the technical and practical aspects. Third, school and subject leaders need to work out how to provide ICT to their pupils in the most effective way possible, so that they both receive instruction in hardware and software, and also use ICT in their subjects as a natural available tool. Given the financial limitations faced by schools, this will not be easy:

CASE STUDY

Arkwright School had two ways of trying to deal with the problem of maintaining an ageing system in the light of increased demands for use. The first was by running a thin client on their 'old' machines. Though it was recognised that this had limitations, it worked fine for applications such as word processing, so that increased performance could be extracted from less powerful machines. The second tactic was to buy second hand machines only, when they were down to one quarter to one fifth of price. The school would purchase them for £50 and then throw them away when they were just too old to serve. They would also buy one or two new machines for specialist use (for example, the art department needed high resolution). The management did not see a future where they would be buying many new machines, because the budget for all their hardware, even as a Technology College, was just under £30k. They were just not able to replace a class set of old machines at £1000 per machine.

Taken from *ImpaCT2* (see Comber et al., 2002).

Teaching and learning styles

The understanding of the impact of networked technologies on the relationship between teacher and learner is still in its infancy, but it is clear that they do change the way that learners learn and teachers teach. The nature of the internet for example is such that no teacher can hope to know everything that is available about a topic. Indeed, one of the strengths of the internet is the multiplicity of points of view that is contained within it. This means that the teacher can no longer take the stance of the conveyor of knowledge, but rather must facilitate the learner to access as much information as is relevant and then develop the skills for them to deploy it in appropriate ways.

This does not mean that the teachers are being made redundant but that they will have to adopt a different style in the twenty-first century. That style will have to be a more democratic one, in which the teacher and the learner grapple with unfamiliar information and mould it to their mutual purposes (see the case study below). This is part of the citizenship agenda to the extent that the individual pupil begins to take more responsibility for his or her own learning, while being guided by the teacher. The teacher's role will be to equip their pupils with the investigative, problem-solving and evaluation skills needed to make use of ICT in a responsible fashion as befits the digital citizen. As more and more governmental information and political participation (such as internet-voting) becomes available through digital technologies, then these skills will become vital for the citizen in making decisions about policies and the political issues of the day.

CASE STUDY

In the session, Year 11 students were engaged in the creation of a database that would carry out stock control functions. The lesson began with an interactive white-board segment, in which the students were brought into the centre, away from the machines, so that they could all see and contribute interactively as requested with the whiteboard. The teacher modelled a problem that they had to solve. However, the teacher used a non-returnable example of stock (in this case, wine) as an exemplar of tracking stock and the use of re-order levels. While the modelling was taking place, the students were involved in answering questions and demonstrating possible solutions on the whiteboard.

When the modelling segment was complete, the students were told to return to their computers and to access some support material that had been placed on the shared area of the network, and which they could use to continue to develop their own databases. However, this material was also about non-returnable goods, while the assignment was to create a database for stock control of returnable items, such as library books, videos, car hire etc.

The teacher was thus providing supporting material for the students that was not simply to be copied and pasted into their own databases. Rather, the teacher provided a 'scaffold' of material that moved students on but which did not give them answers. The activity was explicitly contextualised within the key skill of problem-solving and the students were given a long-term time target for solving the formulae for this type of stock control.

In order to solve the problem, students had to think through what was needed and find a software solution to it. As this itself would take some time and would involve the students in trial-and-error work as they debugged any problems with their proposed solutions, students were encouraged to use e-mail to post their database to home. They were to work on it there in their own time 'for homework', returning it to school via e-mail for the next lesson in a week's time.

Taken from *ImpaCT2* (see Comber et al., 2002).

Censorship

The point at which Citizenship and ICT intersect most sharply is over the issue of censorship. It is one of the more contentious issues that face school and subject leaders in grappling with the potential of networked technologies, because of the enormous media interest in the dangers of the internet (see Lawson and Comber, 2000). Well-publicised accounts of the dangers that accompany the use of the World Wide Web, most notably pornographic sites and paedophile grooming incidents, have made schools wary of unfettered

4.2

Citizenship Education and the Social Implications of Science and Scientific Learning

Professor Mary Ratcliffe

Introduction

Why is Science not as prominent as it could be in the Citizenship Curriculum? This chapter explores this question. It proposes some strategies which allow students to consider socio-scientific issues as part of their entitlement to a curriculum which prepares them for future challenges.

The problem

Science does not seem to feature strongly as a context for Citizenship Education. If teachers use the QCA schemes of work as a guide they can be forgiven for thinking that developments between Science and Citizenship were an afterthought. For example, Science only features in the final two units (20 and 21) in the Key Stage 3 Schemes of Work and few links are made to Science in the Key Stage 4 Schemes (DfES, 2002). School inspectors have found little evidence of Science contexts in the first phase of implementation of the Citizenship Curriculum (Ofsted, 2003). In preparing teachers through initial teacher education for teaching Citizenship, Science (unlike History and English) was not identified as a joint subject with Citizenship for Qualified Teacher Status. There may be good reasons for this training decision, unrelated to the potential of Science as a context for Citizenship Education. For example, the workload in preparing to teach across the sciences in a one year postgraduate course is very substantial. Nonetheless the alignment of Citizenship with a limited number of subjects in giving formal 'licence to teach' indicates the disciplines which are expected to take a major role in Citizenship Education.

At one level the lack of emphasis on Science is unsurprising – Science can be seen as a body of content and not a set of creative processes for exploring and evaluating evidence. Science teachers are used to classroom interactions based on developing conceptual understanding and not those which allow discursive and personal dialogue.

At another level, however, the apparent sidelining of Science is puzzling and shortsighted. Scientific issues are very much in the media. People are expected to make judgements on socio-scientific issues at a personal level – note the ongoing debate about the MMR vaccination. Such issues also feature in public policy decisions. Discussion of socio-scientific issues provides a very appropriate forum for enabling students to distinguish between personal and public morality (Warnock, 2001). Social responsibility and political literacy are features which can both be developed through Science contexts and are important in dealing with contemporary science. Environmental issues, the part of science that does get clear recognition in the Citizenship Curriculum orders, encourage community involvement. Most scientific issues are national and global as well as local. So why aren't scientific contexts more to the fore in national activities supporting Citizenship Education and in schools' practice? The main reasons may stem from the compartmentalisation of the secondary curriculum and the expectations and practice of teachers of different disciplines.

The problems are illustrated by considering one of the units in the suggested Key Stage 4 Scheme of Work – *global issues, local actions* (DfES, 2002). This unit proposes activities for students in considering Local Agenda 21 and issues of sustainable development. Although links are made to the Science Curriculum, the impression is given that the focus is on extensions to the Geography Curriculum. Knowledge and understanding of sustainable development is a specific requirement of the Key Stage 4 Citizenship Programme of Study. Sustainable development also features prominently in both the Science and Geography curricula and Nigel Zanker discusses sustainability as a key Citizenship theme within the Design and Technology curriculum in Chapter 4.3. Given that at Key Stage 4 all students study sustainable development in Science but not all students study Geography, basing Citizenship experience in sustainable development predominantly on the Geography Curriculum has limitations in allowing all students access to the relevant knowledge and understanding.

The education for sustainable development website (www.dfes.gov.uk/aboutus/sd) shows the complementary skills which Geography and Science can encourage. It is worth noting, however, that the expectation that through using Science contexts students 'learn to question and discuss science-based issues' is not borne out in current practice. Levinson and Turner's (2001) questionnaire and interview study exposed Science teachers' reluctance to engage students in the discussion of the social and ethical aspects of biomedical science. They noted that

> *a large proportion of teachers across the curriculum perceive the teaching of science to be about the delivery of facts, and not about values, opinions or ethics. Almost half of all science teachers interviewed feel that their teaching of science should be 'value free', that it does not yield issues that have social or ethical implications*. (Levinson and Turner, 2001).

There are thus some Science teachers who have an antipathy to engagement with the Citizenship Curriculum. Even those Science teachers who are open to considering elements of Citizenship, whether in Science lessons or through contribution to a dedicated Citizenship scheme, may be unfamiliar with useful pedagogic knowledge and skills. Developing students' abilities to 'express, justify and defend orally and in writing a personal opinion' (DfES, 1999:15) is not commonly associated with Science teaching.

Changes in the Science Curriculum are, however, encouraging a greater emphasis on ethical issues and the use and evaluation of evidence. The very recent revisions to the Key Stage 4 Science Curriculum, for example, place 'How science works' at the heart of students' experiences. These Science themes include a detailed consideration of 'how and why decisions about science and technology are made, including those that raise ethical issues, and about the social, environmental and economic effects of such decisions' (QCA, 2004). There are thus increasing opportunities to link with the Citizenship Curriculum.

The Science Curriculum distinguishes between the concepts of 'science', such as forces, electricity etc., and 'ideas-about-science' – 'How science works' in National Curriculum terms. A recent research project explored the barriers and opportunities for teachers of Science in explicitly teaching 'ideas-about-science' (Bartholomew et al., 2004). In describing and evaluating teaching practice which allowed students to engage with 'ideas-about-science', five dimensions were identified (Figure 1).

Figure 1
Five dimensions of practice in teaching 'ideas-about-Science'

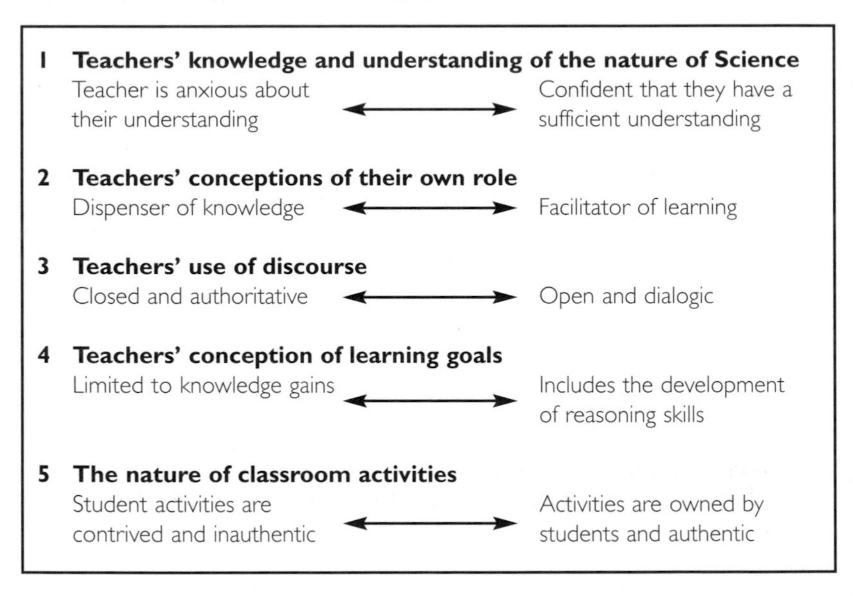

Teachers of Science who were seen as effective in promoting learning about 'how science works' tended to be towards the right on these dimensions. They were able to set clear learning goals which they shared with students and were willing to develop and support students' discussion. Some of the difficulties for Science teachers in developing open and reflective discussion stem from the traditional emphasis in the Science Curriculum on promoting the understanding of scientific knowledge. Shifting from a focus on 'what we know' to 'how we know' presents dilemmas for teachers. On the one hand, they are being asked to promote Science as a body of well-established consensual scientific 'facts'. On the other hand, they are encouraging students to recognise that scientific developments bring with them a degree of tentativeness and that their applications may have social consequences. As one of the teachers in the study put it: 'You don't want them to be uncertain of what they need to write in the exam. And yet you do want them to be critical of things they read in the newspapers or see on TV'.

This tension between two different purposes is perhaps not so acute for teachers of other disciplines who use Science contexts for Citizenship Education. Humanities and English teachers may feel well placed to teach Citizenship concepts and skills using contemporary scientific issues. Such teaching still brings dilemmas, however. Do such teachers have sufficient knowledge and confidence in dealing with the Science base of the issue to promote students' engagement with underlying concepts? If the ethical and social implications of Science are not dealt with by Science teachers, how does this affect students' views of the relevance of the Science Curriculum to their future experience as a citizen? There are no straightforward ways out of the problems raised. Some strategies, however, have been tried and the lessons from these may prove valuable in considering socio-scientific issues.

An integrated or collapsed day

A powerful way of using a Science context to teach the strands of Citizenship is through specific cross-curricular collaboration. As a trial, eight schools in the South of England participated in a cross-curricular or 'collapsed' day to enable Key Stage 4 students to examine the social and ethical implications of genetics (Ratcliffe et al., 2004). This activity was funded by the Wellcome Trust and followed from recommendations of Levinson and Turner's study (2001). A cross-curricular research team from the University of Southampton developed a framework of activities for addressing specific learning goals (Table 1), which was then shared with teams of Science and Humanities teachers on a development day. Not all the learning goals related to the Citizenship Curriculum, but with social and ethical issues at the heart of the event, there was considerable potential for students to voice and evaluate opinions and consider aspects of social responsibility. The day included such questions as: Should any individual with a disabling genetic condition be able to have gene therapy? Should genetic testing to eliminate a severe genetic disorder be encouraged? Students thus had the opportunity, in principle, to develop skills of enquiry and communication relevant to the Citizenship Curriculum and develop some understanding of human rights and responsibilities. Cross-curricular teams of teachers in each of the eight schools used the framework and adapted some suggested activities to plan and deliver a stimulating event for the whole year group. Schools delivered the day to both Year 10 and Year 11 students.

Table 1
Outline of an 'integrated' or collapsed day programme

Activity	Purpose
Introduction (team building)	To encourage team working; to identify pupils' initial views of genetics issue.
Stimulus (external speaker)	To engage pupils' interest in a human dilemma involving genetic disorders. To identify key questions about the science and its impact on individuals and society.
Science – what is possible? (science activity)	To gain a better understanding of genes, genetic crosses, genetic engineering.
Exploring viewpoints What do we think about genetic testing? (group discussion)	To identify individual views and share these. To recognise the range and diversity of views and some of the issues that these might raise.
How should we decide? (ethical reasoning activity)	To understand principles of ethical reasoning and decision-making. To practise using ethical reasoning tools.
Can we? Should we? – Our views (debate, posters, role-play, script)	To synthesise and present arguments related to: What is possible? How should we decide?

Students' responses to the integrated experience were positive. In particular, they were supportive of group discussion of genetics issues because it allowed students to voice their own opinions and to appreciate different points of view:

> *P2* *You learn it but you don't just write it down so it's more interesting*
> *P4* *Yeah it is more informal getting to know what other people actually think*
> *P1* *You get to know others people's views and you discuss a lot*
> *P5* *It broadens your mind a lot more instead of just one view. You learn other people's view and you think oh yes it could be this way or it could be that way so you are more broad minded*
>
> Source: Focus group, School 5 (Ratcliffe et al., 2004)

Some activities had a format which was more inclined than others to provoke critical discussion. For example, in School 3 pupils were given information about a particular genetic dilemma:

> *They then each clarified their own views on a 1–10 continuum – e.g. It is wrong to create a baby so that it can be used to save the life of another child (1 = I*

> *strongly disagree; 10 = I strongly agree). Each group of pupils was then asked to discuss the extent to which they agreed with the statements and why, noting reasons for agreeing and disagreeing*. (Ratcliffe et al., 2004)

Even here, however, teachers had to work hard in asking questions to each group that provoked clear debate rather than leaving students to complete the task with little critical thought. This issue was particularly evident where there was ready consensus.

Researchers noted that critical discussion was only really evident in one school, where it was apparent that ground rules had been explained and students were used to self-regulated and probing discussion. In the other seven schools, there was little to show that teachers were used to promoting *critical* discussion. Science teachers and Humanities teachers both missed opportunities for engaging students in critical reasoning, distinguishing evidence from values. Limitations showed particularly in ethical analysis, a teaching strategy unfamiliar to the majority of teachers. The synthesis activities at the end of the event took a number of forms, from large group formal debate to poster production. Tasks which had a tangible outcome proved to be the ones students approached with the most enthusiasm and thought. For example, in one school students demonstrated the pros and cons of genetic engineering using a range of methods: powerpoint presentation; drama production; article for newsletter; TV newsround presentation; photostory. The opportunities to display and share opinions and evidence through these means were very well received by students and teachers.

Teachers across disciplines found the collaboration fruitful. For some teachers such a cross-curricular event was a new venture. This meant that considerable effort was spent on organising the logistics, perhaps at the expense of focusing on how students' learning was going to be supported effectively. The potential for genuine sharing of pedagogical expertise across disciplines was harnessed where all of the following were apparent:

- there was prior collaboration between teachers whether formal or informal – i.e. a strong ethos of sharing already existed
- several planning meetings were held with *all* teachers who were involved in delivering the programme
- teachers who planned particular activities were able to document and explain the purpose of the activity to each other and exemplify in detail a suitable method of conduct.

There are, therefore, management issues in promoting effective cross-curricular collaboration.

Teachers gained ownership of the programme, investing time and effort in planning for an intensive experience. Was it worth it? Thirty per cent of teachers spontaneously declared how positive they and the students felt about the event. There was a majority view that the opportunity for students in the collapsed day was in being able to consider in depth one issue which brought together genetics and social considerations. Overall 75 per cent of teachers felt suspending the timetable had been a 'very useful' method for considering the issue, with the remaining 25 per cent considering it 'useful'. For teachers, the collapsed day had been a positive experience with intentions to repeat. For many of the teachers such organisation and collaboration was the first time they had addressed socio-scientific issues in such a focused way. That the event proved a generally very positive learning experience for students suggests that cross-curricular days around a socio-scientific issue could form a very useful method of promoting Citizenship Education through Science.

Developing Citizenship skills while exploring 'science in the making'

There are also other teaching strategies that are valuable in considering socio-scientific issues. These include consequence-mapping; ethical analysis; evaluation of media reports; consensus projects and community projects (Ratcliffe and Grace, 2003). One of the aspects which is common to such activities is the potential for students to gain an understanding of 'science in the making' by exploring and evaluating evidence. These activities not only contribute to the development of Citizenship skills but also address important aspects of the modified Science Curriculum (QCA, 2004). For example, students can be encouraged to collect reports of Science stories from the papers and magazines they read. The reports can then be used to highlight and discuss the features (or lack of them) of the conduct of Science. At the same time students can explore features which hook the reader – emotions; surprising life-changing events; important new findings; visual presentation. Concentrating on these and other features, such as the role of editors, can allow students to gain more insight into the nature of media-reporting itself.

Ways forward

There are persuasive arguments for using socio-scientific issues as a context for Citizenship Education. Indeed, if Science is marginalised students are not being well prepared for engagement in personal and public decision-making as informed citizens. *Senior managers should recognise the potential of Science contexts for delivering the Citizenship Curriculum and strive to integrate socio-scientific issues in their Citizenship programmes.* The encouragement of integrated approaches has benefits in teachers sharing pedagogic skills and students' recognition of the contributions of different disciplines. Teachers of Science, and perhaps of humanities, have a need for professional development in using teaching strategies which allow ethical analysis, debate and critical reflection. Supporting Science teachers through professional development will not only enable them to contribute to the Citizenship Curriculum but will also allow them to tackle the changing Science curriculum with confidence and ability. The increased emphasis on scientific literacy, methods of scientific enquiry and evaluation of evidence will require variety in teaching and learning strategies. For many teachers, support in extending their teaching repertoire will be rewarded through effective curriculum implementation. Science teachers should be encouraged to reflect on their skills and knowledge base for teaching both Science and Citizenship. Do you really believe that, in Science classrooms and across the curriculum, students should experience an education that is relevant to their future as informed and active citizens? If the answer is yes, then use the professional development opportunities that are available to try new approaches and encourage students' active participation in considering socio-scientific issues.

REFERENCES

Bartholomew, H., Osborne, J. and Ratcliffe, M. (2004) 'Teaching students 'ideas-about-science': five dimensions of effective practice', *Science Education* 88: 655–82.

DfES (1999) *Citizenship National Curriculum*. London: DfES/QCA.

DfES (2002) *KS3 Citizenship schemes of work; KS4 Citizenship schemes of work*. Available at http://www.standards.dfes.gov.uk/schemes2/citizenship/ (Accessed 13 November 2004).

Levinson, R. and Turner, S. (2001) *Valuable Lessons: Engaging with the social context of science in schools*. London: The Wellcome Trust.

Ofsted (2003) *National Curriculum Citizenship: planning and implementation 2002/03*. London: Office for Standards in Education.

QCA (2004) *KS4: Programme of study for science for 2006* – published 15 November 2004 at http://www.qca.org.uk/2586_10334.html

Ratcliffe, M. and Grace, M. (2003) *Science Education for Citizenship*. Maidenhead: Open University Press.

Ratcliffe, M., Harris, R. and McWhirter, J. (2004) 'Teaching ethical aspects of science – is cross-curricular collaboration the answer?', *School Science Review* 86(315): 39–44.

Warnock, M. (2001) *An Intelligent Person's Guide to Ethics*. London: Duckbacks.

FURTHER READING

Levinson, R. and Reiss, M. (eds) *Key issues in bioethics: a guide for teachers*. London: RoutledgeFalmer.

Ratcliffe, M. and Grace, M. (2003) *Science Education for Citizenship*. Maidenhead: Open University Press.

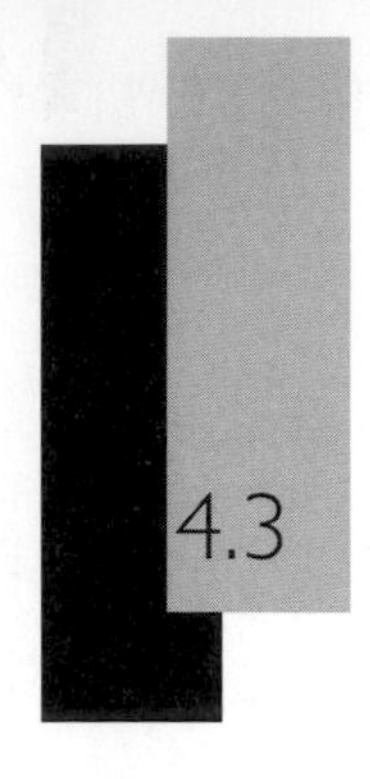

Designed for Citizenship? Innovation, Technology and Social Responsibility

Nigel Zanker

Introduction

Design is concerned with innovation. It is a field of study in which designers, from their imagination, create two- or three-dimensional models of products that they think people want or need. Technology is concerned with the use of tools, materials and processes. It is also a field of study in which technologists or industrialists bring products into working reality from designers' imagination. These products may be objects, systems or environments. Both these fields of study have, therefore, become one subject, Design and Technology, in our school curriculum. It is through this subject that pupils are taught how to design and to make products.

Designers and technologists have become much more aware in recent decades of the social and environmental aspects associated with the designing, making, use and disposal of products. There is now an increased social responsibility – shared by consumers, designers and politicians – not to destroy life and the environment in the process. Similarly, in schools, teachers of Design and Technology foster an awareness of social responsibility through their students' designing and making. It is this that forms the basis of the link between the school subjects of Citizenship and Design and Technology.

This chapter explores this link by reviewing the literature and resources currently available to Design and Technology teachers. It proposes some strategies, through illustrative examples, for teachers to develop their students' active citizenship skills of participation and responsible action through designing and making.

Planning Citizenship Education through Design and Technology

Whilst Citizenship may be delivered as a subject in its own right there are strong links with the established Humanities subjects, notably History, Geography and RE, and also with the range of other subjects cited in Part Two of this collection. However, Design and Technology is also a Humanities subject, a matter often overlooked by policy-makers, because of the impact that designing and making has on human life. Anthropologists chart this impact, in terms of the use of technology, through historical periods or stages:

- 10,000 years ago – *homo sapiens* var *agricola* (farming)
- 250 years ago – *homo sapiens* var *industria* (industrial)
- 50 years ago – *homo sapiens* var *technologica* (microprocessor).

As outlined above, the advancement of this technological impact brings with it an increased social responsibility, especially as our endeavours begin to have a wider effect, producing global consequences, some of which stretch beyond our own planet. The strongest links made between curricular programmes in Design and Technology and Citizenship are through product sustainability and environmental consequences, issues directly referenced in the Programmes of Study for each subject (DfEE/QCA, 1999a). There are also wider links to values, in particular to legal processes and health and safety and around issues about the use to which products and manufacturing effort is put.

In attempting to develop the knowledge and skills of Citizenship in their teaching, Design and Technology teachers are faced with a complex model, as indeed are teachers of any subject. Interpreting the Programmes of Study for both their own subject *and* for Citizenship is already a daunting task, before they might begin to do so in terms of other contextual documents, for instance the *Statement of Values* produced by the National Forum for Values in Education and the Community (DfEE/QCA, 1999c).

However, a less daunting approach to planning for the introduction of a Citizenship Education perspective or component in Design and Technology is not to start with the Programmes of Study but to consider other sources of available guidance. This has the advantage of allowing teachers to follow the key principles of Citizenship by ensuring they are built-into rather than bolted-onto designing and making. These principles are outlined in *Making Sense of Citizenship: A CPD Handbook* (DfES and Citizenship Foundation/ Hodder Murray, 2006), a text in which some of my co-contributors to this volume have helped to produce:

> *. . . for contributions from other subjects to be officially classified as part of the school Citizenship Curriculum, simply identifying common concerns or points of contact between subjects is not enough. The citizenship element must be the significant part of the lesson. (Ibid: 1 (Chapter 8))*

Making Sense of Citizenship does not make specific reference to Design and Technology when offering guidance about the teaching of Citizenship through other subjects. Similarly, there are no examples of Citizenship Education opportunities in Design and Technology, a matter that this chapter will redress. However, the guidance in the handbook for Art and Design can be readily translated into Design and Technology (and, indeed, other subjects) as I have set out in Figure 1:

Figure 1
From Art and Design to Design and Technology: adapting the advice in Making Sense of Citizenship

> The key question for you as a *Design and Technology* teacher is how formal a contribution do you wish to make to Citizenship?
>
> All *Design and Technology* makes references to Citizenship issues from time to time.
>
> Learning objectives should be expressed in terms of the National Curriculum Programmes of Study for Citizenship and made explicit in lesson planning.
>
> If you wish to make a definite contribution in this way then your work should be linked to the rest of the Citizenship Curriculum and planned in association with the Citizenship Coordinator.
>
> Source: *Adapted from* Making Sense of Citizenship *(2006: 23–24 (Chapter 8))*

The relationship between the three strands of National Curriculum Citizenship have been much stated in this collection but they are worth recalling here:

- Knowledge and understanding about becoming informed citizens.
- Developing skills of enquiry and communication.
- Developing skills of participation and responsible action.

It is in this context that Design and Technology is described in *Citizenship – A scheme of work for Key Stage 4: Teacher's Guide* (QCA/DfES, 2002):

> *Through design and technology, pupils learn to think and intervene creatively to improve the quality of life. During key stage 4 they do this through taking part in design and make projects linked to their own interests and those of the wider community. They consider how technology affects society and their own lives and that new technologies have both advantages and disadvantages.*
>
> *A project may be linked to active citizenship either directly, where the resulting product benefits other members of the community, or indirectly, where, as a mini-enterprise project, it raises money for a community or charitable cause.*
>
> *The requirement to think about issues such as the needs and values of users and any moral, economic, social, cultural and environmental considerations creates explicit opportunities for links with citizenship.*

Citizenship styles and values in Design and Technology teaching

The styles of teaching and learning that are required to promote active, effective Citizenship are those that every good teacher of Design and Technology will be familiar with. They can be summarised as:

- active – emphasises learning by doing
- interactive – uses discussion and debate
- relevant – focuses on real-life issues facing young people and society
- critical – encourages young people to think for themselves
- collaborative – employs group-work and co-operative learning
- participative – gives young people a say in their own learning.

(DfES and Citizenship Foundation/Hodder Murray, 2006: Chapter 1)

Similarly, the values central to good Citizenship Education are also central to good Design and Technology. They require young people to be:

- aware of their rights and responsibilities as citizens
- informed about the social and political world
- concerned about the welfare of others
- articulate in their opinions and arguments
- capable of having an influence on the world
- active in their communities
- responsible in how they act as citizens.

(DfES and Citizenship Foundation/Hodder Murray, 2006: Chapter 1)

Having considered the key features of effective Citizenship teaching within a Design and Technology context, we can now consider the National Curriculum provision itself. However, rather than moving straight to the Programmes of Study statements, a more productive approach is to consider the Statements of Importance, which preface the Programmes of Study, and the Descriptors for Key Stages 3 and 4. In Figure 2 they are placed alongside each other to show the relationship between the two subjects and to provide a good precursor to the kind of Design and Technology project planning that encompasses active, effective Citizenship learning.

Figure 2

Statements of Importance and Key Descriptors for Citizenship and Design and Technology at Key Stages 3 and 4

Design and Technology	Citizenship
The Importance of Design and Technology	**The Importance of Citizenship**
Design and Technology prepares pupils to participate in tomorrow's rapidly changing technologies. They learn to think and intervene creatively to improve quality of life. The subject calls for pupils to become autonomous and creative problem solvers, as individuals and members of a team. They must look for needs, wants and opportunities and respond to them by developing a range of ideas and making products and systems. They combine practical skills with an understanding of aesthetics, social and environmental issues, function and industrial practices. As they do so, they reflect on and evaluate present and past design and technology, its uses and effects. Through Design and Technology, all pupils can become discriminating and informed users of products, and become innovators.	Citizenship gives pupils the knowledge, skills and understanding to play an effective role in society at local, national and international levels. It helps them to become informed, thoughtful and responsible citizens who are aware of their duties and rights. It promotes their spiritual, moral, social and cultural development, making them more self-confident and responsible both in and beyond the classroom. It encourages pupils to play a helpful part in the life of their schools, neighbourhoods, communities and the wider world. It also teaches them about our economy and democratic institutions and values; encourages respect for different national, religious and ethnic identities; and develops pupils' ability to reflect on issues and take part in discussions.
During Key Stage 3: pupils use a wide range of materials to design and make products. They work out their ideas with some precision, taking into account how products will be used, who will use them, how much they cost and their appearance. They develop their understanding of designing and making by investigating products and finding out about the work of professional designers and manufacturing industry. They use computers, including computer-aided design and manufacture (CAD/CAM) and control	***During Key Stage 3***: pupils study, reflect upon and discuss topical political, spiritual, moral, social and cultural issues, problems and events. They learn to identify the role of the legal, political, religious, social and economic institutions and systems that influence their lives and communities. They continue to be actively involved in the life of their school, neighbourhood and wider communities and learn to become more effective in public life. They learn about fairness, social justice, respect for democracy and diversity at

software, as an integral part of designing and making. They draw on knowledge and understanding from other areas of the curriculum.	school, local, national and global level, and through taking part responsibly in community activities.
During Key Stage 4: pupils take part in design and make projects that are linked to their own interests, industrial practice and the community. Projects may involve an enterprise activity, where pupils identify an opportunity, design to meet a need, manufacture products and evaluate the whole design and make process. Pupils use ICT to help with their work, including computer-aided design and manufacture (CAD/CAM) software, control programs and ICT-based sources for research. They consider how technology affects society and their own lives, and learn that new technologies have both advantages and disadvantages.	***During Key Stage 4***: pupils continue to study, think about and discuss topical political, spiritual, moral, social and cultural issues, problems and events. They study the legal, political, religious, social, constitutional and economic systems that influence their lives and communities, looking more closely at how they work and their effects. They continue to be actively involved in the life of their school, neighbourhood and wider communities, taking greater responsibility. They develop a range of skills to help them do this, with a growing emphasis on critical awareness and evaluation. They develop knowledge, skills and understanding in these areas through, for example, learning more about fairness, social justice, respect for democracy and diversity at school, local, national and global level, and through taking part in community activities.

The Qualifications and Curriculum Authority has produced a leaflet that maps the two Programmes of Study (QCA, 2001) and makes links to the DfES Schemes of Work for Design and Technology (DfEE/QCA, 2000). The main Design and Technology contributions to Citizenship are identified as:

- enabling pupils to resolve conflicting demands during their design and make assignments, justify the decisions they make, and begin to take responsibility for their actions when making products
- enabling pupils to take into account how products will be used and who will use them
- providing opportunities to gather information, make choices and reflect on how technology affects society as pupils work co-operatively with a range of people during the design and make assignment
- providing opportunities to think and intervene creatively to improve quality of life.

(QCA, 2001)

The Design and Technology Association (DATA) has produced a worked-up example of a Citizenship unit of work, for developing a product that meets a consumer need (DATA, 2004). This unit, in the context of Food Technology, provides a good template for teachers of all Design and Technology media areas. It shows clear learning outcomes for different abilities and has not been over-complicated by Programme of Study statement links. It follows the principles for curriculum planning in Design and Technology advocated in this chapter by using the Statements of Importance and Key Descriptors for Citizenship and Design and Technology at Key Stages 3 and 4.

Whilst the entire Programmes of Study in the Design and Technology National Curriculum should be referred to for determining sufficiency of coverage, the principal opportunities for Citizenship learning are set out in Figure 3 and Figure 4.

Figure 3

Principal opportunities for Citizenship learning in the Design and Technology Programmes of Study at Key Stage 3

1b) consider issues that affect their planning [for example, the needs and values of a range of users; moral, economic, social, cultural and environmental considerations; product maintenance; safety; the degree of accuracy needed in production]

3c) identify and use criteria to judge the quality of other people's products, including the extent to which they meet a clear need, their fitness for purpose, whether resources have been used appropriately, and their impact beyond the purpose for which they were designed [for example, the global, environmental impact of products and assessment for sustainability]

7a) product analysis

7b) focused practical tasks that develop a range of techniques, skills, processes and knowledge

7c) design and make assignments in different contexts. The assignments should include control systems, and work using a range of contrasting materials, including resistant materials, compliant materials and/or food.

(DfEE/QCA, 1999a)

Figure 4

Principal opportunities for Citizenship learning in the Design and Technology Programmes of Study at Key Stage 4

1b) consider issues that affect their planning [for example, the needs and values of a range of users; moral, economic, social, cultural and environmental considerations; product maintenance; safety; the degree of accuracy needed in production]

3c) ensure that their products are of a suitable quality for intended users [for example, how well products meet a range of considerations such as moral, cultural and environmental] and suggest modifications that would improve their performance if necessary
4e) that to achieve the optimum use of materials and components, they need to take into account the relationships between material, form and intended manufacturing processes
6a) product analysis
6b) focused practical tasks that develop a range of techniques, skills, processes and knowledge
6c) design and make assignments, which include activities related to industrial practices and the application of systems and control.

(DfEE/QCA, 1999a)

In recent years, internet websites have been developed to support Design and Technology based Citizenship projects in schools. This resource base is increasing all the time. However, links between these sites are in need of development to increase their usability. The penultimate section of this chapter focuses on key areas for Citizenship learning in Design and Technology contexts with examples of the web-based resources available and how they link to the three strands of Citizenship, especially strand 3: developing skills of participation and responsible action. First, though, I want to explore the particular Citizenship learning opportunities presented by the growing profile of sustainability and environmental impact, both in education and in the broader policy agenda.

Citizenship, environmental impact and sustainability

Often the immediate link between Citizenship and the wider social curriculum and Design and Technology is around the use of what is made: the social value of the product, a child's educational toy, a device for a person with a given disability, a security device. This is, though, only a starting point. In the limited space available here I want to continue to explore the more fundamental *Citizenship* issues about environmental impact and sustainability issues that require exploration if we are to produce good Citizenship Education *and* good Design and Technology Education. That is, developing students' (citizenship) skills of participation and responsible action through the process of designing and making.

Environmental impact

At present, the UK produces over one million tonnes of waste electrical and electronic equipment every year, or three tonnes per British citizen in their lifetime. The waste is toxic and landfill sites are fast running out. As McDonough and Braungart put it: 'Everything . . . is designed for you to throw away when you have finished with it. But where is "away"? Of course, "away" does not really exist. "Away" has gone away'. (McDonough and Braungart, 2002, cited at www.weeeman.org, 2005).

On 1 January 2006, manufacturers and retailers in the European Union (EU) became responsible for financing the collection of ten categories of product at the end of their life cycle. The categories, with their recovery and recycle rates, are summarised in Figure 5. The legislation covering this is the European Waste from Electrical and Electronic Equipment (WEEE) Directive. To restrict the use of toxic substances the WEEE Directive is supported by the Restriction of Certain Hazardous Substances (RoHS) Directive, which is set to come into force in the EU in 2006. The substances restricted include the metals lead, cadmium and mercury. One immediate implication for Design and Technology education is the use of lead-based solder in electronics.

Figure 5

Categories covered by the WEEE Directive

	Electrical and Electronic Product Category	Minimum recovery rate	Minimum recycling of components, materials and substances
1	Large household appliances	80%	75%
2	Small household appliances	70%	50%
3	IT and telecommunications equipment	75%	65%
4	Consumer equipment	75%	65%
5	Lighting equipment	70%	50%
6	Electrical and electronic tools (with the exception of large scale industrial tools)	70%	50%
7	Toys, leisure and sports equipment	70%	50%
8	Medical devices (with the exception of all implanted and infected products)	70%	50%
9	Monitoring and controlling instruments	70%	50%
10	Automatic dispensers	80%	75%

Source: www.weeeman.org

The immediate links between Citizenship and Design and Technology are through activities whereby students consider and learn about the principles underpinning the environmental impact of products designed by them and for them. Such activities include:

- disassembling products to study materials and manufacturing processes and their relevance to environmental impact
- selecting materials and components that have reduced environmental impact in their own designing and making

- using more recycled materials and components in their own designing and making
- investigating product life cycles.

The Weeeman website (www.weeman.org) provides an excellent basis for developing such activities.

Sustainability

The term 'sustainability' is better considered as 'sustainable development' or 'sustainable design' or 'sustainable technology'. Whichever term, it means the same thing – 'change':

> *Development is about change. Every time a new product is introduced, and people buy it and use it, the world changes a little bit . . . All changes or developments are designed to make the world a better place* (Capewell et al., 2002: 21)

Sustainability, therefore, is concerned with how products can be designed to improve the quality of life without adverse global impact in both the short and the long term. Sustainable design can be considered through three aspects: environmental, social and economic considerations. It is inappropriate to separate these aspects entirely from each other. However, each aspect may have its own focus in individual lessons to assist students' knowledge and understanding about becoming informed citizens. Key moral (or citizenship) questions in relation to each of the aspects are summarised in Figure 6. Each should be considered through looking at the whole life cycle of a product – from the extraction of raw materials, manufacturing and distribution through to its use and ultimate disposal.

Figure 6

Environmental, Social and Economic considerations in designing and making as Citizenship questions

Environmental considerations
What is the environmental impact?
What toxic emissions are there?
How is energy generated and used?
How much water is used?
What is the environmental impact of any packaging?

Social considerations
Is the product really needed?
How does it make life better for people?
Is it culturally acceptable to the people who will use it?
Does it build on the traditional wisdom and technology of the community?
What is the impact on social relations?
Will it enhance or diminish cultural diversity?
Does it bring people together in a friendly way and encourage creativity?
Does it have a long-term impact on future generations and the way they live together? If so, is this impact positive or negative?

Economic considerations
Does making, using and disposing of the product create jobs?
What sorts of jobs are created: do other jobs disappear?
Who is employed?
What is the economic impact on other people, now and in the future?
Is the product fair-traded?

Web-based resources for Citizenship learning in Design and Technology

The reader is strongly advised to visit the websites in this section. They represent an outstanding resource for developing students' skills of enquiry and communication using ICT-based resources and many will be as useful in the dedicated Citizenship classroom – and, indeed, elsewhere – as in the Design and Technology workshop. And each offers a range of links that can lead to further investigation.

Design Against Crime – www.designagainstcrime.org

The Home Office and the Design Council fund the *Design Against Crime* programme. The website contains information suitable for secondary schools, higher education and professional designers. The information on the website is useful to students in their designing and making of products that are less vulnerable to theft and which give protection to users. There are some example projects, which include:

- alarm systems such as personal attack alarms
- security tags
- crime prevention/awareness posters.

There are examples of good practice in design covering crime issues. These are presented as case studies using research data from the UK, USA, Scandinavia and South Korea. The purpose of the case studies is to develop a 'new perspective of socially responsible design, embracing social inclusion, crime prevention and other key areas of public policy' (Davey et al., 2002).

Fairtrade – www.fairtrade.org.uk

As the Fairtrade website states (2005), the FAIRTRADE Mark is a certification label awarded to products sourced from developing countries that meet internationally recognised standards of fair trade. By participating in Fairtrade, producers are able to use the additional income to strengthen their organisations and invest in social, environmental and business improvements. Just as importantly, they are able to learn more about markets and marketing, and take more control of their lives.

The Fairtrade website does not, at the time of writing, provide examples of school-based projects. However, there are downloadable lists of fairtrade food products and producers. These are a useful resource for food technology in schools because they can be used to make a direct link between the rights and responsibilities of the consumer, employers and employees. Possible projects include:

- designing and making food products using only fairtrade ingredients
- encouraging preferential purchase of fairtrade products at school and home
- designing material to raise awareness of fairtrade.

Sustainable Technology Education Project (STEP) – www.stepin.org

The Sustainable Technology Education Project (STEP) website was produced by the Intermediate Technology Development Group (ITDG). ITDG, now called Practical Action, is a development organisation that aims to build the technical skills of disadvantaged people in developing countries, helping them to improve the quality of their own lives without damaging the environment. The STEP website contains:

- a range of case studies drawn from around the world, focusing on practical, sustainable solutions to real problems
- a pop-up glossary
- downloadable teachers' notes
- feedback forums to allow people to express views on the issues of today and tomorrow.

This material provides an invaluable resource to develop students' knowledge and understanding about becoming informed citizens through Design and Technology education. In the month accessed (May 2005) there were 37 case studies appropriate to food, graphic products, resistant materials, systems and control and textiles.

Sustainable Design Award (SDA) – www.sda-uk.org

The Sustainable Design Award (SDA) scheme was launched in 2003 in response to the government's action plan for sustainable development in education. The three main partners of the SDA scheme are the Intermediate Technology Development Group (ITDG – now called Practical Action, as stated above), the Centre for Alternative Technology (CAT) and Loughborough University. Registration with the scheme is through ITDG.

The purpose of the scheme is for Advanced level students to explore environmental economic and social issues in Design and Technology through their coursework. However, the activities and resources available on the SDA website are suitable for all students of secondary school age and take the form of starter activities and eco-design tools. Examples include:

Starter Activities

- What's wrong with the world? – to help students put sustainability into perspective

- Belief Circles – to help students develop ideas and understand other possible viewpoints
- Line-ups – to encourage students to think about sustainability issues in day-to-day activities
- Product Pairs – to help students think about values behind choices as consumers
- The Bigger Picture – to show how consumer choices can impact on the lives of future generations.

Eco-design Tools

- Eco-design Web – a qualitative method of analysis used for assessing and improving a product's sustainability
- Design Abacus – a qualitative method of analysis for identifying areas where a product or a design could be improved in terms of sustainability
- Eco-Indicator – a more detailed qualitative analysis of products or designs to calculate their environmental and social impacts
- Footprinting – a tool to illustrate a person's impact on the world
- Sustain-a-balls – a checklist that aims to guide students through their projects.

In addition to the activities and tools, the SDA website is a rich database of information on environmental and social issues and, especially, on the sources and sustainability of different materials.

Waste from Electrical and Electronic Equipment – www.weeeman.org/

The website that supports the European Union's recently introduced *Waste from Electrical and Electronic Equipment* (WEEE) Directive contains a wealth of information on the environmental impact and sustainability of utilising different materials in the design process. It supports the kind of activities referred to earlier in this chapter and provides the necessary information in a very accessible format to enhance students' (and teachers') knowledge and understanding about 'becoming informed citizens', to put matters in QCA's language.

An evaluative conclusion: 'doing' Citizenship in the workshop and classroom

This chapter has provided an overview of the strategies and available resources for raising students' awareness of the importance of social responsibility in the design and environmental impact of products. However, the responsibility ought to start with individual teachers and students. Here lie the links with personal development, social responsibility and practical, *actual* citizenship: developing a culture relating to social environmental issues in school workshops. It is not enough to simply bemoan the lack of corporate or civic social responsibility (or 'corporate citizenship') shown by some businesses and public bodies or by *other* individuals and societies or, even, to focus merely on the design and making of items of social worth. There must be a Citizenship perspective to how Design and Technology is 'done' in the school. So, to end this chapter, some questions, to which the answers raise even more questions – answers that rest with an analysis that begins much closer to home and which might call for some immediate action:

- Are the tools, processes and materials being used in the Design and Technology workshops the most environmentally and socially friendly? If not, how can they be made so?
- Do materials and components purchased and used include recycled and fairtrade products and materials?
- Are materials and components recycled through the disassembly of unwanted student projects?
- Do design and make activities encourage the minimum use of and minimum waste of materials?
- Do students consider sustainable issues in their designing and making?
- Do they consider the social worth, purpose and impact of what they are making?

REFERENCES

Capewell, I. et al. (2002), *Sustainable Design Award Teachers' Handbook*. Rugby: ITDG.

DATA (2004) *Citizenship Unit of Work* – members section of DATA website, www.data.org.uk – Accessed 16 May 2005.

Davey L. et al. (2002) *Design Against Crime: Design leadership in the development of emotional values*. Boston: Design Management Institute Conference (June) www.shu.ac.uk/schools/cs/cri/adrc/dac/DACemotionalvalues.pdf – Accessed 1 June 2005.

DfEE/QCA (2000) *Schemes of work for Design and Technology*. London: QCA.

DfEE/QCA (1999a) *Design and Technology: The National Curriculum for England*. London: DfEE.

DfEE/QCA (1999b) 'Statement of values by the National Forum for Values in Education and the Community', in *The National Curriculum Handbook for secondary teachers in England: Key Stages 3 and 4*. London: DfEE.

DfEE/QCA (1998) *Education for citizenship and the teaching of democracy in schools: Final report of the Advisory Group on Citizenship*. London: QCA.

Huddleston, T. and Kerr, D. (2006) *Making Sense of Citizenship*. London: Hodder Murray/Citizenship Foundation.

McDonough, W. and Braungart, M. (2002) *Cradle to Cradle*. New York: North Point Press. Cited at www.weeman.org

QCA (2001) *Citizenship Through Design and Technology at Key Stage 3*, http://www.standards.dfes.gov.uk/pdf/secondaryschemes/citsubject_designtech.pdf – Accessed 30 May 2005.

QCA/DfES (2002) *Citizenship – A scheme of work for Key Stage 4: Teacher's Guide*. London: QCA Publications.

Figuring out Citizenship: Support from the Mathematics Classroom

Geoff Tennant

Introduction: Mathematics and Citizenship working together

As subjects in the school curriculum, Mathematics and Citizenship can exist in a powerful symbiotic relationship. Studied as a discrete subject, Citizenship draws extensively on mathematical ideas: 'showing an awareness of the use and abuse of statistics' is mentioned quite specifically in the Key Stage 4 Programme of Study for the Citizenship National Curriculum (QCA, 1999) whilst, 'analysing information and its sources' and '[justifying] orally and in writing a personal opinion about [political, spiritual, moral, social and cultural] issues, problems or events' (both in the Key Stage 3 Programmes of Study) might very well draw upon statistical and other quantitative data.

Justifying the converse relationship takes a little more work. Some years ago I did a small survey asking Mathematics teachers questions about their feelings with regard to the need to think about equality of opportunity, multiculturalism and other such issues within Mathematics teaching and learning. Almost exactly, my sample split into two halves: those who were sympathetic to these ideas and considered them important, and those who felt very strongly that Mathematics should have nothing to do with these issues.

The second view is worth considering in more detail, and can be argued something like this. The whole essence of mathematics is decontextualisation: a simple example of this would be that one can generalise from 2 people and 5 people making a total of 7 people, 2 pens and 5 pens making a total of 7 pens, to the sum $2 + 5 = 7$, in which it is not specified what is being referred to. From this point of view the second group as above were correct: Mathematics in its purest form does not engage with contexts, therefore elements of equality of opportunity, multiculturalism, and so on, do not apply.

In practice, I would want to suggest that this argument is wrong, disingenuous and dangerous. Wrong because it glosses over the process of learning Mathematics: only the most exceptional mathematicians are able to make sense of the decontextualisations Mathematics works with without having seen many examples first. Disingenuous because it removes a powerful tool for teaching: in my experience, understanding, for example, that $2 - (-4) = 6$ is much easier based on a story such as having demerits taken away than by any other means. And dangerous because if we don't face up to the reality that we almost certainly are using contexts in our teaching, then those contexts will then end up unexamined, so that, according to Brown and Dowling (1989), many of the questions in textbooks they looked at used examples more familiar and accessible to boys rather than girls, middle class rather than working class, and white children rather than those from minority ethnic backgrounds.

Contexts, then, greatly facilitate the learning of Mathematics in the first instance. But once mathematical concepts have been learnt, they can then be applied back to contexts. An example of this would be data representation. In first learning about pie charts, an example might be how a child in another country spends his/her time in a typical day. Whilst initially the example is a means to an end in learning how to draw a pie chart, once it has been learnt, pie charts can then be used as a means of comparing this child in another country with the child's own day: pie charts are not just drawn but used in analysing data. This illustrates something of the power of the relationship between Citizenship and Mathematics: the context provided by Citizenship facilitates the learning of Mathematics, whilst the mathematical concept then aids the presentation and analysis of issues within Citizenship. Combine this also with the power of ICT in enabling students to draw many graphs very quickly, and a powerful learning environment is set up whereby the differing shapes of the graphs can be analysed, initially in mathematical terms, leading to a fuller understanding of the Citizenship issues underpinning the data: the distribution of the tax burden; the allocation of hospital beds by gender or age or ethnicity; expenditure on public transport; arms or foreign aid, and so on.

In exploring, within this chapter, the opportunities and challenges presented by working at the Mathematics–Citizenship interface, I want to do four things:

1 Briefly consider approaches that have been used thus far.
2 Assess, in this context, the particular challenges presented as Citizenship as a National Curriculum subject is delivered, in part, through Mathematics.
3 Demonstrate possible future directions through considering two case studies arising from the *Beyond the Bar Chart* project, which is currently being undertaken through a partnership between the Mathematical Association and the Association for Citizenship Teaching with support from the Citizenship Foundation.
4 Convince at least a proportion of readers (be these school leaders, curriculum managers or classroom teachers) that such an alliance is worthwhile and can meet the objectives of the various partners concerned.

Approaches to date

In tracing the background to what we would now consider to be issues on the Mathematics–Citizenship interface, there are three main strands which emerge: multicultural mathematics, anti-racist mathematics, and mathematics within global citizenship.

The multicultural approach is, in effect, two-pronged: it is concerned with avoiding bias on the one hand, and promoting positive images on the other. Regarding the former, Shan and Bailey (1991) is one text which critiqued then existing textbooks on the grounds of conveying Mathematics as a white, middle-class, male activity, albeit without reference to any empirical data on students' attitudes towards this, and suggested a variety of alternatives of varying quality. At their best, their ideas involve looking at Mathematics around the world and considering how Mathematics can be applied to topical issues. At their worst, their suggestions appear to tell students what to think through giving contexts which actually throw no light on the Mathematics itself: 'In Britain over 6 billion glass bottles and jars are used each year. These could be recycled. Write down this huge number using a 6 and noughts' (1991: 164).

What is striking in examining the literature for positive suggestions is that it is the same alternative activities which keep on coming up: Islamic patterns, Rangoli patterns, and alternative counting systems particularly. Used well, students' understanding of Mathematics is enhanced whilst they are also learning that mathematical activity goes on, and has always gone on, right across the world. However, there is the danger here that the actual impression conveyed is that non-Europeans are backward and use Mathematics in non-standard and restricted ways and that the resultant materials are good only for end of term lesson fillers.

The anti-racist approach within Mathematics, rather than, in effect, substituting one set of materials for another, is concerned with the whole teaching methodology, looking for approaches which are 'practical, investigative, and problem solving in nature, so that the approach will encourage analytical and questioning frames of mind' (Cotton, 1990). In addition, this author goes further: '. . . an anti-racist approach addresses the needs of all pupils in helping them to question values, have a truer understanding of the worldwide sources and applications of mathematics, and gain true equality of access to the curriculum'.

Thus, for example, when considering the use of images within mathematical resources, a multicultural approach might be restricted to avoiding (or re-writing) those resources which show a bias or insensitivity in the choice of male/female images or images of people of different ethnic origin. An anti-racist approach, on the other hand, might encourage students to explore this bias and insensitivity and try to explain the reason for its presence. At its best, this can give powerful insights into Mathematics and Citizenship issues. At its worst, it can be telling children what to think, and even giving students with a racist disposition the information they need to be better informed racists. And ultimately, how far are we prepared to go in encouraging 'analytical and questioning frames of mind' if the conclusions students reach are sexist or racist?

More recently, with Citizenship becoming compulsory in secondary schools, a number of resources have become available aiming to support work on the Mathematics–Citizenship interface. These include a collection of prompts for work looking at human rights from a mathematical perspective (Wright, 2004), and structured statistical projects with real life contexts including world statistics and the environment (SMILE Mathematics, 2003). Alongside what is, at present, a very small amount of material of this nature, are a considerable number of sources of data on many Citizenship issues – the United Nations Children's Fund website, www.unicef.org, would be one of only many examples here. In practice, however, the information and data is often hard to identify or extract and can require a great deal of preparatory work by the teacher before it can be used in the classroom, thus providing a disincentive to the majority of teachers to make use of such ideas. There are many other considerations relating to the teaching of contentious issues such as the sensitivity (and possibly vulnerability) of individual students when raising certain issues, the way that images are presented, the balance between the need to provide background context to complex issues and the need to keep the language accessible to students, the desirability of providing open-ended and differentiated tasks in order to tackle thought-provoking issues. These important considerations merely serve to make the task of preparing resources even more time-consuming.

An agenda for moving forward: the challenges

As is argued elsewhere in this book, there is a strong case for delivering Citizenship as a discrete subject in UK secondary schools in order to ensure that students' entitlement is met. For the time being, it is clear that many schools are either not doing this at all, or are not allowing sufficient time to enable this to be done fully. There is going to be, therefore, the expectation that Citizenship is delivered through other curriculum areas, including Mathematics, and this needs to be thought through carefully.

One key issue here is winning the hearts and minds of Mathematics teachers. This is going to be particularly difficult when dealing with the 'abstractionists' as outlined above. But teachers trained in Mathematics who are well disposed to the idea of working on the Mathematics–Citizenship interface are likely to need support in this area. This was illustrated when the secondary Mathematics PGCE group at the University of Leicester, for whom I act as tutor, went out into schools to work with children on materials on this interface, following a preparation day at the end of the PGCE year in 2004. Whilst, overwhelmingly, the experience was a positive one, with excellent feedback from the student teachers, teachers in schools and the children themselves, PGCE students reported back that they did not feel entirely comfortable dealing with the debates, uncertainties and opinions expressed, which working with Citizenship issues brings up. This would appear to reflect both the nature of their training, which is primarily, but not exclusively, geared towards Mathematics in isolation of consideration of Citizenship issues, and also the degree backgrounds of the students, in Mathematics or a related subject, in which debates, opinions, attitudes, are not up for consideration in the same way as they would be within, for example, the Social Sciences. The change to the GCSE five or more A*–C measure necessarily to include English and Mathematics as from 2007 represents yet another pressure on all teachers, particularly those in these subjects, to be obtaining results from their students; any additional expectations need to be communicated sensitively.

In practice, a major 'selling point' is that mathematical objectives and statements of attainment can be met by working on the Mathematics–Citizenship interface. In terms of the Mathematics Programmes of Study, it is likely that work will involve data handling, creating hypotheses and testing them, percentages, ratio and proportion, and so on. But perhaps the most important contribution that work of this nature can make in terms of addressing the Statements of Attainment in the Mathematics National Curriculum lies in Attainment Target 1, 'Using and applying mathematics'. For example, at Level 6, 'Pupils carry through substantial tasks and solve quite complex problems by independently breaking them down into smaller, more manageable tasks. They interpret, discuss and synthesise information presented in a variety of mathematical forms. Pupils' writing explains and informs their use of diagrams. Pupils are beginning to give mathematical justifications' (DfEE, 1999: 87). It is easy to see how, for example, undertaking a project researching the viability of introducing a Fairtrade tuckshop into the school could be enabling children to demonstrate competencies under this heading.

In looking to support Mathematics teachers in working with the Citizenship interface, the following points are likely to be helpful:

- Write resources into departmental schemes of work, with clear National Curriculum references.
- Arrange for team teaching as part of a training programme, either with a Mathematics teacher experienced in this respect or, with suitable preparation, with a Citizenship teacher. (Citizenship teachers are often confident in just those issues that Mathematics teachers are nervous about and vice versa.)
- Provide resources which start with closed-ended exercises and become increasingly open-ended, to give a clear sense of direction but also flexibility for students to develop their own lines of thinking.
- Provide enough information, both in the resources and background notes, for teachers to get started without a huge amount of preparation on their part.
- Provide exemplar pupil work.

It is important also to ensure coordination with other curriculum areas to ensure that similar topics – for example, water conservation – are not being covered in a similar way in other subject areas – for example, Geography. Planned reiteration yes; duplication no.

An agenda for moving forward: 'Beyond the Bar Chart'

The *Beyond the Bar Chart* project, with teaching materials on the Mathematics–Citizenship interface, will be disseminated during 2006. Whilst no great claims are made for originality, the materials were written with the above criteria in mind, in trying to provide materials which facilitate good quality project work that develops skills and knowledge in *both* subjects, which give clear direction whilst leaving space for students to develop their own ideas, with sufficient background information to enable teachers to work with children without the need for a large amount of prior preparation. Whilst written to a high standard, part of the agenda was to give a sense of empowerment to teachers using the materials, in leaving them feeling able to generate further such materials for themselves.

To illustrate the approach, two examples are given of the materials that have been written by the team, one in the context of budgeting, and the other in world trade.

EXAMPLE A: EMILY'S TRIP

Information

- Emily is going on the school trip to France in June. She has 20 weeks to save the money she needs.
- The cost of the trip is £280 and she will need an extra 25 per cent of this amount for her pocket money.
- Emily gets £7.20 each week pocket money but she also has a paper delivery round.
- She gets paid £3 for a weekday delivery round and £5 for a Sunday round for 5 months before she goes away.
- Emily normally spends 15 per cent of her pocket money on snacks and sweets, 25 per cent on CDs and 60 per cent on clothes.

Key questions

1 How much pocket money will she take on the trip?
2 How much does she normally spend on clothes each week?
3 Emily decides to save one quarter of her clothes money each week towards her holiday. How much does she save each week? Over 20 weeks?
4 How much will Emily earn from her paper rounds?
5 If she saves part of her clothes money and all her earnings, how much does she save altogether?
6 How much more does she need to save? Suggest how she can do this.

Discussion point

The trip is priced on the basis of 30 students paying the full cost. One student has trouble paying the full amount due to an illness in the family. Think about the arguments for or against the other students paying extra to cover his costs. How would you feel about paying extra? Would the reason the student couldn't, or wouldn't, pay make a difference?

Extension

Plan a school trip and work out how you will pay for it. You may like to consider the following:

- How you will decide where to go?
- What alternatives are there for travelling? How much do each cost? How will you decide which method to take?
- What possibilities are there for accommodation?
- What could you do once there? How much will it cost? How will you decide what to do?
- How many staff will you need to take? Can you ask them to pay to go?
- What other expenses need to be met?
- What is the total cost per person of the trip?
- How will you cope with people who wish to go but either can't or won't pay?
- Would it be possible to organise fund raising events to finance the trip? If so, what? Who would contribute, to what and how much?
- How could you raise the remaining money you have to find yourself?

There are a number of issues here. One is the move from the specific to the general: the initial questions are closed ended in order to set the scene for what's coming. The question about one or more individuals not being able, or willing, to pay for the trip, needs careful thought about how to set the discussion up, particularly in view of the children actually there in the group for whom this could easily be a sensitive area – as considered above, Mathematics teachers may well need help in considering how to lead such a discussion. As regards the extension activity, the greater the extent to which students can generate for themselves the questions that need answering, and the methods for answering them, the better.

EXAMPLE B: THE TRADE GAME

Organisation

Divide the class into six groups. Explain to each group that they are representing a country. The aim of the game is to make as many shapes that fit a certain criteria according to what they have studied recently, e.g. shapes with an area of $24cm^2$.

Tell the groups what resources each group will start with, for example:

Group 1 No paper, 6 rulers, 6 pens and £30
Group 2 2 sheets of squared paper, 2 rulers, 2 pencils and £20
Group 3 3 sheets of squared paper, 1 ruler, 1 pencil and £10
Group 4 3 sheets of squared paper, 3 sheets of plain paper, 1 ruler, 1 pencil and £5
Group 5 4 sheets of squared paper, 4 sheets of plain paper, no rulers, 1 pencil and £5
Group 6 10 sheets of squared paper, 10 sheets of plain paper, no rulers, no pencils

Each shape can be sold to the business team (which could be teachers or students) for up to £5 according to the quality of the shape (and, if you wish, according to current economic conditions). The objective is to maximise the profit. Trading between groups is allowed. At the end, the groups of students are each asked to prepare a presentation explaining how they felt during the game, what they have learnt, and the countries that the different teams might represent.

In the trialling of materials undertaken by PGCE students at the end of the year, this activity proved universally popular. It can be adapted endlessly, including the sudden invention by one of the groups of scissors, communications black-outs necessitating working in silence for a specified time, group members becoming ill meaning they have to take time out from working, and so on. As indicated, the products being made can be varied depending on what students have been studying recently. Their experiences within the game can then be compared with the trading power of countries rich in natural resources (particularly Group 6) as opposed to those with the means of production and large financial resources (particularly Group 1). This was found to be a very powerful learning experience, in coming to understand some of the issues involved in world trade, and particularly the difficulties of working with only 'natural' resources – the experience, of course, of people and organisations in many developing countries.

Not just Mathematics in a Citizenship context but genuine Application of Number

The two examples above give some sense as to the opportunities for working at the Mathematics–Citizenship interface. Moreover, they begin to frame Mathematics much more in terms of, to use the language of Key Skills, *Application of Number*. And as Patrick McNeill argues in Chapter 5.6, there is both accreditation and pedagogical opportunity here. Considered as starting points in need of adaptation for local situations, they are activities which enable the Mathematics and Citizenship Statements of Attainment (and often the Key Skills specifications) to be met at the same time, whilst supporting the Mathematics teacher who is not entirely confident working in this area, particularly with the use of closed questions as in the first example.

Ultimately, children's experiences are as good as what happens in individual classrooms up and down the country. In the context of many other pressures and expectations upon Mathematics teachers, their hearts and minds need to be won in making work on the Mathematics–Citizenship interface enjoyable, challenging, meaningful, thought-provoking and attitude changing. To win an entire department to such a project may be too much; to win one or two innovative colleagues should be achievable in most schools. To use the terminology of the editors, Mathematics is less a *carrier* for large slices of the Citizenship curriculum and more a *tool* for bringing Citizenship issues to life in the Mathematics classroom (a process that enlivens and renders as *felt* relevant Mathematics itself) and a *tool* for assessing and understanding the implications of data on social, economic and political issues in the Citizenship classroom (building the numerical confidence of the Citizenship practitioner in the process). In exploring ways of working with Mathematics teachers, and in looking at samples of materials in the light of criteria for what they might look like, it is hoped that this chapter has gone some way to suggest how this might be done.

REFERENCES

Brown, A. and Dowling, P. (1989) *Towards a critical alternative to internationalism and monoculturalism in mathematics education*. London: Institute of Education.

Cotton, A. (1990) 'Anti-racist mathematics teaching and the National Curriculum', *Mathematics Teaching*, 132: 22–26.

DfEE (1999) *Mathematics: the National Curriculum for England*. London: HMSO.

QCA (1999) *Citizenship: Key Stages 3 and 4*. London: HMSO.

Shan, S.J. and Bailey, P. (1991) *Multiple factors: classroom mathematics for equality and justice*. Stoke-on-Trent: Trentham Books.

SMILE Mathematics (2003) *Real data: statistics projects for Key Stage Three*. London: SMILE Mathematics.

Wright, P. (2004) *Human rights in the curriculum: mathematics*. London: Amnesty International UK.

FURTHER READING

Adams, M., Arnaouti, S., et al. (1993) *Summing up the world: mathematical activities with a global perspective (Key Stages 3 and 4)*. Bournemouth: Development Education in Dorset.

Dodd, P. (1989) *Mathematics from around the world: a multicultural resource book*. Newcastle-upon-Tyne: Rutherford School.

Dodd, P. (1993) *Global mathematics: a second multicultural resource book*. Newcastle-upon-Tyne: Rutherford School.

Lumpkin, B. and Strong, D. (1995) *Multicultural science and math connections: middle school projects and activities*. Portland, Maine: J Weston Walch.

SMILE Mathematics (2003) *Real Data: Statistics Projects for Key Stage 3*. Smile Mathematics, London. See www.smilemathematics.co.uk

White, N., Riding, M., et al. (1988) *Mathematics for all*. Trowbridge: Wiltshire Education Authority.

Wright, P. (2004) *Human rights in the curriculum: mathematics*. London: Amnesty International UK.

Zaslavsky, C. (1993) *Multicultural mathematics: interdisciplinary cooperative learning activities*. Portland, Maine: J Weston Walsh.

Zaslavsky, C. (1996) *The multicultural math classroom: bringing in the world*. Portsmouth, New Hampshire: Heinemann.

ACKNOWLEDGEMENTS

Many thanks to the *Beyond the Bar Chart* team – Alice Dorsett, Andolie Marguerite, Carole Buxton, Graham Morris, James Nicholson, Jenny Brown, Jenny Orton and Peter Wright – on whose work part of this chapter is based.

For further information on the *Beyond the Bar Chart* project please contact the author at School of Education, 21 University Road, Leicester, LE1 7RF, e-mail: gdt3@le.ac.uk

PART FIVE

OBJECTIVES FOR CITIZENSHIP CROSS-CURRICULAR THEMES, DIMENSIONS AND SKILLS

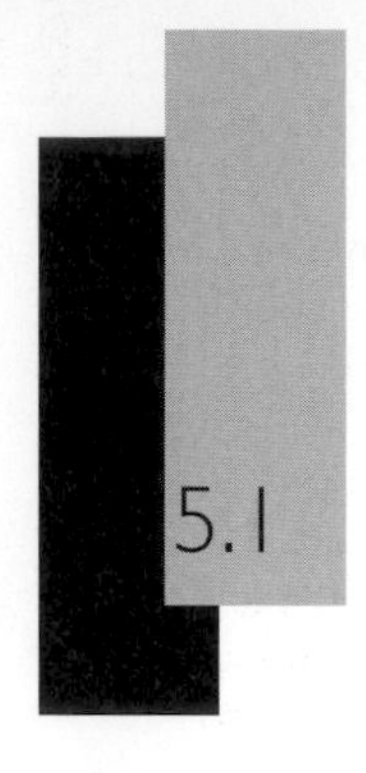

5.1 Education for Diversity and Equality

Don Rowe

Education for equality: from the 'personal' to the 'public'

Equality issues have been central to the concerns of many teachers for a long time. These have expressed themselves in two main ways. First, there have been huge changes in the past 20 years in how schools have faced up to the challenges of eradicating institutional discrimination, particularly in relation to gender and race. With the development and increasing formalisation of PSHE programmes, it also became widely accepted that equal opportunities issues should form part of the empowerment curriculum, which underpins the rationales of both PSHE and Citizenship to a considerable degree.

Within the context of mainstream PSHE approaches, equality issues have tended to focus on inter-personal rather than social and political domains. Thus strategies which teachers have favoured include:

- raising awareness of personal attitudes towards race and gender issues
- examination of stereotyping and its effect on behaviour
- raising self-confidence in individuals to resist social typecasting
- teaching inter-personal strategies to deal with discriminatory behaviour.

Such an inter-personal focus has left these approaches open to the charge, especially from those working within social science and anti-racist traditions, that they have ignored the structural and institutional dimensions to inequality. The advent of National Curriculum Citizenship, as Campbell and Craft note in Chapter 6.2, has pointed up the need for equality education to include the public as well as the personal by introducing a wider set of elements drawn from social studies, politics, law, ethics and philosophy. Citizenship Education helps young people answer the question 'What kind of society do I want?.' But this is a highly contested matter. Even if the whole class agrees to the statement 'we want a fair society, free of discrimination', the good Citizenship teacher will recognise that this still needs exploration in terms of the wide divergence of views over what is meant by fair, who would count as belonging to society and what counts as discrimination.

School policy, classroom practice and curriculum aims

Equality issues are challenging for teachers and schools. Not the least of the difficulties is the fact that although it is easy to give lip service to education for equality, and to produce aspirational policies on anti-discrimination, it is not so easy to be confident that institutional discrimination has been eradicated, that all staff are free from prejudicial attitudes (Wilkins, 2001) or that the implementation of policy is itself fair and consistent.

Pedagogically, education for equality has particular characteristics which make it a highly complex task. For one thing, the concept of equality has a clear moral component and teachers can easily feel put in the position of adopting the moral high ground in relation to their students. This is problematic for a number of reasons. First, teachers generally do not claim to be morally superior to anyone else. Teachers are members of society and few would want to suggest they are completely free from any form of prejudice. Second, once a teacher adopts such a position, the mode of pedagogy shifts from scaffolded, exploratory talk, towards directed discourse where students are ushered towards pre-determined conclusions. Worse, the lessons can become 'preachy'. In such contexts, teachers sense the loss of open dialogue between themselves and students and know that there is an increased likelihood of their audience switching off. Once this happens, it is impossible to hope for any kind of attitudinal or behavioural change, since this can only happen when students willingly and reflectively explore an issue in such a way that this fundamentally challenges their thinking. Too little is known as yet about which strategies are most likely to achieve attitudinal change whilst still remaining acceptable in terms of not being manipulative or propagandist. If teachers wish students to adopt more tolerant attitudes towards ethnic minorities or gay and lesbian people, how is this to be achieved without the unethical manipulation of students' views, especially when these reflect the legally held views of their parents?

The revised National Curriculum launched in 2000, offered, for the first time, a statement of values, aims and purposes for education as a whole which appeared to legitimise the pursuit of social justice by educational means. According to this statement, one of the central purposes of the school curriculum is to help 'all pupils to learn and achieve' – which means the school should not discriminate. At the same time education is described as a 'route to equality of opportunity' and a means of achieving 'a healthy and just democracy' (DfEE/QCA, 1999). The school curriculum should aim to 'develop pupils' integrity and autonomy' at the same time as helping them become 'responsible and caring citizens'. These statements look, on the face of it, to be above criticism – they are motherhood and apple pie aims. But precisely what constitutes a healthy and just society is a contested subject about which citizens do not agree. It is not clear what precisely education for equal opportunity should amount to, or what measure of equality might exist in a just society. What does equality actually mean, to whom should it be given and how should it be achieved? Citizens disagree on these issues and Citizenship Education, as Huddleston among other contributors to this text argues, must acknowledge these disagreements.

Education for equality: leading change or following trends?

Education can claim to have made a considerable contribution towards improving the lot of some discriminated groups, particularly in the areas of race and gender, but we should be cautious about claims that education has actually led the way. There are grounds for believing that the curriculum has reflected, rather than instigated, social change – for example, Parliament legislated equality rights for disabled people some 20 years after making race and gender discrimination unlawful – and the PSHE and Citizenship Curriculums have, by and large, reflected, not anticipated, this trend. Further, the ambivalences that remain around gay, lesbian and trans-sexual discrimination continue to be reinforced by the neglect of these issues in school. Where certain attitudes are strongly held in the community, teachers have traditionally found it very difficult to challenge them in the classroom or deal with them in ways that can be robustly defended if challenged by parents or governors.

How legitimate is it for teachers to attempt to shift the attitudes of young people in the direction of the liberal agenda? On the face of it, this is beyond the remit of schools and the Citizenship Curriculum. Common schools, welcoming parents of all religious, cultural and political beliefs, are obliged to treat issues which are controversial outside of the classroom as equally controversial inside the classroom – this is, to a degree, less true of faith schools where there may be a confluence of political and religious views, e.g. on abortion or homosexuality. Teachers, instead, need to base their approaches on the fact that every young person is entitled to understand that all social issues are controversial and that subjecting them to critical scrutiny is a legitimate and necessary preparation for life in a democratic, pluralist society. Young people are entitled to know that views they, or their parents, hold are contested and why. Further, they should learn how to defend these views rationally, on grounds which are valid within a democratic framework, i.e. using arguments which people with different values or philosophies can accept as reasonable. Of course, liberal minded teachers are privately entitled to hope that subjecting what they believe are intolerant views to critical scrutiny in this way may help students to moderate these ideas, but this is not necessarily a publicly acceptable justification for the exercise.

Education for attitudinal change, then, needs to be based upon trust in the power of rationality, honesty and consistency to bring about more reflective, tolerant and critical thinking within individual students. A more detailed consideration of the pedagogies underlying education for race equality articulates and illustrates this position.

Achieving equality in practice: education for race equality

Despite the fact that race equality has been on the political agenda for decades now, it is still fair to claim that racism and diversity are amongst those Citizenship issues most often avoided by teachers. This is not only against the spirit of the National Curriculum, which expects young people to be taught about diversity and the 'need for mutual respect and understanding', it is also to ignore vital aspects of the 'legal and human rights and responsibilities underpinning society' (DfEE/QCA, 1999). But for many teachers it presents an uncomfortable challenge, especially in areas where there appears to be no overt racism (Hamilton et al., date unknown; Gaine, 1995) or where racial tensions are high. However, this is not the only reason for avoidance and it is useful to try to understand the reasons why the subject is approached with such caution.

Uncertainty about how to tackle race equality issues can arise from the fact that:

- teachers often feel uncertain of their own knowledge of different cultures and religions and may feel it is better to say nothing than unwittingly to cause offence. Teachers often feel that pupils themselves know more about issues of prejudice and multi-culturalism than they do
- teachers in largely white schools may feel that dealing explicitly with race has the effect of singling out the few ethnic minority students in the class as potential victims, creating divisiveness that was not there before. Many minority students have expressed their unease at being singled out in this way
- 'doing racism' is often construed as addressing the negative attitudes of some (probably white) students which can be uncomfortable for a teacher because it can alienate these students, making the teacher's role problematic
- many teachers fear that the normal ground rules for the open and democratic discussion of controversial issues cannot apply when race-related issues are debated. They fear that open discussion encourages or even legitimises pupils' racist views, causing offence to others in the class and possibly even spreading unacceptable ideas in the school.

Some of the above assumptions, if they are correct, are based on ideas about racism which have been shown by recent research to be out-dated. In schools the dominant anti-racist model portrays racism as something that is 'done' to black or Asian people by whites. This approach over-emphasises one element of racism (i.e. colour) to the detriment of a more comprehensive understanding of racism's true and complex nature. It also has the serious disadvantage of being divisive, casting one section of the class as potential perpetrators and the other as likely victims. Furthermore, it is just too simplistic, resisting any exploration or acknowledgement of the real feelings and reservations held by many 'ordinary' citizens.

From racism to 'racisms'

In fact, rather than discuss racism, it is more useful to think of 'racisms' (Bhavnani, 2001) since the forms and origins of racial prejudice are many and varied. Intolerance or friction between members of different national or ethnic groups can arise from widely differing causes. For teachers, this implies the need to recognise that racial prejudice in some form (weak or strong) is something to which people of every ethnic group are likely to succumb. Racism in some shape or form will be found in every classroom in the land. Asking the question, 'what exactly constitutes racism?' therefore is not a question that implies moral ambiguity but rather admits the contested nature of a question to which every citizen should give some thought. If the Welsh and the Scots dislike the English, is this entirely unfair? This is not such an easy question. And what about other types of racial prejudice and stereotype, including views about the Irish, the French, Germans, Belgians, Americans, various traveller communities, Jews, the Japanese, the Chinese and Africans, as well as Pakistanis, Bangladeshis, Indians and people of African-Caribbean origin?

How easy is it to say all these forms of racism are equally wrong? For example, you would have to be a saint to be able to forgive people who had slaughtered your parents or raped your daughters – so are there some forms of racism which, if not actually right, are at least understandable or forgivable? The exploration of issues in this way raises real questions about where we draw the lines and on what grounds, and can stimulate engaged thought in ways that pre-packaged moral messages cannot. Here, the research findings of social scientists can throw light on the issues, enabling young people to become more aware of the influences on their own lives and of the evidence that underpins the experiences, claims and attitudes of others. Bhavnani points to recent research showing that racisms can be gender-, age- and class-related. For example, working-class white young men tend to express their racism more violently than their female counterparts. For the middle classes, racism may be less confrontational but it expresses itself strongly through choice. 'White flight' (the term used to explain the exiting of urban areas by whites for the suburbs as the former become identified as 'black' areas) is one well-recognised illustration of this.

Students are entitled to understand the different guises of implicit and explicit racism which they may encounter locally or observe in society at large. To deconstruct racism in this exploratory and less judgemental fashion is to help young people become more aware of the influences on their own attitudes, allowing them to critically evaluate their own views without loss of face.

Promoting attitudinal change: practical strategies

Every teaching activity has an implicit set of aims and a theory of learning: the clearer teachers are about the methods they use, the more effective they are likely to be. An analysis of teaching materials about race and racism (Citizenship Foundation, 2003) reveals a number of strategies that are commonly drawn on and these are set out below. Each is distinctive and each attempts to promote a different kind of learning but they can be used together, if not within a lesson, then certainly across a teaching programme. Moreover, individual models may offer approaches that can be usefully applied in other areas of the education for equality sphere: gender, sexuality, disability, age or social class.

Knowledge and understanding

This method aims to increase understanding of the complexities of the issues. It aims to counter prejudice and media bias through better factual knowledge of the issues. This approach also aims to develop an appropriate grasp of technical vocabulary, enabling students to be more aware of how language may be used emotively or inaccurately.

Public discourse

This strategy introduces controversial issues through a third party analysis of the way issues are discussed in the public domain. In effect, it inducts young people into the nation's conversations. This allows prejudicial or offensive statements to be critically examined whilst avoiding the need for students to claim such ideas as their own in class debate. In this way, the teacher is more in control of what is said and how. Exploratory talk is always more enlightening than the oppositional stances adopted in traditional debates. The public discourse approach asks students to examine how arguments are used, what people see as key issues, whether claims made can be substantiated, how statistics are used, how arguments are 'spun' and so on. These may well be positions which students themselves identify with, but in this approach this need not be acknowledged publicly.

Legal and human rights

This approach is based on the political and legal equality of citizens. It is based on the belief that students should understand not only their own rights but appreciate that other people have similar rights. The legal rights stance looks at what rights are embedded in law, how law works and how citizens access such rights and whether the justice system actually delivers the equality citizens are entitled to. Human rights issues often underpin legal issues – indeed many human rights are embodied in the law. But the law does not always work in intended ways and human rights values need to inform the judgements of those who enforce the law. If not, it may deny some people the human rights they deserve.

The human rights approach is important because it introduces the fundamental idea that even democratic governments (as opposed to individual citizens) can be oppressive, especially to minority groups. Citizens need the important protections of human rights instruments. Human rights values and the international codes, such as the European Convention on Human Rights and the United Nations Declaration of the Rights of the Child, offer a perspective with which to critically evaluate the actual level of equality in society. In the UK, it is not easy to teach about the importance of human rights since our society scores well in international comparisons and many basic rights are taken for granted by students. However, human rights issues still need to be critically evaluated because they too are contested. Most have limits beyond which it would be wrong to take them and even human rights can come into conflict with other people's rights, for example in relation to freedom of speech. This is not to question the basic value of these rights but it is to equip young people with the necessary ability to think critically about them, without which they will never be able to implement them with sound judgement.

Moral reasoning

Teachers are often wary of engaging in moral education, and many confuse it with moral instruction. We need to distinguish between the promotion of a particular set of moral values and improving students' ability to discuss moral questions in general. Social and political issues are full of moral questions but teachers rarely see the need to give students the necessary moral language and concepts to debate them adequately (Huddleston and Rowe, 2001). Young people should be helped to acquire the language and procedures to enable them to ask questions such as 'What views do people hold on this issue and why?', 'What does justice mean?', 'How can we decide what is the common good?' and so on. Moral questions involve ideas such as good, bad, right and wrong, fairness, rules and laws, consequences, motivation and so on and raise crucial but difficult questions requiring specific forms of thought and vocabulary without which they cannot be properly addressed.

Empathy

This approach is very closely allied to the moral reasoning approach. Indeed, without empathy and perspective taking, moral reasoning will be defective. Empathic approaches, such as the use of first hand accounts from people who have experienced racism or prejudice, are often used to encourage students to identify with the suffering of victims and develop their ability to see particular issues from another's standpoint. Empathy-based approaches are best used not on their own (where the aim is merely to engender sympathy) but in conjunction with moral reasoning and other cognitive strategies.

Modeling good practice in the race sphere and beyond

As we have seen, behaviour, attitudes and values can all be usefully deconstructed in the classroom. Without doubt, behavioural change follows from increased understanding of an issue, improved empathic awareness and more mature moral thinking. If you change the way a person conceptualises a situation, you inevitably influence the kind of reaction that follows. But moral learning is also very strongly influenced by observing others and reflecting on the example they set. For this reason, teachers and schools should seek to ensure consistency between the values they claim to uphold and those underpinning whole school practices and policies. Few things are more undermining to claims of respecting all students than the disproportionate representation of a particular ethnic or gender group in the school's exclusion statistics.

A chance to renew the equalities agenda?

I have argued in this chapter that teaching for attitudinal change about equality issues is complex and full of philosophical and psychological challenges. It is hard to ask a teacher to take an exploratory stance regarding what decent people see as an obvious social evil. Yet this fundamental position need not be compromised by the willingness to admit that issues like racism need to be subjected to critical enquiry. Even if, as a society, we say that prejudice and inequality are wrong, the question of what we mean by these terms still stares every citizen in the face and it is right that these issues are explored within the classroom and the wider school. While there is no suggestion that this sort of learning should be restricted to the Citizenship classroom in particular, the space opened up by National Curriculum Citizenship provides an opportunity to take a fresh look at work in the equalities education field.

I have also suggested that an open-ended exploratory approach is not only philosophically right, but that it is educationally more robust and defensible against attacks of liberal bias. I have, finally, tried to argue (see also Citizenship Foundation, 2003), and this is probably the crucial point, that such an approach is far more likely to cause students to re-appraise their thinking and, therefore, more likely to achieve a shift towards mature, reflective thinking than any amount of well-intentioned preaching.

REFERENCES

Bhavnani, R. (2001) *Rethinking Interventions in Racism*. Stoke-on-Trent: Trentham Books.

Citizenship Foundation (2003) *Education for Citizenship, Diversity and Race Equality: a practical guide*. London: Citizenship Foundation and DfES websites (see Organisations and Websites section on page 352).

DfEE/QCA (1999) *The National Curriculum*. London: DfEE – Qualifications and Curriculum Authority.

Gaine, C. (1995) *Still No Problem Here*. Stoke-on-Trent: Trentham Books.

Hamilton, C., Rejtmen-Bennett, R. and Roberts, M. (date unknown) *Racism and Race Relations in Predominantly White Schools: preparing pupils for life in a Multi-cultural society*. Essex: The Children's Legal Centre.

Huddleston, T. and Rowe, D. (2001) *Good Thinking: Education for Citizenship and Moral Responsibility, Volumes 1, 2 and 3*. London: Evans Brothers/Citizenship Foundation.

Wilkins, C. (2001) 'Student Teachers and Attitudes towards 'Race': the role of citizenship education in addressing racism through the curriculum', *Westminster Studies in Education*, 24(1). Oxford: Carfax Publishing.

FURTHER READING

Gillborn, D. (1995) *Racism and Antiracism in Real Schools: Theory, Policy, Practice.* Milton Keynes: Open University Press.

Osler, Audrey (ed.) (2000) *Citizenship and Democracy in Schools: Diversity, Identity and Equality.* Stoke-on-Trent: Trentham Books.

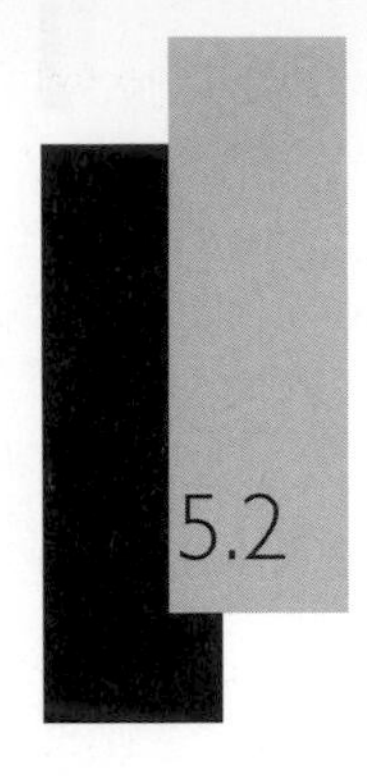

Education for a Green World: Learning about the Environment and Sustainability

Barry Dufour

Environmental Education, Citizenship and the National Curriculum

Environmental Education is a key component of Citizenship in the revised National Curriculum for 2000 as part of the knowledge base at Key Stages 3 and 4. In Key Stage 3, it is located within the context of learning about the environmental implications of the world as a global community, and in Key Stage 4, it appears as *the wider issues of global interdependence including sustainable development and Local Agenda 21* (DfEE/QCA, 1999a). Local Agenda 21 refers to local action plans on sustainable development based on Agenda 21 which formed part of the deliberations and agreements at the Rio Earth Summit in 1992. As such, this summit made the very link that underpins this chapter: between the local and environmentally friendly and the global and sustainable. I deal with 'Development and Global Education' in the following chapter.

Environmental Education: a recent history

Environmental Education has been of interest to teachers and pupils in primary and secondary schools long before it became an element of the National Curriculum Council's cross-curricular issues from 1990 onwards, as *Curriculum Guidance* 7 (NCC, 1990), or part of the subject of Citizenship implemented in secondary schools in 2002. Since the late 1960s, there has been a growing political and public concern about the environment, and the modern environmental movement in Britain dates from this time (Huckle, 1990). All of the great social and political movements of the twentieth century have inevitably made an impact on the school curriculum and this is certainly the case with Environmental Education.

During the late 1960s and early 1970s in England, there were many educational materials on the full range of environmental issues available to teachers and students including educational games, films, school texts and topic books and these were complemented by various official curriculum projects (Lawton and Dufour, 1973). The common concerns then were very similar to today's: the impact of population growth, the local and world environment, natural resources, food, the land, the atmosphere and biosphere, the conservation of nature, the impact of the motor car, the impact of towns, technology, the consumer society, and debates about the future. In the 1980s, several key publications underlined the importance of Environmental Education in schools including the HMI document *Environmental Education from 5–16* (HMI, 1989). The 1990s began with the publication of a series of National Curriculum Council booklets on cross-curricular themes, skills and dimensions including the one on Environmental Education cited above (NCC, 1990). Although there was, by this time, a growing divergence of 'green' perspectives, the notion of sustainability was now firmly established worldwide as *the* key concept for an understanding of the environment. This can be seen especially in Geography as a subject in the National Curriculum in England.

Geography from the 1990s: Environmental Education, sustainability and Citizenship

In Chapter 2.4, David Barrs deals with Geography's contribution to the current Citizenship agenda at length. Here, I want to emphasise a particular point: as a school subject, Geography has always made an important contribution to Environmental Education and Citizenship. In the pre-2000 National Curriculum, it was assumed that Environmental Education would be embedded in Science and Geography. Indeed, during the 1990s, at Key Stage 3, the Cambridge Geography Project included a text by David Lambert called *Green Pieces* (Lambert, 1992) which contained a major emphasis on the environment including sections on organic food and farming, pollution, environmental disasters, climate and the greenhouse effect, water as a scarce resource, and the consumption of finite resources. Lambert, formerly based at the University of London Institute of Education, is one of the leading Geography specialists on Environmental Education.

The revised Geography National Curriculum of 2000 made Environmental Education more explicit with statutory objectives on 'knowledge and understanding of environmental change and sustainable development' with students required to '. . . explore the idea of sustainable development' (DfEE/QCA, 1999b). Teachers and students therefore have a brief to engage in wide-ranging critical investigation. Lambert has also co-edited a key resource to guide Geography teachers in their exploration of Citizenship (Lambert and Machon, 2001).

Environmental Education and Citizenship today

Important sources on Environmental Education today, which will be helpful for Citizenship co-ordinators, include the 1995 OECD study of Environmental Education which illustrates developments in several countries, *Environmental Learning for the 21st Century* (OECD, 1995). Also, the (Conservative) government strategy for Environmental Education in England entitled *Taking Environmental Education into the 21st Century* (DfEE, 1996) is an important document because achieving government policy status is a key landmark in the progress of any subject's status and viability. Major handbooks written for teachers and educational decision-makers include the two books associated with Joy Palmer. The first is *The Handbook of Environmental Education* by Palmer and Neal (1994), both key activists in the National Association for Environmental Education in the UK. It is a wide-ranging guide to teaching and learning resources, curriculum development, and creating school policies. Joy Palmer's later book, *Environmental Education in the 21st Century* (Palmer, 1998) is a thorough study of the issues, theory and practice and includes a comparison of work in different countries which demonstrates that Environmental Education, at varying levels of intensity, is now a feature of school curricula across the globe. Her summary of the key issues in the world environmental agenda (in Part 2 of her book) includes:

- population growth, poverty and inequality
- food and agriculture
- tropical forests
- biological diversity
- desertification and drought
- freshwater
- oceans and coasts
- energy
- atmosphere and climate
- managing solid wastes and sewage
- hazardous substances (including nuclear waste)
- development and environment.

And critically, in Palmer's view, this last theme should either be first or seen as being the common link between all of the environmental issues.

There are hundreds of sub-topics within each of the above themes, including the analysis of local, national and global dimensions, that school students can investigate and involve themselves in as part of their Citizenship studies. Of course, more modern terminology would be used nowadays, such as investigations into:

- the Rio Summit of 1992, the Kyoto Protocol of 1997 and the subsequent progress up to the Johannesburg Summit in 2002, being the ten-year follow-up to the Rio Summit
- junk food (the *Jamie's School Dinners* TV series presented by Jamie Oliver on Channel 4 in 2005 had an enormous effect on raising awareness of food issues – see the Food Commisssion website for general issues on food – www.foodcomm.org.uk)
- recycling
- renewable energy
- global warming and climate change
- threats to habitats and species decline (such as the campaign in 2005 to save the orang-utan from extinction because of rainforest clearance in Borneo and Sumatra to exploit palm-oil production – see *The Oil for Apes Scandal* at www.foe.co.uk).

Students might also wish to look at the history and activities of some of the major environmental lobbying organisations such as Friends of the Earth, the Worldwide Fund for Nature, Greenpeace, and many others; the websites and publications of these organisations contain a wealth of information and are listed in the Organisations and Websites section on pages 352–8.

Government (and other) initiatives in the twenty-first century: ESD takes centre stage

Environmental Education has the support of the Labour administration and in 2002 the Qualifications and Curriculum Authority published its curriculum guidance and a new website on Education for Sustainable Development (QCA, 2002), using seven core concepts:

- Citizenship and stewardship
- Sustainable change
- Needs and rights of future generations
- Interdependence
- Diversity
- Uncertainty and precaution
- Quality of life, equity and justice.

In addition, the House of Commons Select Committee on Environmental Audit published its Sixth Special Report (House of Commons, 2003) and received an official response to this by the DfES for schools in September 2003 when it published its Sustainable Development Action Plan for Education and Skills (DfES, 2003[1]). This coincided with an Ofsted report in 2003 reporting on good practice on ESD (which has become the short hand for this area of work) in a range of secondary and primary schools (Ofsted, 2003). There are now many successful projects on ESD in English schools including the Learning for Sustainable Cities Project run by the Manchester Development Education Project. The project links schools in Greater Manchester with schools in several other countries and involves teachers and students working on various environmental and related activities, all of which is summarised on the web at www.dep.org.uk/cities. As this book goes to press in May 2006, the DfES is reported to be taking the sustainability agenda further with the publication of guidance on the development of 'sustainable schools'. Certainly, sustainability is a key dimension of the kind of Citizenship-rich schools called for in these pages.

The issues and challenges for Environmental Education and Citizenship

Environmental Education, along with many other areas of discourse which do not enjoy the status of 'subject' in the National Curriculum, encounters the problems of all peripheral and cross-curricular issues: how to move from the

DfEE/QCA (1999b) 'Geography Key Stages 1–3', in *The National Curriculum for England*. London: DfEE/QCA.

DfES (2003) *Sustainable Development Action Plan for Education and Skills*[1].

HMI (1989) *Environmental Education from 5–16*. London: HMSO.

House of Commons (2003) *Government Response to the Committee's Tenth Report, Session 2002–03 on Learning the Sustainability Lesson. Sixth Special Report of Session 2002–03*. Produced by the House of Commons Audit Committee. HC 1221. London: The Stationery Office.

Huckle, J. (1990) 'Environmental Education: Teaching for a Sustainable Future', in B. Dufour (ed.) *The New Social Curriculum*. Cambridge: Cambridge University Press.

Lambert, D. (1992) *Green Pieces*. The Cambridge Geography Project. Cambridge: Cambridge University Press.

Lambert, D. and Machon, P. (2001) *Citizenship Through Secondary Geography*. London: RoutledgeFalmer.

Lawton, D. and Dufour, B. (1973) *The New Social Studies*. London: Heinemann Educational Books. (See pages 342–46 for a brief summary of school approaches and resources on the environment in this period.)

NCC (1990) *Environmental Education – Curriculum Guidance 7*. York: National Curriculum Council.

OECD (1995) *Environmental Learning for the 21st Century*. Paris: Organisation for Economic Co-operation and Development.

Ofsted (2003) *Taking the First Step . . . Towards an Education for Sustainable Development*. Ofsted, HMI 1658.

Palmer, J. and Neal, P. (1994) *The Handbook of Environmental Education*. London: Routledge.

Palmer, J. (1998) *Environmental Education in the 21st Century*. London: Routledge.

QCA (2002) *Education for Sustainable Development*. London: Qualifications and Curriculum Authority. This was a short pamphlet outlining the principles of ESD but was also intended to launch the ESD website now run by QCA. See www.nc.uk.net/esd

NOTE

1 The DfES document noted above, *Sustainable Development Action Plan for Education and Skills*, has yet to find formal publication. There is no date or ISBN on the publication but it was launched at the *Sustrans Safe Routes to School* Conference in Leicester in September 2003. A critical account of the document appeared in *The Guardian* newspaper on 14 October 2003, suggesting that it is not an action plan, was rushed out and contains no targets. The article was called *Unsustainable* and was written by John Crace. Once published, any document should be available from the DfES or The Stationery Office.

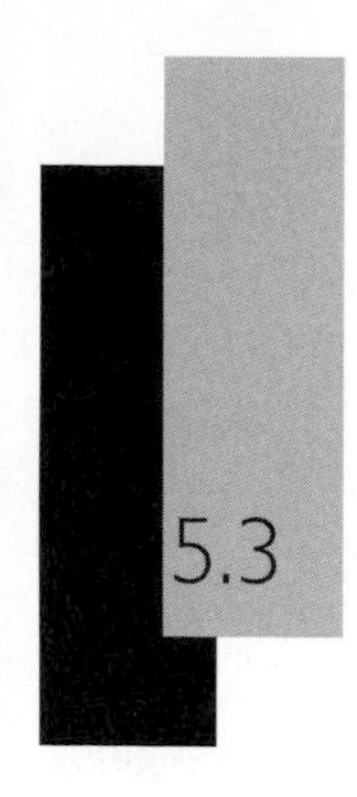

Education for a Just World: Development Education and Global Education

Barry Dufour

Development and Global Education and National Curriculum Citizenship

There are specific references to students needing to learn about the global community and global interdependence at both Key Stage 3 and Key Stage 4 in the Citizenship Programmes of Study (DfEE/QCA, 1999). The content and skills prescribed therein for 11–16 year olds fall within the broad remit of Global Education. The themes include human rights, cultural diversity and the importance of playing a part in democratic processes; and the skills to be encouraged include studying and debating political and social issues. The QCA Key Stages 3 and 4 Schemes of Work for Citizenship (QCA, 2001 and 2002) also offer exemplar units from these areas, such as Unit 12 for Key Stage 4 pupils of 14–16 years of age and entitled *Global Issues, Local Action* which explores ways of involving students in Local Agenda 21 issues emerging from the 1992 Rio Earth Summit, which I discuss in Chapter 5.2 devoted to Environmental Education.

There are many definitions of Global Education, from UNESCO, Oxfam and various academics and educationists in the field (Osler and Vincent, 2002) but all agree it is about educational programmes that attempt to develop young people's critical understanding of global interdependence in its many forms, grounded in principles of fairness and justice, and exploring a wide range of themes that are featured below. An early and abiding area of focus was that of Development Education, and many now see this as forming a key aspect of Global Education.

Development Education and the global perspective

Development Education in UK schools had its origins in the 1960s in teaching about poverty in Third World countries. The movement was active throughout the 1970s and 1980s and was responsible for an impressive range of teaching ideas and resources for schools (Dufour, 1982) but its aims and curriculum coverage have gradually broadened into a comprehensive treatment of world development and global issues. In short, Development Education has progressed from a study of *poorer* societies to a global consideration of the interdependence of *all* societies; a shift given a new pertinence by the protests that have emerged at a succession of world trade summits since the early 1990s.

Against this background, the Development Education Association (DEA) was set up in 1993 and is now an umbrella organisation for over 240 partner organisations in the UK and overseas, all actively committed to promoting Development (and Global) Education in schools and beyond. The journal of the DEA, *The Development Education Journal* (published three times a year), continues to be an outstanding source of debate and ideas for teachers and Development Education professionals. Exploring the developed–developing/North–South link remains the key priority but this is now framed much more securely within a global context, especially around a critical analysis of global trade and commerce and the public policies of western governments, western trade and political alliances and western-based multi-nationals. Thus, the connection with Citizenship Education is clear: the personal and political choices and actions of citizens, policy-makers and organisations in one society influence not just those in that society but those elsewhere and, indeed, those much further away.

A brief history of Global Education

Global Education has for a long time flourished in the USA, Canada, Australia and some European countries. In the UK, Global Education in schools has its roots in the activity and later influence of the Council for Education in World Citizenship (created in 1939) and the subsequent World Studies Project set up in 1973 and the Schools Council World Studies 8–13 Project in the 1980s, with nearly half of all LEAs in England having some kind of involvement with this project (Dufour, 1990). Much of this work was carried forward for teachers by INSET initiatives run in the 1980s and 1990s by David Selby and Graham Pike of the Centre for Global Education at the University of York and through their influential publication, *Global Teacher, Global Learner* (Pike and Selby, 1988). During the 1990s, with the National Curriculum prescribing a strictly subject-based programme (apart from the cross-curricular issues), World Studies and Global Education and Development Education struggled to survive in many schools. However, where these themes or courses have survived, they find themselves at the centre of a genuine renewal of interest at the start of the twenty-first century, in response to an increased public awareness of globalisation, global threats and inequalities and partly as a result of the arrival of Citizenship in the National Curriculum.

Global Education and Citizenship today

There are now many programmes in Global Education and Citizenship. A vital background book for teachers, to further their understanding of the definitions, developments, research, concepts and practice in relation to Global Education in England and three other European countries, is Osler and Vincent's book *Citizenship and the Challenge of Global Education* (2002). An important publication from the DfEE, DFID, QCA and the DEA in 2000, *Developing a Global Dimension in the School Curriculum*, gave an official recognition to Global Education (DfEE, 2000). This short booklet outlines how the different subject areas can tackle it and how wider school activities, such as a whole-school policy, community activities and school-linking projects with schools in less economically developed countries, can play a part. It defines the core concepts of Global Education as:

- Citizenship
- Sustainable development
- Social justice
- Values and perceptions
- Diversity
- Interdependence
- Conflict resolution
- Human rights.

Oxfam produced its own brief guide, *A Curriculum for Global Citizenship* (Oxfam, 2002) with similar concepts but divided into teaching objectives grouped around three areas: knowledge and understanding; skills; and values and attitudes. In 2001, the DEA published a further brief but helpful booklet, *Citizenship Education: the Global Dimension – Guidance for Key Stages 3 and 4* (DEA, 2001). It explores how the three strands of Citizenship Education – political literacy, social and moral responsibility, and community involvement – can each be given a global dimension and suggests a range of ideas and activities, with some case study examples from different schools and subjects.

Indeed, many school subjects have incorporated global dimensions. National Curriculum Geography for 11–14 year olds requires pupils to learn about interdependence, global citizenship and sustainable development. National Curriculum Citizenship programmes are *required* to include a global dimension. GCSE Integrated Humanities courses explore core concepts related to Global Education, and World Sociology – a new option in AQA Advanced Level Sociology – is gradually increasing in popularity (there is an excellent text on the latter from Cohen and Kennedy, 2000).

Similarly, in relation to the social sciences, the Royal Anthropological Institute (RAI) approved in 2003 a new Strategic Plan that includes a commitment to explore the potential of the subject, which has the study of comparative societies at its core, in pre-university settings such as schools and FE colleges. Already, progress has been made on a number of areas including plans for updating *Discovering Anthropology*, a resource guide for schools, looking at how comparative perspectives can be built into Citizenship for 11–16 year olds, and drawing up early plans for a proposed A Level in Anthropology. Global Education should take account of life in small-scale societies and the fact that many school students of all ages are interested in the threats to indigenous peoples. Organisations such as Survival International can be useful in providing information on successful development and transition as well as the plight of many of these peoples in countries around the entire globe.

While many of the Global Education publications discussed above provide suggested concepts, ideas, activities and case studies of good practice in schools, it is still the case that teachers and students need hard information and resources that address these ideas. Commercial publishers are producing topic books on some of the major themes but, beyond this, four main sources can be located:

1 Activities linked with local development projects can be inspirational for local teachers and students but also for those who may not be in the particular local areas of operation. Nationally, the DEA website offers an overview of these approaches – www.dea.org.uk.
2 A wide range of other websites, only a few of which can be mentioned, provide current information. For example, the DFID (the Department for International Development) operates a special DEA-endorsed website for schools (www.globaldimension.org.uk) and features a vast range of available school resources reviewed by teachers and lecturers.
3 Major monthly publications such as the *New Internationalist* provide an excellent resource for older students.
4 And last but not least, Oxfam itself, through its website, www.oxfam.org.uk, its publications, its helpful and knowledgeable staff and the famed *Oxfam Catalogue for Schools: Resources for Global Citizenship*, (Oxfam, 2006, produced each year) continues to make a major contribution to the global awareness of school students and adults. Amongst their recent publications, *The Challenge of Globalisation* (Oxfam, 2003) is a teaching and resource book for secondary schools which explores the complex issue of globalisation, now a central feature of the modern post-communist world and exercising the concerns of academics, politicians, protesters and people across the globe.

Active teaching and learning in Development and Global Education

One of the fundamental features of both Development and Global Education as these have developed in the UK in recent decades has been the emphasis on the process of teaching and learning as much as on the content. As with Citizenship, active, co-operative and experiential learning has been at the heart of all the good practice and curriculum projects outlined above. While it is certainly not the case that *all* of the Citizenship agenda can be taught and learnt in this dynamic manner, much of it *should* be and, therefore, Citizenship teachers have much to benefit from the methods employed and developed by development and global educators. For example, the Get Global! programme is a skills-based approach to active Global Citizenship for Key Stages 3 and 4 and contains dozens of worksheets, games and activities (Actionaid, 2003). Large numbers of secondary schools in England are using these approaches to address aspects of the Citizenship Curriculum. Another example is the United Nations Association which supports the MUNGA – the Model United Nations General Assembly – programme whereby groups of schools come together for a day-long simulation with students representing different countries to argue a position on various themes including poverty and Third World debt. Likewise the Citizenship Foundation's Giving Nation programme involves a critical look at charitable aid, not least in international projects, through promoting innovative school-based programmes and activities including *g-week*.

Styles of teaching and learning therefore are fundamental if we are to address the concern of a teacher at a school in Leicester who was overheard saying to a colleague, 'How do you teach international trade to 15 year old girls on a wet Friday afternoon?' Some aspects of the content and skills in Citizenship and in Development and Global Education are new to most teachers but if the teaching is uninspired then these major areas of learning, like any other school subject, have the power to disengage – whereas their mission is the opposite. The best practice in Development and Global Education can point the way.

The World in 2005

World events in 2005 provided much for the student of Global Education to ponder. The G8 summit of world leaders in Scotland during July attracted wide interest from everyone including lobbyists and protesters determined to ensure that the leaders listened to the people. The Live 8 pop and rock concerts linked with the summit also hammered home the concerns of millions of people, along with the activities of the campaigns for Trade Justice, Drop the Debt and the hugely popular Make Poverty History.

As a result, significant moves were made on commitments to increase aid, on debt reduction and on the cancellation of the debts of 18 extremely poor countries.

From globalisation to justice: meeting students' aspirations

In 1998, a MORI research project for the DEA on secondary school students' attitudes found that 81 per cent of them believed it important to learn about global issues at school. But 54 per cent felt powerless to change the world (MORI, 1998). And yet thousands of school students were involved and were empowered in the 2005 protests and campaigns. It may be hoped that the impact of these kinds of events and campaigns and the impact of Development and Global Education in schools will lead to greater confidence amongst students in their willingness and ability to speak up, to take action and to contribute towards making the world a more just place.

CASE STUDY
Botanica

This is a simulation exercise on global education available on the internet at http://botanica.clc-leicester.org.uk

This highly engaging and effective educational game can be played by primary or secondary school students and adults in any setting. It works as a one-hour workshop or day-long simulation preceded by a series of preparatory sessions. It can be modified to suit different scenarios. In the original version, 'Botanica' is a country, rich in natural resources but economically poor and with a national debt. Students form citizen groups with different jobs and points of view within the country such as government officials, media people, plantation workers, shantytown dwellers, builders and so forth. The simulation involves a day of voting on whether Botanica should host a major international sporting event (such as the Olympic Games). Different groups lobby each other. Students work alongside teachers and invited members of the local community, all in role. Major issues on the environment, tourism and development are explored and citizenship skills practised. The game was devised by Peter Batty and Sue Baughan in partnership with the University of Leicester Botanic Garden.

REFERENCES

Actionaid (2003) *Get Global! A Skills-based Approach to Active Global Citizenship for Key Stages 3 and 4*. London: Actionaid (Available for purchase from several of the global/development organisations but also available in PDF format from a number of sites including www.actionaid.org/schoolsandyouth)

Cohen and Kennedy (2000) *Global Sociology*. London: Palgrave.

DEA (2001) *Citizenship Education: the Global Dimension – Guidance for Key Stages 3 and 4*. London: Development Education Association.

DfEE/QCA (1999) 'Citizenship Key Stages 3–4', in *The National Curriculum for England*. London: DfEE/QCA.

DfEE (2000) *Developing a Global Dimension in the School Curriculum*. London: DfEE. (DfEE Ref. 0115/2000).

Dufour (1982) See Fyson, N.L. 'Development Education: Teaching About The Third World', by Nance Lui Fyson, in B. Dufour (ed.) *New Movements in the Social Sciences and Humanities*. London: Maurice Temple Smith.

Dufour, B. (1990) See Pike, G. 'Global Education: Learning in a World of Change', in B. Dufour (ed.) *The New Social Curriculum*. Cambridge: Cambridge University Press.

MORI (1998) *Children's Knowledge of Global Issues*. London: MORI.

Osler, A. and Vincent, K. (2002) *Citizenship and the Challenge of Global Education*. London: Trentham Books.

Oxfam (2002) *A Curriculum for Global Citizenship*. Oxford: Oxfam.

Oxfam (2003) *The Challenge of Globalisation. A Handbook for Teachers of 11–16 year olds.* Oxford: Oxfam.

Oxfam (2006) *Catalogue for Schools 2006 – Resources for Global Citizenship.* Oxford: Oxfam. This is an annual publication updated each year.

Pike, G. and Selby, D. (1988) *Global Teacher, Global Learner*. London: Hodder and Stoughton.

QCA (2001) *Citizenship. A Scheme of Work for Key Stage 3*. London: QCA.

QCA (2002) *Citizenship. A Scheme of Work for Key Stage 4*. London: QCA.

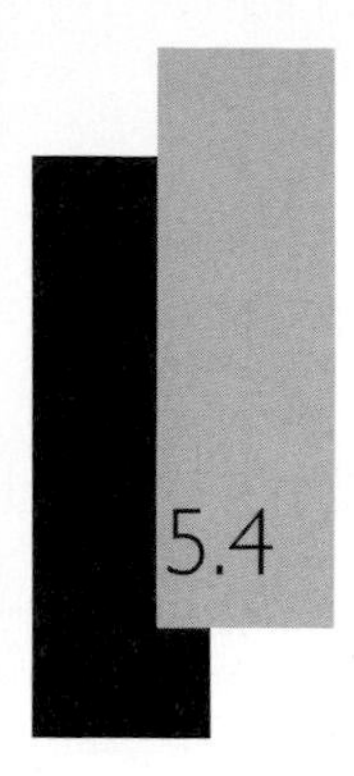

Education for a Safe World: Conflict, Peace Education and Conflict Resolution

Barry Dufour

Dealing with issues of war and conflict in the classroom has a special urgency today in the post-9/11 world and yet there has been little activity at the official DfES level or in most schools to promote peace education, conflict studies and conflict resolution. It is truly amazing that the lowest priority in the curriculum in schools in England has been given to the systematic discussion and exploration of current world conflicts. Yet, education for peace and international understanding has been a central component of key UNESCO pronouncements on education and Citizenship for many years (UNESCO, 2000). Audrey Osler and Kerry Vincent rightly include the issue of peace within their definition of Global Education (which I cite in Chapter 5.3) and then go on to say how:

> *The terrorist attacks of 11 September 2001 and their aftermath serve to reinforce the need for an education which prepares young people to live together in an interdependent world. The scale and shock of the attacks left many young people (and adults) feeling vulnerable and powerless. The repercussions are not only felt at national and international levels but also within local communities across the world.* (Osler and Vincent, 2002)

There is also very little mention of war and conflict or education for peace in the Citizenship National Curriculum subject document. The Key Stage 3 Programme of Study refers to children knowing about 'the importance of resolving conflict fairly' and, in the section on learning about the world as a global community, there is a brief reference to the United Nations. Key Stage 4 is similar – just a mention of the United Nations and global interdependence. Wars, terrorism and education for peace do not, explicitly, feature (DfEE/QCA, 1999).

There is slightly more specificity in the QCA Citizenship Schemes of Work. In the Key Stage 3 folder, there are two relevant booklets – one entitled *Citizenship and History: Why Is It So Difficult To Keep Peace in the World Today?* and *Citizenship and Religious Education: How Do we Deal with Conflict?* (QCA, 2001). But the Key Stage 4 Scheme of Work is devoid of reference to this major area. This low level of prioritisation has not always been the case in schools.

A lot of work was conducted in the 1970s and 1980s in British schools in World Studies and, as I have discussed in Chapter 5.3, Development Education. During this time, the Centre for Peace Studies at St Martins College of Higher Education in Lancaster was operating along with another influential unit, the Centre for Global Education at York University. Many schools were involved in their programmes. During the 1990s, partly related to the narrow prescriptions of the National Curriculum, much school activity in this area declined. However, the Bradford University Peace Studies Department was active and influential throughout this period and still is, and currently, at the academic level, peace education and studies of conflict resolution have never been more popular. An internet search for 'peace studies' offers nearly one million site references with many major academic courses and specialist centres across the world involved in research, teaching, consultancy and political representation. In the UK, two of the most important centres are the Department of Peace Studies at Bradford University and the Quaker-linked Richardson Institute for Peace and Conflict Research at Lancaster University. Unfortunately, at the secondary school level, there have been only a few initiatives in the recent period, some in Northern Ireland, some associated with the Quakers and some through a few schools linked with UNESCO projects.

Conflict resolution at the interpersonal level at school is an important area: usually and correctly framed within the context of PSHE rather than Citizenship and sometimes explored through circle time, especially in primary schools. Typical areas include anger management, dealing with bullying, mediation, co-operative games and reconciliation. The Quaker Bookshop in London (Friends House, 173–77, Euston Road, London, NW1 2BJ) has a wide selection of background books for teachers and teaching resources including the delightfully titled *A Volcano in My Tummy (Helping Children to Handle Anger)*. However, using the more public conflicts that fall properly within the remit of Citizenship (between countries or communities and/or over political issues), and to which I now turn, can create a positive backwash into the personal domain: students understand their own conflicts – and the potential for and barriers to resolution – having considered a broader conflict at one remove. Just as the personal can become public, the public, too, can become personal. And, given the diversity of many classrooms and the personal-political histories therein, they are often one and the same.

Key themes and episodes in international and armed conflict

In spite of the current low profile of peace education, it could be argued that there are several fundamental themes that would form an essential part of any school work on peace, wars and conflict resolution. They feature the inclusion of some of the bleakest periods in twentieth and twenty-first century history but, as always, there are opportunities for considering forces for good, for reconciliation and for peace – and it is vital that pupils are encouraged to consider these aspects as part of their general focus along with the details of atrocities and disasters. History, English, PSHE, Humanities and Citizenship lessons are all areas where these themes can and should be explored more extensively.

While commercially-produced school books, other materials and curriculum projects for studies of peace and conflict are few and far between, peace and conflict studies is one of the key areas where the worldwide web plays an instant and crucial role. Teachers and students can gain access to the most current information and can investigate the activities, efforts and recent information from the major humanitarian organisations including Oxfam, Amnesty International, Save the Children, the United Nations and hundreds of other organisations, a few of which are listed in the Organisations and Websites section on pages 352–8. These organisations often lead the field in providing research, training and educational resources in the broad field of peace and conflict resolution.

A set of suggested key themes or episodes are briefly discussed below. In addition to these, teachers and students may wish to investigate other areas. The aims of confronting these themes are not only to understand what happened but to develop ideas and concepts on why these tragedies occur, how they are or might be resolved and how they can be prevented in future. This involves a mix of factual understanding and the development of moral perspectives about human dignity, worth and peace. Of course, two things go without saying: first, that teachers need to approach these aspects with care given the sensitivity of these topics for many of their students; and second, that their consideration should play a key part in any Citizenship programme worthy of the name.

Hiroshima and Nagasaki

Although in a catalogue of horrors of the twentieth century, we could start with World War I – and the general degradation of World War II, including the Holocaust, would not be far behind – the impact of the use of nuclear weapons on Hiroshima and Nagasaki in August 1945 is still burned on our consciousness in the twenty-first century, both for the Japanese nation and for all of humanity. It would be hugely remiss if secondary school pupils did not have the opportunity to study this in history or as a case study in their Citizenship work. The Mayor of Hiroshima said on 6 August 2000, the 55th anniversary of the dropping of the atomic bomb on Hiroshima, that this very act and Hiroshima itself should be the symbol of peace for the twenty-first century. There is no shortage of school history books and topic books on this subject, and a web search for 'Hiroshima Peace Museum' brings up 10,000 internet links, with the 'Hiroshima Peace Site' being one of the main ones.

Nuclear weapons and weapons of mass destruction

Although the Cold War is now over – the prime *raison d'être* for the nuclear arms race – several countries still possess nuclear weapons. Similar destructive power exists in the form of biological and chemical weapons. It is worth noting that the suggestion that Iraq possessed weapons of mass destruction was one of the reasons for the invasion in 2003 by the United States and its allies including the UK. Most countries in the world adhere to the 1972 Biological and Toxic Weapons Convention and the 1993 Chemical Weapons Convention with both Conventions banning the development, production and stockpiling of these agents and weapons – but some countries have not subscribed.

The arms trade

The proportion of Gross Domestic Product (GDP) that many countries spend on arms along with concerns about their supply and demand are among the key debates. The USA dominates the world supply but many other countries are involved. The global supply of small arms is also an issue, some of it illegal. The trade continually places the world, and its communities, at risk by providing the means for conflict and has repercussions on other areas, such as development, as outlined in a recent report by Oxfam entitled *Guns or Growth: Assessing the Impact of Arms Sales on Sustainable Development* (Oxfam, 2004), published as part of Oxfam's contribution to the campaign entitled Controlarms. Some informative books for school students include *The No-Nonsense Guide to the Arms Trade* (Burrows, 2003) and *Shattered Lives: the Case for Tough International Arms Control* (Oxfam/Amnesty International, 2003). Key websites on this theme are Campaign Against Arms Trade (www.caat.org.uk), and controlarms.org. Local campaigns around gun crime, especially in inner city areas characterised by high levels of deprivation, provide a rich if tragic source of Citizenship learning and, just maybe, a force for social change.

Landmines

Landmines and unexploded ordinance kill or injure 2000 people worldwide every month, often women and children working in the fields of recently war-torn countries. The Mine Ban Treaty of 1997 has greatly reduced the production of landmines and there are now extensive programmes for mine clearance. But some countries have not signed the treaty and they hold 90 per cent of the world stockpile – these countries include the USA, China and Russia, with the latter two countries still manufacturing mines. Many devices similar to landmines, such as fragmentation weapons, are not covered by the treaty (Smith, 2003). Further information can be obtained from several of the campaigning organisations including The Halo Trust, Landmine Action, and the Mines Advisory Group (see Organisations and Websites on page 352).

Current conflicts across the globe

The BBC2 television documentary, *One Day of War*, screened in the UK on 27 May 2004 calculated that there were at least 70 major conflicts in operation around the globe at that time. They were mainly internal to the countries and included Nepal, Chechnya, Somalia and 67 others. Poverty or scarce resources were common themes, and these will surely continue to be so in future. As part of these conflicts, two people were killed every minute worldwide. In Sudan, for example, there were accusations of genocide involving Muslim Arabs against black Africans. Children are hugely involved in many of these conflicts, often armed and not even in their teenage years. Many of the aid agencies provide up-to-date information on these conflicts and run funding appeals. By consulting the websites of the aid agencies, teachers and students, if inclined, can become active in learning about these problems and can work together in generating awareness and in active humanitarian support such as fund-raising. A key example was the Sudan crisis in 2004 which brought wide-scale interest from schools, not least through the *Giving Nation* programme outlined at g-nation.co.uk.

Refugees and asylum seekers

There are millions of refugees in the world escaping war and persecution. Many relocate but remain in their own country, such as in Angola or Sudan, but many seek refuge abroad. The largest numbers, in their millions, have moved to Pakistan and Iran fleeing from the constant fighting in Afghanistan, and to Jordan and the Palestine Authority fleeing from Israel. Since refugee and asylum panics often occupy sections of the British press and with tighter laws against settlement in many parts of Europe, it becomes important that school students are given an opportunity to look at the issues in a considered manner, not only when some of the young people in the class or the school are themselves asylum seekers or refugees. The Home Office website (www.homeoffice.gov.uk) offers statistics, procedures and policy outlines while a number of materials from the *Oxfam Catalogue for Schools* offer case studies and analyses of the refugee position. The Refugee Council website (www.refugeecouncil.org.uk) also contains important information. An outstanding audio-visual resource entitled *The Refuge Project: Learning about Refugees with Refugees* was published in 2003 by the Aegis Trust (see Figure 1) and, as this book goes to press, a major new resource for young refugees and asylum seekers is in preparation at the Citizenship Foundation.

Figure 1
The Refuge Project: Learning about Refugees with Refugees
Aegis Trust, 2003

This project, which consists of a multi-media pack of materials for teachers and students, explores issues of conflict, genocide and peace as a background to a study of refugees and asylum seekers. As well as these themes, it covers dozens of major issues such as racism, xenophobia and the role of the mass media. The pack features a DVD, information and teaching ideas, lesson worksheets, documents for classroom use, and personal profiles of actual refugees. The project was based on students and teachers from Nottinghamshire schools working together and talking with refugees. It is an attractively produced and highly powerful pack and deserves to be in every secondary school.

More information and purchasing details can be obtained from the website: www.aegistrust.org

The wider implications of learning about conflict and peace

Throughout this work, it is important that students should not only learn about the causes and development of the conflicts but also about resolution. There are moral reasons and reasons of historical balance for ensuring this, with the constant perspective that wherever there are conflicts, horrors and unspeakable human degradation, there are always countervailing efforts for reconciliation, resolution, settlement and peace, sometimes motivated by strategic need but often by high moral purpose and humanitarianism. There are countless examples of this related to the aftermath of all of the historical events and topics covered above. Just one small example of this is the work of Médecins Sans Frontières (www.msf.org) providing medical relief during and after wars and disasters – many pupils will be inspired by this selfless and often hazardous intervention. The many activities and relentless efforts of the various humanitarian campaigning organisations discussed here and listed in the Organisations and Websites section, so often a source of valuable contemporary information for teachers and pupils, are also an example of a larger purpose of care and concern for people and the planet.

On a wider note, Lynn Davies in her important book *Education and Conflict* (Davies, 2004) analyses various international settings and presents a persuasive case that education for peace and conflict resolution is not just a curriculum matter but is related to school ethos and organisation, just as is the case with Citizenship Education itself. The way we conduct ourselves in school, both as teachers and students, has a *direct* bearing on the kind of future citizens that the students become. In this sense, education for a safe school is also education for a safe world.

REFERENCES

Barker, J. (2003) *The No-Nonsense Guide to Terrorism*. London: New Internationalist/Verso.

Burrows, G. (2003) *The No-Nonsense Guide to the Arms Trade*. London: New Internationalist/Verso.

Davis, L. (2004) *Education and Conflict*. London: RoutledgeFalmer.

DfEE/QCA (1999) 'Citizenship Key Stages 3–4', in *The National Curriculum for England*. London: DfEE/QCA.

Osler, A. and Vincent, K. (2002) *Citizenship and the Challenge of Global Education*. London: Trentham Books.

Oxfam (2004) *Guns or Growth: Assessing the Impact of Arms Sales on Sustainable Development*. Oxford: Oxfam.

Oxfam/Amnesty International (2003) *Shattered Lives: the Case for Tough International Arms Control*. Oxford: Oxfam/Amnesty International.

QCA (2001) *Citizenship: a Scheme of Work for Key Stage 3*. London: QCA.

Smith, D. (2003) *The Atlas of War and Peace* (4th edn). London: Earthscan.

Thorpe, T. and Jarvis, R. (2006) *A Guide to the Law for Young Asylum Seekers and Refugees*. London: Citizenship Foundation.

UNESCO (2000) *Fifth session of the Advisory Committee on Education for Peace, Human Rights, Democracy, International Understanding and Tolerance: final report, 25 March*. Paris: UNESCO.

FURTHER READING

Oxfam's recent conflict resource book for teachers working with 13–16 year olds was published in 2005. It is called *Making Sense of World Conflicts* and was written by Cathy Midwinter. It provides activities and source materials for teaching within English, Citizenship and PSHE and suggests teaching ideas around explorations of the origin and nature of conflict as well as strategies for conflict resolution. This is a unique resource for teachers and pupils.

Oxfam also produces a major resources guide: the *Oxfam Catalogue for Schools 2006: Resources for Global Citizenship*, available from Oxfam.

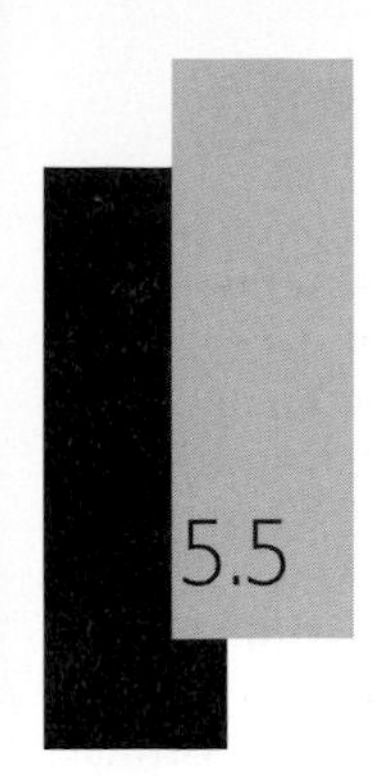

Education for Employability and the Workplace

Linda Prince

Bridging Citizenship and Work-Related Learning

This chapter seeks to bring to the attention of a Citizenship Education audience the potential and importance of the full range of practice in vocational, work related and careers education. In particular, it looks to these as possible strands through which citizenship skills might be developed and it reminds the designers of Citizenship Education programmes about the relationship between the development of what are increasingly referred to as 'employability' skills and effective citizenship. Being an effective, informed employee or employer is a key element of being an effective citizen – as many of those older students in part time employment are already discovering; students for whom the rights and responsibilities of employment are already in sharp focus.

Citizenship and work experience: the early days

There is an extensive literature on work experience. Governments have published guidelines and advice, individual organisations like Project Trident, the Schools Curriculum Industry Partnership (SCIP), and Education Business Partnerships (EBPs) have produced local and national documentation about it and commentators have written whole books on the subject.

The 1973 Education Act (Work Experience) gave schools the right to carry out work experience for those 'in the last year of compulsory schooling'. It did not explain how or why this should be done and it was over a year later that Circular 7/74 was published with some suggestions of good practice. Realistically, the introduction of work experience in 1973 was a response to the Raising of the School Leaving Age (ROSLA) in 1972. Educationalists had to find a more 'relevant' curriculum for students who had suddenly found themselves with an extra year of schooling. Indeed, as the whole post-Tomlinson debate proves, we are still talking about finding a relevant curriculum today (QCA, 2005; Tomlinson, 2005; DfES, 2005).

Yet, in the 1980s it was not the 'educationalists' that took the lead on this; rather this vacuum was filled by the Department for Trade and Industry under Lord Young[1] which announced in 1988 that it would send all students out on work experience and a high proportion of teachers on industrial placements.

Announced in November of 1982 and launched in 14 pilot schemes in the following September, the Technical and Vocational Educational Initiative (TVEI) had as one of its main targets to introduce, expand and embed Work Experience Schemes so that they were seen as the norm rather than an 'extra' to schooling. Up to this point, as I shall outline below, work experience programmes were much less ambitious.

Especially with regard to gender, TVEI was to become one of the first educational programmes to champion workplace derived models of equal opportunities and notions of breadth, balance and relevance in school settings: a perspective that the editors of this collection might define as 'Citizenship-rich'. However, many in the educational community were suspicious and resentful of the engagement that other government ('non-educational') agencies were managing to gain in schools and the Department for Education and Science (DES) was determined to regain its influence. The 1988 Education Act signalled this intent and paved the way for the National Curriculum followed by an associated set of ill-fated Cross-Curricular Themes shortly afterwards (NCC, 1991a).

Pre-TVEI, work experience has not always been an unmitigated success. Confusion regarding the aims and objectives of work experience has often led to misplaced students and failed schemes. Early schemes were focused on students who may have exhibited classroom 'behavioural problems'. Schools justified work experience on the grounds that students would be better off in a place they really wanted to be (a damning indictment of the curriculum offer in school and one repeated with the flirtation with 'disapplication' in the late 1990s[2]. Hence, there was an unspoken agreement that it was about testing out vocational areas, career sampling and even about 'getting a job'. Moreover, it was targeted at the less successful and the educationally reluctant rather than the economic elite.

TVEI disputed this. Prior to TVEI, most work experience had been for post-16 students or for 'non-academic' Year 11 leavers who were in their last year of compulsory schooling. TVEI redrew the definition of the 'last year', so that students a year earlier (those in Year 10) could go on work experience but the aims of these schemes were very different. In a valiant effort to show progression through work experience, pre-16 TVEI programmes had to have a different and more generic focus to those designed for the post-16 learner. Thus, TVEI work experience was about 'working as a team', 'working with adults', 'improving personal and social skills', 'equality of opportunity', 'problem-solving', 'health and safety at work' – reflected in Units 6, 9 and 10 of the QCA Schemes of Work for Citizenship (QCA, 2003) – but with little emphasis on careers.

However, employers and often parents were more interested in the 'careers' approach. No employer wanted a student who was not interested in her or his company. Parents wanted daughters and sons to be able to try out jobs that they might one day aspire to. Students did not the see relevance of working in a supermarket when they wanted to be a dentist. Only teachers identified work experience as being about the wider personal and social skills and personal and corporate responsibility.

Worse was to follow. Inundated with requirements for literacy, numeracy, PSHE, Science and so on, schools pressurised students into writing essays in English about 'My Work Experience', writing about employment law in Careers sessions, completing sections of the Work Experience Diary in French, completing GNVQ customer care modules – until the student was left with no time to do any work experience at all or to enjoy it.

What precludes work experience from having the development of both vocational skills and social and personal skills as aims for the schemes? It is reasonable that the balance should switch towards the vocational post-16 – but isn't it better, in any case, to undertake work experience at any age that both improves the personal and social skills of the learner and places them where they might have an interest?

Citizenship through work experience: an opportunity?

Key Stage 4 Citizenship requires students to acquire 'knowledge and understanding about becoming informed citizens', to develop 'skills of enquiry and communication' and to develop 'skills of participation and responsible action' (DfEE, 2000). Work experience can provide a valuable site for doing so. Questions of political literacy, social and moral responsibility and community involvement have always permeated the workplace, whether the issue concerned is one of ethical business practice, trade union membership or corporate social responsibility.

One way forward is to build links between Citizenship, PSHE and Careers Education through work experience rather than to present these as conflicting and multiple demands, overloading students so that they miss the seminal point of work experience. The suggestion is not that work experience can *deliver* Citizenship but that it can support its development. And an effective Citizenship programme can enhance any Work Experience Scheme, preparing students with some of the knowledge that they need to make sense of the workplace.

The Cross-Curricular Themes: the Cinderella of the National Curriculum

The Cross-Curricular Themes (NCC, 1990a) were published under a Thatcher government and the fourth theme, Economic and Industrial Understanding (EIU) (NCC, 1990b), is very much about responsibilities rather than rights and about supporting the business community and the status quo rather than questioning either. Throughout there is a strong focus on economic concepts, enterprise, creating wealth, consumer decisions, technological developments and the role of government in regulating the economy. Many practitioners felt that other themes such as Careers Education and Guidance had the same slant and even with Education for Citizenship designated as a theme, there proved to be relatively little opportunity for the exploration of contentious issues or political debate, especially as these themes were to be delivered across the curriculum, 'everywhere but nowhere' as the editors of this collection put it.

for themselves and others. Both ensure that Employment Law and Health and Safety regulations are understood. Both challenge any sort of prejudice in employment and training. And both offer a distinct but complementary take on these issues.

Careers focused work often focuses more on the individual (in, as it were, the PSHE tradition) whilst Citizenship tends to address employment matters though a public or policy based lens – looking at the need for regulations and policies in fields such as equal opportunities and workplace rights. The need is for PSHE, Citizenship and Careers practitioners to work together in real collaboration and to remember that schools should not be doing this in isolation. The views and expertise of employers, work-based training providers and those offering Modern and Foundation Apprenticeships should be sought. Parents and carers are important and the views of young people crucial.

Like Citizenship, there are discrete parts of Careers Education and Guidance that will need to be taught but much of the work is complementary. The aim of curriculum planners needs to be to identify where learning areas are complementary and strengthen integration.

Citizenship and the broader vocational domain: the past is not such a foreign country

Callaghan's Ruskin speech[3] was a watershed and tried to bring the goals of education into line with those of national economic revival. It resulted from several years of criticism of schools and colleges by those who felt that society and the economy were not being served well. Employers, especially, were critical of standards and attitudes towards industry, about the lack of appropriate skills and lack of values being promoted about industry and commerce[4]. Recent 14–19 and related policy papers echo the same thoughts (DfES, 2003a; DfES 2005; Tomlinson, 2005). They also bring an additional thrust: that young people need to be 'responsible citizens and workers, able to contribute to a productive economy' (DfES, 2003b). The current focus on 'employability' and functional skills in the post-Tomlinson literature underlines this thrust. It is important that young people become more rounded, motivated and responsible citizens for their own benefit and for that of society as a whole. Callaghan's concern was with the development of a productive economy. The current literature still seeks this but it seeks and values effective citizenship too.

With the 14–19 agenda, the Key Stage 3 (now 'Secondary') Strategy and an emphasis on transition issues coupled with personalised learning, the individualisation of programmes and multi-site delivery, what can we expect of the future? If learners are progressing at their own pace, possibly in multiple geographical locations, including virtual ones, how will we monitor attendance, punctuality or progress? Monitoring these things has always been problematic. Perhaps we need a new definition of 'attendance'.

The flexible curriculum has been round the block before in different guises – remember 365, CPVE, TVEI? What we need to do is learn from the past and see where previous initiatives failed. Whilst some would point to the 'short termism' of government initiatives and associated funding as being the main reason for the disappearance of some of these initiatives, it is also true to say that there were things that could be improved upon this time around.

Students now have entitlements to work-related learning and to Enterprise Education but, beyond this, how will schools deliver vocational qualifications? Do we need better partnering agreements with Further Education, Higher Education and other high schools? The Leadership Incentive Grant (LIG) emphasises the need for collaboration. Local Skills Councils (LSCs) are already responsible for post-16 and may well have a bigger say in Key Stage 4 and look to collaboration across a wider area. E-learning means the opportunities for study are limitless. It would be all too easy for a school to ask the timetable coordinator to fit in a couple of modules on hairdressing and car mechanics and think the vocational element of the new 14–19 agenda has been met. But as we know, the curriculum should influence the timetable – not the reverse. Accepted there are constraints of recruitment and retention but, even so, now is the time to be brave. If Citizenship is about 'enhancing democratic life for us all, both rights and responsibilities, beginning in school and radiating out'[5] then Senior Leadership teams need to review the core purpose of their organisation, provide a framework and opportunities for learners (staff and students) in the organisation and to do so in conjunction with other providers.

Granted that this is no easy task. Many schools are in challenging circumstances as are the communities that they serve. But if we really are to exploit the combination of Careers, work related learning, PSHE and Citizenship then we need to think outside the box and use the strengths of each to support the Holy Grail of education – the appropriate curriculum.

Your starter for ten!

All of the above areas of school life (work experience, Careers Education and Guidance and vocational education) link with Citizenship. Citizenship has a particular strength to add to each of these areas and vice versa, each area can add to the body of knowledge that is Citizenship. But this is not an exhaustive list of mutual partnership and support. We recognise that there are links with PSHE, sports development, drugs awareness, healthy schools, Science, Sociology, English, Art – all of the things we do at school. If this collection as a whole has a message, it is that no subject is an island. What, then, can Senior Leadership Teams, middle managers and individual teachers do to ensure that we get cohesion rather than overload?

With this challenge in mind, I will finish with ten questions that you might wish to consider – whether as whole school, at departmental level or for the individual classroom.

1. Do we do things to prepare our students for the world of work and beyond? How do we know?
2. Do we ever reinforce work from another area of learning or are we really guilty of duplication? How do we know?
3. Do we build on work in Key Stage 3 that was done in primary school? How do we know?

- they have points values up to Level 2 in the Achievement and Attainment tables.

In addition, all six Key Skills are included in the UCAS tariff at Levels 2 and 3.

All this is, of course, in line with the move towards a 14–19 curriculum, embodied in the work of the Working Group on 14–19 Reform (the Tomlinson group) whose interim report and proposals were published in February 2004 (Tomlinson, 2004) and which endorsed the importance of skills-based learning. The apparent rejection of Tomlinson in the pre-election 14–19 White Paper of February 2005 (DfES, 2005a) has, in practice, meant no slackening of the drive towards a skills-based curriculum and the emphasis on the wider Key Skills continues to grow.

Skills for Citizenship: an opportunity to share

In this chapter, I will show how these two initiatives, Citizenship and Key Skills, relate to each other and how much they have in common. I will argue that they can work together to their mutual benefit, and that failing to co-operate would be to miss an opportunity and potentially to disadvantage learners. In arguing this, I will endorse the views of Campbell and Craft who, in Chapter 6.2 of this text, maintain that Citizenship and PSHE require and promote similar skills, which they list on page 297. They include Key Skills, especially the wider Key Skills, in their list.

From Callaghan to Curriculum 2000: a recent history of skills-based learning

The roots of Key Skills, like so much of the current educational scene, can be found, as Linda Prince notes in Chapter 5.5, in James Callaghan's Ruskin College speech in October 1976. 'I am', he said, 'concerned on my journeys to find complaints from industry that new recruits from the schools sometimes do not have the basic tools to do the job that is required.' He went on to make a similar point about graduates, and the Great Debate that he called for has rumbled on (even if it has never properly sprung to life) ever since.

In line with the 'New Vocationalism' of the 1980s and the range of programmes developed in those years (TVEI, YOPS, TOPS, YTS etc.), the National Council for Vocational Qualifications (NCVQ) was founded in 1986 and developed the first version of the six Key Skills (then known as Core Skills) that we have today. NCVQ (since merged into QCA) developed these Core Skills for delivery in the context of occupational qualifications such as NVQs, but the first three found their way into the school and college context via their integration in General National Vocational Qualifications (GNVQs) in the early 1990s. The fact that the wider Key Skills were not a requirement of GNVQ contributed to their lack of status and significance at that time. The Core/Key Skills specifications were revised in 1995 and again in 2000.

Dearing, Curriculum 2000 and the skills agenda

The Dearing Review of 1996 (Dearing, 1996) recommended the introduction of Key Skills (as Dearing chose to call them) into the 16–19 curriculum as a whole, across both the 'vocational' and the 'academic' pathways. In doing this, he was beginning to fill the gap between the literacy and numeracy strategies in primary schools and the 'graduate employability' agenda in higher education, where a vigorous debate was further stimulated by the report of the National Committee of Inquiry into Higher Education (Dearing, 1997). Today, Quality Assurance Agency (QAA) policy identifies Key Skills (though not necessarily the QCA version) as essential elements of all HE programmes. HE institutions must demonstrate how they will develop and assess students' key (or 'transferable') skills in preparation for employment and lifelong learning.

As a result of Dearing (1996), the Key Skills Qualification was included in the Curriculum 2000 reforms that were introduced in England, Wales and Northern Ireland in September 2000. This was a 'profiled' qualification whereby students had to achieve Communication, Application of Number and Information Technology at any mixture of Levels, usually from 1 to 3. Assessment was by a combination of a portfolio of evidence and an external test. The wider Key Skills were again given short shrift, being 'encouraged' but not accredited as qualifications and not being allocated points in the UCAS tariff.

Curriculum 2000 in crisis: a testing time for Key Skills

Within a year, Curriculum 2000 had run into trouble. The introduction of the AS/A2 and the modular structure of A levels with which this was associated, coupled with the drive to increase the number of subjects that students studied at this level, led almost immediately to a perceived 'assessment burden' that was unacceptable. How far this perception was justified or how far it was a response to a radical curriculum change introduced to a profession that was under-prepared and institutional arrangements that were unfitted for it, remains debatable but, when coupled with the spectre of 'grade inflation' and the alleged dumbing down of the 'gold standard' at the altar of inclusion, the Key Skills initiative became one of the casualties. The upshot was the abolition of the stand-alone Key Skills Qualification, the introduction of proxy qualifications for some aspects of the Key Skills assessment requirements (for instance, stated GCSE equivalencies) and reduced expectations of how many Key Skills 16–19 year old students should achieve. Following a period of uncertainty and confusion, government policy is now (in late 2005) that 16–19 year old students who have not achieved GCSE Maths and/or English at grades A*–C should achieve the relevant Key Skills at Level 2 (and have an entitlement to this) and that students aiming to proceed to higher levels of study should be encouraged to achieve at least one of the first three Key Skills at Level 3. This policy applies to all students and trainees, whether at school, college, or in apprenticeship programmes.

In work-based training, all apprentices must achieve Level 1 in Communication and Application of Number, and Advanced Apprentices must achieve Level 2 in these Key Skills. Each apprenticeship framework specifies any additional Key Skill requirements, often including one or more of the wider Key Skills, which many employers see as being at least as important as the first three.

These developments have been accompanied by continuous and often lively debate, carried on through a truly huge number of conferences, research papers, government reports, curriculum projects and development programmes. The debate has revolved around four main questions.

1 Is there a set of transferable skills that underpin competence in all areas of study, employment and life in general?
2 If so, what are these skills?
3 How can they best be developed? (i.e. What teaching and learning strategies and pedagogies are required?)
4 How best can their achievement be recognised? (i.e. How can we assess skills-based learning?)

The answer to the first question is almost universally 'yes' but this unanimity breaks down almost as soon as the second question is asked. A period of relative stability since 2000, during which the six QCA-specified Key Skills have been delivered in the context of a wide range of education and training programmes, has recently given way to yet another review. QCA is working on the development of the new 'functional skills' in Maths, English and ICT which will build on the existing Key Skills, basic skills and GCSEs. In addition, at the time of writing, QCA is conducting a consultation on a single framework, suitable for all 11–19 year olds, for what they are now calling PELTS (personal, employability, learning and thinking skills). These appear to embrace the wider Key Skills.

The third question has prompted a variety of responses (which is as it should be) and it would require a full text not a chapter to assess these. The fourth has become the Achilles' heel of the entire skills initiative.

Key Skills and Citizenship: the shared ground

A starting point for establishing the shared ground for Key Skills and Citizenship is to map the Key Skills Standards (as revised for September 2004) against the two skills strands within the Citizenship Programmes of Study. This is done in Figure 1 with *Developing skills of enquiry and communication* (Table A) cast in terms of the first three Key Skills and *Developing skills of participation and responsible action* (Table B) cast in terms of the wider Key Skills.

Figure 1

Mapping the Citizenship Programme of Study at Key Stage 4 to Key Skills

Table A: Developing skills of enquiry and communication and the first three Key Skills

Pupils should be taught to:	Communication	Application of Number	Information and Communication Technology
	For this Key Skill, students need to know how to:		
a *Research a topical political, spiritual, moral, social or cultural issue, problem or event by analysing information from different sources, including ICT-based sources, showing an awareness of the use and abuse of statistics*	Read and summarise information.	Interpret information. Carry out calculations. Interpret results.	Find and select information. Develop information.
b *Express, justify and defend orally and in writing a personal opinion about such issues, problems or events*	Give a short talk. Write documents.	Present results.	Present information.
c *Contribute to group and exploratory class discussions, and take part in formal debates*	Discuss.		

Table B: Developing skills of participation and responsible action and the 'wider' Key Skills

Pupils should be taught to:	Working with Others	Improving own Learning and Performance	Problem-Solving
	For this Key Skill, students need to know how to:		
a *Use their imagination to consider other people's experiences and be able to think about, express, explain and critically evaluate views that are not their own*	QCA guidance on the wider Key Skills suggests that students should develop a range of interpersonal skills and personal qualities, including the ability to: • communicate ideas • listen to others • handle disagreement and conflict • empathise • avoid discrimination • be open to feedback • consult with others • listen to others • communicate needs and ideas.		
b *Negotiate, decide and take part responsibly in school and community-based activities*	Plan work with others and work co-operatively.	Help set targets and plan how these will be met.	Help identify a problem and identify different ways of tackling it. Plan and try out a way of solving the problem.
c *Reflect on the process of participating*	Review your contributions and agree ways to improve working with others.	Take responsibility for some decisions about your learning. Review progress and provide evidence of achievements.	Check if the problem has been solved and identify ways to improve problem-solving.

Embedding Key Skills: the lessons for Citizenship Education

The central irony for the Key Skills initiative is why, with so much agreement on the value of these skills, the 'carrots' provided by funding mechanisms via the Learning and Skills Council (LSC), and the 'sticks' that can be wielded by the inspectorates (Ofsted and the Adult Learning Inspectorate), there has been such a struggle to embed skills-based schemes in schools and colleges. While some 940,000 Key Skills qualifications were awarded to 572,000 individuals in England, Wales and Northern Ireland between October 2000 and September 2004 (DfES, 2005b), the fact remains that, while there are many centres of good practice, there are also many 16–19 centres where Key Skills practice is notional, token or non-existent. Moreover, there has as yet been little take-up of Key Skills programmes at Key Stage 4. The literacy and numeracy strategies are rising into the secondary sector through the Key Stage 3 Strategy (which also carries a welcome focus on the sort of Thinking Skills that Ted Huddleston and Will Ord address in Chapters 3.5 and 2.7 respectively), but Key Skills, if they are to be seen in part as a development from those strategies, as I have argued above, have only very slowly moved down into Key Stage 4 to complete the links, a failure which has implications for a skills-rich Programme of Study such as Citizenship.

Drawing in part on Hodgson and Spours (2003), I suggest that there are five main reasons for this failure.

1 The notion of Key Skills as having a 'deficit agenda' i.e. that their task is to make good the weaknesses, particularly in literacy and numeracy, that many 16 year olds bring to their studies and employment.
2 The low status of Key Skills resulting from their association with employability and vocational qualifications.
3 The assessment regime for Key Skills, which is experienced as cumbersome in terms of the portfolio and inappropriate in terms of the tests for the first three Key Skills.
4 The emphasis on assessment rather than development of the Key Skills.
5 The extent to which the Key Skills lobby, among whom I number myself, under-estimated the work that needed to be done to introduce subject teachers, especially of A level, who were more or less expert in the transmission of a subject- and knowledge-based curriculum assessed largely through examinations, to the concept and practice of an integrated and skills-based curriculum assessed largely by portfolio. Teachers from a BTEC or GNVQ background have had noticeably less difficulty in delivering the Curriculum 2000 version of Key Skills than those from an A level background, the latter often doing little more than claiming 'students are doing these skills anyway' – but they weren't.

Proponents of Citizenship will recognise the similarities: important only for the disaffected, low status, difficult to assess, done anyway. The Citizenship lobby should be wary of celebrating the arrival of Citizenship as a Foundation Subject in the National Curriculum before it addresses these issues. In hindsight, the Key Skills lobby may have celebrated too soon their welcoming at the Curriculum 2000 table. Citizenship would face these questions whether or not it featured a strong skills dimension. That it does, and therefore poses real challenges as to how teaching and learning is done in schools, makes these points all the more pressing.

Citizenship and the wider Key Skills

Another irony of the Key Skills initiative since 2000 has been the near-universal agreement that the wider Key Skills are at least as important as the first three and the equally widespread absence of their take-up. The explanation is straightforward: until September 2004, they were not recognised as formal qualifications in the National Qualifications Framework (NQF) so they lacked status, did not attract funding, and did not attract points in the UCAS tariff.

And yet they were regularly identified by teachers in schools and colleges, by employers and by higher education institutions, as being the most valuable skills that learners and trainees can bring to their work. They are also, quintessentially, citizenship skills. Citizenship happens because we work with others; it is effective because we develop insight into our own ways of learning and doing (i.e. improve our own learning) and because we solve problems in the process.

And why were these skills excluded from the National Qualifications Framework? Because there was no independent or external component to their assessment regime. And why was there no such component? Because no one could come up with an assessment model that was both appropriate to these skills and met the then-perceived requirements of the National Qualifications Framework. The vision of a school hall filled with students sitting alone at desks at least two feet apart, in silence, and taking a test in Working with Others, is too much even for the most traditionally-minded assessment expert. The same vision could be applied to Citizenship: how about assessing Community Involvement by a written and unseen exam?

This anomaly has been resolved since September 2004, with the wider Key Skills becoming available as full qualifications on equal standing with the first three. The assessment regime requires candidates, in addition to completing the portfolio of evidence, to give satisfactory answers to questions asked by an assessor. The assessor will select these questions from a list supplied by the awarding body and will use them to confirm candidates' knowledge and understanding where this cannot be inferred from the portfolio. This is considered to meet the NQF requirement for an independent/external component in the assessment regime. This interpretation of the NQF requirement should be of great interest to those concerned with the assessment and future status of Citizenship.

Citizenship and Key Skills: shared opportunities and shared troubles

Of course a mapping exercise such as that outlined in Figure 1 is purely an auditing exercise. It reminds us of linkages but, as Linda Prince reminds us in

Chapter 5.5, the recent history of Cross-Curricular Themes warns us against the notion that the audit is itself the job done. More profoundly, the real shared ground is in the introduction of what Tony Breslin refers to in his chapters elsewhere as 'not just a new subject but a new type of subject' and it is from this kind of newness that Key Skills both gains its energy and has met its problems. This is the real common ground with Citizenship. Let us then summarise this common ground.

Innovation

Both initiatives face the usual range of responses to curriculum innovation, ranging from the evangelical through the realistic to the cynical and the downright hostile, compounded by their being introduced at a time when 'innovation fatigue' is widespread in the educational world. These pressures should not put curriculum innovators off but they are wise to be conscious of them, as the editors emphasise elsewhere in this book.

Teaching and learning

Citizenship and Key Skills are both committed to active and student-centred styles of teaching and learning. Indeed, they make no sense if delivered in any other way. Ord, Hannam, Huddleston, Rowe and other contributors to this volume emphasise this point. I will not repeat their words here but will simply emphasise that, just as you cannot teach about democracy undemocratically, so you cannot teach about skills didactically.

Assessment

In principle, there should be no great problem with assessing the first three Key Skills, where the emphasis is on the product of work the student has produced. Similarly in Citizenship, assessing a student's knowledge and understanding poses few problems in principle, though, in practice, it may be a challenge to make such assessments intrinsically interesting.

Assessment of the wider Key Skills, and of the moral responsibility and community involvement aspects of Citizenship, however, pose problems, or at least call for a broader range of assessment tools. The first reason for this is that both are concerned with processes and experiences rather than products, so outcomes are more difficult to specify. The second reason is that the assessment of some aspects of both comes uncomfortably close to assessing the candidate's worth as a person. Working with Others, for example, calls for particular personal qualities. If a candidate lacks these qualities, despite a programme of skills development and assessment for learning, does failing to achieve the standard mean they are any less valuable as a person? Similarly, assessing Citizenship should not judge the worth or personality of an individual or their community, or fail them as citizens.

For both the wider Key Skills and for Citizenship, assessment should focus on process, on what the student has experienced, what they have learned and how they have developed. It should include self-assessment, peer assessment, assessment by tutors and teachers, witness statements from employers and community leaders, diaries and logbooks. There is much to be learned about this form of assessment from the pilot of the Welsh baccalaureate qualification, whose core includes all six Key Skills and many aspects of Citizenship.

Integration or bolt-on?

Both initiatives have to confront a tendency to 'bolt them on' to an already crowded curriculum, rather than to integrate them into mainstream subjects and enrichment activities. Full integration is difficult and complex and risks the 'everywhere but nowhere' status identified by other contributors to this volume; bolting on leads to marginalisation. Both initiatives have found that the solution lies in having clearly timetabled slots, with specialist teachers, as a 'home base' while at the same time gradually developing integration over time.

Image and perception

Both Citizenship and Key Skills suffer from an image problem, based on misperceptions (sometimes wilful) of what they are about. Citizenship has to distance itself from the old-style civics: Key Skills has to distance itself from Maths and English. Civics was about knowledge; Citizenship is also about the skills that are needed to make use of this knowledge. Maths and English are about underpinning techniques; Key Skills are also about using these techniques in real situations. Both are about application and the active and committed use of knowledge and understanding to tackle problems and get things done.

Status, recognition and currency

Citizenship and Key Skills both experience a contradiction between the rhetoric that repeatedly stresses their importance and the reality of an unwillingness in some schools and colleges to give them the practical support to match the rhetoric. There is widespread agreement that young people are disengaged from the political process, but less readiness to devote resources to the problem. There is widespread agreement that young people lack the skills they need to be independent learners and for employment, but less readiness to devote resources to the problem. In the unofficial hierarchy of qualifications, GCSEs and A levels still come top, vocational qualifications below them, and Key Skills, PSHE and Citizenship in the bottom ranks.

Developing skills for developing citizens: a way forward?

The aim for both Citizenship and Key Skills is to find the right balance between being integrated into the curriculum and preserving their identity as areas of expertise that require particular professional skills from teachers.

The citizens of the twenty-first century will need to appreciate, evaluate and, where appropriate, embrace the new, rather than stay with the familiar and safe habits of the past. They must be able to plan and manage their own learning and performance, tackle the problems they will encounter, and work with others. Among the skills they will need for this are communication, numeracy and a confidence and competence with ICT.

The question is not whether Key Skills (or however they might be rebranded following the current reviews) should be delivered through Citizenship or whether Citizenship should be delivered through Key Skills. The question is how can the two be delivered in such a way that their interdependence, both with each other and with the curriculum as a whole, is recognised, exploited and clearly apparent to students.

What might help us succeed?

Perhaps it is fitting to close with the ten *Critical Success Factors* identified by the Key Skills Support Programme as effective in supporting successful curriculum innovation. They are:

- promoting a positive agenda
- implementing an effective curriculum model
- establishing clearly defined roles and responsibilities
- co-ordinating activity within teams and across the centre
- delivering effective teaching and learning
- establishing clear assessment procedures
- using resources efficiently and effectively
- embedding quality assurance
- delivering appropriate staff development
- reviewing and planning ahead.

If the proponents of Citizenship can bring these attitudes and this political savvy to their practice, then the aims of the 'Citizenship movement' may be achieved. We owe this to the developing citizens that we work with; we owe it also to the cause of building a model of schooling that can meet their needs. The political culture may indeed be changing; the culture of schooling must help it on its way.

REFERENCES

Dearing, R. (1996) *Review of Qualifications for 16–19 Year Olds: Full Report*. London: SCAA Publications.

Dearing, R. (1997) *Higher Education in the Learning Society: Report of the National Committee of Inquiry into Higher Education*. London: The Stationery Office.

DfEE (1998) *Education for Citizenship and the Teaching of Democracy in Schools: Final Report of the Advisory Group on Citizenship; 22 September 1998*. Suffolk: QCA Publications.

DfES (2005a) *14–19 Education and Skills*. Cm 6476.

DfES (2005b) *Awards of Key Skills Qualifications: 2003/04*. London: National Statistics First Release, DfES (ref: SFR 15/2005).

Hodgson, A. and Spours, K. (2003) *Beyond A levels: Curriculum 2000 and the reform of 14–19 qualifications*. London: Kogan Page.

Tomlinson, M. (2004) *Working Group on 14–19 Reform: Interim Report. London:* DfES (ref: DfES/0013/2004).

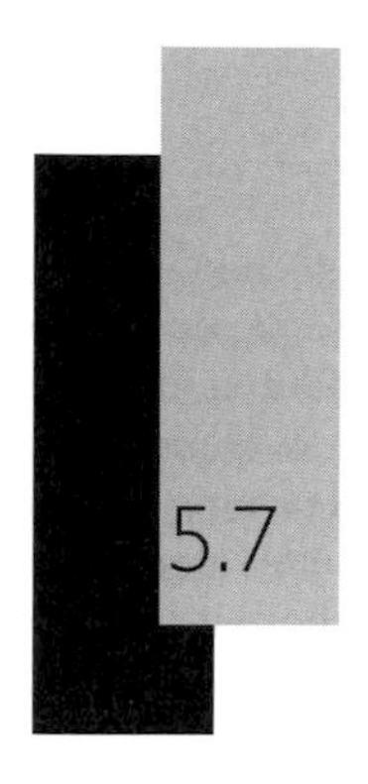

5.7

Education for Democracy and as a Democratic Process

Derry Hannam

Student participation: time for Citizenship to 'get real'?

There are some, amongst whom I would firmly include myself, who have long argued that if Education for Democratic Citizenship is to have any hope of success in preparing young people to play an active part in a democratic society then the necessary learning in school must be at least in part experiential. For this to happen many, if not most, schools have to change. They have to become more democratic than they currently are in the everyday lived experience of their students. Some are trying and achieving some success. My own research (Hannam, 2001) explored associations between unusually high levels of democratic participation in a small sample of (12) secondary schools and academic attainment, attendance and exclusions. The findings were encouraging.

Participation and successful learning: the evidence

The evidence to support the case for experiential learning in democratic participation is growing. It began to emerge from the IBE study (Abela-Bertrand, 1997). It is inescapable in both recent IEA studies, *Citizenship and Education in Twenty-eight Countries* (Torney-Purta et al., 2001) and *Civic Knowledge and Engagement in Upper Secondary Students in Sixteen Countries* (Torney-Purta et al., 2002), which conclude that 'Schools that model democratic values by . . . inviting students to take part in shaping school life are most effective in promoting civic knowledge and engagement . . . and they are more likely to expect to vote as adults than other students.' The authors add a 'sting in the tail' that supports my case for the need for change – '. . . this approach is by no means the norm in most countries'. *The component IEA English Report* (Kerr, 2002) endorses these findings for 14 year olds in English secondary schools and agrees that a democratic approach 'is by no means the norm' here either. Further supportive evidence is contained in the *Citizenship Education Longitudinal Study: First Cross Sectional Survey 2001–2002* (Kerr et al., 2003) and *Citizenship Education Longitudinal Study: Second Annual Report: First Longitudinal Survey* (Kerr et al., 2004). A very similar picture is emerging from recent research into effective and ineffective service learning in the US (Billig, 2000a, 2000b, 2000c).

(Clay et al., 2001; Davies, 1998; Hannam, 2001; Inman and Burke, 2002; Taylor and Johnson, 2002; Trafford, 2003). It is encouraging that two of these works were published by professional associations, one by ATL (Association of Teachers and Lecturers) and another by SHA (Secondary Heads Association), and that a third was funded by the DfES. They are driven by both principle and pragmatism.

The first absolutely clear point is that a council that is felt by students to offer serious and effective opportunities for participation in school decision-making cannot be an add-on extra to a fundamentally authoritarian and coercive institution. *It must spring from a deep belief in the right of young people to have a voice.* The literature indicates that this belief must be held by the school leadership, the headteacher in particular, and at least a significant minority of the teaching staff. When I conducted a pilot study for CSV/DfES in 2001 (Hannam, 2001) to explore associations between student participation, attendance, exclusion and achievement, I found this commitment to the students' voice *as of right* in all of the 12 selected 'more than usually participative' secondary schools. Some of the schools actually referred to the student council as the principal means for implementing Article 12 of the UN Convention on the Rights of the Child in the school prospectus. This commitment to students' rights shines from the pages of Bernard Trafford's excellent book, *School Councils, School Democracy, School Improvement*. It is the mainspring of his success with democratic innovation at the independent Wolverhampton Grammar School (Trafford, 2003).

A close second to this commitment to the right of students to have a voice comes the recognition that a democratic participative ethos is associated with enhanced learning, and that some important learning can only take place through the experience of participation in democratic decision-making. The most obvious, and supported by large-scale research, is an understanding of and commitment to democracy itself as supported by the research already mentioned. The lesson is clear. As Tony Breslin argues elsewhere in this volume, you can't teach about democracy without some sense of democracy itself.

Schools with effective student councils also seem to understand that many other contributions to school improvement follow from effective listening to the student voice and open-hearted sharing in decision-making. There is hardly any problem affecting the day-to-day running of a school on which the students do not have a unique and valuable 'take' (hence, Ofsted's interest in seeking their views at inspection time!). These schools take issues of concern to management to the student council and reciprocally listen carefully and positively engage when students bring their issues to the senior management or leadership teams.

Schools with effective student councils do not attempt to restrict and constrain what can be discussed though they may well negotiate sensible guidelines. Some would argue that it is necessary to set clear boundaries for what may be discussed but I stand by the view expressed in the 'Toolkit' that I co-authored for the DfES/School Councils UK (Clay et al., 2001), which is supported by Bernard Trafford (Trafford, 2003):

> *Most effective councils do not exclude anything from being discussed, apart from matters of personal confidentiality. The power of councils to make decisions and take action are likely to expand as students become more confident . . . If rigid limits are imposed on councils at the outset, students are unlikely to develop any enthusiasm for them.* (Trafford, 2003)

Figure 1 draws on the collected literature to summarise the criteria common to the most effective student councils.

Figure 1
Effective student councils

The collected literature suggests that effective school or student councils are likely to emerge when:

- there is high profile support for the student council from the school's leadership drawing in the support of teachers, non-teaching staff, parents and governors;
- there is conspicuous reference to the importance of student councils in key school documentation including prospectus and development plan;
- the structure of, and support for, the council is such that effective meetings of the full council, and any subgroups, are possible;
- there is the opportunity for meetings to be as frequent and of sufficient length as the business requires (i.e. not squashed into break or lunchtimes);
- there is the possibility for at least some of the meetings to be in 'curriculum time', and thus configured as a part of 'real' learning;
- there is provision of appropriate accommodation for meetings and access to computing/reprographic facilities – in some Scandinavian Upper Secondary schools the student council has its own office with telephone, computer and photocopier);
- there are sufficient opportunities for effective meetings to take place in every constituent class and tutor group;
- there is, therefore, excellent communication and feed-back to and from representative council meetings;
- there are skill development activities for student councillors and teachers who work with them;
- there is regular communication with governors through the presence of elected students as 'associate members' of the governing body. (Now formally set out as an option for governing bodies in the new regulations that slipped, almost unnoticed, into operation for State Schools in September 2003);
- there is a budget for the student council;
- there is thoughtful integration of the student council's activities and experience into the broader Citizenship Curriculum.

the Governing Body or associations such as a national school students' body. The 12 schools in my pilot study (Hannam, 2001) took participation beyond the overtly democratic structures of councils and governorship. Many other examples of student participation in decision-making in a wide range of extra curricular and curricular activities were found, and often they were to be found in the 'no-man's-land' or border zone between the formal and the informal curriculum. One school, for example, ran a vast range of mixed-age 'electives' built around the common enthusiasms and interests of both students and teachers, which took over the curriculum for a whole afternoon every week. Central to the process was the participation of the students in decision-making about which activities should run and how they should be evaluated. The teachers faced the challenge of discovering how to function in the role of coach or learning facilitator, one that most found both challenging and very rewarding.

The 12 schools were also exploring ways of involving students in normal subject lesson and departmental planning decision-making in a wide range of subjects. Perhaps predictably students in all 12 schools were involved in planning and delivering the PSHE course, but some schools were moving into interesting new territory such as experimenting with student participation and negotiation over setting decisions in subjects like Maths and Modern Languages and lesson delivery in Drama and Science. In other schools, students regularly attended departmental planning meetings to contribute feedback on the effectiveness of courses and teaching methods. There is not space here to describe all these activities in detail. Others involved students on interview panels for staff appointments, a practice now common through other youth services such as Connexions. I called these schools 'more than usually participative'. In fact they very closely match the schools described as 'progressing' in the four point typology developed by the authors of the *Second Annual Report on Citizenship Education* (Kerr et al., 2004). The authors identify these 'progressing schools' as being the 25 per cent or so of English secondary schools that are beginning to implement the Citizenship Curriculum with some signs of success.

The emergence of 'students as researchers' provides another powerful vehicle. Such groups were at work in one of the pilot study schools and students reported that the experience was more powerful than school council membership even though the council was very effective in their school. In a recent study for QCA/CSV I looked closely at the work of 'students as researchers' in four schools across all phases. The power of using tangible skills to gain expert knowledge that was taken seriously by staff, governors and peers and led to real change and improvement to the school was impressive (Hannam, 2004). Possibly the most impressive example was that carried out by 7–10 year olds at Brackenhill School, Bradford, which was used as a case study by Fielding and Bragg in their, *Students As Researchers: Making A Difference* (2003).

New developments at the National College for School Leadership give one cause for optimism. The NCSL's advocacy of the notion of dispersed leadership, one that includes the students as potential leaders in schools, is an exciting development. Schools, such as those in my study, that truly believe in the potential of their students, led by headteachers willing to innovate and take risks, so as to allow this potential to develop, can play a key role not simply in developing models of participation that the more conservative might, in time, draw on but in casting the institutional shapes for the school of the future.

From participative schooling to democratic renewal

As we move into an uncertain future with already emergent crises over energy and water supply, carbon emissions and the possibly catastrophic implications of global warming, we as a species face a choice between unleashing our as yet unrealised potential for learning and creativity or retreating into authoritarianism, xenophobic, fundamentalist and probably species-terminating violence. For the optimistic outcome to be realised we have to create and sustain democratic, open and cohesive, though diversity-tolerating, participative societies. This requires school systems that model such societies for our young. If they are to be change agents these schools have to lead us into the future with democratic vision. It is not good enough for them to merely reflect the status quo of the society around them. This is a hard but not impossible task. Some schools are showing us the way they are Citizenship rich. Government and the teaching profession must support them.

REFERENCES

Abela-Bertrand, L. (1997) *What Education for What Citizenship?* Geneva: UNESCO-IBE.

Alderson, P. (1999) *Civil Rights in Schools; Briefing Paper 1 of the ESRC Children 5–16 Research Programme*. Hull: University of Hull.

Baginsky, M. and Hannam, D. (1999) *Report on School Councils in England*. London: NSPCC.

Billig, S. (2000a) 'The Effects of Service-Learning', *School Administrator,* August, pp. 14–18.

Billig, S. (2000b) *Service Learning Impacts on Youth, Schools, and Communities: Research on K-12 School-Based-Service-Learning, 1990–1999*. Denver: RMC Research Corpn.

Billig, S. (2000c) 'Research on K-12 School-Based-Service-Learning: The Evidence Builds', *Phi Delta Kappan,* May, pp. 658–64.

Clay, D., Gold, J. and Hannam, D. (2001) *Secondary School Councils Toolkit*. London: School Councils UK.

Davies, L. (1998). *School Councils and Pupil Exclusions: Research Project Report*. Birmingham: The University of Birmingham.

DfES (2003) *Working Together: Giving Children and Young People a Say*. London: DfES.

Fielding, M. and Bragg, S. (2003) *Students As Researchers: Making a Difference.* Cambridge: Pearson Publishing.

Hallgarten, J., Breslin, T. and Hannam, D. (2004) *I Was a Teenage Governor: Project Report Phase 1: Pupil Governorship: Initial Thoughts and Possibilities.* London: IPPR.

Hannam, D. (2001) *A Pilot Study to Evaluate the Impact of the Student Participation Aspects of the Citizenship Order on Standards of Education in Secondary Schools.* London: CSV – Available at www.csv.org.uk/csv/hannamreport.pdf

Hannam, D. (2004) *Involving Young People in Identifying Ways of Gathering Their Views on the Curriculum*. London: QCA – Available at http://www.qca.org.uk/ages3–14/downloads/involving_young_people.pdf

Citizenship Education, Active Citizenship and Service Learning

So, what is the link between 'Active Citizenship', Citizenship Education and social capital? And what role might Service Learning play in delivering the objectives of Citizenship Education? As readers will be aware, Crick's first and seminal report, *Education for Citizenship and the Teaching of Democracy in Schools* (DfEE/QCA, 1998), resulted in the addition of Citizenship to the National Curriculum. This report also recognised the importance of active learning in the community – learning that is, by definition, experiential in nature.

This pedagogy of experiential learning is based on the learning cycle of David Kolb (1998) and is now beginning to establish itself in schools, colleges and in higher education and in professional development and training programmes. As a form of learning it is based not just on experience but on a structured learning activity with measurable learning outcomes. A key element of Kolb's model is that learning emerges from the structured reflection of the learner. Thus, as applied to Citizenship Education, the student learns not just through, for instance, volunteering or civic engagement but through their reflections on this. Thus, Carnegie Young People's Initiative, CSV Education for Citizenship, Continyou, Changemakers, the Citizenship Foundation, Envision and other voluntary sector organisations have highlighted the importance of encouraging the development of, for example, Citizenship Education through reflective service learning. Many schools in the UK and the US now provide school students with the opportunity to engage in this kind of Service Learning (to use the prevalent US terminology), learning that derives from the offering of service in the community: 'active learning in the community', 'community based learning for active citizenship', or active citizenship in the community', as different UK based programmes frame such activity (Wade, 1997; Annette, 2000; Potter, 2002). A key challenge facing such programmes is to go beyond traditional volunteering and the doing of good works so as to link service learning with political knowledge, skills and understanding: to shift, as the title of one of the Citizenship Foundation's First Friday seminars put it, '. . . from doing good to good citizenship'[1].

While there has been a tradition of community-based internship and experiential education since the 1960s, the new emphasis in the USA since the early 1990s has been on the link between Citizenship Education and Service Learning (Rimmerman, 1997; Battistoni, 2002). There is also an increasing emphasis on the need for Service Learning programmes to meet the needs of local community partners (Cruz and Giles, 2000; Gelmon et al., 2001). Thus, Service Learning helps to build a type of 'bridging as well as bonding social capital' (Putnam, 2000) and may also develop the capacity for building for democratic Citizenship within civil society (Annette, 2000; Kahne and Westheimer, 2000 and 2003). An important research question that needs to be examined, albeit one beyond the reach of this chapter, is: 'what are the necessary elements of a Service Learning programme which can build not only social capital but also active citizenship?' (Eyler and Giles, 1999; Kahne and Westheimer, 2000 and 2003).

Excellent examples of youth-led service learning which involve reflective experiential learning for Active Citizenship are the REAL programme developed in the UK by Changemakers, a voluntary sector organisation which works with young people, and Youth Act!, a Citizenship Foundation programme inspired by a range of work under the same title developed by Street Law in the US[2] that seeks to provide young people with the citizenship skills to effect real change in their communities (see Figure 1). The volunteering dimension of the Citizenship Foundation's Giving Nation programme and their research with IPPR[3] into the work of pupils as associate members of governing bodies, both of which provide opportunities for Service Learning, are also worthy of note.

Figure 1

The Youth Act! Process

Service learning as political activity: a lesson in empowerment and civil renewal

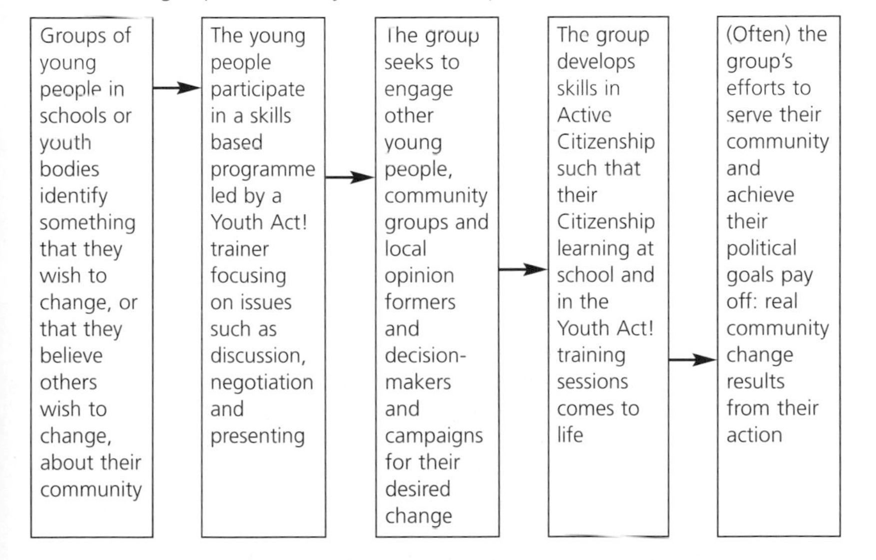

Active Citizenship, Service Learning and the delivery of the National Curriculum

In schools, the problem for teachers is to integrate Citizenship Education, including the opportunity to engage in Service Learning, into a (*national*) curriculum, which many view as already overcrowded (although this is less the case at Key Stage 4 and post-Tomlinson changes may help further here). And the Service Learning element poses an additional burden: providing the opportunity for students to participate in Service Learning requires strong partnerships with local community-based organisations, businesses and service providers and timetable flexibility. Nonetheless, it is important if Crick's oft-quoted ambitions are to be fulfilled:

> *We aim at no less than a change in the political culture of this country both nationally and locally: for people to think of themselves as active citizens, willing, able and equipped to have an influence in public life and with the critical capacities to weigh evidence before speaking and acting; to build on and to extend radically to young people the best in existing traditions of community involvement and public service, and to make them individually confident in finding new forms of involvement and action among themselves.* (DfEE/QCA, 1998; and DfEE/FEFC, 2000)

The vision of Crick's Advisory Group is a formidable one and there are, of course, many challenges to be faced if it is to be realised. Terence McLoughlin, among others, has raised a number of issues arising from the Advisory Group's report (McLaughlin, 2000; Osler, 2000). Here, I want to build on these and encourage further debate and discussion about how Citizenship Education through Service Learning might help to bring about the more participative democratic political culture that Crick seeks.

Civil renewal, deliberative democracy and Active Citizenship

David Blunkett in his Edith Kahln Memorial Lecture (CSV/Blunkett, 2003), and in his more recent publications and speeches, has called for a new civic renewal, which emphasises new forms and levels of community involvement in local and regional governance. This new democratic politics, which would include referendums, consultative activities, and deliberative participation, has found support from organisations as diverse as the Local Government Association, various trades unions and a range of educational bodies, support that has encouraged the prominent think tank IPPR to call for greater and more creative forms of civic engagement (IPPR, 2004).

One outcome of this shift in thinking, which might be termed a switch from government to governance, is the obligation upon local authorities to establish Local Strategic Partnerships, a duty arising from the Local Government Act 2000. These partnerships bring together a range of local organisations and seek to involve local communities in the development of Community Strategies. A more informal model – local Citizenship Education community forums – performs a similar but school specific task. Developed by Carrie Supple at the Citizenship Foundation, the forums are networks of local organisations (NGOs, public service providers, statutory bodies, youth offending teams, local football clubs, businesses) that, with LEA support, convene with teachers on a regular basis so as to inform and support the delivery of the Citizenship Curriculum in local schools[4]. More recently, the Home Office has established a Civil Renewal Unit, which has begun to develop an adult learner focused *Active Learning for Active Citizenship* programme through which it is intended that participants will develop the capacity to engage in deliberative democracy at a local level. In parallel, another Home Office team, the Community Cohesion Unit, is proposing the establishment of a national Citizenship (or Citizens') Day, as a means of celebrating a full range of local Active Citizenship projects while the newly formed Department for Constitutional Affairs is proposing a range of activities to enhance the legal and political awareness of citizens of all ages.

Generally the intention of these initiatives, especially where they are targeted at poorer areas, is to tackle social exclusion and promote regeneration and civil and civic renewal by promoting engagement and the building of social capital through active citizenship projects. As such, these projects provide important pegs on which schools and other educational institutions can hang Citizenship-focused education programmes, not least those based around real Service Learning. Moreover, they enable (and sometimes implore) the school or college to take a leadership role. The work of Gladesmore School in Tottenham, in leading a local anti-gun crime initiative through the Youth Act! framework, provides a practical example of this (see Figure 2).

Figure 2

From student action to curriculum (and community) change

The Youth Act! anti-gun crime project at Gladesmore Community School in Tottenham

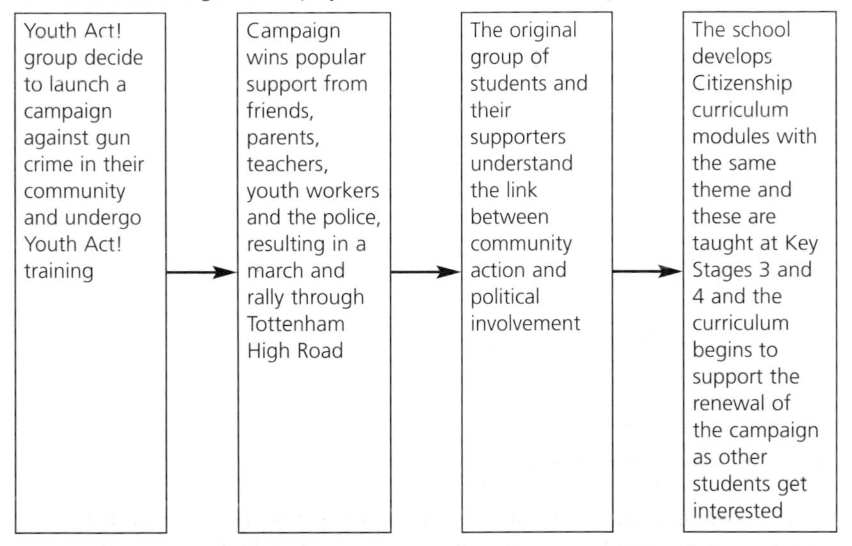

Service Learning and political awareness: the evidence

Until recently there has been relatively little empirical research into Citizenship and Citizenship Education beyond some pioneering studies of youth political socialisation. Ivor Crewe and his colleagues noted that much of the debate about Citizenship is 'conducted in what is virtually an empirical void' (Crewe et al., 1997). There has been, more recently, an increasing amount of research into Citizenship Education and its learning outcomes internationally. In the UK there have been a number of small-scale studies since 1998 and more recently the eight-year Citizenship Education Longitudinal Study (which is outlined in Chapter 1.2) has been launched. This is, for the first time in the UK, providing a comprehensive understanding of the outcomes of Citizenship Education as a compulsory core National Curriculum subject at Key Stages 3 and 4 and complements the Post-16 Citizenship Education Survey that is also being funded by DfES and undertaken by NFER. There are a number of contextual factors raised in the first report of the longitudinal study, and in other research. Critically, these focus on the competing definitions of Citizenship with which practitioners contend, the lack of a coherent vision for Citizenship Education in schools and colleges and the coherence of Citizenship programmes – concerns made all the sharper given the competing claims on Citizenship's purpose: promoting equality, identity and diversity, building global citizenship, getting the vote out, developing community cohesion and so on. Tony Breslin's concept of the Citizenship Manifesto, outlined elsewhere in these pages and now the subject of development work at the Citizenship Foundation[5] (Breslin, 2002), promises to do something to pull together the different dimensions of the Citizenship Curriculum and to thus bring coherence to work based in the classroom, the wider school and the outside community. This coherence is vital if Service Learning is to be seen as a key part of the Citizenship offer rather than a bolted on afterthought, probably for a minority of learners.

If, though, research into Citizenship Education in the UK remains in its infancy, there is an extensive range of research studies in the USA into the learning outcomes of Service Learning programmes for students in both secondary schools and higher education. What is especially interesting about this research is that the almost universal finding is that Service Learning, where volunteering is part of a formal Citizenship Curriculum, is more effective in its link with 'Citizenship' outcomes than with 'Community Service' or volunteering itself. That is, it serves to develop just the type of political awareness and literacy that Crick and his colleagues intended the new UK curriculum to do: a Service Learning, which builds Citizenship knowledge and develops Citizenship skills (Melchoir and Ballis, 2002).

'Real' community involvement: the case for Service Learning

Crick's three strands of Citizenship (Social and Moral Responsibility, Political Literacy and Community Involvement) are interwoven into a set of knowledge and skills within the National Curriculum that has subsequently emerged. I remain concerned, though, that the interpretation of 'community involvement' that underpins the Citizenship Curriculum will involve a conception of the community that sees it simply as a place or neighbourhood where students are merely 'active': *doing* good rather than as a *political good*, the outcome of which is informed, effective citizens. That is, the new curriculum will result in forms of volunteering that will fail to challenge the students to think and act 'politically': volunteering without Service Learning (Crick, 2002).

This raises the issue of how we develop through community involvement, especially on the local level, a more deliberative and democratic politics that can also provide a more active and political framework for enriching Citizenship Education. Thus, learning about Citizenship through active Community Involvement within the framework of the new curriculum should, at least in part, be based on the pedagogy of overtly reflective experiential Service Learning. Here, the key to success is to be found in asking how community-based or -focused learning experiences can best be structured to challenge students to become 'political' such that they become more aware of the political significance of civic engagement in local communities. As Breslin and Dufour argue in the opening pages of this text, digging a pensioner's garden is itself an act of doing good rather than an act of good Citizenship. The Citizenship learning begins when the student gardener begins to question why the pensioner is in the position that they are: in short, they may learn a thing or two about gardening, but the greater lessons are less about the pansies and more about the politics.

REFERENCES

Annette, J. (2000) 'Education for Citizenship, Civic Participation and Experiential Service Learning in the Community', in D. Lawton, R. Gardner and J. Cairns (eds) *Education for Citizenship*. London: Continuum.

Annette, J. (2003) 'Community and Citizenship Education', in A. Lockyer, B. Crick and J. Annette (eds) *Education for Democratic Citizenship*. London: Ashgate.

Battistoni, R. (2002) *Civic Engagement Across the Curriculum*. Providence, RI: Campus Compact.

Breslin, T. (2002), 'A Citizenship Manifesto for Every School?', *Teaching Citizenship*, 1(2). Birmingham: Assocation for Citizenship Teaching (ACT)/Questions Publishing.

CSV/Blunkett, D. (2003) *Civil Renewal: a new agenda; the Edith Kahn memorial lecture*. London: Community Service Volunteers.

Crewe, I., Searing, D. and Conover, P. (1997) *Citizenship and Civic Education*. London: Citizenship Foundation.

Crick, B. (2002) *Democracy*. Oxford: Oxford University Press.

Cruz, N. and Giles, D. Jr. (2000) *Where's the Community in Service-Learning Research?*. Michigan: Michigan Journal of Community Service Learning.

DfEE/QCA (1998) *Education for Citizenship and the Teaching of Democracy in Schools: Report of the Advisory Group on Citizenship*. London: QCA.

DfEE/FEFC (2000) *Citizenship for 16–19 Year Olds in Education and Training: Report of the Advisory Group on Citizenship*. Coventry: Further Education Funding Council.

DfES (2004) *Education and Training 14–19: Report of the Independent Advisory Group*. London: DfES.

Eyler, J. and Giles, D. Jr. (1999) *Where's the Learning in Service Learning?*. San Francisco: Jossey-Bass.

Gelmon, S. et al. (2001) *Assessing Service-Learning and Civic Engagement*. Providence, RI: Campus Compact.

IPPR (2004), *The Lonely Citizen*. London: Institute for Public Policy Research.

Home Office (2003), *The New and the Old: The Reports of the 'Life in the United Kingdom' Advisory Group*. London: HMSO.

Home Office (2004) *The Russell Report*. London: Home Office.

Kahne, J. and Westheimer, J. (2000) *Service-Learning and Citizenship: Directions for Research*. Michigan: Michigan Journal of Community Service Learning.

Kahne, J. and Westheimer, J. (eds) (2003), 'Special Section on Education, Democracy and Civic Engagement', *Delta Kappen,* 85(1).
Kolb, D. (1998) *Experiential Learning*. Englewood Cliffs, New Jersey: Prentice Hall.
McLaughlin, T. (2000) 'Citizenship Education in England: the Crick Report and Beyond', *Journal of Philosophy of Education,* 34(4).
Melchoir, A. and Ballis, L. (2002) 'Impact of service learning on civic attitudes and behaviours of middle and high school youth: findings from three national evaluations', in A. Furco and S. Billig (eds) *Advances in Service Learning Research*. Greenwich, Conre: Information Age Publishing.
Osler, A. (2000) 'The Crick Report: difference, equality and racial justice', *The Curriculum Journal*, 11(1).
Potter, J. (2002) *Active Citizenship in Schools*. London: Kogan Page.
Putnam, R.D. (2000) *Bowling Alone in America*. New York: Simon and Schuster.
Rimmerman, C. (1997) *The New Citizenship*. New York: Westview Press.
Wade, R. (ed.) (1997) *Community Service-Learning*. New York: SUNY Press.

NOTES

1 First Friday is a regular free-to-attend seminar for Citizenship Education teachers and advisers staged on the first Friday of every month during the academic year.
2 More information on Youth Act! programmes is available (in the UK) from the Citizenship Foundation and (in the US) from Street Law. Youth Act! is a trade mark of Street Law inc.
3 In 2002, IPPR and the Citizenship Foundation initiated the 'I Was A Teenage Governor' project to assess the learning and governance outcomes of involving young people as associate members of the governing bodies of their schools. Reports from this ongoing project, now managed solely by the Citizenship Foundation, are available on their website (www.citizenshipfoundation.org.uk).
4 More details about the Community Forum model are available from Carrie Supple at the Citizenship Foundation.
5 The Esmee Fairbairn Foundation is funding a three year practice development project at the Citizenship Foundation from Summer 2005.

FURTHER READING

Annette, J. (2003) 'Community and Citizenship Education', in A. Lockyer, B. Crick and J. Annette (eds) *Education for Democratic Citizenship*. London: Ashgate.
Crick, B. (2002) *Democracy*. Oxford: Oxford University Press.
Faulks, K. (2002) *Citizenship*. Oxford: RoutledgeFalmer.
Potter, J. (2002) *Active Citizenship in Schools*. London: Kogan Page.

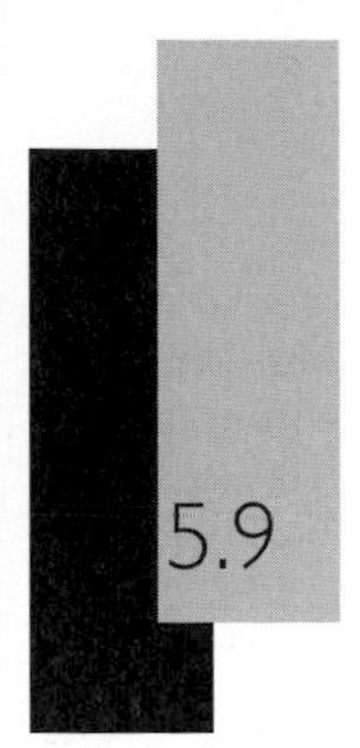

Education for Health and Well-being: Citizenship within the National Healthy School Programme

5.9

Jayne Wright

Background

Those of us who have long worked within PSHE and Citizenship, the pastoral area and the social curriculum welcomed the arrival of the National Healthy School Programme (NHSP) with a sigh of relief: at last a programme geared towards educating the whole child and caring about school staffs' well-being too! The programme is the umbrella that sits over a plethora of subjects, whole school approaches, initiatives and support mechanisms. In essence, it has been a 'carrier' process for the improvement of Citizenship provision in schools. Schools undertaking Healthy Schools work have the opportunity to work on a programme driven by 'Education' (Department for Education and Skills – DfES) and 'Health' (Department of Health – DH). This partnership has helped to raise the profile of many key issues rewarding success in areas such as Citizenship. Healthy Schools complements existing and increasingly mainstreamed efforts to promote PSHE, physical activity, healthy-eating and emotional health and well-being in schools.

The government's stated belief that schools are one of the key settings in which to promote the health of young people and the wider community prompted their decision to introduce the National Healthy School Standard in 1999. The programme was created to support and complement both the non-statutory PSHE framework available to schools from 2000 and, thereby, the statutory implementation of Citizenship in secondary schools as part of the National Curriculum from August 2002.

The government's White Paper *Excellence in Schools*, produced by the then DfEE in 1997, outlined an intention to help all schools to become 'healthy' schools. The Department of Health (DH) later announced the arrival of the National Healthy School Standard in its Green Paper *Saving Lives: Our Healthier Nation* (DH, 1998), reinforced by an announcement on 14 May 1998 by Ministers Tessa Jowell (Public Health) and Estelle Morris (School Standards) prior to its formal launch on 6 October 1998. From then on all Local Education Authorities (LEAs) and their health counterparts, Health Authorities, were invited to submit local healthy school programmes to be accredited to the National Healthy School Standard. Since then the NHSP has evolved and developed both nationally and locally. In December 2002 the DfES and DH decided on specific targets for Phase 2 of the programme. These were since superseded in 2005 by new targets.

The arrival of new guidance

2005 marked the arrival of new national guidance and criteria for what is now called 'National Healthy School Status' (NHSS) which is found within the new *National Healthy Schools Programme* (NHSP). This aims to introduce 'more rigorous and nationally consistent criteria' (DH/DfES, 2005c) as outlined in the Public Health White Paper of November 2004 – *Choosing Health*. In this, the Government's intention for all schools to become healthy schools was outlined (see Figure 1). This objective is also included in the *Five Year Strategy for Children and Learners* (DfES, July 2004), the *Healthy Living Blueprint* (DfES, September 2004) and the *National Service Framework for Children, Young People and Maternity Services* (DH/DfES November 2004). Healthy schools (and, indeed, as part of this, Citizenship) can also make a significant contribution towards achieving the five national outcomes for children set out in *Every Child Matters* and the subsequent Children Act of 2004.

Figure 1
National targets for the NHSP

- By December 2006, half of all schools in England to achieve national healthy school status.
- By 2009, the Government wants every school to be working towards achieving national healthy school status.

In this new guidance, Citizenship is not overtly identified as one of the four new core themes (see Figure 2), but local programmes and, indeed, the national team are keen to see schools developing and improving their Citizenship provision. Citizenship is part of the PSHE and Citizenship non-statutory framework at Key Stages 1 and 2 entitled 'preparing to play a role as active citizens'. As such, primary schools are still expected to demonstrate good practice in Citizenship in order to be recognised as a 'Healthy School' under the new criteria (see Figure 3). Following the introduction of Citizenship as part of the statutory curriculum in secondary schools, there would appear to be some tension emerging between PSHE and Citizenship, a point discussed elsewhere in this volume in chapters by Jan Campbell, Liz Craft and by Tony Breslin. The pressure on schools to ensure coverage of the Citizenship Programme of Study at Key Stage 3 and 4 has meant PSHE curriculum time in many schools has been squeezed. Most would agree that it is vitally important for schools to keep both subjects high on their agendas. The new Healthy Schools core themes and criteria continue to ensure that PSHE is given a high profile by schools in all phases. The challenge is to ensure that Citizenship and PSHE are not set in competition, but are given equal status and delivered, as Campbell and Craft argue in Chapter 6.2, as part of a coherent whole school approach that recognises both their distinctiveness and their complementariness as areas.

The aims of the National Healthy Schools Programme

The NHSP is designed to give practical support to schools in creating an enjoyable, safe, effective learning environment – one that minimises potential health risks thereby enhancing life chances. So what is a healthy school? In the words of the NHSP Guidance for Healthy Schools Coordinators:

> *A healthy school is one that is successful in helping pupils to do their best and build on their achievements. It is committed to on-going improvement and development. It promotes physical and emotional health by providing accessible and relevant information and equipping pupils with the understanding, skills and attitudes to make informed decisions about their health. A healthy school understands the importance of investing in health to assist in the process of raising levels of pupil achievement and improving standards. It also recognises the need to provide both a physical and social environment that is conducive to learning.* (DH/DfES, 2005b)

In this context,

> *the aims of the NHSP are:*
> - *to support children and young people in developing healthy behaviours*
> - *to help to raise pupil achievement*
> - *to help to reduce health inequalities; and*
> - *to help promote social inclusion.* (DH/DfES, 2005c)

The editors of this collection point to the tension between achievement and inclusion that sits at the heart of much education policy. The NHSP aims to bridge this divide. As such, Healthy Schools has been widely welcomed nationally and locally. Every Local Education and Health Partnership in the country now offers schools the opportunity to take part in an nationally accredited Healthy Schools Programme.

A recognised strength of the original Healthy Schools programme was that schools and their local communities could target their areas of greatest need first: 'the strength of the National Healthy School Standard is that it combines a national quality standard with the flexibility for local partnerships and schools to decide on what they need and what works for them' (DfES, 1999). As such, each school and, indeed, each local partnership had a slightly different flavour. This stemmed from the existence of those 'Health Promoting Schools' which preceded the National Healthy Schools Programme. The 2005 National Healthy Schools Status marks the end in many ways of this local variety; although schools will still be encouraged to work on matters that are important to them, they will also be expected to demonstrate particular evidence in the four core themes (see Figure 2) and meet set criteria (see Figure 3) using a whole school approach (as part of the process outlined in Figure 4). It would appear that the spirit of the original National Healthy Schools Standard has been very much retained and celebrated both by schools and by local Healthy Schools partnerships, something evidenced by the common featuring of the original Healthy Schools logo on school note paper and in school foyers (Figure 5).

Health as a policy priority in the context of *Every Child Matters*

If the NHSP did not exist there would still, undoubtedly, be pockets of good health focused practice taking place in schools around the country; the NHSP does provide a means of recognising and validating *existing* good practice in a number of crucial aspects of school life, including Citizenship. Teachers have always cared about these issues although it could be argued that the profile of these approaches has been eroded to a certain extent by the current obsession with academic subject targets, testing and league tables. Without the NHSP, however, would children's health feature as highly on schools' agenda? Recent headlines in the media on obesity, voter apathy, sexually transmitted infections amongst teenagers, binge drinking, drug taking, teenage pregnancy rates (to name but a few) serve as a reminder of the importance of this work. Educationalists and politicians would be wise to ensure that health (physical, social and emotional) in its broadest interpretation remains top of the agenda in schools if the UK is serious about tackling these issues effectively. Funding continues to be paramount if local Healthy Schools Programmes are to achieve their targets and offer schools proper support.

Moreover, Ofsted has confirmed that schools that have vigorously adopted the NHSP are more improved than those that have not embraced the NHSP at all or with less enthusiasm: 'an increasing number of Ofsted Inspection Reports are specifying the NHSP as having an effect on their school' (Health Development Agency (HDA), 2003a).

From September 2005, Ofsted expects schools to demonstrate how they are contributing to the five national outcomes for children stipulated by Every Child Matters and the Children Act 2004 – being healthy; staying safe; enjoying and achieving; making a positive contribution, and economic well-being. They will be expected to include in their Ofsted Self-Evaluation Form (SEF) their progress under these five outcomes: 'Gaining national Healthy School status provides rigorous evidence of this, and will assist you in evidencing your self-evaluation and completing your new school profile' (DH/DfES, 2005c).

Thus, whilst teachers fine tune their delivery and focus on their subject-specific agendas in an attempt to improve exam results, small amounts of progress will undoubtedly ensue. Greater gains, however, will be made if the teaching profession can ensure that pupils:

- feel safe and secure in their environment
- feel valued and have a voice in their school
- are free from hunger and thirst at school
- understand and are empowered to participate in the political and legal system of their country
- feel able to make informed, healthy lifestyle choices
- are given responsibility and have their rights respected.

Where this takes place, concentration improves in classes and relationships become valued – resulting in improved motivation and performance.

Anecdotally, teachers report that a pupil whose mind is elsewhere because, for example, they fear bullying, they have not eaten, or have taken drugs, cannot learn effectively. Surely educationalists have a duty to ensure that the above issues are addressed in our schools? The NHSP provides a platform from which to work towards this vision and here the arrival of statutory Citizenship Education has a key part to play.

The importance of Citizenship to a healthy school

Citizenship provides learning opportunities for pupils, from the Foundation Stage, through Key Stages 1 to 4 and in the post-16 sector, to gain the knowledge, skills and understanding necessary to play an effective role in society at local, national and international levels. Moreover, the key strands of Citizenship Education (social and moral responsibility, political literacy and community involvement) and the associated National Curriculum requirements at Key Stages 3 and 4 have been embedded in the NHSP (*Managing Teaching Citizenship Through the National Healthy School Standard*, HDA, 2003b). The Healthy Schools Programme has, in many ways, encouraged the development of a curriculum that:

- enables the preparation of pupils such that they play an active role as citizens
- helps pupils to become informed, thoughtful and responsible citizens who are aware of their duties and rights
- develops the skills of enquiry and communication
- promotes pupils' spiritual, moral, social and cultural development, making them more self-confident and responsible both in and beyond the classroom
- develops the skills of participation and responsible action
- encourages pupils to play a helpful part in the life of their schools, neighbourhoods, communities and the wider world
- supports the knowledge and understanding that young people require to become informed citizens
- teaches pupils about our economy and democratic institutions and values
- encourages a respect for different national, religious and ethnic identities
- develops pupils' ability to reflect on issues and take part in discussions.

The key strands from the National Curriculum Programmes of Study can all be 'taught' in any allocated Citizenship Curriculum time and through other 'carrier' subjects and this is important, but to deliver Citizenship effectively is to do more than this: it is to employ a whole school approach and to develop an ethos which is conducive to bringing the statutory requirements to life. Thus, the NHSS helps the school to develop a context in which Citizenship is *lived* as well as *learnt*. Thus, the Citizenship Curriculum is '. . . effectively embedded into the whole school ethos as well as delivered coherently and effectively through designated lessons' (HDA, 2003b).

Here the *School Self-Evaluation Tool For Citizenship Education* (DfES, 2004) can help to establish strengths and areas in need of development under the following six headings:

- Leadership
- Resources and their management
- Teaching and learning
- Staff development
- Monitoring and evaluation
- Parental/community involvement.

The self-evaluation tool, developed in partnership with the National College for School Leadership and the Association for Citizenship Teaching, works well with the requirements of NHSS and enables their application within the context of developing Citizenship Curriculum provision. As such, it allows Citizenship Coordinators to formulate an approach that can form part of a school's Healthy School action plan.

It should also be noted that NHSP also encourages schools to recognise pupil voice, so central in taking forward the Citizenship agenda, and to work in partnership with parents. Without this partnership with home and engagement with the pupils' real needs and views, pupils' readiness to learn is often compromised.

The new *Guidance for Healthy Schools Co-ordinators* (DH/DfES, 2005b) continues to advocate the same approaches but as Citizenship is no longer one of the four core themes, there is obviously less emphasis. The new National Healthy Schools database does, however, provide local programmes with a mechanism to record achievement against Citizenship provision. The following (Figure 6) can be found within a section entitled 'Other work outside the NHSS':

Figure 6

Criteria for Citizenship set out in the new Guidance to Healthy Schools Co-ordinators

Citizenship

- The school has completed the *School Self-Evaluation Tool for Citizenship Education* and uses this to inform planning.
- A Citizenship Coordinator with sufficient status in the school to fulfil the role is in post and Citizenship is discussed in line with the curriculum areas, with the Leadership team in the school.
- There is an up-to-date policy for Citizenship which reflects the school's work, aspirations and vision.
- There are sufficient resources including funding to meet the minimum standards and entitlement of the National Curriculum in line with statutory requirements, non-statutory guidance and NHSS guidance.
- There are schemes of work providing a tangible core programme supplemented by lessons/activities in the broader curriculum which have clearly focused Citizenship learning objectives.
- A wide range of teaching and learning approaches are used to deliver Citizenship with recognition given to different styles of learning and an awareness of the controversial nature of some issues, which are responded to appropriately.

- A consistent approach to assessing and recording progress in Citizenship is used, taking evidence from across and beyond the school environment and celebrating achievement.
- Parents and community members are used to support the Citizenship Curriculum and receive clear guidance on their role and purpose.

Lessons to learn from primary schools

In my experience as a Healthy Schools Line Manager in Hertfordshire and more recently as a Healthy Schools and Citizenship consultant in Buckinghamshire, it would appear that primary schools often lead the way in successfully creating a whole school vision around both Citizenship and health. In secondary schools there are often pockets of excellent practice taking place but embedding it in the school's ethos and as a genuine whole school approach is a much greater challenge. Generally speaking, secondary schools would do well to build on the success taking place in their feeder primary schools. This would enable pupils from these successfully validated primary schools to build more effectively on their knowledge, skills and understanding. Pupils often arrive at secondary school as previously highly valued members of their primary school, whose views are listened to and acted upon, only to be anonymous members of a large community in which they have little real say. All secondary schools need to give pupils the opportunity to continue to flourish as active citizens and, as Derry Hannam points out in Chapter 5.7, to participate in the life and decision-making of the school. The recognition of the skills that pupils bring from primary level is not apparent in every secondary school. Secondary school teachers and school leaders are missing a golden opportunity here. If teachers are to welcome pupils effectively into a larger, new community, then they need to build on their current successes experienced in primary. Implementing the NHSP in the secondary school can play a key part here and may help to address issues such as the dip in achievement that occurs across primary–secondary transfer – the justification for the rightly lauded Key Stage 3 Strategy.

The very structure of secondary education is less effective at successfully initiating and embedding whole school approaches in this area. As a range of contributors to this volume note, often PSHCE (Personal, Social, Health and Citizenship Education) does not have a high profile in the school and is delivered by teams of teachers that are less than pleased at the prospect of teaching an additional subject. Secondary schools operate on tight deadlines for coursework and exams and, sadly, non-examined subjects are often viewed as less important by staff, and this can be projected to pupils. The introduction of GCSE courses in Citizenship Studies goes some way to tackling these issues but must not do so at the expense of the broader Citizenship and PSHE curriculum. Learning is not just about examinations. The NHSP reminds us of the importance of schools as emotionally and physically healthy places.

Working towards a shared vision: the NHSP as a benefit to pupils and teachers

This is not to say that secondary teachers are not advocates of everything that the NHSP and PSHCE stand for; it is simply the lack of time and often limited training that often prevents these areas from flourishing. The PSHE Certification Programme has made, in my experience as a PSHE Lead, National Assessor and Regional Certification Adviser, a considerable impact on the confidence and abilities of secondary school PSHE teachers, thereby beginning to tackle the training issue.

With time at a premium, some teachers see NHSP as 'just another initiative' or a 'bolt-on'. Here, it is important for the full school community to understand the benefits of an effective whole school approach to NHSP for both their pupils *and* school staff. It is for this reason that the school's leadership team must possess a clear vision that gives direction and motivation to their staff. The NHSP, and the role that it plays in the improvement of the school's Citizenship practice, is a process that needs to be steered, and a vision that needs to be shared by all staff. Heads that think the Healthy Schools Programme is a quick fix, tick box way to obtain a logo for their school letter heading need to re-evaluate their approach. The audits of current levels of activity in the four core themes often reveal woeful inadequacies that need urgent attention. This, coupled with the results of seeking the actual opinions of their own pupils, parents and staff, often unveil a host of issues that need addressing if the school is to move forward. Lip service is not an option. A head ignores the school's views at their peril!

Carried out thoroughly, the NHSP permeates all aspects of a school curriculum, its ethos, its policies, its procedures; influencing and re-engaging the very heart of the school. This may sound daunting (and fanciful) to the overworked, stressed teacher, losing the work–life balance battle and dealing constantly with behaviour issues. However, in providing the opportunity to take things (and thinking) back to the drawing board, the NHSS provides schools with a unique opportunity and framework to reflect and do things differently. Thus, again it can be an engine for positive change; for thinking outside of the box – especially in respect of those things that the stressed teacher and the vexed school community battles with most. Moreover, it provides a means of consolidating activity across many other initiatives, approaches, strategies, awards, planning processes, drives and programmes: Safer Routes to Schools; the Teenage Pregnancy Strategy; Young People's Substance Misuse Plans; School Achievement Awards; Investors in People; Sport England's Activemark and Sportsmark awards; the Duke of Edinburgh programme; key aspects of the behaviour and attendance strategy (SEBS – Social, Emotional and Behavioural Skills, and SEAL – Social and Emotional Aspects of Learning) and so on.

It has been my privilege to observe classroom provision across a wide variety of primary and secondary schools. Seeing life through the eyes of pupils is very enlightening and often a liberating experience. Observing the fruits of change and the successes of schools achieving NHSS has been one of the most rewarding professional experiences of my career. To have played a part in helping a school to make changes that benefit the lives of hundreds of pupils and staff has been challenging but thoroughly worthwhile. As a profession we can sometimes be cynical; indeed, I have heard every argument levied against working on the Healthy Schools Programme. However, when carried through thoroughly, the benefits justify the means (and any toil) many times over. It is wonderful to see a school's work recognised. Pupils and staff need to have pride in their school. The NHSP provides a golden opportunity for a school to work as a community in pursuit of a positive goal and one that is central to the Citizenship agenda.

The benefits of the Healthy Schools Programme: the experience of two schools

Evidence of impact and success is often, in many ways, anecdotal. Not all things that schools do can be measured but that certainly does not mean that they lack impact! Proving the success of NHSP has been a tricky issue for the local and the national Healthy Schools teams. As noted, Ofsted findings have thrown weight behind the programme but it is the words of headteachers, teachers, parents and most importantly pupils that reveal the extent of its impact. On one memorable visit to a secondary school I stopped a pupil in the corridor and asked what they thought of the Healthy Schools Programme. I half expected him to look at me blankly, so I was really pleased when he replied, 'It's really good! We have a buddy system that I'm part of and there's not as much bullying. Things have got better at lunchtime too. There's places for us to go out of the cold and lockers so we don't have to carry our stuff everywhere. The school council have worked well hard at making that happen. So are you going to pass us then?' I suppose the badge gave it away and I did successfully validate the school!

I have literally seen schools turn themselves around using the NHSP as a framework for school improvement. It is a long process that can be uncomfortable at times as it moves a school out of its 'comfort zone', especially in the early consultation phase. But if a school is determined to listen to all concerned and is really prepared to make things better, then it is often the smallest of changes that can have the biggest impact. In the words of one secondary headteacher, 'I don't think you can improve academically unless you become a healthy, happy school' (HDA, 2003c) or as the official documentation puts it 'Its basic tenet is that pupils, like adults, learn better when they are in a condition to learn – when they feel safe and secure, valued, stimulated, challenged and rewarded for their learning' (HDA, 2003a). And it follows that if the pupils are motivated and happy then they are likely to be better behaved and achieve more academically. This in turn improves the contentment of the staff that positively impacts both on teaching and learning and on recruitment and retention issues. At a time when TLR (Teaching and Learning Responsibilities) are under negotiation, and staff morale is fragile, the NHSP can provide positive support for staff.

The two case studies below provide a description of how, differently applied, the NHSS (and now the NHSP) can bring about whole school improvement. It is this reality in schools that I would like to leave you with. Working on the NHSP really can make a difference to a school!

CASE STUDY 1
Bishop's Hatfield Girls' School in Hertfordshire

The school is an 11–18 comprehensive girls' secondary school that has been involved in the Healthy Schools Programme from the early stages.

PSHE and Citizenship including Sex and Relationship Education, Careers Education and Drug Education are all taught in a programme aptly entitled 'Life Skills'. Components are carefully designed to be mapped in a cross-curricular way that enables staff and pupils to see the links.

The topics are sub-divided into eight key areas that are seen as essential knowledge, skills and understanding that enable a person to function as a healthy citizen. These are visually demonstrated to pupils in the form of a jigsaw to show how they fit together to make a whole, thereby demonstrating the different facets of us.

Components of the Life Skills Programme:
- My Relationships – My social, sexual and moral self
- My Career – My vocational self and use of leisure
- My Environment – My environmental self
- Me – My self-awareness, philosophic, bodily and moral self
- My Community – Myself as citizen, political, social and moral self
- My Finances – My financial self
- My Education – Myself as a learner
- My Health and Safety – My physical self, healthy self, safe self

Citizenship is, therefore, delivered partly through discrete units of work within the Life Skills programme, and partly through mapped links across the curriculum. Students at Key Stages 3 and 4 have one weekly 50-minute 'Life Skills' lesson taught by a member of the Life Skills team, all of whom have volunteered to teach the programme. The team attend one or two days' INSET annually in a residential setting. This protected time allows for creative planning and structuring of the year's Life Skills Programme. In addition, half-termly planning, assessment and evaluation meetings are built into the school's calendar of meetings. This ensures that the delivery of PSHCE is cohesive and that the staff are keen to be part of the team. Feedback from pupils has been very positive and is used to inform planning. Pupils play a key part in the assessment process too. Formative assessment opportunities are built into the programme and at the end of the academic year students write a report of their progress and achievements. This report forms part of the final end of year report to parents.

Awards to recognise student achievement in voluntary work are offered through the Millennium Volunteers programme in the Sixth Form. Students can gain a 100-hours award, and subsequently the award for excellence, which recognises 200 hours of voluntary work. This has enabled active Citizenship to flourish in the school by providing a positive focus that has a high profile with other staff and pupils too.

The school is currently establishing a Curriculum Planning Group, which will include pupil representatives from every year group to give input into schemes of work and lessons. The pupils will then have a real voice about how and what they are taught.

The Life Skills Programmme Coordinator is responsible for Citizenship and for Healthy Schools. She feels that a number of successful processes have been embedded in whole school practices that enable the school to address the Citizenship Programmes of Study as part of their work on the NHSS. She comments: 'the pupils, staff and parents hold the Life Skills Programme in high regard probably because we all believe in its value and it is delivered by a dedicated team of enthusiastic PSHCE teachers. NHSP has provided us with a positive structure that has also given us some reward for all our hard work.'

CASE STUDY 2

Tring School in Hertfordshire

Tring School is an 11–18 mixed comprehensive in Hertfordshire. It is working on the Hertfordshire Healthy Schools Programme. The Life Skills Coordinator, an Assistant Headteacher, notes: 'the benefits seemed obvious because if children are not happy and healthy in school they are less likely to achieve their potential. In addition the (old) seven NHSP themes are common to most schools and all involved aspects we wanted to improve and develop.'

The accreditation process required the involvement of pupils and teachers, support staff, caterers, governors and parents. The already active School Council was given the opportunity to get involved in a number of key issues ranging from Healthy-Eating to Health and Safety. In fact, the HDA (Healthy Development Agency) has named the school in documentation that praises the use of healthy vending machines. The school council were keen to play a part in introducing these to the school as part of the food agency's pilot scheme to see how popular healthier products would be compared to the high fat, high sugar alternatives.

A computer consultation package has been used by 200 pupils in Years 7–13 providing the opportunity to listen to the pupils' views on a range of issues that cover all of the NHSP key themes. The lively, colourful and fun graphics meant that pupils enjoyed answering the questions too. The school is in the process of analysing the results to improve areas identified in the questionnaire. Dealing with bullying more effectively and the delivery of SRE appear to be areas that will be focused on next as a result of the consultation.

The school has implemented PSHCE Primary Liaison meetings. The school liaises closely with its seven main primary feeder schools. The opportunity to discuss PSHCE-related issues with the primary coordinators has been invaluable. They have looked at continuity and progression across the Key Stages with particular reference to SRE, where both primary and secondary policies now have areas of commonality. Materials are therefore more consistent and introduced at planned times to avoid overlap and repetition. In the future, the group plan to develop consistent drug education work and will continue to work on the Healthy Schools Programme together.

Much effort has been devoted in the last couple of years to developing their Citizenship programme. Audits have been undertaken and time devoted to the development of pupil portfolios. Sessions have also been provided that enable pupils to identify where they have gained Citizenship skills in other areas of the curriculum. Through the Duke of Edinburgh Award Scheme, Millennium Volunteers and charity work the school has been able to encourage 'active' Citizenship opportunities. A highly successful area has also been the organisation of elections connected with School Councils, Youth Town Councils and UKYP (UK Youth Parliament). Posters, candidates campaigning, voting using real booths and ballot boxes have all helped to raise the status of these councils and pupils have greeted the elections with real enthusiasm.

Finally, peer education projects have been expanded in the school. Year 12 pupils have delivered SRE and drug education sessions to Year 9 and at present the school is working with a Year 10 ASDAN group on Conflict Resolution with a view to delivering a session to a Year 7 form from another school. Training of the pupils and staff to ensure the success of the peer educators has taken place and 30 teachers from a number of European countries have observed some of the Citizenship sessions and peer education projects.

The coordinator is clear about the impact of the NHSP on all of this: '. . . the real advantage of the programme is the process it takes you through and the opportunities therefore provided for real and continued improvement'.

Enhancing Citizenship provision through the NHSP framework: a closing observation

In summary, the NHSP provides schools with the opportunity to focus on areas that really matter. This is demonstrated in the case studies provided here and in schools up and down the country. The Healthy Schools Programme is successful when it forms part of the school's ongoing self-evaluation and consultation processes. It is not new, nor is it a 'magic wand' to make things instantly better. It is a programme that rewards and actively supports school success through providing an environment where pupils feel valued, feel safe and are able to make healthy lifestyle choices as active, responsible citizens. Schools not working on a Healthy Schools Programme do so at their peril and risk missing an opportunity to enhance and indeed improve their Citizenship provision too.

REFERENCES

DfES (1999) *National Healthy School Standard: Guidance*. Nottingham: DfES Publications.

DfES (2001) *National Healthy School Standard: Getting Started – A Guide For Schools*. DfES/Department of Health.

DfES (2004) *The School Self-Evaluation Tool For Citizenship Education*. DfES/ACT/QCA/NCSL.

HDA (2003a) *How the National Healthy School Standard Contributes to School Improvement*. HDA/DH/DfES.

HDA (2003b) *Managing Teaching Citizenship Through the National Healthy School Standard*. HDA/DH/DfES.

HDA (2003c) *National Healthy School Standard: A Toolkit for Local Co-ordinators*. Wetherby: HDA/DH/DfES.

DH/DfES (2005a) *National Audit Tool and Guidance for local education and health partnerships on validating school achievement of national healthy school status*. DH/DfES.

DH/DfES (2005b) *Guidance for Healthy Schools Co-ordinators*. DH/DfES.

DH/DfES (2005c) *National Healthy School Status – A Guide for Schools*. DH/DfES.

ACKNOWLEDGEMENTS

The author would like to thank Sue Carter at Bishop's Hatfield Girls' School and Andrew Dobberson at Tring School for their permission to include and input into the case study material.

PART SIX

STRUCTURES FOR CITIZENSHIP MEETING THE LEADERSHIP AND MANAGEMENT CHALLENGE

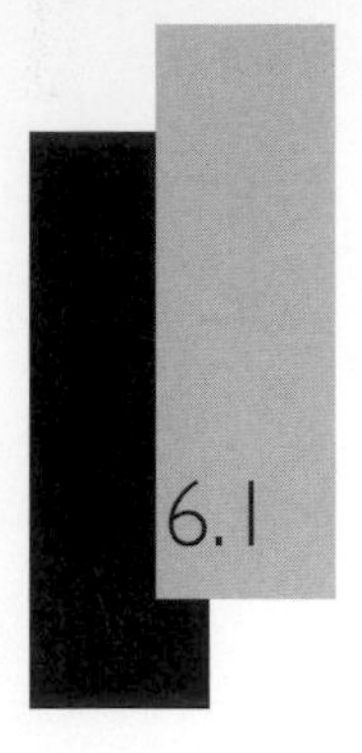

6.1 Citizenship in Secondary Schools: Management, Organisation and Identity

Graham Morris

The introduction of Citizenship as a National Curriculum subject in secondary schools in 2002 was, in a number of respects, a unique event in post-war educational history. Whilst the arrival of a National Curriculum itself brought a degree of statutory prescription previously applied only to Religious Education, it consisted, with the possible exception of Design Technology, of a range of familiar subjects with recognisable identity and long pedigree. The subsequent largely failing attempt to promote 'cross-curricular themes', of which Citizenship was one, left the secondary curriculum of ten subjects together with PSHE, RE and Careers Education and Guidance relatively untouched. A number of adjustments have been made as to the requirements within Key Stage 4, but the advent of a new subject to be studied by all is unprecedented.

Citizenship is, however, a 'new subject' in more than one sense; newly introduced, yes, but also new in that it is not as yet fully defined with the clarity of other subjects, nor rooted in widely understood concepts, theory and conventional practice. The 'Crick Report' (QCA, 1998) provides a powerful steer in this respect, going far beyond its rhetorical much quoted aim of bringing about 'a change in the political culture of this country'. Yet it is when one turns to the Programmes of Study produced by the QCA (DfEE/QCA, 1999), with the 'light touch' which David Blunkett asked for, that one can discern a series of features which render the subject unique beyond the fact that it is newly introduced. They might be summarised and listed as follows:

- Remarkable brevity and lack of detail compared with other National Curriculum programmes of study.
- A rubric indicating that 'teaching should *ensure* that knowledge and understanding about becoming informed citizens are acquired and applied when developing skills of enquiry and communication and *participation* and *responsible action*' (emphasis added).
- Indications of cross-curricular links with other subjects.
- A requirement to 'negotiate, decide and take part in school and community-based activities'.

Each of these brings with it an important implication for the provision and management of education for Citizenship within the school:

- The need and scope for devising the precise content and mode of provision in individual schools.
- A degree of prescription with regard to pedagogy.
- The possible need to manage cross-curricular provision.
- A unique stipulation with regard to learning leading to action and involvement in the school and the community.

Leading and managing change

Taken together, the above considerations indicate clearly that the introduction of Citizenship and its subsequent development hold significance for the whole school, no matter what particular form of provision may be decided upon, a matter I shall come to later. Whether experienced through wrangling over curriculum time allocations at Senior Staff meetings, the requirement of tutors to embark upon teaching topics with which they are unfamiliar, a greater attention to the voice of the pupil or student through an increasingly effective school council or the request that other, perhaps all, subject departments contribute to the school's Citizenship provision, all members of staff will be involved and have concerns if not specified responsibilities. Thus, we are dealing with substantial and uncharted change and all the characteristic responses which accompany it. There exists an extensive literature on the management of change which I shall not cite here. Suffice it to say that a number of themes run through it, none in themselves surprising, but all relevant in the current context. Perhaps most important is the need for all involved to recognise the need for change, or at least to have some understanding as to what those leading it are aiming to achieve by it. Second, there is the need for managers to recognise the levels of insecurity and uncertainty which are commonly experienced at times of change and to provide a collaborative and supportive environment on which people may rely. Such insecurity is most frequently related to fears of inadequacy when faced with new and unfamiliar tasks or responsibilities or of one's previously proven skills and activities being undervalued. From this emerges a third need to actively assist people to fulfil new responsibilities through adequate training, mentoring and feedback.

What I am attempting to draw attention to here is the distinction between 'managing Citizenship', so to speak, as an ongoing and integral part of the school's provision, challenging enough in its own right given its complexities, and the need to take particular account of the effects of its still recent introduction, which should be regarded as a process *spanning* a number of years rather than as something which *occurred* in September 2002. Initiating and sustaining such a period of change through to successful implementation requires not merely management, but *leadership*, a more than semantic distinction implied in the title of this part of this volume. Accumulating evidence from the QCA (QCA, 2004) and Ofsted (Ofsted, 2002; 2004) indicates beyond doubt that the stance and actions taken by headteachers in particular and their senior colleagues in establishing a shared, positive vision backed by facilitating time and resource is the crucial factor in moving towards high quality Citizenship Education. Such senior management teams have recognised that far from being a belated appendix to a standard list of established curriculum subjects, Citizenship has a major part to play in reconsidering curriculum provision overall, with a potential for engaging with pupils and students in ways which promote and nurture not only their own development as individual citizens but also the healthy development of the school as a community. They have allocated time for whole staff discussion prior to taking key decisions, have identified and supported teams charged with elements of planning led by appropriately rewarded coordinators, have made full use of initial funding intended to support the introduction of Citizenship and supplemented it, have readily released key teachers to attend relevant courses and conferences and have devoted significant amounts of time to in-school INSET. And soon, if not already, they will be reviewing arrangements in the light of experience and making modifications. In other words, they have recognised that in the early stages of a development of this kind an enhanced, even disproportionate, degree of resource is required, not only because of its self-evident importance, but also as a clear expression of the leadership's commitment, thereby engaging progressively the commitment of others. At the other end of the spectrum is the headteacher who has done little more than inform the PSHE Coordinator that she should add the letter C to the first part of her title and left her to get on with it. Sadly, I quote.

Curriculum provision

Nobody is likely to contest the proposition that the decision as to what form Citizenship should take within the school's curriculum structure is of profound importance. It has obvious implications with regard to the time allocated to Citizenship and thus also to other subjects. It crucially bears upon who will teach the subject, in what context and with what degree of competence. It has significance for the lines of responsibility and accountability which need to be established and for the way in which resources will be allocated. Less obvious, perhaps, is the importance of the way in which this decision is taken and of the rationale lying behind the particular solution adopted. Given the average head of department's understandable position of seeking to defend, if not enhance, allotted curriculum time, it would come as no surprise to find a headteacher looking from the outset at the possibilities of inclusion in pre-existing PSHE time or of cross-curricular potential. Indeed, the former alternative has been found to be the most commonly adopted initial means of inclusion in the timetable. One has to ask, however, to what extent this is likely to lead to high quality teaching and learning and to a necessary identity for the subject, most particularly where PSHE is handled by group tutors, some, or even many, of whom may feel themselves to lack confidence or competence in dealing with elements of the programmes of study. Significantly, this model enlists teachers to work in fields which they might otherwise not have chosen. In practice one finds a spectrum of response ranging from enthusiastic embracing of a new and valued opportunity, through resigned acquiescence ('OK. Where's the worksheet?'), to resentment expressed in unprintable terms. I am not contending that this approach is inevitably doomed to mediocrity or worse, but that much preliminary and ongoing training is normally required to turn a conscript army into effective units sharing a common understanding of the purposes, values and practices which they serve. If time is indeed at a premium as everybody alleges, then we cannot afford to misuse it through less than fully committed, competent teaching and must therefore take the necessary steps to secure it.

The relationship between Citizenship and PSHE is powerfully elucidated by Jan Campbell and Liz Craft in Chapter 6.2 and needs no rehearsal here. It is worth noting, nevertheless, that the model of provision discussed above usually involves a PSHE and/or Citizenship Coordinator working with Year Heads on a school-wide strategic plan which the Year Heads then mediate with and through their tutor teams. Based on a notion of 'pastoral care', there is at least some correspondence between the role of the tutor as the person with a delegated responsibility for oversight and guidance of a particular group of pupils and his or her role within a tutor-based PSHE programme, concerned as it will be with issues of personal development, self-esteem, healthy lifestyles, personal relationships and so forth. Such correspondence is difficult to perceive, however, when turning to much of the knowledge and understanding required by the Citizenship Programmes of Study. That is not to say that a tutor could not be a first-rate teacher of Citizenship; many will be. I wish to assert, nevertheless, that the subject of Citizenship is not a corollary or spin-off of pastoral care and requires an identity of its own whether within a PSHE programme or elsewhere. One might add that, whilst those filling Year Head positions are likely to have displayed generic skills of team management and leadership or the potential for developing them in post, they may or may not have a particular interest in or aptitude for crucial curriculum responsibility in the field of Citizenship.

As many of my co-authors have noted, Citizenship, as one of five non-statutory cross-curricular themes set out in the early 1990s, did not provide an encouraging introduction to this approach. The very fact that the themes lacked the statutory status enjoyed by the subjects of the then only recently launched National Curriculum was probably as significant as any other factor in the relative lack of impact. The perception that other subjects had the potential to contribute nevertheless survived and was signalled clearly in the publication containing the Programmes of Study (DfEE/QCA, 1999), then in the initial guidance provided by the QCA (QCA, 2000) and, most noticeably, in the schemes of work (QCA, 2001a and 2001b) with their pull-out sheets indicating ways in which each subject might play a part. This has led some to carry out audits designed to identify as many topics as possible which might find a place in the work of other departments, leaving a residue of unplaceable items to be dealt with either within PSHE or some discrete Citizenship time. In a few cases the attempt has been made to deal with curriculum provision on an entirely cross-curricular basis.

The management of cross-curricular provision presents a range of self-evidently problematic issues to be resolved. Creating, developing and maintaining coherence, not merely in a curriculum plan document, but crucially in the perception and experience of pupils, requires the strongest possible identification and labelling of that which forms part of the school's provision for Citizenship. This corresponds to Ofsted's insistence that prior, precise information is afforded an inspection team as to within which lessons Citizenship Education may be observed. Systems for collation of assessments and reporting to parents need to be devised in ways that avoid the real danger of bureaucratic overload, especially where a large number of departments are involved (and here the editors' preference for a smaller number of 'carrier' subjects is surely right). The role, status and delegated authority of the Citizenship Coordinator vis-à-vis heads of department becomes of signal importance in leading and managing within a cross-curricular approach, raising questions about the degree of autonomy enjoyed by heads of department with regard to teaching in their own subject area. Moreover, one question is never far from the surface: to what extent are particular subject departments willing collaborators in the enterprise or reluctant participants? This issue of status and authority is one to which I will return.

Much of what I have said might be read as outlining exclusive alternatives; some have treated them as such and there are, indeed, choices to be made. However, most readers will be aware that advice and guidance from the DfEE/DfES, the QCA and from Ofsted have consistently indicated that a variety of approaches is necessary, including some so-called 'discrete' provision and also planned opportunities for active participation beyond the time-tabled curriculum – 'school and community-based activities'. For example, QCA's initial guidance (1998), having suggested a number of topics which might be taught through other subjects, goes on to say: 'In key stage 4, where pupils might not take subjects or courses that offer these opportunities, discrete provision of Citizenship will be necessary to meet the programmes of study.' Clearly the term 'discrete' stands in contradistinction to 'cross-curricular', but to what extent does the inclusion of modules or individual lessons within a PSHCE programme, albeit labelled as Citizenship, represent 'discrete' provision? I suggest that the answer depends upon the degree to which pupils experience the Citizenship element as a consistent thread linking regularly occurring, distinctive lessons and activities, capable of being logged or recorded and reflected upon, rather than apparently randomly distributed modules between others to which they do not relate. There are many topics which may provide the basis for study both from a PSHE and a Citizenship angle, as exemplified in the useful table in Campbell and Craft's chapter on page 296. I am suggesting, however, that clear signals need to be provided when the focus moves from the personal and inter-personal realm into the area of public policy if the notion of Citizenship and Active Citizenship within the public domain is to gain real purchase in the minds of pupils.

Citizenship and middle management

In an earlier section above I drew attention to the essential role of the headteacher and senior management team in creating and sharing a sustaining vision and in committing resource, mainly in the form of time, necessary during a period of innovation or change. I have also considered some, though certainly not all, of the issues surrounding the decision with regard to curriculum structure, since this holds the most significant implications for the way in which Citizenship is to be managed. The dominant structure and culture within secondary schools is that of the subject department. Heads of department lead teams of subject-trained professionals with responsibility for teaching *their* subject in most cases to all year groups vertically, so to speak, throughout the school. Across this structure, horizontally, lies a pastoral system most commonly comprising Year Heads and teams of tutors who, for a relatively small proportion of their time, perform duties and provide services unrelated to their specific subject specialism. Whole school co-ordination of pastoral work has frequently been the responsibility of one deputy head, whilst another may have held curriculum coordination responsibilities. However, there have developed, over time, a number of activities, provisions and related responsibilities which do not fit easily into this structure, most notably tutor-led PSHE, but also encompassing, for example, Careers Education and Guidance and GNVQ coordination, the new family of subjects as Tony Breslin calls them elsewhere in these pages. Now, for the first time, we have a National Curriculum subject requiring status and identity equal to that of other subjects without, as yet, some of the attributes which characterise them: a well defined department with a departmental head, shared educational histories involving degree study or its equivalent and subject specific teacher training, an established curriculum time allocation, developed and thoroughly tested classroom practice, detailed Programmes of Study and related lesson plans and resources.

Whilst a Head of Citizenship leading a dedicated department of several committed teachers providing core discrete provision presents at first sight a much more manageable proposition than does a Citizenship Coordinator working with a number of departments or perhaps directly or indirectly with 40 or more tutors, there still remains for the said Head of Citizenship the issue of some degree of cross-curricular coordination and/or liaison with heads of other departments or, at the very least, with whoever may be responsible for PSHE.

Whichever of these may be the case, the person responsible for Citizenship needs, I suggest, a dedicated and regularly meeting team of people with whom to discuss, plan, review and develop what is offered to pupils. He or she needs also to be accorded the status, reflected in the appropriate salary, equivalent to other heads of major departments. Furthermore, if the level of co-ordination extends, as it should, to all kinds of arrangements for related activity within the school and in the community which it serves, then the task is at least as demanding as that of any head of department and probably more so. Forms of line management, accountability and performance review differ from school to school. However, it would seem important that an appropriate member of the senior management team hold not only a particular brief but a personal commitment with regard to Citizenship if the person responsible is not already a member of that team. This is particularly relevant when, as is currently not uncommon, responsibility has been given to someone who has not necessarily sought it and is self-confessedly not yet entirely confident of meeting all the demands of the post.

Citizenship and subject identity

I have already used the word 'identity' several times and suggested its importance, since without it Citizenship is unlikely to register within the priorities of the school or in pupils' experience, let alone the perception of parents and the community. The creation of that identity implies not only visibility but also widely recognisable coherence, shape and form. Whilst we speak of Citizenship as a new 'subject', it is manifestly more than a subject in the conventional sense: a new subject and a new *type* of subject as the editors of this volume put it. If it is in practice to embody 'the teaching of democracy in schools', part of the title of the Crick Report, through genuine and valued participation in which pupils 'negotiate, decide and take part responsibly in school and community-based activities', as the Programmes of Study put it, then the dimensions of the school's provision for this will include a range of activities, procedures and conventions beyond those to be found in Citizenship lessons, irrespective of curriculum structure.

It is safe to say that every secondary school already provides or organises some activities which can potentially contribute powerfully to Citizenship learning, though they may not previously have been seen in that light. One thinks, for example, of work experience schemes, charity projects, police liaison schemes, properly functioning School Councils, Young Enterprise. Readers will be able to add many more. Some such activities involve all pupils at some stage in their progress through the school whilst only some may take part in others. In the latter case it may legitimately be argued that, because they do not involve all, then they cannot be regarded as part of the Citizenship entitlement. However, a thorough audit of all the activities, schemes and community relationships in which the school is involved, including its internal procedures through which public responsibilities are offered to pupils, is likely to provide at least the basis for constructing what Tony Breslin has called a 'Citizenship Manifesto' for the school (Breslin, 2001). Whilst some may wish to avoid the campaigning resonance of his title, the notion of a single, twice folded A4 sheet setting out in broad terms the school's approach to Citizenship, where in each year group it is clearly located in the curriculum, the additional experiences provided for all and the range of further opportunities available at different stages together with the community, civic, commercial and voluntary organisations who assist, is a powerful one. The process of creating such a document is one which will, perforce, involve some, perhaps many, members of staff and lead them to a fuller recognition of the scope of Citizenship. The document itself will be a significant means of informing and raising the consciousness of pupils, parents, governors and the wider community. It will also, incidentally, provide the Ofsted inspector with a comprehensive summary of the school's policy and practice and a manageable starting point for his or her programme of observation.

School self-assessment and continuous professional development

Surveys conducted by Ofsted (Ofsted, 2004) and the Second Annual Report of the Citizenship Education Longitudinal Study (Kerr et al., 2004) reflect the considerable disparities between individual schools' progress in implementing Citizenship Education. The latter, building upon an initial baseline survey, the subject of Chapter 1.2, identifies the factors underlying successful Citizenship in schools and suggests that all schools need to review how they teach Citizenship two years after its introduction. The need for such a review and for subsequent action in response to its outcomes will be required on a regular basis. *The School Self-evaluation Tool for Citizenship Education* (DfES, 2004a) provides a valuable matrix within which to structure a review, including, among others, sections on leadership and on staff development. It goes on to recommend appropriate action depending on the stage of development which the school has reached in each respect.

Whilst responsibility for managing the conduct of the review might well lie in the hands of an individual or small group, it would seem important that all members of staff and some representative pupils be provided with the opportunity to engage in appropriate parts of the review in order to ensure that varying perceptions are taken fully into account. With the emphasis upon a holistic approach running through all that has been said above and all publications cited, a review carried out on this basis can be yet another means of securing clarity, understanding and commitment to what, at best, should be a major advance not only in the quality of Citizenship Education but also in the life of the school in a more general sense.

The need for continuous professional development with regard to Citizenship is, and will continue to be for some time, greater than in any other subject as a result of its unfamiliarity for many involved. A school seriously intent on achieving high quality learning in Citizenship will be giving a degree of priority to releasing key members of staff to attend relevant courses or seminars. However, as with other subjects, the main thrust of professional development will take place within the school, supplemented and perhaps steered by the insights and knowledge acquired by those so released. The official DfES CPD Handbook for Citizenship and the related video (DfES, 2004b) is a further tool which should enable schools to undertake that task supported by advice, guidance and resource. There nevertheless remains the management issue of allocating an adequate proportion of INSET time for this purpose, which will, again, be indicative of the school leadership's determination, or lack of it, to implement effectively a decision, which emerged through our British democratic procedures, we perhaps should remind ourselves, that Citizenship should become part of the National Curriculum in England.

REFERENCES

Breslin, T. (2001) 'A citizenship manifesto for every school?', *Teaching Citizenship, Issue 2*. Association for Citizenship Teaching.

DfEE/QCA (1999) *The National Curriculum for England: Citizenship*. London: DfEE/QCA.

DfES (2004a) and Lloyd, J. with Kerr, D., Maclean, S. and Newton, J. *The School Self-evaluation Tool for Citizenship Education*. London: DfES, QCA, NCSL, ACT.

DfES (2004b) *Teaching Citizenship: a CPD handbook*. London: DfES.

Kerr, D., Ireland, E., Lopes, J., Craig, R. with Cleaver, E. (2004) *Citizenship Education Longitudinal Study: Second Annual Report: First Longitudinal Survey – Making Citizenship Education Real*. Nottingham: DfES Publications.

Ofsted (2002) *Citizenship: Survey Report: Preparation for the introduction of Citizenship in secondary schools 2001–2002*. HMI 730, E-publication only. London: Ofsted.

Ofsted (2004) *Subject Reports 2002/03: Citizenship in Secondary Schools*. HMI 199. London: Ofsted.

QCA (1998) *Education for Citizenship and the Teaching of Democracy in Schools*. London: QCA.

QCA (2000) *Citizenship at Key Stages 3 and 4: Initial guidance for schools*. London: QCA.

QCA (2001a) *Citizenship: a scheme of work for Key Stage 3*. London: QCA.

QCA (2001b) *Citizenship: a scheme of work for Key Stage 4*. London: QCA.

QCA (2004) *Citizenship 'Annual report on curriculum and assessment 2002/03'*. London: QCA.

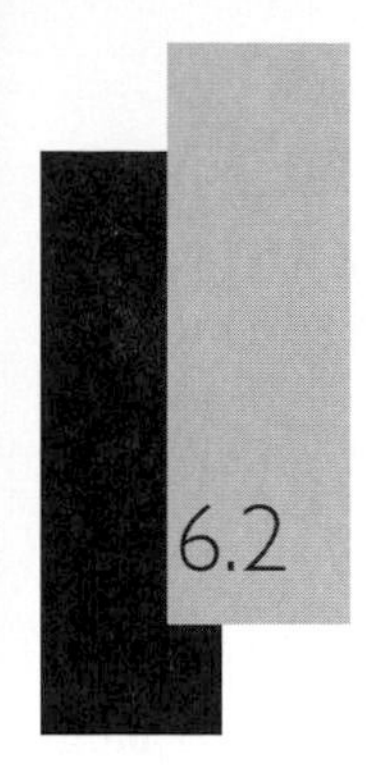

Citizenship and Personal, Social and Health Education: Clarifying and Managing their Roles and Relationship

6.2

Jan Campbell and Liz Craft

At the time of writing, Citizenship had been a statutory National Curriculum subject at Key Stages 3 and 4 for only a few years and schools are at very different stages of implementation. Whilst many are delivering Citizenship as a component of an existing Personal, Social and Health Education (PSHE) programme, a growing number give the subject more and separate curriculum time. The numbers using the GCSE Citizenship Studies specifications to recognise achievement has resulted in the subject becoming the fastest growing qualification subject[1]. Using a joint PSHE-Citizenship approach carries a dual risk: the dilution of PSHE provision *and* non-compliance with the requirements of the programmes of study for Citizenship, especially as there remains confusion about what constitutes PSHE and what constitutes Citizenship (Ofsted, 2003).

This chapter will explore the relationship between Citizenship and PSHE and the essential, distinctive and complementary contributions of each to enabling young people to be personally effective, socially responsible, healthy and active members of their communities. It will identify common ground between the two and suggest areas where planning, training and delivery can be linked.

The focus is on the school curriculum for pupils aged 5–16. It is beyond the scope of the chapter to explore in detail early years or post-16 issues although some aspects of the chapter are also relevant to them. In addition, no attempt has been made to consider the broader political Citizenship agenda. It is important, therefore, to stress that the focus is on Citizenship Education in schools. On occasions we refer to personal and social education (PSE) rather than PSHE. This is where text relates to actual programmes or quotations that pre-date the revision of the National Curriculum when PSE was a common term.

The aims, values and purposes of education

Education is

> *the route to spiritual, moral, social, cultural, physical and mental development, and thus the well-being of the individual . . . a route to equality of opportunity for all, a healthy and just democracy, a productive economy and sustainable development . . . education must enable us to respond positively to the opportunities and challenges of the rapidly changing world in which we live and work. In particular, we need to be prepared to engage as individuals, parents, workers and citizens with economic, social and cultural change . . .* (QCA, 1999).

With the publication of the revised National Curriculum in November 1999, the aims and purposes of the curriculum were, for the first time, fully described. An expansion and explanation of requirements of section 351 of the Education Act 1996 made clear the requirement for schools to provide a curriculum that promotes the development of all learners and 'prepares pupils for the opportunities, responsibilities and experiences of life' in a rapidly changing world.

Such aims are whole organisation responsibilities and are achieved through the ethos of the school, its curriculum and its wider and extra curriculum provision. Each subject has its part to play. But before the revision of the National Curriculum in 1998, it could be argued that the sum of the subjects and statutory requirements did not fully prepare pupils for life in the real world.

Prior to the revision of the National Curriculum, most schools had some provision called PSE or PSHE. In addition to personal and social education, this frequently included some aspects of Citizenship together with health education, careers education and guidance, industrial and economic understanding and environmental education. In all but a few schools this provision failed to ensure that young people understood the political and economic realities of their communities and how to engage with and act within them. They were not, therefore, equipped to contribute to society as citizens with rights, responsibilities and duties.

Towards Citizenship *and* a new framework for PSHE

In 1999, the then Secretary of State for Education and Employment, David Blunkett, took the decision to make Citizenship a new National Curriculum subject at Key Stages 3 and 4 with effect from August 2002. New national frameworks for PSHE and Citizenship for Key Stages 1 and 2 and for PSHE for Key Stages 3 and 4 were also introduced and took effect from August 2000 alongside the introduction of the revised National Curriculum in schools.

These frameworks, whilst themselves non-statutory, contained statutory elements of sex and careers education, included areas of health education, for example drug education, that was compatible with the programmes of study for science and addressed statutory policy areas such as behaviour, anti-bullying, equal opportunities and race relations.

The introduction of the national frameworks for PSHE and the new subject of Citizenship provided schools with challenges and opportunities. They needed to review their provision to ensure that the values, aims and purposes of the school curriculum were carried through into teaching and learning activities that would be appropriate, relevant and meaningful to the pupils in their particular school community.

So what is the difference between PSHE and Citizenship?

Bernard Crick wrote in 1998 that 'PSE is a necessary but not a sufficient condition for good citizenship'[2]. He went on to elaborate on the links between

PSE and the three guiding principles of Citizenship Education: Social and Moral Responsibility, Community Involvement and Political Literacy. The first constituted common ground between the two subjects, being an essential pre-condition for Citizenship, the second had much common ground between the two but the third, Political Literacy, had distinct and different content from PSE.

Citizenship and PSHE are, therefore, related but different subjects. Each has an essential, but distinct, role in promoting the personal and social development of pupils through planned, coordinated, monitored and evaluated provision.

There are many definitions of both PSHE and of Citizenship. We attempt here to build on some of them to clarify the differences and identify some common ground.

PSHE relates to planned learning opportunities provided by a school to promote the personal and social development of its pupils and their health and well-being. PSHE is likely to be provided through discrete lessons as well as through opportunities provided by the subjects of the National Curriculum, assemblies, the tutorial programme, circle time, special projects and other events that enrich pupils' experiences.

PSHE is concerned with qualities, attitudes, knowledge, understanding and behaviour in the personal domain. It promotes abilities, competencies and skills in relation to oneself and others and deals with issues of social responsibility and morality including respect for the differences between people. PSHE leads to the fostering of self-esteem, self-confidence, independence and empowerment. It promotes informed decision-making. Knowledge and understanding includes that which is concerned with career and education opportunities; personal finance; health – including sexual health and drugs, alcohol and tobacco; safety – including personal safety; relationships and lifestyles – including those different from their own.

Citizenship also contributes to pupils' personal and social development. It has a body of knowledge and skills that is concerned with enabling pupils to engage with political and public policy issues, participate in society and in the democratic process. As well as social, moral and cultural aspects, Citizenship addresses the political, legal and economic dimensions of everyday issues, problems and events within the context of local, national and global communities. Knowledge and understanding includes that which is concerned with legal and human rights and responsibilities; the origins and diversity of the UK; central and local government and public services; elections, voting and the role of parliament in democracy; the world as a global and interdependent community; and the UK's relations with the EU, the Commonwealth and the UN. Citizenship knowledge is underpinned by key concepts and principles[3] and must be acquired as pupils are developing and applying skills of enquiry and communication, participation and responsible action. This interrelationship between knowledge and skills is essential. Citizenship skills must be developed in the context of learning Citizenship knowledge, for Citizenship is an active subject where pupils need opportunities to use and apply their knowledge, understanding and skills to take action with others on issues that concern them and as informed, critical and responsible members of communities.

PSHE and Citizenship: some common ground

Both Citizenship and PSHE address contemporary issues of relevance and importance to young people and should involve pupils actively throughout the learning process. Both work best where school approaches to planning, review and provision are supported by senior management and a positive organisational ethos which recognises pupils as partners and decision-makers in the education process rather than merely as recipients.

Both Citizenship and PSHE benefit from separate lesson time as well as teaching across the curriculum and through activity in wider school and community life. They are best taught by dedicated, knowledgeable teachers skilled in facilitating active learning approaches who plan teaching and learning activities with clear, measurable outcomes. Both subject areas require all involved to have high expectations of what pupils can achieve in terms of knowledge, skills and understanding. The standards in Citizenship and in PSHE should equate to those in other subjects.

The following sections explore some areas in which schools could plan and co-teach aspects of both subjects whilst retaining the distinctive nature of each, ensuring that both Citizenship-specific and PSHE-specific learning outcomes result.

Responding to pupils' needs and priorities: why a coherent whole school approach is required

Both PSHE and Citizenship develop best where there is a whole school approach to planning and review. Schools can develop a clear and coherent curriculum by using the whole school processes promoted through the National Healthy School Programme, the teacher's guides in the QCA schemes of work for Citizenship and the teacher guide in the PSHE units for Key Stages 1 to 4.

When planning or reviewing the curriculum for PSHE and for Citizenship, the needs and priorities of the pupils should be considered. For example:

- the characteristics of the school community including geographical context, local political context, diversity, inclusion and equal opportunities
- local data on, for example, crime, community safety and health issues such as teenage pregnancy and drug misuse
- school data on, for example, behaviour, bullying and racial incidents
- the views of pupils themselves who should be involved in the identification of curriculum priorities to ensure that provision is relevant and valued by them
- consultation with parents, teachers, governors, the wider community.

Schools may place particular emphasis on those aspects of PSHE and Citizenship that address pupils' needs and concerns. This does not remove the requirement to address all statutory requirements, but does provide scope to go into more depth where topics or issues are of particular relevance or to use approaches that best capture pupils' interest.

Both Citizenship and PSHE benefit from some separately timetabled, dedicated curriculum time. The contribution of other subjects is important and school and community-based activities, required in Citizenship, are also important to PSHE provision. Other chapters examine how different subjects contribute to Citizenship. Here we focus on how some aspects may be addressed within PSHE without losing the integrity of either.

Doing Citizenship and PSHE: opportunities for 'real' experiences

Citizenship and PSHE have in common the need to provide opportunities for pupils to learn from real situations with relevance to their lives, now and in the future. In addition, Citizenship requires the active participation of pupils in taking real decisions and actions in the school and wider community context. Pupils should develop skills, knowledge and understanding to:

- *take responsibility* for their learning
- *explore and discuss*[4] issues of topical and personal relevance and consider the varied attitudes and values they encounter
- *make real choices and decisions* in both personal, public and community contexts
- *find information and advice*, for example, related to health or to the law
- *participate in groups* of different sizes and composition, for example, those of same and mixed gender, those including younger or older people, those with people of different abilities
- *meet and work with adults* other than teachers, for example, through visits and with external contributors to lessons and events
- *participate*[4] in learning outside the classroom, taking responsibility and action both in the school and in the wider community
- *manage change* whether changing relationships and social circumstances, changes in learning environment, changes in community involvement
- *have time to reflect*[4] on what they have learnt about each subject through their experiences in the classroom and beyond.

Addressing Citizenship and PSHE through topics or issues

Some topics or issues have the potential to engage pupils in learning about both Citizenship and PSHE. For example, issues relating to crime in the community and drug use and misuse can be approached from the personal perspective relating to health and personal responsibility and the public perspective as issues with political, legal, economic and societal or public policy implications.

Some topics relevant to the lives of pupils can be planned from both PSHE and Citizenship angles by using a questioning approach as is demonstrated in the QCA Scheme of Work for Citizenship at Key Stage 3 (QCA, 2001). Table 1 illustrates how PSHE questions promote enquiry into the personal, social and health aspects of a topic or issue while Citizenship questions promote enquiry into public policy and political aspects of the topic[5]. This distinction between the *personal and social dimension* and the *public and* (therefore) *political dimension* lies at the crux of the distinction between PSHE and Citizenship.

Table 1
Approaching an issue from PSHE and Citizenship perspectives

Topic or issue	Examples of PSHE-specific questions	Examples of Citizenship-specific questions
Drugs	What are the effects of different drugs on my health and on my relationships with others? How could I resist unwanted pressure to smoke or drink alcohol?	What is the law relating to different drugs? How are such laws made and changed? What effect does alcohol-related crime have on my local community? How can we lobby for change?
Sex and relationships	What are the characteristics of a friend? How do different forms of contraception work? Where do I go for advice about relationships?	Who decides how local sexual health services are funded? How is the public consulted about services? How can I get them improved?
Bullying	What do I understand by the term bullying? How should I respond when I see or experience bullying?	How can I help to develop and consult on the anti-bullying policy in my school? How does a bully infringe the human rights of the victim? When does bullying become a crime?
Crime	Do I have the skills to resist pressure to break the law? What is my reaction when I see the results of vandalism?	What do I know about crime in my community? Why should law-breakers be punished?
Diversity	How does stereotyping and racism affect me and people I know? How can I challenge discrimination assertively?	How do I understand diversity and how is it represented locally and nationally? How does the law protect people from racism? How can we raise awareness of diversity issues in our schools and wider communities?
The economy	What influences how I spend my money? Who can advise me on budgeting and saving?	What happens to the tax I pay when I buy a CD or DVD? What is the role of financial services in the economy? What impact do government spending decisions have?

Skills for both Citizenship and PSHE?

Citizenship and PSHE have in common the need to engage pupils actively in the learning process, enabling them to develop the skills to work co-operatively with a wide range of people, to deal with changing relationships in widening social contexts, to explore issues, problems and events that concern them personally, socially and as members of communities, to take responsibility for their actions, and those that affect others, and to take action with others on issues that concern them.

Skills in Citizenship are set out in the National Curriculum programme of study as skills of enquiry and communication, participation and responsible action. To date, the skills in PSHE are less clearly set out and this is likely to be addressed as the national framework develops in future years.

Both Citizenship and PSHE *do* require and promote some similar and some distinct skills – indeed many subjects in the curriculum promote some common skills. Schools should plan how and where opportunities to develop and practise these skills will be provided, how pupils will reflect on these opportunities and how they will be helped to apply what they have learnt and developed to other subjects and situations. The skills include:

- communication skills – including listening, discussion, and providing information to others including peers
- thinking skills – especially critical thinking skills needed to weigh information and evidence and to substantiate arguments
- research skills – investigation and enquiry, asking questions
- analytical skills – evaluation, analysis, interpretation, reflection
- decision-making skills – group and individual
- negotiation and problem-solving skills
- creativity skills – generation of ideas/solutions/suggestions
- improving own learning and performance, working with others, problem-solving.

In addition, Citizenship requires specific skills relating to participation and action within the school and wider community context. This may involve the use of a wide range, some of those above and some additional skills, including:

- initiating, planning and carrying out change/action
- advocacy, pleading a case or cause for self or others
- representation skills, speaking or acting on behalf of others
- voting and other forms of democratic decision-making
- debating (as an extension of mere *discussion* skills), such that young people are able to construct and present coherent arguments and lobby for causes effectively.

The following example illustrates how skills in both Citizenship and PSHE may be developed and practised.

A group of pupils demonstrated that their research and analytical skills needed improving. In Citizenship lessons they were taught how to plan and undertake an investigation. Step by step they were supported in investigating the types of crimes committed in their local area. They collected statistics, interviewed police and magistrates, researched local newspaper stories. They were shown how to analyse and interpret the information, discuss their views and present their findings to others. They reflected on the skills they had developed and undertook self and peer-assessment.

In a PSHE lesson later in the term they referred to the skills learnt and used them to research the effects of smoking on health. This time they worked in groups, reminding each other of the skills and approaches previously developed and transferred them to the PSHE investigation.

A brief consideration of continuing professional development (CPD)

As for any subject, staff teaching either Citizenship or PSHE need to be confident that they have the knowledge and skills appropriate to the subject. It is beyond the scope of this chapter to address teacher-training issues in any depth but it is appropriate to look briefly at areas where Citizenship and PSHE need separate training provision and where schools can offer CPD that supports both subject areas.

At the time of writing, in contrast to most other subjects, few of the teachers delivering either Citizenship or PSHE have received relevant initial teacher training. However, demand and interest in teacher training and CPD opportunities in both subjects are growing. Uptake of the *National Certificate of CPD for PSHE Teaching*, which was launched in 2002, has been strong and a similar *National Certificate of CPD for Citizenship Teaching* has been piloted. PGCE courses in Citizenship for new teachers have been offered since 2001 and have proved popular and successful in raising the quality and status of the subject in schools. However, most of the training for existing teachers with responsibility for the new subject has been left to schools to organise. Teachers need to be supported in developing knowledge and understanding related, for example, to government, parliament, the economy and the law. These are the areas that were neglected in provision prior to the introduction of Citizenship as a National Curriculum subject and they remain the areas about which teachers report that they feel least comfortable. Those teaching PSHE have different knowledge requirements. For example, they need secure knowledge and understanding related to health issues such as sex and relationships and drug education. The co-publication by Hodder Murray alongside this collection of *Making Sense of Citizenship: a CPD Handbook*, which has been developed by the Citizenship Foundation in collaboration with the Association for Citizenship Teaching and a range of other Citizenship organisations and follows a development project funded by the DfES, should further support those seeking to develop best practice in Citizenship (Huddleston and Kerr, 2006) but they will need the support of colleagues and the allocation of significant resources if they are to achieve their goals.

Both subjects require teachers who are confident to handle sensitive and controversial issues. Training, and *Making Sense of Citizenship* addresses this, should also address ways of:

- consulting pupils and planning teaching to respond to, for example, learning needs and styles, existing levels of knowledge and skills, the attitudes they hold or encounter
- establishing ground-rules – enabling pupils to discuss, negotiate and agree rules for discussing and working together
- responding to spontaneous issues raised by pupils, perhaps in relation to a topical issue or event
- challenging prejudice and discriminatory language and behaviour
- managing discussion about sensitive and controversial issues such as racism.

The role of the teacher in PSHE and Citizenship is frequently that of facilitator and supporter rather than instructor. Training should promote an understanding of how active learning cycles work so that pupils plan activities, participate in them and review them afterwards to establish what happened, what was learnt and how the learning can be applied to future situations.

Training should also help teachers of both Citizenship and PSHE to develop confidence in using participatory teaching and learning approaches such as discussion and debate, enquiry, role-play and simulation, use of ICT, using photographs and photography, learning from visits and visitors, involving pupils in issues or activities related to the wider community.

CPD can be effectively provided through opportunities for teachers to observe colleagues, through coaching and through the establishment of teacher networks as well as participatory courses and workshops. If the focus of such activities is the development of skills or the management of active learning they may be used to develop teacher competence in both Citizenship and PSHE (and indeed other subjects). If it is to illustrate how to plan and deliver specific knowledge and understanding, training provision may be better made separately.

Conclusion

Some have seen the relationship between Citizenship and PSHE as a contest. This is damaging for both, confusing for schools and irrelevant to pupils. This chapter has attempted to illustrate that Citizenship and PSHE are both essential components of the school curriculum with complementary but different content, sometimes around common themes. Together they make a major contribution to the personal and social development of pupils, helping to prepare them for the opportunities, responsibilities and experiences of life.

By recognising their importance, clarifying their roles and planning rigorously for each, schools and those who support them can provide a curriculum that is valued by pupils as being relevant to their lives. Provision is likely to be most effective where there are regular, discrete lessons for each of PSHE and Citizenship, complemented by planned and coordinated contributions within other subjects and aspects of school life. Whatever forms of provision are used, Citizenship and PSHE should be planned to ensure pupils are always clear about which subject they are being taught and assessed in. Including activities where areas of learning for Citizenship and for PSHE are linked around topical issues can help pupils make sense of them. However, trying to address all of both subjects through joint provision would prevent them from achieving their full entitlement to learning in both.

REFERENCES

Huddleston, T. and Kerr, D. (2006) *Making Sense of Citizenship: A CPD Handbook*. London: Citizenship Foundation/Hodder Murray.

Ofsted (2003) *National Curriculum Citizenship: planning and implementation 2002/03*. London: HMI.

QCA (1999) 'The school curriculum and the National Curriculum: values, aims and purposes', in *The National Curriculum: Handbook for secondary teachers in England*. London: QCA.

QCA (2001) *Citizenship: A Scheme of Work for Key Stage 3 Teacher's Guide*. London: QCA.

FURTHER READING

Calouste Gulbenkian Foundation (2000) *PASSPORT: A framework for personal and social development*. London: Calouste Gulbenkian Foundation.

Department for Education and Employment (1999) *Preparing Young People for Adult Life: A Report by the National Advisory Group on Personal, Social and Health Education*. London: DfEE.

Department of Health and Department for Education and Employment (1999) *National Healthy School Standard: Getting Started*. London: DH/DfEE.

Health Development Agency (2003) *Certification of the teaching of PSHE (Personal, Social and Health Education) Handbook*. London: Health Development Agency.

QCA (1998) *Education for Citizenship and the Teaching of Democracy in Schools* (the Crick Report). London: QCA.

NOTES

1. It is likely that awarding bodies will offer a full GCSE course in Citizenship Studies and a full AS and A level qualification in Citizenship Studies from 2008.
2. The comment was contained in a letter from Professor Sir Bernard Crick, chair of the advisory group on Citizenship, to Professor John Tomlinson, chair of the advisory group for the Passport framework for Personal and Social Development, dated 12 May 1998.
3. Here the concepts might include democracy and autocracy; co-operation and conflict; equality and diversity; fairness, justice, the rule of law; rules, the law and human rights; freedom and order, individual and community; power and authority; rights and responsibilities.
4. 'Exploring and discussing', 'participating' and 'having time to reflect' are all National Curriculum requirements for Citizenship at Key Stages 3 and 4.
5. This dual approach was first developed by Jan Newton, Don Rowe, Ted Huddleston and the team at the Citizenship Foundation.

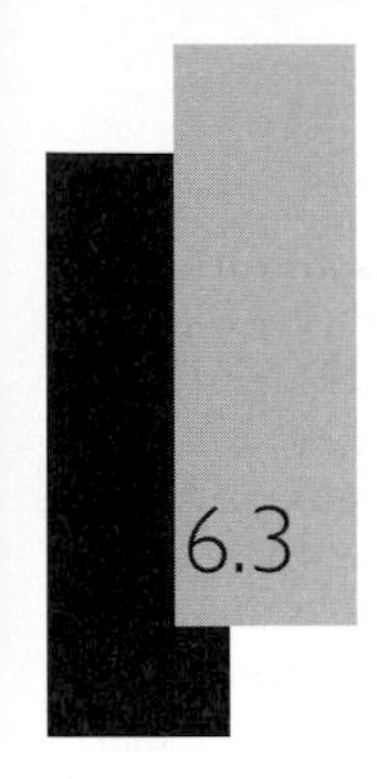

Religious, Moral and Spiritual Education and Citizenship: Managing and Building on the Interface

John Keast

Citizenship and RE: the shared territory

Whatever the complexity of conceptualising it, Citizenship is closely linked with religious education, moral education and spiritual education. It entails moral responsibility, assumes ethical values, and involves questions of identity, allegiance and authority. All these issues are foundational to the concept and practice of religion and religions. Citizenship Education is thus intricately connected with the Religious Education Curriculum. The approach of both Citizenship and the majority of the world's religions to neighbourliness provides one example of their shared territory. Many, if not most, religions teach their followers, either directly in sacred writing or indirectly in the ethical outworking of faith, to 'love your neighbour'. Questions of who are neighbours, what it means to love them, and why – are all religious questions as well as Citizenship issues. Most religions, if not all, teach their followers to also 'love God' or adopt equivalent attitudes to the creative power believed to be the ultimate meaning of life. How this is done, and with what consequences for ordering society and for other people who may believe or practise differently, again impacts directly on aspects of Citizenship.

Religious, moral and spiritual education: a word on definition

If these fundamental conceptual links are accepted then the roles played by religious, moral and spiritual education are crucial to the effective provision of Citizenship. Before looking at how these roles may be developed, a word about the curriculum areas covered in this chapter. Religious, moral and spiritual education are not identical but they are intimately and inextricably connected. It may be helpful to think of them as concentric circles, with spiritual education being the largest. This is not the place to define spiritual education, but it may certainly be characterised as developing fundamental human qualities, aptitudes and sensitivities concerning the nature, purpose and meaning of life and achievements. These may be appreciated and articulated in general human terms (a 'humanist' spirituality) or religious terms, with the main religions of the world consisting of historical, traditional and contemporary systems of spiritual understanding, belief and practice. Religious Education is thus a circle within spiritual education, as it focuses specifically on the nature and role of religions as particular forms of spiritual development and practice. Moral education is more problematic as it is both entailed by spiritual and religious education, but also stands on its own as a dimension of all education. Then there is the question of 'values'. The whole curriculum, indeed the whole school, is value-laden, because education itself is an activity that rests on and promotes values. Truth, honesty and integrity are fundamental to academic pursuit and study. Consideration for others, social and moral responsibility, and respect are essentials for any effective school community. Self, others, society, the environment are four values identified by the Forum on Values in Education and the Community (popularly known as The Values Forum) set up by Sir Ron (now Lord) Dearing and Nick Tate at the School Curriculum and Assessment Authority (SCAA) in 1996, and which have found their way into the National Curriculum Handbooks for teachers, published by HMSO in 1999 as part of the revised National Curriculum for England. Values are not then the preserve of spiritual, religious and moral education, though they are again essential elements of this kind of education. For ease of reference, then, I will use the term Religious Education (RE) to refer to all three: spiritual, religious and moral education as well as to values in general. However, this term must be understood as designed to educate about all religious traditions and ethical life stances and not as religious instruction or nurture.

Ethics, skills and content: connections between Religious Education and Citizenship

It will be clear by now that RE has basic connections with the whole Citizenship curriculum, including its more political, economic and constitutional aspects. The debates over the draft constitution for the European Union have illustrated the implicit connections that cultural and religious heritages or traditions have with contemporary societies and political developments. However, some parts of the Citizenship Curriculum have explicit links with RE and these need to be articulated so the contribution of RE can be clear and effective.

First, there is the spiritual, religious and ethical base for the political, social and contemporary issues that Citizenship will inevitably deal with. These cover a wide spectrum from attitudes to asylum seekers to policy on genetically modified food, to drug liberalisation, to war in Iraq. All these issues involve questions of right and wrong as well as political judgement, and so are clearly connected with moral, religious and spiritual issues.

Second, there are skills and attitudes of social and community involvement in the Citizenship Curriculum that also link with religion and thus with RE. With the possible exception of sport, participation in faith communities probably constitutes the dominant form of community involvement by young people outside schooling, especially in minority ethnic communities. How and why young people are, become and remain part of community life is linked with their religious identity. This is seen in their reception and growing up in religious traditions, their belonging and practising as members of these traditions (overtly or by allegiance, through worship, community groups and activities, charities and political involvement) and by the way in which they contribute to a sense of place and community through places of worship, community centres and cemeteries.

Third, there is the specific requirement in the Citizenship Programmes of Study dealing with the diversity of different identities in the UK, especially religious identity. This requirement is notable for two reasons. First is that it is part of the National Curriculum for all secondary school students, and is not subject to a parental withdrawal clause as is RE. This means that all pupils should learn about the nature, origin and relevance of people in Britain of all major religious traditions. The withdrawal clause notwithstanding, RE is one way in which this part of the Citizenship Curriculum is being and will continue to be taught, irrespective of how the rest of the Citizenship Curriculum is being delivered. In the language of the editors of this volume, RE, as a statutory provision, provides an excellent carrier for this element of National Curriculum Citizenship. Second, RE teachers have a long tradition and much expertise and skill in providing this kind of education and in addressing the issues of diversity, respect and multi-culturalism therein. Under current legal requirements RE teaches pupils about Christian, Buddhist, Hindu, Jewish, Muslim and Sikh identity, accounting for some three-quarters of the population in England and Wales according to the census of 2001.

Within each of these elements of the Citizenship Curriculum, RE has roles to play and contributions to make. If there is a core or discrete programme of Citizenship in a school, delivered by a specialist team of teachers or by form tutors, RE teachers should play a key role in its planning and evaluation and, timetable allowing, its delivery. Where provision is *entirely* cross-curricular, and other contributors to this collection have warned of the drawbacks of this, it is even more important that the RE team should be involved in the planning and evaluation processes.

Linking RE teaching with the delivery of Citizenship

How might this contribution of the RE teacher and RE team shape up in practice? This will, of course, in part depend on the school's approach to Citizenship, but there are various options. To ignore these is to 'cut off' a vital supply line of expertise that can only strengthen the Citizenship programme as a whole, especially as it moves through what Tony Breslin identifies elsewhere in this volume as its 'subject building' phase. I will now explore these options in a little more detail.

First, there is the linking of specific areas of content. Some of this has been mentioned above, such as the learning about diverse identities, but there are other examples, including aspects of human rights. Very often GCSE Religious Studies courses (taken by about half the pupils in each cohort) include material on human rights, especially in relation to religious teachings about humanity, its origin, nature and destiny. Flowing from such philosophical and theological understanding come issues of how human beings should therefore regard each other. One example comes from the so-called Abrahamic religions (Judaism, Christianity, Islam), which teach that human beings have been given stewardship of the world, and are accountable to God for their use of the world's resources, their treatment of each other, their own power and talents, and obedience to God's will. This means that the human rights of life and freedom, promoting dignity and basic needs, equality, anti-discrimination and respect are intrinsic to religious views of life. Education in these matters is also intrinsic to the development of understanding and promoting Citizenship. Examples like this can be found also in Sikhism, which lays great stress on the equality of men and women, Buddhism, which promotes a middle way between asceticism and indulgence, and Hinduism, which promotes non-violence (ahimsa). Such issues also help deliver content on the world as a global community, the work of international groups, especially development and environmental charities, many of which have links with religious traditions, for example, Christian Aid and Islamic Relief[1].

Second, there are many skills common to both Citizenship and RE. These include the general skills of research, enquiry, debate, evaluation and communication, but beyond them are more specific skills. These include empathy (using the imagination to put oneself in the position of others), reflection (for example on the ideals, goals and purposes that motivate human life and activity), and dealing with bias and polemic in sources, understanding and seeking authority. There is the skill of synthesis, which relates issues to greater contexts of philosophical, religious, political or ideological systems, deepening understanding of diverse viewpoints within single systems, and of issues of power, loyalty, allegiance, identity, solidarity and obligation. This list, which moves from *skills* to *types* of understanding, covers vital areas of competence and effectiveness in understanding society, what makes it function or malfunction, and how and why people are or are not engaged.

Third, there are aspects of practical involvement that are common to both. RE in school is linked with the faith communities around the school, drawing on them, for example, for resource, reality and relevance. These communities have developed in relation to each other and react with each other. How they function in a multi-faith society is an important question for social cohesion and inclusion. RE in school therefore has a practical dimension in helping pupils to understand the practical agenda for faith communities in our societies. Many pupils are involved in faith communities, and even the majority who are not, are linked by identity with them. Pupils visit and are visited by faith communities. Citizenship's essential active dimension, where pupils are involved in their communities through contributing to activities and decision-making, is of direct importance to RE and offers a vehicle for practical RE work. Local faith forums, for example, replicating that of the Golden Jubilee Young People's Faith Forum in June 2002, are to be promoted by the National Association of Standing Advisory Councils for RE (NASACRE). Such involvement also helps cover the Programme of Study in Citizenship on voluntary groups and resolving conflict.

These three ways can apply equally to a cross-curricular approach to

Citizenship or to a model in which RE acts as a strong or supporting 'carrier' for Citizenship, though the way in which RE makes its contribution might be differently conceived and 'planned in', depending on the specifics of the school's precise curriculum framework. For example, teaching and learning about different identities may be a specific RE contribution in a cross-curricular approach, complemented by work in, say, History on political development of the franchise and elections and in, say, English on the media, whereas with a discrete Citizenship programme, the RE contribution might be supportive, introductory or reinforcing of some basic coverage in the Citizenship time.

RE, Citizenship and whole school activities

Whole school activities with which RE is concerned range across a spectrum ranging from the less definable but extremely important (for instance, those seeking to foster an ethos of respect and the valuing of diversity) to specific activities (such as fund-raising for charities, perhaps through the Giving Nation programme (Citizenship Foundation, 2005), visits to specific faith institutions or a social enterprise day). How far and in which ways schools choose to develop the links between these activities and their RE and Citizenship programmes is very likely to be influenced by whether the school is a religious foundation. These so-called 'faith schools' are very variable in character, but they have in common a link between the establishment and nature of the school and a religious faith. Most such schools are Roman Catholic or Anglican Christian, but there are significant and growing numbers of other faith schools, including Jewish and, more recently, Islamic schools. It is inevitable (and appropriate) that the concept of Citizenship in these schools is coloured by the approaches to Citizenship of the faith that 'owns' the school. Christians are regarded as citizens of two cities, earthly and heavenly, with an allegiance to God and Caesar; Muslims are members of the 'ummah', a worldwide brother- and sisterhood of the faithful; Jews are subject to the overriding requirements of the Torah. Such fundamental values will guide the kind of Citizenship offered in the school and the kind of RE but, whatever the faith concerned, the issues that arise from its discussion and practice can provide a *positive* starting point for Citizenship learning. Perhaps for this reason faith schools figure strongly as those delivering good Citizenship Education in the early reports of the NFER Citizenship Education Longitudinal Study (Kerr et al., 2003; Kerr et al., 2004). And remember, whatever the type of school, headteachers in all schools are required to provide an act of collective worship daily for all their pupils. Even though this is often problematic, assemblies are whole school activities with a religious connotation, and many RE departments are concerned with the quality of such activities. They offer opportunities for questions of Citizenship to be reflected on in a context of values, articulated through worship or silent reflection. Contemporary political or other events provide obvious examples of this. In this context, the editors of this collection argue strongly that the assembly space can be significantly enriched by reference to the Citizenship Programmes of Study.

Senior leadership team support for RE and Citizenship

How school leaders and senior management support RE itself is sometimes a contentious issue, let alone how they may support RE in itself supporting Citizenship. RE departments sometimes feel that they lose out on funding levels, time allocation, representation in school management structures and staffing matters. If this is so, RE needs to be further supported, both for its own sake and so as to enable it to fulfil its potential in supporting Citizenship. The need to deliver quality Citizenship Education offers, therefore, a (further) rationale to positively support and lead RE.

What kind of support can school leaders supply for RE to help it support Citizenship? Although the answer may vary according to type and tradition of the school, school leaders need to make opportunities available to all RE departments to consider the implications and nature of the Citizenship Curriculum and they need to ensure that these have been taken. A whole school approach is needed to make Citizenship Education effective; RE must be included, not simply as one among many subjects but as a potentially very significant contributor. School leaders need to have asked whether their implementation of Citizenship might not be jeopardised by low quality RE in their schools or by the teaching of conflicting messages through the two programmes. Staff responsible for the respective curriculum areas need to have been put into a positive, creative and effective working relationship to maximise the support from RE to Citizenship and vice versa. Here, pairing GCSE RE and Citizenship Studies short courses into paired joint delivery programmes or complementary but distinct courses offers one option for collaboration at Key Stage 4 and, in any case, time for the joint consideration of curricula, methodology and resourcing should be made available, not just at the beginning of programmes or in the curriculum design stage but in an ongoing way that informs and renews classroom delivery. This is not to say that Citizenship and RE are identical subjects or should be amalgamated into a common curriculum. A ship's engineer is not the same as its navigator, but both need to be in a positive working relationship with the other if a voyage is to be successful.

Citizenship, the role of the RE Coordinator and the non-statutory National Framework for Religious Education

What action points should an RE Coordinator have taken or be taking in support of Citizenship? These are likely to depend, at least to some degree, on what sources of support he or she may have received from the LEA or its Standing Advisory Council for RE (SACRE), for the RE curriculum is largely controlled by local authority syllabuses. For example, an analysis of the Citizenship Curriculum in terms of its links with the local agreed syllabus might already have been produced for all schools in the authority, and other training and information events might have been held.

Whatever has been provided already, the first action point should be for the RE Coordinator or manager to familiarise him or herself with the purpose, nature and contents of the Citizenship Curriculum as delivered in their school. This should be done both generally and specifically with the senior leadership or management team and the Citizenship Coordinator. Interestingly, one essence of National Curriculum Citizenship, following Crick (Crick, 1998), is that Citizenship too should come in a 'localised' flavour: fit for the purpose of the school, its students and its community.

Second, there should be detailed planning of curriculum provision, content and coverage, with joint and mutual understanding of the respective contributions, in terms of knowledge, understanding and skills. The whole of the RE Programme of Study in the school should have the Citizenship and PSHE contributions indicated, with their extent and nature, and vice versa. This will help to ensure that both staff and, more importantly, students are aware of the way learning in each subject area reinforces the other.

Third, to make the second more effective, the RE Coordinator should collect, over time, relevant resources, in the form of primary sources, quotes, media articles, journals, books, posters, leaflets, case studies, notice boards, etc. to support, exemplify and illustrate these connections.

The fourth action point is the use of the first three. The role of RE in a school is not simply to *support* Citizenship. It has its own discrete aims and purposes, which can, in return for supporting Citizenship, be supported by Citizenship. One of these is the difference RE itself makes to students' understanding of, skills for and involvement in inter-religious dialogue and the valuing of diversity. Here, the aims of RE can be greatly supported and complemented by the largely secular drive behind Citizenship Education. RE has for a long time claimed a central place in the theory of the purpose of the school curriculum, but has often failed to fulfil the promise it has held out. Links with practical activity in religious worship have often been discredited or poorly achieved, but links with inter-religious dialogue, on a practical level, are part of the national and international agenda for action by education and the community. Here RE must fulfil its potential. The RE Coordinator needs to identify every area of the RE Curriculum where this promise and agenda for action may be supported by Citizenship Education. It will be good Citizenship *and* good RE. Put 'practical activity possible' beside every issue, item and element of the RE Curriculum which could have a Citizenship connection. This may be described in terms of a community link, a person link, an internet link, a local link, a national link, an international link, through letter writing, a Q&A session, an on-line debate, petitions, poster campaigning, lobbying, or publications such as a faith newsletter. The possibilities may not quite be endless, but they are rich and varied and supportive of both RE and Citizenship.

The capacity for this potential to be supported on a national level has been greatly enhanced by the development of the non-statutory National Framework for Religious Education which was published in October 2004. This quasi-national curriculum for RE represents a significant agreement by all the major faith communities and RE professional associations nationally on what RE is and the standards to be expected in schools, and will influence the development of local agreed syllabuses and faith school RE programmes. The

Framework identifies clear links with the Citizenship curriculum. Its programmes of study include aspects of learning that reflect the importance of RE's contribution to Citizenship and the development of an inclusive and cohesive society.

Finally, there should be pro-active and longer-term thinking on where the various curricula for Citizenship, RE and other related areas are going in terms of students' spiritual, moral, social and cultural development, including their involvement in the school, local, national and/or global community. In other words, there should be a coherent understanding of the school's social curriculum and role, and how this links with the school's aims and ethos. Leadership from the Coordinator and the senior managers is critical if this is to be achieved but the benefits are clear for learners, teachers and managers alike.

REFERENCES

Citizenship Foundation (2005) *Giving Nation Resource Pack*. London: Citizenship Foundation.

Crick, B. (1998) *Education for Citizenship and the Teaching of Democracy in Schools*. London: DfES/QCA.

Kerr, D., Cleaver, E., Ireland, E. and Blenkinsop, S. (2003) *Citizenship Education Longitudinal Study: First Cross-Sectional Survey 2001–2002*. Nottingham: DfES Publications.

Kerr, D., Ireland, E., Lopes, J., Craig, R. with Cleaver, E. (2004) *Citizenship Education Longitudinal Study: Second Annual Report: First Longitudinal Survey – Making Citizenship Education Real*. Nottingham: DfES Publications.

NOTE

1 See for example *Islamic Relief: Reacting to Poverty* (Islamic Relief, 2001).

FURTHER READING

Blaylock, L. (ed.) (2002) *Secondary RE and Citizenship*. Birmingham: Christian Education Publications.

Crick, B. (2000) *Essays in Citizenship*. London: Continuum.

Gearon, L. (ed.) (2003) *Learning to Teach Citizenship in the Secondary School*. London: RoutledgeFalmer.

Gearon, L. (2004) *Citizenship Through Secondary Education*. London: RoutledgeFalmer.

Herbert, D. (2003) *Religion and Civil Society*. Aldershot, Hampshire: Ashgate.

Pestridge, J. (ed.) (2002) *Citizens of Faith: Making a Difference*. Birmingham: Christian Education Publications.

Sachs, J. (2002) *The Dignity of Difference*. London: Continuum.

UEA (2003) *Citizens of the Future,* Conference Report. Keswick Hall RE Centre, University of East Anglia.

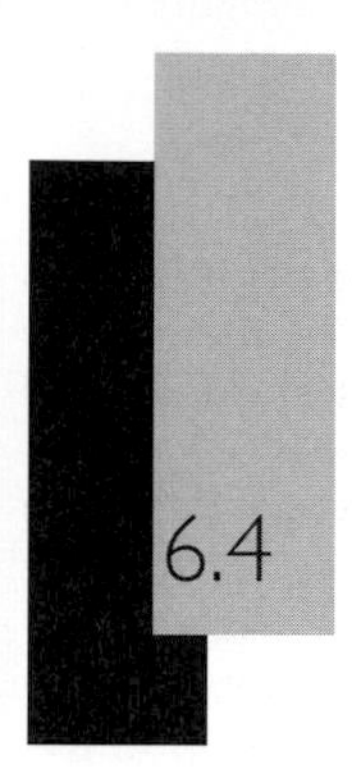

6.4 Delivering National Curriculum Citizenship: Comparing and Applying Curriculum Models

Tony Breslin

The multi-faceted nature of Citizenship

If the various contributors to this volume share one view, it is about the multi-faceted nature of Citizenship Education. In England, Citizenship may now be a Foundation subject of the National Curriculum, while in Wales, Scotland and Northern Ireland it also enjoys a newly enhanced status, if not as a subject, then as a subject by any other name. But it remains much *more* than this. That is, it needs to find expression in a *range* of ways, through, for instance:

- discrete subject based delivery
- clearly identified modules within PSHE or 'PCHE'
- as a Cross-Curricular Theme (notably through other Foundation Subjects as identified 'carriers')
- the tutorial and assembly programme
- a range of events, activities and forums for student participation and community involvement that impact on the school both *as* a community and *in* the community.

The challenge is not to decide *which* approach to deliver Citizenship through but to work out the *mix* of approaches to use. And in coming to this decision, a range of factors will need to be considered: the shape of the wider timetable, the identification and availability of key members of staff, the traditions of the school and the needs of the community that it serves. Certainly, if the early reports from the NFER study that David Kerr is leading, and which he and his colleagues outline in Chapter 1.2, tell us one thing, it points to a clear need for:

- a clear core Citizenship programme that addresses the key themes of National Curriculum Citizenship
- a recognisable, appropriately qualified and resourced citizenship 'team' of subject specialists
- a range of activities across the school and in the community through which students can rehearse and develop the skills that are central to National Curriculum Citizenship.

In this chapter I want to do two things. First, I will outline three curriculum strategies through which Citizenship might successfully be delivered: core-plus-carrier; partnership; and surrogate. Each of these has a clearly identified Citizenship programme at its heart. This is not to argue *against* cross-curricular approaches but to argue *for* a strong, identifiable central Citizenship programme, serving as an anchorage point around which *additional*, reinforcing cross-curricular provision might be based and on which the latter might build.

Second, I want to argue for the encapsulating of any approach to curriculum within a 'Manifesto' framework (Breslin, 2004) that draws together what Pattison calls the 'three Cs' of Citizenship: Citizenship in the curriculum; Citizenship in the culture of the school; and Citizenship in terms of the school's relationship with its surrounding community (Pattison and Barnett, 2005). This analysis is represented in Figure 1.

Figure 1
The 'three Cs' of Citizenship

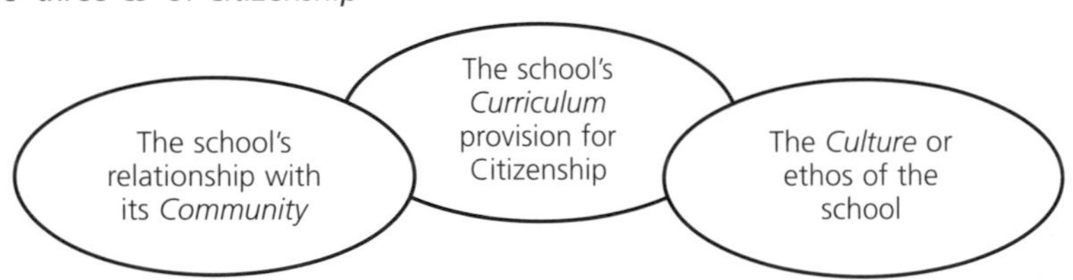

A core programme supported by 'carrier' subjects

A number of contributors have called for practitioners to think in terms of combining a strong 'core' programme with 'carrier subjects' (Breslin, 2004; Rowe, 2004; Huddleston and Kerr, 2006) as an alternative to traditional 'Cross-Curricular' delivery. Generally, there is a growing acceptance (Ofsted, 2005; NFER/Kerr et al., 2003; 2004; 2005) of the conclusions initially presented by Whitty, Rowe and Aggleton (1994) that the conventional cross-curricular approaches deliver neither rigour nor profile to the themes or subjects that they are seeking to serve. Instead schools need to signal the importance of these themes or subjects through granting them a place on the timetable if not in the wider life of the school: everywhere (or anywhere) is nowhere. Thus, a place on the timetable gives Citizenship an identity in the minds of students, teachers, parents and inspectors, a resourcing stream and a location in related structures such as the staffing framework. Or, in the words of the inspectorate:

> *. . . there is a strong and identifiable core programme, irrespective of how it is delivered . . . [and] . . . teachers have good subject knowledge and are up to date with subject thinking . . . [and] . . . some or all pupils are following accredited courses . . .* (Ofsted, 2005).

A 'Core-Plus-Carrier' model provides this identity but it does not pretend that one or two 45 minute lessons a week can 'do' Citizenship. Rather, this Core programme is supported by a small number of carrier courses.

Thus, a designated group of subjects – and these will differ from school to school depending on the skills and interests of teachers and the programmes of study and specifications followed – are 'carriers' for specific elements of the Citizenship curriculum with modules of work dovetailing with the Citizenship core. Although the language of 'carrier' subjects tends to allude to notions of physical illness rather than curricular health, such an approach does guard against the 'everywhere but nowhere' threat while not isolating Citizenship in the way that an approach over-focused on a discrete Citizenship course might do. This Core-Plus-Carrier (or CPC) model might look something like that set out in Figure 2. Such a model makes a range of further assumptions. These may be summarised as follows:

- The core Citizenship programme is delivered by a dedicated Citizenship team.
- This team is likely to be largely drawn from the social sciences and humanities.
- The carrier subjects are core subjects followed by all students in the Key Stages in which they 'carry' Citizenship.
- A subject such as English is selected as a 'Strong Carrier' because of its capacity to contribute to the Citizenship learning of all students.
- For the same reason, subjects such as Geography and History are selected as 'Supporting Carriers' and are used only at Key Stage 3 because they may become options at Key Stage 4.
- GCSE Citizenship Studies is selected as the spine of the Core programme at Key Stage 4 not simply because of the assessment option that it offers but because it offers, 'off the shelf', a stable main entitlement that offers a good basic, and distinctly public, coverage of the main National Curriculum requirements but a range of other possibilities might be taken up here: an ASDAN based programme; a GCSE programme in one of the social sciences; an in-house developed programme.
- Taught lessons provide the main but not the only part of the core programme: the assembly programme, dedicated themed 'Citizenship Days' and whole school events such as school council elections make a formal and acknowledged contribution to teaching and learning activities.
- Additional ad-hoc curricular enrichment and extra-curricular activities make a further contribution to the Citizenship learning of those students involved in them.
- Finally, and critically, there is a two-way relationship between the carrier subjects and Citizenship: the arrows work each way because the 'carrier' modules deliver for the Citizenship programme of study and for English, Geography and History programmes – this is not English (or whatever) doing Citizenship's work; it is English and Citizenship working in partnership to best meet the needs of each subject.

Figure 2
Citizenship through a Core-Plus-Carrier (CPC) framework

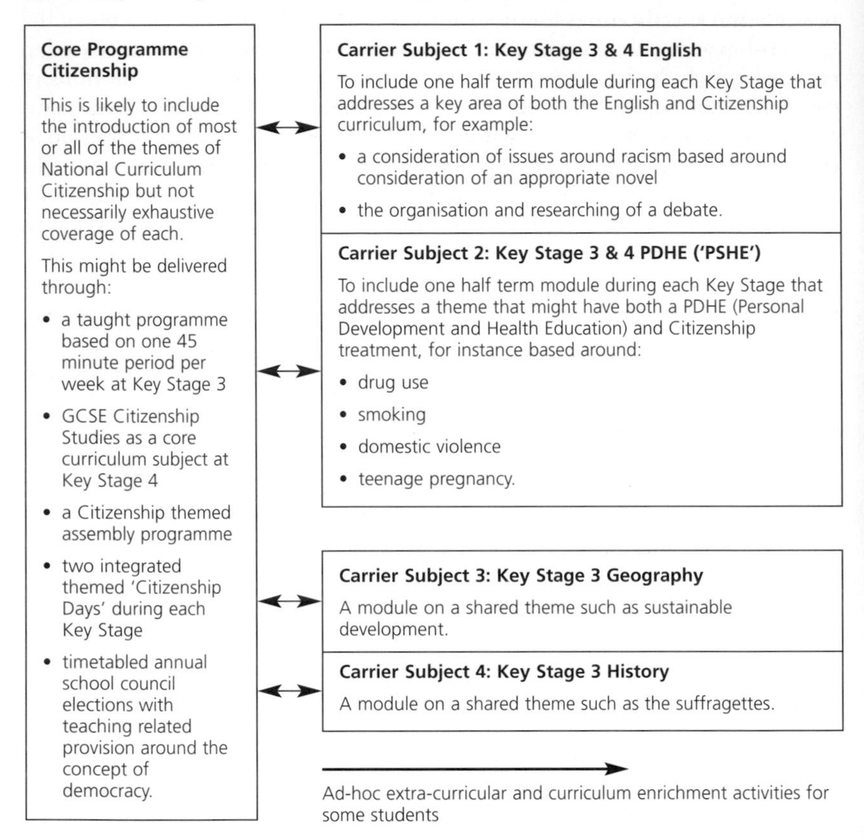

Citizenship and PSHE revisited

Of course, one of the pertinent issues about the framework presented in Figure 2 is the representation of PSHE and the fact that in this representation Citizenship is taught in a discrete programme to PSHE. So as to distinguish the two programmes a little further, PSHE is recast as Personal Development and Health Education. Jan Campbell and Liz Craft in Chapter 6.2 and others elsewhere (Rowe, 2005; Huddleston and Kerr, 2006) provide a much more sophisticated distinction between what is 'Citizenship' and what is 'PSHE' and, of course, the two sit properly along a continuum on which the 'social' dimension to PSHE sits close to the centre. The nub of this distinction is around the notion of public or community policy; when the discussion turns to policy (for example, 'What should we do about drugs, smoking in public places, domestic violence or teenage pregnancy in our community or society?' rather than 'How do these things impact on my health, personal life and social relationships?'), the perspective is a Citizenship rather than a PSHE issue.

These are, though, complex distinctions not easily articulated in the classroom without significant CPD activity, skilled delivery teams and carefully structured delivery frameworks (Figures 4 and 5). Therefore, especially where the PSHE tradition is weak and/or where it is taught (ignoring the earlier cited advice from the NFER longitudinal study and elsewhere) by 'generalists' (usually form tutors) rather than specialists, there is a case for separating the two and teaching each as *complementary* to the other rather than *integrating* them, if only to give Citizenship a new identity as a *real* subject. I shall return to this in the discussion of curriculum strategies based around Subject Partnership later. For now, though, I want to say a little more about the aspects of Citizenship Education that sit outside, albeit alongside, conventional curriculum delivery: matters of 'culture' and 'community' as Pattison puts it; matters of enrichment as I define it here.

Citizenship and the role of enrichment

Enrichment, in this context, might be thought of as including:

- optional courses and activities that might contribute to or enhance Citizenship learning
- whole school activities that often take place largely outside the classroom
- aspects of the school's culture or ethos that have a manifest impact on the Citizenship learning of students
- aspects of the school's community activities that have a manifest impact on the Citizenship learning of students
- extra-curricular activities that all or some students have the chance to participate in
- frameworks and mechanisms that enable students to participate in the school's decision-making processes
- accreditation frameworks that recognise those Citizenship skills which students develop away from the school in community projects and part-time employment.

Figure 3 builds on the CPC model with a formal rather than ad-hoc enrichment programme. It is through this enrichment programme that students individualise the Citizenship Curriculum to meet their own needs and interests. And through this very real application of *Personalised Learning*, students learn and apply the skills at the heart of the Citizenship Curriculum and effective Citizenship itself: active citizenship made real and with purpose. (For the sake of the example the strong and supporting carrier subjects are different to those that appeared in Figure 2.)

Figure 3

Citizenship through a Core-Plus-Carrier framework with a complementary enrichment programme

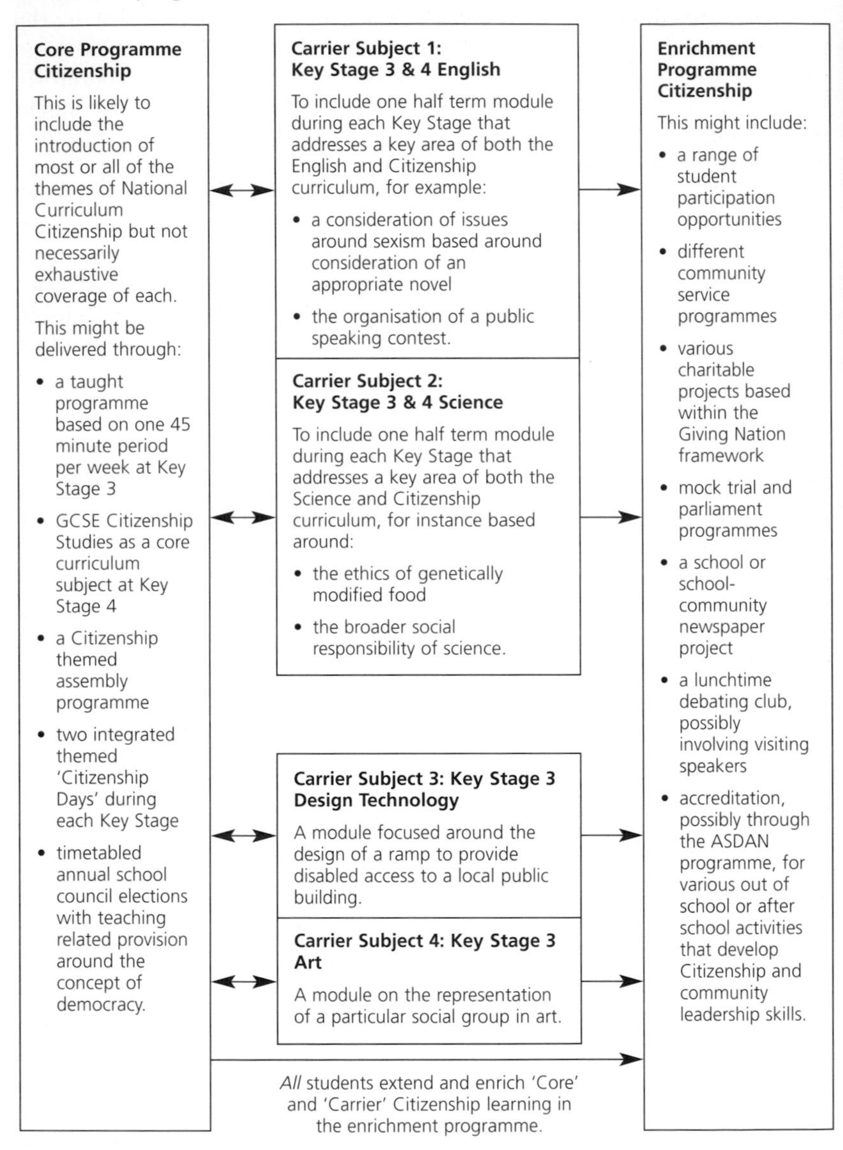

Critically, the framework presented in Figure 3 gives status to the additional learning undertaken in a range of settings beyond the core programme and the carrier subjects. As such, it places a healthy pressure on the school to encourage all students to participate in some form of enrichment and to seek Citizenship accreditation for a range of activities within and beyond the curriculum and the school. Thus, there is some attempt both to 'share out' enrichment activities (so that the same learners do not dominate the school council, the charity projects and the young enterprise and mock trial competitions) and to get students to render explicit (and seek credit for) the Citizenship learning that might be happening elsewhere in the curriculum (in Business Studies or Economics or Sociology) and in their broader lives (for instance, the skills that they are developing as a supervisor in a part-time job or a sports leader in a youth club). This enriched Core-Plus-Carrier model can do much to lay the foundations for the whole school Citizenship Manifesto framework (Breslin, 2002; Watchorn, 2005), which I shall discuss towards the close of the chapter. And, in any case, both the Partnership and Surrogate models that are discussed in what follows require a similar enrichment strand to run alongside them.

A subject partnership approach

A second curricular strategy is provided through a Subject Partnership model. This is less dispersed than the Core-Plus-Carrier model set out thus far. As such a subject partnership approach may offer a narrower model for the delivery of Citizenship but it is, arguably, more focused and it may be easier to put in place when no obvious team of Citizenship 'experts' exists in the school. Here, the Citizenship Curriculum is addressed by a partnership between Citizenship and one other subject or subject cluster. The usual variants are:

- Citizenship and PSHE ('PDHE' as framed earlier), common at Key Stages 3 and 4
- Citizenship and RE, common at Key Stage 4
- Citizenship and Humanities, common at Key Stage 3 and an emerging possibility at Key Stage 4.

The most common of these is the PSHE–Citizenship partnership. Here, the key task is to articulate in curricular form how PSHE/PDHE and Citizenship are distinct but complementary; the danger is to simply meld them together and assume no difference: bad PSHE doesn't produce good Citizenship Education; Citizenship Education does not deal with the important issues around health, welfare and relationships or Careers Education and Guidance that are often best considered on PSHE programmes and which schools are legally obliged to address.

Nonetheless, timetabling pressure often forces Citizenship and PDHE (if I may persist with the term) to cohabit. This presents two options: across a single three term year, Figure 4 presents a modular framework and Figure 5 an integrated one.

Figure 4
Citizenship through a joint modular Citizenship and PDHE Programme

Half Term 1 **Citizenship Module A** Courts, Trials & Justice	*Half Term 2* **PDHE Module A** Drugs Awareness	*Half Term 3* **Citizenship Module B** Discrimination & the Law

Half Term 4 **PDHE Module B** Personal Financial Planning	*Half Term 5* **Citizenship Module C** Participating in Local Politics	*Half Term 6* **PDHE Module C** CV Development

Figure 5
Citizenship through an integrated thematic Citizenship and PDHE Programme

Term 1 **Drugs and public policy**	**Term 2** **The impact of teenage pregnancy**	**Term 3** **Smoking as a public and private issue**
Term 1A: PDHE The personal impact of the use of proscribed drugs in terms of relationships and health	*Term 2A: PDHE* The personal consequences of teenage pregnancy	*Term 3A: PDHE* The consequences of smoking in terms of health and the notion of smoking as a 'social lubricant'
Term 1B: Citizenship An analysis of how the law approaches drug taking, the rationales for this and a consideration of alternative approaches	*Term 2B: Citizenship* How society supports and stigmatises teenage pregnancy and what public policy responses could or should be	*Term 3B: Citizenship* The stigmatisation of smoking and emerging organisational and public policy on smoking

In the modular model, the modules are free-standing and non-sequential and might be delivered by a specialist team or a year group team on a carousel basis with one teacher leading each module and repeating this to a different class each term. In the integrated model the private–public distinction between PDHE and Citizenship is articulated conceptually through the dual focus of the linked PDHE and Citizenship thematic blocks. However, across

Key Stages 3 and 4, certain items on the Citizenship and PDHE Curriculum may not lend themselves easily to this integrated treatment. Nonetheless, such an approach to certain issues (i.e. some paired integrated PDHE–Citizenship modules within a broader modular framework) can underline the distinctions and links between the two approaches.

PDHE is not the only prospective partner for Citizenship. As John Keast notes in Chapter 6.3, at Key Stage 4, a number of schools now partner the RE GCSE Short Course with the Citizenship Studies GCSE Short Course in a programme that delivers two accredited courses, sometimes through a shared (or at least jointly planned) teaching programme. Likewise, integrated Humanities programmes at Key Stage 3 can provide a partnering opportunity for Citizenship and a specialist team highly skilled in delivering the complex, controversial and challenging issues at the heart of the Citizenship Curriculum.

Citizenship through a 'Surrogate' programme

A third option, probably again alongside a partner course or carrier programme, is to identify a surrogate programme that meets a significant proportion of the totality set out in the National Curriculum documentation or its equivalent elsewhere. Here, the social sciences – notably GCSE Social Science, Sociology or Politics – suggest themselves as natural candidates and, as this book goes to press, leading figures in the Historical Association and the Geographical Association are working with one of the awarding bodies (OCR) to develop a joint History and Geography specification (with a title still to be decided) specifically seeking to address the Citizenship programme of study from the perspectives of these two long established subjects. Likewise, existing Humanities specifications, as Deidre Smith discusses in Chapter 2.6, can provide an excellent core or foundation on which to base good quality Citizenship Education.

A surrogate approach provides existing, proven qualifications with which colleagues are comfortable and for which a skilled team is in place (often in the Humanities or Social Science area). The risk though is obvious: those teaching will not conceive of their work as 'Citizenship' itself but as a *proxy* for *covering* Citizenship. Such fixes easily communicate themselves to students, parents and inspectors. If the surrogate model is used, the course (whatever the *examination* title) must be 'branded' Citizenship and delivered in terms of the subject's formal, *statutory* requirements. Citizenship cannot afford to be too modest to 'shout its name'.

Profile and coherence: the role of the Citizenship Manifesto

As stated at the outset to this chapter and at various points by various contributors to this text, one of the key challenges for all who are involved in organising Citizenship Education programmes is to recognise and address the multi-faceted nature of Citizenship learning. Thus, teachers and trainers are asked to create programmes that cover knowledge and understanding drawn from a number of disciplines and to support the development within students of a range of skills. Successful courses are therefore likely to mix traditional classroom teaching, activities such as mock trials, mock elections and community involvement initiatives with a strong service learning strand, a point that the Ofsted guidance, summarised in Chapter 6.6, makes clear.

To reiterate, the requirement is for a mixture of approaches, a mix that will vary from one school, college, or training provider to another. The danger of such a balanced, multi-faceted approach is that the outcome will lack coherence and identity for both learner and teacher. This is one reason why it is important to be specific about the contribution of carrier subjects, the purpose of subject partnerships and the branding of any surrogate programmes. It is also why enrichment activities and processes must be clearly located in terms of their contribution to Citizenship learning and to the community that is the Citizenship-rich school. Here, the concept of the 'Citizenship Manifesto' might have something to offer.

Usually presented in the form of a concise leaflet or pamphlet, the Citizenship Manifesto summarises a school's or college's approach to Citizenship Education and sets out, in a very public way, the sort of core and optional activities that students can expect to undertake.

Within such a framework, the core Citizenship activities (those required by the statutory curriculum and any additional ones that the school believes all of its learners should participate in) are made explicit. These are likely to relate closely to the knowledge, understanding and skills set out in the National Curriculum requirements for Citizenship and amount to a Citizenship *entitlement* for students. In some settings, the Citizenship Studies GCSE Short Course will form a key part of this entitlement. In other settings, where any such specification is a Key Stage 4 option for instance, the Short Course will form part of the optional element of the Manifesto. These optional enrichment activities offer students additional opportunities to develop citizenship skills in particular areas of interest and to be accredited for these efforts: environmentalism, the media, business and enterprise, community involvement, political activity and so on.

To reiterate the point made earlier, it is through the enrichment activities that students are able to individualise the Citizenship Curriculum for themselves, allowing it to be aligned to their abilities, preferred learning style, personal interests and career aspirations. The Manifesto, similarly, 'individualises' the approach to the Citizenship Curriculum taken by the school. As such, the combination of 'core' and 'enrichment' learning enables students to take a personal track through a common curriculum, providing in the process the basis for a *Citizenship Portfolio* in which individual learners record their achievements and experiences, whether these be gained on a GCSE Short Course, as a member of a volunteering programme or through membership of the school's or college's Student Council.

REFERENCES

Breslin, T. (2002), 'A Citizenship Manifesto for Every School?'. *Teaching Citizenship*, (Issue 2). Spring 2002. London: Association for Citizenship Teaching.

Breslin, T. (2004), 'New Subject: New Type of Subject'. *Teaching Citizenship,* (Issue 8). Spring 2004. London: Association for Citizenship Teaching.

Citizenship Foundation (2005) *Giving Nation Resource Pack*. London: Citizenship Foundation.

Huddleston, T. and Kerr, D. (2006) *Making Sense of Citizenship: a continuing professional development handbook*. London: Hodder Murray / Citizenship Foundation.

Kerr, D., Ireland, E., Lopes, J., Craig, R. with Cleaver, E. (2003; 2004; 2005) Annual Reports from the *Citizenship Education Longitudinal Study*. Nottingham: DfES Publications.

Ofsted (2003) *National Curriculum Citizenship: Planning and Implementation*, London: Ofsted.

Ofsted (2005) *Citizenship in secondary schools: evidence from Ofsted inspections (2003/04)*. London: Ofsted.

Pattison, P. and Barnett, A. (2005) 'A School for Citizenship', *Teaching Citizenship*, (Issue 10). London: Association for Citizenship Teaching.

Rowe, D. (2004) 'Building on Strengths: a national strategy for CPD', *Teaching Citizenship,* (Issue 9), Summer 2004. London: Association for Citizenship Teaching.

Rowe, D. (2005) 'Citizenship and PSHE in Teaching Citizenship', (Issue 10), Spring 2005. London: Association for Citizenship Teaching.

Watchorn, E. (2005) *Citizenship Manifesto Project Briefing Papers*. London: Citizenship Foundation.

Whitty, G., Rowe, D. and Aggleton, P. (1994) 'Subjects and themes in the secondary school curriculum', *Research Papers in Education*, Volume 9; Number 2.

NOTES

- In September 2005 the Citizenship Foundation, after securing funding from the Esmee Fairbairn Foundation, launched its *Citizenship Manifesto Development Project*. The project, which follows the publication of an earlier article in the Association for Citizenship Teaching's journal *Teaching Citizenship* (Breslin, 2002) is led by Emma-Jane Watchorn at the Citizenship Foundation and currently involves 12 secondary schools drawn from a range of areas across the UK and will publish outcomes in summer 2008. Further information is available at www.citizenshipfoundation.org.uk/manifestos.
- David Lambert at the Geographical Association and Martin Roberts at the Historical Association are working with OCR to explore the possibilities of a combined humanities programme that might meet the requirements set out in the Citizenship curriculum and offer an alternative to GCSE Citizenship Studies, one with which some Geography and History practitioners might feel more comfortable.

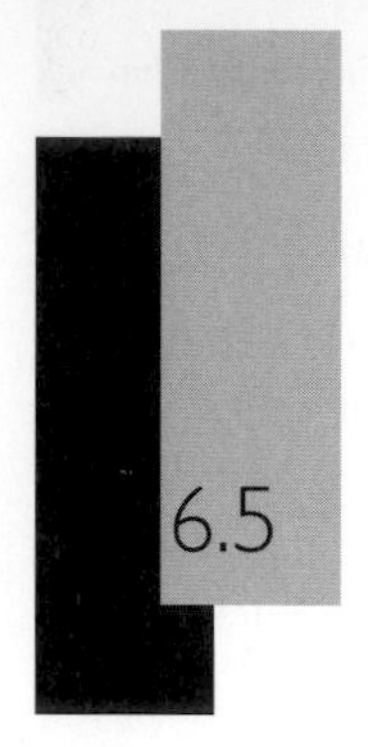

Calling Citizenship to Account: Issues of Assessment and Progression

Tony Breslin

'Assessing' (or worse still *examining*) Citizenship, in the curriculum or elsewhere, is, to say the least, a contentious exercise. 'Failing' in Citizenship carries a different baggage than probably any other subject and the recent launch of Citizenship 'lessons' and 'tests' for newcomers to the UK (Home Office, 2003; Home Office, 2004) has served to emphasise the following: Citizenship as exclusive rather than inclusive; Citizenship as nationality rather than empowerment; Citizenship as legal status rather than political process. Indeed, the very process of 'assessing' Citizenship seems to transfer it from a process to a status, from an activity to a grade. In short, *assessing* Citizenship seems to go against the grain of what active, effective Citizenship is. And yet this is of little use to the working teacher who must be able to make judgements about students' progress if only to make judgements about the effectiveness of their own teaching. That Ofsted have recently acknowledged that 'assessment is currently a weak aspect of Citizenship' (Ofsted, 2003) only serves to underline a plethora of anecdotal evidence and the scale of the challenge in this vital but difficult area.

Assessing Citizenship at Key Stage 3: the statutory requirements

As is the case with any National Curriculum subject, the statutory requirement for Citizenship is that schools should record students' progress throughout Key Stage 3 and that there should be a formal teacher assessment towards the close of the Key Stage. The purpose of the formal assessment is to produce a statement of attainment against the Key Stage descriptor. In addition, again as with other National Curriculum subjects, Citizenship must feature in the annual progress reports to parents during Years 7, 8 and 9 (and indeed during Years 10 and 11). However, the statements of attainment arising from the formal teacher assessment carried out towards the close of Key Stage 3 do not have to be included in the reports to parents (although, of course, they may be). Thus, in terms of the formal assessment, there is an obligation to assess and record but not to report.

In this context, Don Rowe, who has contributed elsewhere to this volume and who leads the DfES National Strategy for CPD in Citizenship, advises that assessment addresses:

- the knowledge and understanding that underpins Citizenship
- citizenship skills (enquiry, debate, participation)
- aspects of students' written and oral work
- citizenship learning in different contexts (for instance that which takes place in discrete, Citizenship lessons *and* in other subjects and contexts)
- 'active' Citizenship (in school and in the wider community).

Here, some schools have found it useful to develop a matrix covering the range of knowledge and skills against a notional grading scale that shows where a student:

- shows understanding of course content
- can argue a case in writing
- can argue a case orally (plenary/small group)
- demonstrates research skills
- demonstrates skills of participation
- demonstrates responsibility in school/community matters.

It is important to emphasise, though, that while the assessment should identify where Citizenship is being taught substantially rather than tangentially (either in a core programme or in other subjects or contexts), it is not necessary to assess more than a sample of work. Rather, as Rowe (2004) puts it: 'Be selective – identify 1 or 2 pieces of written course work, 1 or 2 oral tasks and some group work in each year, give students the chance to review their own work at that time and use techniques based on self and peer assessment, using *summative* techniques for *formative* purposes.' Assessment *for* learning is at least as important as assessment *of* learning. In acknowledging this, the recently issued QCA guidance on assessing Citizenship (QCA, 2006) draws on the earlier work of the Assessment Reform Group (1999) in acknowledging that improving learning through assessment depends on five key principles:

1 Providing effective feedback to pupils
2 Actively involving pupils in their own learning
3 Adjusting teaching to take account of the results of assessment
4 Recognising the profound influence that assessment has on the motivation and self-esteem of pupils, both of which are crucial influences on learning
5 Pupils being able to assess themselves and understand how to improve.

This chapter dwells primarily on formal assessment and examining. It is on this that teachers feel most insecure and, as noted above, it is in this approach to assessment that controversy persists. However, this controversy and insecurity (which is shared as much by an inspectorate and examination establishment that is 'feeling its way') is an opportunity to innovate. Such innovation might take three forms:

1 Testing out conventional assessment tools (such as GCSE) on this new *type* of subject

2 Using alternative tools (such as the ASDAN or Key Skills frameworks) as a means of demonstrating life beyond GCSEs, something that, as argued later, other areas of the curriculum might benefit from
3 Drawing into formal assessment, as Rowe suggests, those approaches that have traditionally been marginalised (the assessment of group tasks, oral and video based assessment, portfolio based models, self and peer assessment) because of their appropriateness to the assessment of Citizenship but raising their status and mainstreaming them in the process.

In short, while the focus here is on the traditional formal approaches, reconsidering what formal assessment should be and 'thinking different' on this is a key part of the assessment challenge in Citizenship. Certainly, while QCA do set out a statutory requirement, both QCA (2006) and Ofsted (2002) bring perhaps an untypical openness of mind to the task.

Assessment, progression and the problem of 'levelling' Citizenship

The requirement to assess Citizenship at Key Stage 3 raises the thorny problem of measuring attainment in Citizenship learning noted in the introduction and again above. Citizenship generates neither the precision correctness of Mathematics at this level nor the factual certainty of scientific experimentation. Nor can it rely on the framework of National Curriculum levels used to assess attainment and progression in most other subjects, although Liz Craft and her team at the QCA continue to explore the possibilities of extending this kind of framework to Citizenship. Indeed, drawing on social psychology and the work of Kohlberg (1958) in particular, Rowe has argued persuasively (Rowe, 2005) that our knowledge of how learning progresses and how young people develop the intellectual capacity to make moral decisions might be used to construct a level-based framework for the assessment of Citizenship learning. Thus, as set out in Figure 1, Rowe, drawing on the work of others (Connell, 1971; Furnham and Stacey, 1991; Gibbs et al., 1992), correlates stages in the development of social and political thinking with age and with progression through the Key Stages of the curriculum and offers this as a basis for devising a framework for assessing learning in Citizenship.

Rowe's colleagues at the Citizenship Foundation, Huddleston and Kerr (2006) translate this kind of thinking into a set of learning activities, using the example of learning about the law (Figure 2). From an assessment perspective, the subsequent task is to devise a set of mechanisms for testing this learning: a piece of writing to assess the ability to analyse and interpret, a short pen and paper test to assess basic knowledge, making a presentation to assess communication skills, a class debate to assess the ability to reason and debate and so on.

Figure 1

The development of social and political thinking in young citizens

Age – very approximate	Nature of social and political thinking	Stage
Below 9 years approx. (some overlap with KS1)	Children do not recognise politics as a distinct part of social life. Rules and laws are understood as prohibitions from people in authority to prevent bad consequences. Reasons for obeying the law would be to obey authority or to avoid getting into trouble. There is no understanding of the *social* purpose of laws and little empathic understanding or ability to be 'in other people's shoes'. Thinking is 'embedded' in concrete examples, is egocentric and concrete. Nevertheless, children can recognise and discuss quite complex social situations, e.g. of rule breaking, punishment and mitigation based on personal experience.	**'Pre-political stage'** 'Implicit' social and moral thinking. The development of social and moral concepts, e.g. fairness, equality, rules, justice takes place in the context of personal relations.
Age 9 to early adolescence approx. (some overlap with KS2)	At this stage, children's ideas about the social and political world are growing rapidly. However, their thinking about the social world generally lacks reality or detail. Also, children seem unable to see politics in terms of the *tensions* between interested parties with different interests (their solutions to problems are simplistic and non-problematic). Some ideas (e.g. about the role of kings and queens) are still more influenced by stories than real life. Much social and moral reasoning goes on but it is still implicit at this stage – it needs to be embedded in recognisable situations. Politically, for most children, there is now the beginning of the recognition of social roles and institutions, including, for example, the Prime Minister, 'Queen', and 'police officers'. So the political world begins to emerge but it is 'personalised' and not yet about institutions, organisations, or social forces. Children of this age do not recognise the conflicts of interests and their thinking about political problems is simplistic. Reasons to obey the law are still egocentric and largely lacking in empathy or awareness of other people's interests or rights. Laws are still seen as authority-based, and generally prohibitive. At this stage children develop a new form of moral thinking which is influenced by the nature of peer relationships which are developing rapidly. Children will say 'it's OK to steal if everyone else does' or 'if they hit you, you can hit them back'. Equally, stealing could be wrong because 'if you steal from others, they might steal from you'. On the positive side, children will suggest it is right to help others because one day they will do the same for you.	**'Simple realism'** Children begin to take in aspects of the social world as it really is, but these ideas are rudimentary at first such as recognition of the PM as embodiment of government.
Age 10–14 approx. (some overlap with KS3)	Political issues come to be seen as increasingly realistic and complex. Politics begins to be seen as more 'problematic' than before (i.e. concerning people with conflicting interests). Political thinking becomes more realistic as social issues become better understood but, for many students, political issues are still understood in *personal* terms (e.g. crime is more about individual law-breaking than a social phenomenon). However, laws begin to be seen as positive as well as negative and as changeable if they do not achieve the purpose for which they were devised.	**'Inter-personal social and political thinking'** Ability to recognise political issues as they show up in the lives of individuals.

Age – very approximate	Nature of social and political thinking	Stage
Age 10–14 approx. (some overlap with KS3)	Awareness of government and social structures (e.g. the local council) is developing but this lacks institutional detail and whilst there is understanding of the broad role of state institutions (e.g. to provide housing, hospitals or education) there is little knowledge of the way these institutions actually operate. This gradually modifies as they learn more about them. Some young people at this stage think in fairly simple terms about political issues, identifying only one or two factors, whilst others are able to recognise several elements to a political problem. Economically, wages are seen as originating in the manager of a business, or 'they come from the till'. The economic nature of political issues is barely recognised at this stage. Unemployment, for example, is more likely to be thought of as caused by personal traits such as laziness rather than economic or social forces. Reasons given for obeying the law at this age begin to show greater awareness of the effect of actions *on other people* (empathic awareness). Behaviour can be motivated by the desire to win approval or *not to hurt* other people. Children begin to speak of anti-social actions as damaging the trust between people (an idea not mentioned in earlier stages). Young people still understand society to be a community of individual people who live together and help each other, nothing more.	
Age 13 plus (some overlap with KS4)	This phase is marked by the emergence of the idea that a *society* is something in its own right (something like a machine made up of interconnecting elements). This brings greater sophistication to political understanding (though many young people remain at the inter-personal stage in their thinking). Problems begin to be understood from society's perspective. Individual citizens are increasingly understood as 'a part of the whole' and actions are interpreted as such. The tensions between individual interests and society's interests begin to be recognised and competing interests can now be balanced against each other, e.g. 'this should be allowed – but within limits or with exceptions'. Economically, wages are now understood to come from company profits. Economic inequalities are more understood as relating to type of work rather than the amount of work different people do. The idea of an inter-related economic system as an integral part of society begins to be well-established. Reasons for obeying the law now include society-focused reasons such as the need to maintain law and order, or to uphold the democratic will of society, in addition to the inter-personal reasons offered earlier. These reasons were not offered before. Moral and ideological thinking becomes more explicit in many young people of this age as their own personal values and identities (e.g. vegetarian, environmentalist) develop and there is greater internal consistency across a range of personal views and beliefs.	**'Social construction of politics'** Emergence of more generalised thinking about society as something above and beyond individual citizens in its structures and practices. Political problems now begin to be interpreted in the light of how *organisations* work as well as how *people* behave.

Age – very approximate	Nature of social and political thinking	Stage
Early and mature adulthood	At this stage, for some, probably not the majority, there develops a social and political morality which is underpinned by universal moral principles, rather than rules socially constructed by individual societies. Societies, as well as individuals, can now be criticised on the basis of whether they uphold these universal values. The individual re-emerges as important, embodying human rights in the face of potentially corrupt practices by the state. Rules and laws are now seen as implementing (or not) moral principles of justice, equality, respect for human rights, etc. This is sometimes called a 'prior to society' perspective because a citizen's allegiance to his/her society will depend on levels of social justice upheld by that society. In other words, there is an appeal to an authority higher than society which was characteristic of the earlier stage. At this advanced stage of thinking an individual will identify moral principles by which they live and around which they build their identity. Extreme examples of this are demonstrated when people would rather die than betray their principles.	**'Principled perspective'** Societies now come to be seen to be answerable to higher level moral principles, such as human rights.

Source: Rowe/Citizenship Foundation (2005).

Figure 2
Progression in Citizenship learning: understanding the law

Learning Activity *Key Stage 1 (Ages 5 to 7)*	**Learning Activity *Key Stage 2 (Ages 7 to 11)***	**Learning Activity *Key Stage 3 (Ages 11 to 14)***	**Learning Activity *Key Stage 4 (Ages 14 to 16)***	**Learning Activity *Post-16 (Ages 16 to 19)***
Learn about **school rules** and why they exist – by discussing particular examples.	Learn about **what makes a good law** – by discussing whether it would be good to have a law banning fireworks.	Learn about **youth justice** – by discussing the fairness of different types of punishment.	Learn about the **causes of crime in society** – by discussing the implications of crime figures.	Learn about the **underlying causes and costs of crime in society** – by discussing trends in crime figures over time.

Source: Huddleston and Kerr (2006).

While 'borrowing' levels from the assessment of English will probably prove more popular with the hard-pressed teacher, the sophisticated analysis of progression in Citizenship learning that Rowe, Huddleston and Kerr together offer ought certainly to figure in any future development of a level based framework for Citizenship. But let us revisit, for now, why such a framework is absent.

At one level this absence of a level based framework exposes the ambivalence around assessment in this area of the curriculum noted at the outset. On the one hand, teachers in the classroom and in other working contexts require practical, easy to use measurement tools to judge where students are 'at' so that they can appropriately set subsequent assignments, report to parents where necessary and draw comparisons with performance in other subjects. On the other, there is a baggage about failure in Citizenship itself that many practitioners struggle with. As one teacher put it to me, albeit with tongue firmly in cheek, at a CPD session shortly after the National Curriculum requirements were first published, '. . . what happens with the kid who fails Citizenship? Is it like the Monopoly board? Do they go straight to jail?'[1].

Interestingly, though, four years on it appears that it is the practical concerns rather than the philosophical ones that are in the ascendancy; the needs of day-to-day practice are beginning to win out and, with the publication of *Assessing Citizenship: example assessment activities for Key Stage 3* (QCA, 2006) and *Making Sense of Citizenship: a CPD handbook* (Huddleston and Kerr, 2006), guidance is starting to emerge. The former document sets out four units of work of differing length and complexity, each mapped to the requirements of the programme of study and each with suggested assessment activities: a three lesson unit (*Doing democracy*) for Year 8; a four lesson unit for Year 9 (*Getting involved, having a voice*); a five lesson unit for Year 9 (*Refugees and asylum seekers*); a six unit lesson for Year 9 (*Young people and the law*). In each unit the depth and breadth of the learning is assessed through defining student performance as being 'towards', 'at' or 'beyond' the expected level of achievement in terms of the programme of study. In Figure 3, illustrative extracts from the *Refugees and asylum seekers* unit are reproduced.

Figure 3
Assessing learning in Citizenship: towards, at or beyond?

Unit 3: *Refugees and asylum seekers*	**Towards**	**At**	**Beyond**
1 How well do you understand why some immigrants are viewed with hostility and why some media portray this hostility?	Basic description of some reasons for hostility.	Describe a wider range of views in the media and give reasons why some media portray a hostile image of immigrants.	Analyse and justify why different views are put forward. Explain why tolerance is important in a democratic society.
2 How well can you analyse the sources and use information to think critically about a topical issue?	Select and use some correct information from sources. Use limited research to support opinion.	Use sources to show two sides of the argument and how they differ. Use other sources or own knowledge of issues.	Analyse sources to explain different views. Draw on other relevant sources of information to support explanations.

Source: Adapted from QCA (2006).

Of course, such an approach does not provide numerical levels but it does enable the teacher to map and record the progress of a class (and, therefore, the success of the unit in teaching and learning terms) in a systematic manner that reveals the relative performance of different students.

Assessing Citizenship at Key Stage 4: a place for GCSE?

Awarding bodies have not had a good time lately, two of the three being hung out to dry in the tabloid press over so called 'marking scandals', while the other, doubtless, counts its lucky stars; all of them struggling with the examining practicalities of Curriculum 2000, the annual moral panic over 'grade inflation' and the confusion that has followed the Secretary of State's rejection of Tomlinson (Tomlinson 2005, DfES 2005). They have not lost the knack, though, of spotting a new market. Enter, from all three awarding bodies, specifications in Short Course GCSE Citizenship *Studies*. The 'studies' bit is important. Loosely all three specifications address the new National Curriculum requirements and each provides an assessment tool for, in particular, the knowledge base for Citizenship and, through coursework, which contributes 40 per cent of the marks in each case, the skilled application of this. In addition, each of the new specifications helps to provide an underpinning for the study of Citizenship and an 'anchorage' point for its establishment in an academic, or at least *academicised,* curriculum. Each helps to 'brand' Citizenship and give it the kind of visibility and presence that it has rarely enjoyed as a Cross-Curricular Theme and, as one sign of this, major publishers, including Hodder Murray, have published textbooks to support all three specifications, a number of these produced by contributing authors to this collection (Fiehn, 2003; Thorpe and Marsh, 2003; Thorpe and Williams, 2004; Thorpe, Marsh and Breslin, 2004; Mitchell, 2003; Wales, 2003). Finally, as 'Short Courses' these new specifications, as I have noted in the previous chapter, can usefully complement Short Courses in RE, either in the core or as a combined option, and, as with the latter, they do not make exhaustive demands on timetable space, especially if some of the time currently allocated to PSHE, or 'PCHE', is drawn on. Here, a commitment to two standard periods a week across Years 10 and 11 is generally thought to be sufficient.

At the time of writing (February 2006), the awarding bodies have just begun to work on the revisions to these specifications with the revised versions available for teaching from September 2008 and first examination in summer 2009. Here, three issues are pertinent:

1 While the substantive content is likely to remain similar, there may be a stronger read across between some aspects of the content included in newcomers' and GCSE programmes.
2 All three awarding bodies are actively considering the development of both short and full GCSE programmes with the former likely to be a subset of the latter.
3 All three awarding bodies are actively considering the development of AS and A level programmes in Citizenship Studies, thus opening up a public examination framework for Citizenship across the emerging 14–19 continuum – currently AQA offers an AS programme but this is strongly Social Science based and, in its development, originally pre-dated and anticipated Crick rather than emerged from it.

Given that the candidate base for GCSE Citizenship Studies has grown from 9000 candidates in 2003 to 27,000 candidates in 2004 to 39,000 candidates in 2005, an increasing number of schools, many of which are placing Citizenship Studies within a compulsory core programme at Key Stage 4 (and sometimes from the beginning of Year 9), seem to concur on the benefits of bringing Citizenship into the world of examination papers, coursework and, of course, league tables.

However, following a course in GCSE Citizenship Studies (or, post-16, an A level programme) does not act as a proxy for *doing* Citizenship in the fullest sense. In this context, participating in a Student Council, taking part in a mock election, carrying out a school based trial, visiting local civic facilities, undertaking a community service placement or joining a local campaigning group, all of which constitute *experiencing* Citizenship, might be captured in the quality of a student's GCSE answer or, in some cases, the theme of their coursework but Citizenship programmes should involve opportunities to undertake this kind of active work whether or not students are following a GCSE course. Moreover, assessment and accreditation frameworks need to reflect the experiences and the skills gained through them *alongside* any GCSE grade. To fail Citizenship *Studies* is not to fail *Citizenship*, because the two are not synonymous. There is a broader point here. GCSE must not dominate the Citizenship agenda in the way it has other parts of the curriculum but it does have something to bring to the table. Eight, nine or ten GCSEs – the standard offer to most students in most of our secondary schools – does not of itself constitute curricular breadth but rather a range of variations on a theme. Indeed, one can argue that teaching and learning in several artistic, creative and technological subjects has been over-constrained by the demands of a 'one size fits all' GCSE based approach to assessment. Citizenship must not make the same error.

In summary, a GCSE Short Course in Citizenship Studies does not provide a 'one-stop' solution for delivering Citizenship but, as a core or optional course, it can add an academic strand to a school's Citizenship provision, among a broader offer that is assessed and accredited in a range of ways. The GCSE 'brand' can add credibility and status to Citizenship among students, teachers and parents, especially in those schools strong on academic tradition and where examination grades, or their acquisition, is a major driver in the quest for budgets and curriculum time. Those who want to see Citizenship prosper in any particular school are always wise to take account of the local politics of the context in this way. Moreover, in making what might appear to be attendant compromises for the broader good, the individuals concerned should be assured that it is colleagues from a range of social science, arts and humanities backgrounds who have produced the current and emerging specifications.

Beyond GCSE: alternative or complementary options at Key Stage 4

In this context, alternative or complementary assessment tools and courses to the GCSE Citizenship Studies route should also be considered. To reiterate, GCSE Citizenship Studies can make a very significant contribution to the assessment, delivery and public profiling of Citizenship in the National Curriculum at Key Stage 4 but it should not be required to do it all. Here, the Key Skills Framework, ASDAN awards, programmes such as the Duke of Edinburgh's Award Scheme and 'carrier' GCSE and AS specifications, notably in Social Science, Sociology and Politics, might all have a role to play. Again, none provides a sole mechanism for delivering Citizenship, nor should they, but each can contribute to a school's approach to Citizenship and the assessment of this.

Against this background, the decision by Edexcel to abandon development work on a 14–19 BTEC portfolio based framework for PSHE, Citizenship and Careers Education with Foundation, Intermediate and Advanced strands some years ago[2] looks increasingly like a missed opportunity, given both the revival of BTEC qualifications and the emergence of the 14–19 agenda. Under the guidance of Barbara Molog, a Development Manager at Edexcel, Chris Deakin of Banbury School in Oxfordshire and I undertook the development work on the Citizenship Module. Liz Craft's work at QCA on the development of an Active Citizenship Award, now being piloted through AQA, again raises the prospect of a portfolio based approach to the assessment and accreditation of Citizenship learning that embraces the experiential dimension that the GCSE framework can struggle with when it is employed as the sole delivery and assessment mechanism. In the longer term, it is possible that Active Citizenship may become a key strand of – or theme for – the Extended Study that seems certain to become a part of the 14–19 curricular architecture post Tomlinson.

Assessment in Citizenship: remembering the rationale and operating the lever

Huddleston and Kerr (2006), in opening their chapter on 'Assessment, Recording and Reporting' *in Making Sense of Citizenship: a Continuing Professional Development Handbook*, are unequivocal in their position on assessing, recording and reporting Citizenship:

> *Assessment, recording and reporting are essential aspects of learning and teaching in Citizenship Education. They help students to recognise and value what they are learning, provide teachers, parents, employers and others with information about student progress and achievement and, finally, raise the profile of Citizenship Education both in schools and in the wider community.* (Huddleston and Kerr, 2006: 141)

They further remind us that such assessment should always be a balance of 'on-going qualitative feedback' (assessment for learning) and 'occasional checks on performance' (assessment of learning) and that it must capture learning that takes place both *within* and *beyond* the classroom, as it is argued inspection must in the next chapter. Moreover, we cannot afford to *not* assess in Citizenship simply because it is challenging to do so. In meeting this challenge, we operate an important lever in underlining the fact that Citizenship is both a *real* subject and one that is qualitatively distinct from many of the conventional disciplines that have long dominated the school timetable. Those conventional disciplines would do well to look at their own assessment practices through a set of Citizenship spectacles but that is a topic for another chapter, if not another book.

REFERENCES

Assessment Reform Group (1999) *Assessment for learning: beyond the black box*, cited in QCA (2006) *Assessing Citizenship: example assessment activities for Key Stage 3*. London: QCA.

Connell, R. (1971) *The Child's Construction of Politics*. Melbourne: Melbourne University Press.

DfES (2005) *14–19 Education and Skills*, White Paper. London: DfES.

Fiehn, J. and Fiehn, T. (2003) *Citizenship Studies for GCSE*. London: Hodder Murray.

Furnham, A. and Stacey, B. (1991) *Young People's Understanding of Society*. London: Routledge.

Gibbs, J., Basinger K. and Fuller, D. (1992) *Moral Maturity: Measuring the Development of Socio-moral Reflection*. New Jersey: Lawrence Erlbaum.

Home Office (2003) *The New and the Old: the report of the 'Life in the United Kingdom' Advisory Group*. London: Home Office Social Policy Unit.

Home Office (2004) *Life in the United Kingdom: A Journey to Citizenship*. London: The Stationery Office.

Huddleston, T. and Kerr, D. (2006) *Making Sense of Citizenship: a continuing professional development handbook*. London: Hodder Murray/Citizenship Foundation.

Mitchell, M., Jones, D. and Worden, D. (2002) *Citizenship Studies for AQA GCSE Short Course*. London: Hodder Murray.

Ofsted (2002) *Citizenship 11–16: guidance for inspectors*. London: Ofsted.

Ofsted (2003) *National Curriculum Citizenship: Planning and Implementation*. London: Ofsted.

QCA (2006) *Assessing Citizenship: example assessment activities for Key Stage 3*. London: QCA.

Rowe, D. (2004) 'Assessment, Recording and Reporting'. Unpublished Power Point presentation developed as part of the National CPD Strategy for Citizenship team's work in this area.

Rowe, D. (2005) Rowe outlined this analysis in a presentation to the Citizenship Foundation's *First Friday* seminar in December 2004. It is an approach that is likely to be influential in developing work on assessment in Citizenship.

Rowe, D. and Citizenship Foundation (2005). These materials were used as part of the above presentation.

Thorpe, T. and Marsh, D. (2002) *Citizenship Studies for OCR GCSE Short Course*. London: Hodder Murray.

Thorpe, T., Marsh, D. and Jones, L. (2003) *Citizenship Studies for OCR GCSE Short Course Foundation Edition*. London: Hodder Murray.

Thorpe, T., Marsh, D., Breslin, T. and Rowe, D. (2003) *Citizenship Studies for OCR GCSE Short Course Teacher Resource*. London: Hodder Murray.

Tomlinson (2005) *14–19 Curriculum and Qualifications Reform: Report of the Working Group on 14–19 Reform*. London: DfES.

NOTES

1 This discussion followed a presentation I had given at a North London school as part of a Citizenship focused input to a training day. However, the sentiment has been repeated on many occasions – a sentiment that questions the process and purpose of assessing something as fundamental as Citizenship. For the Citizenship Education community the debate has been thrown into particular focus by the decision to 'test' those seeking 'naturalisation' as British citizens from autumn 2005.

2 The initiative was led by Barbara Molog who had done much to develop Edexcel's practice in respect of BTEC style programmes at Key Stage 4 notably in areas such as PSHE and Careers Education. The Citizenship Development strand, on which Chris Deakin and I led, was complemented by programmes with other themes such as Careers Education and Guidance and Economic and Industrial Understanding and anticipated much of the current thinking around portfolio based assessment models in the 14–19 phase. However, the framework, although completed, was never published.

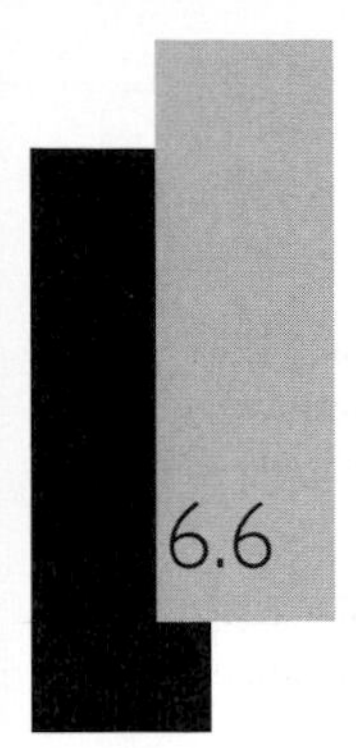

Calling the School to Account for Citizenship: Inspection, Self-Assessment and the Quest for Quality

Tony Breslin

Inspecting Citizenship: what are the inspectors looking for?

The previous chapter considered the role of assessment in measuring and supporting students' progression and performance in Citizenship learning. Another approach, of course, is to look at the institution's performance. As with assessment, inspecting Citizenship gives rise to a similar ambivalence and again the concern is as much a practical as a philosophical one. The questions are multiple: What are the inspectors looking for? How do we articulate Citizenship during the inspection? What about those aspects of Citizenship provision that involve some but not all students? How well prepared are the inspectors to identify and make judgements about Citizenship? How does the new inspection framework introduced in September 2005 change all of this?

Here, the initial advice for inspectors observing the teaching of Citizenship as part of the National Curriculum remains instructive (Ofsted, 2002; Ofsted, 2003a). Following the curriculum order, the guidance emphasises that schools must provide a curriculum that covers the three elements of Citizenship. That is, schools must seek to ensure that students:

- have access to the knowledge and understanding about becoming informed citizens and are able to articulate this
- have the opportunity to develop skills of enquiry and communication and that they successfully do so
- have the opportunity to develop skills of participation and responsible action and that they successfully do so.

(DfEE, 2000)

Beyond this, though, Ofsted's early guidance on Citizenship emphasised autonomy and flexibility, underlining the need for schools to develop approaches to Citizenship appropriate to their circumstances. Thus, while the guidance clearly stated the need for the management of Citizenship to be based upon clear aims, appropriate priorities, targets for implementation and good planning as evidenced by a scheme of work and supporting documentation, there was no compulsion to achieve particular goals in specific ways. Rather, it acknowledged that different schools would have their own starting points and would, therefore, need to '. . . audit their curriculum carefully to identify existing work that can contribute to Citizenship Education . . . and act upon this information in order to ensure that the [Citizenship] requirements of the National Curriculum are met' (Ofsted, 2002). Flexibility and autonomy are, therefore, the key themes and this is, of course, a reflection of Crick itself (DfEE, 1998) and his famed 'light-touch' analysis.

Preparing for the inspection of Citizenship: flexibility and a new challenge

Some would argue that flexibility and autonomy are new territory for both the National Curriculum and for Ofsted. Certainly, there is some recognition of the fact that this is new ground for many teachers. Here, the reminder to inspectors that they should be mindful of, and sensitive to the new status of Citizenship, is worth quoting in full but it should be remembered that the currency of the statement declines with each passing year:

> ... *In most schools, where Citizenship has been newly established, there may be tentative arrangements as teachers develop, modify and refine provision. Inspection and self-evaluation should be helpful to this process. During this stage of development, in inspecting and reporting on Citizenship, allowance should be made for the emergent nature of the subject.* (Ofsted, 2002)

In this context, inspectors should judge the '... appropriateness of the school's [Citizenship] curriculum in the context of the needs of the pupils and the community'. Of course, this flexibility may in part be because Ofsted is as new to Citizenship as the schools facing inspection and this indeed correlates with the author's experience in qualifying as an Ofsted inspector[1]. Just as most Citizenship teachers are not qualified specialists (although some do have dedicated PGCE qualifications and academic backgrounds in related fields such as the social sciences), most Ofsted inspectors are not Citizenship specialists although some have undergone the optional one-day Ofsted training course in Citizenship offered to inspectors prior to the introduction of the new inspection framework in September 2005. The English inspector, the Mathematics inspector and the History inspector generally have academic and professional backgrounds in the teaching and managing of such subjects and the attendant expertise and empathy for the classroom practitioner and departmental head that flows from this. The Citizenship inspector rarely has such a background and this can have consequences for the quality of the judgements made. Even though to refer to inspectors in this subject-defined manner is arguably anachronistic in the era of the new framework, the following update to working inspectors – cited by Jerome in his excellent discussion of the connections between Citizenship Education and History teaching (Jerome, 2005) – acknowledges the risk of not having sufficient Citizenship expertise within inspection teams:

> ... *Touching on topics which are relevant to Citizenship has been accepted by some inspectors as National Curriculum Citizenship when it is not.* (Ofsted, 2003b: update 43)

As records of best practice accrue, we can expect, though, expertise to grow and a rather more directive form of 'guidance'. Certainly, the former Chief Inspector's pronouncements (Bell, 2005) and more recent Ofsted reports (Ofsted 2005a) do not carry the tentativeness of the earlier statements. Hoping to get through with a fuzzy pretence of cross-curricular practice that neither students nor teachers can identify when asked to do so is certainly not an option. Nonetheless, the fact that Citizenship is still developing as a subject offers the real opportunity for teachers and individual schools to be innovative and to play a role in decreeing just what future best practice might be. The fact that Ofsted concedes that '. . . no single approach to delivery is recommended . . . no single approach to assessment is required . . . no specific time allocation is suggested' (Ofsted, 2002) is not a licence for weak practice. Rather, it is a call for *new* practice. With regard to assessment specifically, therefore, while the guidance acknowledges that '. . . schools must . . . have a system for assessing, recording and reporting pupils' achievements in Citizenship' and that '. . . good assessment in citizenship shares the same general characteristics as other subjects', any sense of a conservative or traditional approach finding favour is muted by the acknowledgement that a wide range of methods should be used '. . . if assessment is to be valid'.

And while Citizenship can no longer claim the mantle of an entirely 'new' subject, it remains, as argued by myself and several others within this collection, a new or different *type* of subject (Breslin, 2004) and one that is still in the process of developing or, perhaps redefining, the paraphernalia of what it is to be a school subject. Thus, the very strong suggestion here is that developments in the school's Citizenship programme should be staged and clearly planned rather than immediate but inappropriate and superficial. Simply re-branding an existing PSHE programme as 'Citizenship' will neither convince inspectors nor improve the quality of teaching and learning. Schools will be judged on the quality of what they are doing and the clarity of their planning for further improvement rather than solely on the impact of their earlier efforts.

Inspection, Citizenship and self-evaluation: towards rigour and clarity

The new Ofsted framework introduced in September 2005 is seen as part of a broader 'new relationship with schools' and sets out its guidance for inspectors in three relatively brief documents: *Every Child Matters*, *Using the Evaluation Schedule* and *Conducting the Inspection* (Ofsted, 2005b, Ofsted, 2005c; Ofsted, 2005d). These documents usher in a regime in which the standard inspection cycle is reduced from six to three years, in which weaker schools are visited more frequently and in which the inspection itself is shorter and sharper and assumed to be preceded by a substantial exercise in school self-evaluation that is based around a new on-line School Self Evaluation Form (SEF) completed by headteachers and their management teams and regularly updated, addressing just about every aspect of school life. This focus on the school as a whole shifts the focus away from subject based reporting towards a more holistic approach; one that promises to acknowledge Citizenship if it is sufficiently visible in the curriculum and across the life of the school but risks missing it completely where this is not the case, especially if inspectors in the new smaller teams are insufficiently trained in Citizenship and therefore inadequately attuned to seek it out.

Complemented by the introduction of School Improvement Partners as part of the National Strategies framework, this process commits the school to making judgements about its own practice that the inspectors then verify during the inspection, assessing as they do so the school's capacity to 'self improve'. In a further break with previous practice, the school is given somewhere between 48 and 72 hours notice of the inspection. Weeks and – in the initial Ofsted model – months of 'counting down' to an inspection have been replaced by the edginess of not knowing when notification of an inspection might arrive. Within this new framework, the SEF is a document that both demands a rigorous approach to assessing and recording current school practice and a statement of the school's individual character: the process of self evaluation balancing the principles of autonomy, flexibility and sensitivity with those of rigour and clarity.

Moreover, under the new arrangements the standard inspection visit itself has been reduced from four days to two days, a time frame that will mean that inspectors will want to see that statutory requirements (including those relating to Citizenship) are being met but within which there will be less time for the analysis of individual subjects. This arguably lighter-touch (but definitely not *soft-touch*) approach to whole-school inspection is complemented by a programme of subject inspections – additional visits to schools focused around the more detailed analysis of practice in particular subjects including Citizenship. Where the school visited as part of a subject inspection does not teach Citizenship as a discrete subject, it will need to clearly identify where Citizenship learning is taking place. Underlining the sort of explicit approach to branding Citizenship practice advocated throughout this collection, Huddleston and Kerr put it thus:

> *Where a lesson in another subject is included in your school's citizenship provision, the citizenship content is examined and reported on as though it were a discrete citizenship lesson. Citizenship content should be made explicit to students and citizenship learning objectives included in the lesson plan and assessed separately. The same applies where citizenship is taught through other activities, for example, special events, tutorial/pastoral programmes.* (Huddleston and Kerr, 2006: p.139)

These changes in the broader Ofsted framework, then, have a particular pertinence to Citizenship. Three points are especially notable. First, the reduced time given to classroom observation (and the move away from subject based reporting) in the new arrangements may advantage those subjects that complement classroom teaching with other school-wide learning activities and here Citizenship has a clear advantage, provided these activities are seen as a part of Citizenship learning. Second, the framing of the new arrangements around the principles of *Every Child Matters* and, indeed, the adoption of this wording as the title for the new framework suggests a convergence between school inspection and key Citizenship themes (Brett, 2005). Third, the broader direction of inspection practice seems to be following a trend that practice in Citizenship has done much to shape. What had begun to emerge as the methodology for both teaching and inspecting Citizenship has become the methodology for inspection itself. What some (or at least some successful schools) will see as a 'lighter touch' approach – Crick's term for the autonomy and flexibility within the Citizenship curriculum – to inspection now informs Ofsted's approach to schools and self-evaluation sits at its core.

In this respect, schools would be wise to make use of another important addition to the Citizenship literature, *The School Self-Evaluation Tool for Citizenship Education* (QCA/NCSL/ACT, 2004). Published through a partnership of the Qualifications and Curriculum Authority, the National College for School Leadership and the Association for Citizenship Teaching, and recently updated by Huddleston and Kerr (2006), the tool sets out a framework for evaluating practice that schools may be wise to adapt for other subjects as they seek to compile their SEF data. The self-evaluation tool sets out four stages in the development of Citizenship practice (Focusing, Developing, Established, Advanced) and suggests that any school can be at any of these stages with regard to the following areas:

1 Leadership
2 Resources and their Management
3 Teaching and Learning
4 Staff Development
5 Monitoring and Evaluation
6 Parental and Community Involvement.

Extracts from two strands of the matrix through which the self-evaluation tool is presented are set out in Figure 1. One is drawn from Leadership (Table A); the other from Parental and Community Involvement (Table B).

Figure 1

Extracts from the self-evaluation tool for Citizenship Education

Table A: Leadership

Area No.	Area Title	Focusing	Developing	Established	Advanced
1d	*Citizenship policy statement*	There is no policy statement.	There is an up to date policy statement which reflects the school's work on Citizenship.	There is a detailed policy statement which reflects the school's work, matched to the school's strategic plan.	There is a coherent policy statement reflected in current work, matched to the development plan and school aims. It is reviewed and updated regularly.

contd.

Table A: Leadership

Area No.	Area Title	Focusing	Developing	Established	Advanced
1g	*Key decision-making*	The Head or Citizenship Coordinator responds to initiatives.	The Citizenship Coordinator discusses Citizenship with the leadership team.	A Citizenship Development Group includes a member of SMT, subject teachers, other staff and governors.	There is a pro-active and inclusive leadership group which includes pupil representatives meeting regularly and driving Citizenship forward.

Table B: Parental and Community Involvement

Area No.	Area Title	Focusing	Developing	Established	Advanced
6b	*Non Government Organisations (NGOs) and agencies*	No use is made of other providers.	The school makes some use of local and national agencies as a resource.	Mapping of local community resources has been undertaken and their use is planned for in Citizenship.	Members of the community organise support and initiate activities in the school.
6d	*Keeping parents and local community informed*	Parents and community are generally unaware of the school's approach to Citizenship.	Citizenship is addressed at the governors' and parents' AGM and in school newsletters to the community.	Parents and community are kept informed through regular newsletters, the school website and through participation in Citizenship activities.	Parents and community are invited to participate in workshops on Citizenship related issues specifically for parents.

Source: QCA/NCSL/ACT (2004).

The new inspection framework demands two things: that all school activities impact on the learning of students and that schools 'know themselves' in a way that they have never had to demonstrate before. It also demands that they become skilled in making judgements about their practice. Moreover, the SEF's recurrent themes around student consultation and parental voice move practice towards the kind of 'Citizenship-rich' approach argued for throughout this collection. Indeed, this is the real gain for Citizenship from the new framework; through classroom observation inspectors will make judgements about the quality of provision in the traditional way – recording judgements about teaching, attainment, achievement and the impact on learning. Through scrutinising the school's SEF analysis they will be able to infer and have their attention drawn to much about how the school operates as a community; thus, they will be better equipped to make judgements not just about Citizenship in the classroom but, to draw on Pattison's typology (Pattison and Barnett, 2005), about the extent to which Citizenship is embedded in the culture of the school and in the school's relationships with the communities that it serves. However, schools should not rely on the SEF alone to bring good practice beyond the classroom to the attention of inspectors.

Bringing Citizenship practice to the inspectors' attention

In this context, and as has been noted elsewhere in this collection, Pattison's three-part typology (Figure 2) is vital to the delivery of good quality Citizenship Education. Clearly identified, appropriately timetabled curriculum delivery – much but by no means all of it within the classroom – must be augmented by a range of experiential learning opportunities for students through the culture of the school and through the links the school has established with its community. This experiential learning consolidates the classroom activity and gives students a real opportunity to rehearse and refine their Citizenship skills. Moreover, inspectors need to be able to identify these three strands of Citizenship learning and to *connect* them. For this reason, the school needs to make all three explicit as Citizenship activities and *connect* these, possibly through the Manifesto framework proposed in our Conclusion (Breslin, 2002; Watchorn, 2006).

Figure 2
The 'three Cs' of Citizenship
Citizenship in the Curriculum, the School's Culture and the School's Community

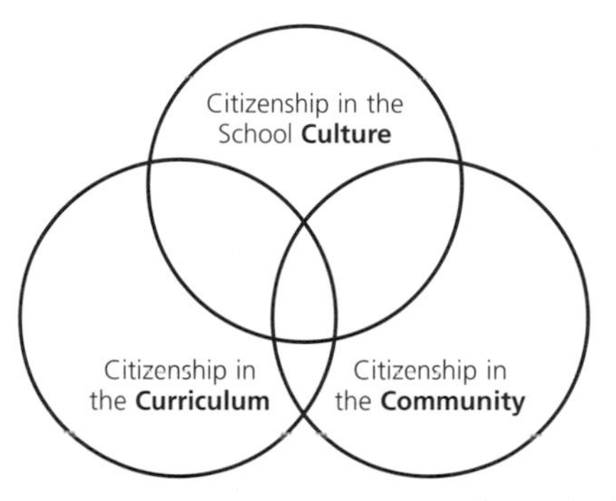

Source: Pattison and Barnett (2005).

Here, a pre-inspection audit of Education Outside the Classroom activities (Breslin, 2006), possibly steered through the SEF process, may be instructive. Two questions need to be asked: first, to what extent is the school enabling students to undertake a range of Citizenship learning experiences beyond the confines of the standard classroom? Second, to what extent do all students engage in these activities? The second point is important because inspectors are primarily interested in those activities that all students experience rather than those that engage small sub groups. Such learning experiences might include:

- participation in mock elections
- membership of the student council
- involvement in a mock trial competition team
- being part of an interview panel for staff appointments
- leading a school based group concerned with a Citizenship issue such as an Amnesty, Agenda 21 or Greenpeace group
- undertaking a social enterprise project
- participating in a charitable giving or volunteering programme
- undertaking a Community Service programme
- undertaking a community based research project
- participating in a school based 'student as researchers' programme
- being part of a debating society or competition
- writing, editing or managing a school newspaper or magazine
- taking part in off site visits to local civic institutions such as the law courts and the town hall or civic centre.

The difficulty, of course, is in responding to the second question not the first: ensuring that either all students take part in all activities (which would seem practically impossible) or, at least, that all students are exposed to a range of these experiences (practical, but difficult to map unless these 'outside the classroom' activities are part of a coherent Citizenship programme). However, there is one short cut to broadening students' experience of these activities that is missed by many schools: utilising frameworks such as student council elections and the assembly programme to expose the wider school to the learning undertaken by the activists on each project. Thus, if community service volunteers feed back their experience to other students through the assembly programme they enhance (and in Ofsted speak 'impact on') the learning of others, namely the wider group. Moreover, through such an approach the school demonstrates that it is a 'citizenship-rich' community. And, critically, it does not leave inspectors to 'find' the hidden gems of Citizenship learning; nor does it allow inspectors to write these off as the indulgences of an activist minority of often rather privileged, middle-class learners.

For the school there is another reason for taking this approach. As this text goes to press, I am involved in a drafting team preparing a national Education Outside the Classroom 'manifesto' to be published by the DfES in late 2006 or early 2007. This work, led by Andrew Adonis[2], is set to give a new prominence to learning outside the classroom and the Youth Community Action programme being developed by David Cameron's team[3] is a move in the same direction. The Adonis initiative, in particular, is likely to give a new prominence to non-classroom learning and to articulate this as a vital component in a broad curriculum. As with 'light touch' and 'self evaluation', Citizenship practitioners may again be among the first to get there, modelling best practice in 'Education Outside the Classroom' (EOTC). Perhaps Citizenship is not so much a 'new *type* of subject' as Barry Dufour and I claim elsewhere in these pages but a model for the future of subject learning in other areas: experiential as well as taught; beyond and within the classroom; delivered through discrete timetable slots and through carrier subjects. Certainly, the new Ofsted framework is much less subject driven; most current inspectors though have a life-time of professional experience built within subject 'silos', defined by single conventional disciplines, delivered through standardised timetables. Identifying and connecting the Citizenship learning that goes on through the culture of the school and through the school's relationship with its community is vital if Citizenship practitioners are to get predominantly non-Citizenship trained inspectors to, literally, 'think outside the (timetable) box'.

Inspecting Citizenship: another burden or a helpful lever?

A developing curriculum subject, especially one that will *need* to be delivered through a variety of conduits and assessed through a variety of mechanisms, deserves such development time. A 'subject' that seeks to educate for social and moral responsibility and develop political literacy while building an ethos of whole school community involvement requires it. Those who abuse this development time or fail to use it may, though, be in for a rude awakening. Autonomy, flexibility and gradualism may constitute a 'light touch' from Ofsted, possibly one inconceivable under one previous Chief Inspector, but, as already stated, a *soft touch* they are not. Schools inspected early in the life of National Curriculum Citizenship may not be hung for failing to have every detail in place; they will if they cannot demonstrate that they are making solid, cautious, thoughtful and purposeful progress towards this goal. Citizenship Coordinators seeking to gain the leverage that they will need to make a success of their responsibility across the school as a whole would do well to remind heads, managers and colleagues of this.

REFERENCES

Bell, D. (2005) *Citizenship through participation and responsible action*, speech for *CSV-Barclays New Futures* conference; 15 November 2005. London: Ofsted.

Breslin, T. (2002) 'A Citizenship Manifesto for Every School', *Teaching Citizenship,* (Issue 2), Spring 2002. London: Association for Citizenship Teaching.

Breslin, T. (2004) 'New Subject: New Type of Subject', *Teaching Citizenship,* (Issue 8), Spring 2004. London: Association for Citizenship Teaching.

Breslin (2006) *Education Outside the Classroom – Citizenship and Volunteering Sector Working Group: Needs, Challenges and Opportunities: Initial feedback on the development of an EOTC Manifesto*, Internal discussion and briefing paper. London: Citizenship Foundation.

Brett, P. (2005) available at www.citized.info

DfEE (1998) *Education for Citizenship and the Teaching of Democracy in Schools*. London: QCA.

DfEE (2000) *The National Curriculum for England: Citizenship*. London: QCA.

Huddleston, T. and Kerr, D. (2006) *Making Sense of Citizenship: a continuing professional development handbook*. London: Hodder Murray/Citizenship Foundation.

Jerome, L. (2005) 'History and Citizenship: getting the balance right', *Teaching Citizenship* (Issue 12). London: Association for Citizenship Teaching.

Ofsted (2002) *Citizenship 11–16: guidance for inspectors*. London: Ofsted.

Ofsted (2003a) *National Curriculum Citizenship: Planning and Implementation*. London: Ofsted.

Ofsted (2003b) *Update 43* available at www.ofsted.gov.uk

Ofsted (2005a) *Citizenship in secondary schools: evidence from Ofsted inspections (2003/04)*. London: Ofsted.

Ofsted (2005b) *Every Child Matters: framework for the inspection of schools in England from September 2005*. London: Ofsted.
Ofsted (2005c) *Conducting the Inspection: guidance for inspectors of schools*. London: Ofsted.
Ofsted (2005d) *Using the Evaluation Schedule: guidance for inspectors of schools*. London: Ofsted.
Pattison, P. and Barnett, A. (2005) 'A School for Citizenship', *Teaching Citizenship* (Issue 10). London: Association for Citizenship Teaching.
QCA/NCSL/ACT (2004) *The School Self-Evaluation Tool for Citizenship Education*. London: QCA.
Watchorn, E. (2005) *Citizenship Manifesto Project Briefing Papers*. London: Citizenship Foundation.

NOTES

1 As part of the training to become an Ofsted inspector, prospective inspectors shadow an inspection team in a school. The observations offered here are derived from my own experience shadowing an Ofsted team, early in 2003. No member of the team had undergone the optional training course on Citizenship offered by Ofsted and none had a subject background in Citizenship or more broadly the social sciences. The school had not 'helped' the inspectors by failing to 'brand' a range of participation and community activities within a Citizenship framework.

2 In early 2005 the DfES, in a move designed to give status to non-classroom learning, announced that it intended to produce an 'Education Outside the Classroom' manifesto and brought together a range of practitioners from diverse areas to pull this manifesto together, organising them in a range of thematic working groups reporting directly to Education Minister Andrew Adonis. I lead the Citizenship and Volunteering Working Group. Adonis is also the minister responsible for Citizenship Education. This work is ongoing at the time of publication.

3 In early 2006 David Cameron, the Conservative Party leader, staged an invitational seminar in which I participated involving 25 voluntary sector leaders, three members of his shadow cabinet and a range of policy advisers. Cameron asked those present to explore his proposal for a community involvement programme provisionally titled the 'National School Leavers' Programme'. By the close of the three-hour event the concept had evolved into 'Youth-Community Action.' Organisations represented included the Citizenship Foundation and Community Service Volunteers.

CONCLUSION

PULLING IT ALL TOGETHER: EFFECTIVE CITIZENSHIP EDUCATION AS A REALITY IN THE SECONDARY SCHOOL

The Way Forward: Building the Citizenship-Rich School

Tony Breslin and Barry Dufour

So, what do we mean by the 'Citizenship-rich' school?

At the outset of this book we posed the question, 'How does the Citizenship-rich school differ from that which is Citizenship-poor?' In so doing, we are building on an earlier writer's work on 'Citizenship' Schools (Alexander, 2000). Rather than simply repeat the advice of our contributors, we want to, in this closing chapter, crystalise their thoughts, recent research and our experience, into a checklist – of recommendations and questions – against which the reader might assess the extent to which any school with which they are familiar is or isn't Citizenship-rich. But first let us clarify what we mean by the term 'Citizenship-rich'.

For us the Citizenship-rich school has five defining characteristics:

1 Citizenship Education is clearly identified in the curriculum model, on the timetable, in assessment frameworks, in CPD provision and in the school's improvement and development plans.
2 It enables young people to develop their Citizenship knowledge through a skills-based and learner-centred pedagogy.
3 Citizenship learning, thus, takes place not only within designated timetable space – important as this is – but through a range of opportunities and activities, on and off the school site, that are valued by students, teachers and the wider community.
4 It encourages and facilitates the active and effective participation of all – students, teachers, parents, the wider community – in its day-to-day activities.
5 It models the principles that it teaches about in Citizenship in the way that it operates as an institution and a community and proclaims this outlook in its documentation.

But why should a school, your school or any school that you identify, seek to become Citizenship-rich? Again, there are a number of rationales but we want to summarise these in terms of the following:

1 Justice: schools seek to be just communities in which all are equally valued and given voice – a Citizenship-rich perspective can help the achievement of this aspiration.

2 Effectiveness: those schools that involve students, parents and the wider community so as to build a better understanding of the needs of each are better placed to meet these needs – a Citizenship-rich perspective places the principles of student participation, community involvement, staff development and family learning at the core of school activity.
3 Achievement: increasingly research (Hannam, 2001; Kerr et al., 2004) shows that a strong focus on these Citizenship-rich principles brings returns in terms of student performance across the curriculum.
4 Inclusion: the same principles deliver practical inclusion – the breadth of Citizenship learning is much wider than that of a conventional subject and reaches a broader range of learners including those often thought of as disaffected, disruptive or both.

In short, the Citizenship-rich school is both a successful school and a community where there is a positive and harmonious ethos that is tangible, where teaching and school organisation demonstrably reflect Citizenship values, where students contribute to the leadership and management of the school by being clearly involved in a wide range of rights, duties and responsibilities, where there is an active and vigorous school council run by students, where students feel safe and content because of the school's anti-discrimination and anti-bullying approaches, where there is a wide involvement in community action and an awareness of local, national and global concerns. It is a school in which all students achieve and feel included rather than one in which some achieve and others feel excluded (Breslin, 2004).

Definitions and rationales do not, though, of themselves lead to outcomes. In what follows we make some key practical recommendations, and pose some key questions, that individually and collectively are likely to enhance the delivery of effective Citizenship Education in the school – any school – and to, as such, render that school more Citizenship-rich. We focus for much of the remainder of this chapter on three key elements: curriculum, ethos and resources.

The Citizenship-rich curriculum: rethinking and renewing subjects

Evidence from the NFER longitudinal study (Kerr et al., 2004) led by David Kerr and discussed in Part One and from research by Whitty, Rowe and Aggleton (1994), Ofsted (2005) and CSV (2003, 2004) clearly shows that a purely cross-curricular approach is inappropriate: it lacks focus, rigour and identity. Thus, while Parts Two, Three and Four of this book provide a rich seam of potential inputs to the Citizenship Curriculum, and PSHE and Religious Education are treated separately in Part Six, the message of the book as a whole is emphatically not to simply deliver Citizenship as a scattering across the existing timetable: everywhere is nowhere (Breslin, 2003) or to bundle it into a hastily re-branded PSHE programme.

Rather, the invitation is to strategically 'pick 'n mix' from a *limited* number of 'partner' or 'carrier' subjects and to combine these inputs with a clear

Citizenship core. At risk of upsetting some of our co-authors, we might distinguish the subjects addressed in earlier chapters into four groups:

- natural partners for Citizenship, notably PSHE, RE, English and the humanities
- other established subjects, such as Mathematics and Science, where the connection might not initially appear obvious or might be limited but quite specific
- often 'forgotten' subjects, notably those drawn from the social sciences (such as Sociology and Politics), to which the 1990s National Curriculum was not kind but which often offer a real legacy for Citizenship, both in their treatment of controversial issues and in the teaching specialisms (and specialists) that they offer
- newer 'areas', especially those members of the new family of subjects (Dufour, 1982, 1990; Breslin, 2004) such as Political Literacy (as opposed to 'Politics'), Personal Finance Education, emotional literacy, Work-Related Learning and Built Environment Education.

In this context, our recommendations are fivefold:

1. Establish some form of explicit core Citizenship programme, either discretely or in a carefully combined arrangement with PSHE or RE as set out in Part Six of this book, and work with a small number of identified carrier subjects in a 'core-plus-carrier' (CPC) framework.
2. By all means prioritise the 'natural' partners as potential 'carrier subjects', or as a source for members of staff who might have something to offer a Citizenship team (e.g. the humanities, English, RE), but do not ignore other subjects (e.g. Science, Design and Technology, Business Studies), or those that are commonly forgotten by curriculum planners (e.g. Sociology, Economics, Politics) and those colleagues that might have once taught these, or those who have expertise in some of the newer areas (e.g. Work-Related Learning, vocational education, Enterprise).
3. Ensure that those teaching carrier subjects have the opportunity to work with the Citizenship Coordinator and team to develop joint modules that deliver the objectives of both subjects – Citizenship and English for instance – rather than one at the expense of the other.
4. Ensure that Citizenship learning is assessed and/or accredited with as much rigour and regularity as any other subject, but not necessarily in the same way.
5. Think of other subjects and specialists not just in terms of their input to that part of the Citizenship programme that sits on the timetable but in terms of other Citizenship activities: mock elections and trials, integrated days, school surveys and so on.

In this way, Citizenship can renew rather than burden other subjects while Citizenship's status as both a *new*, and a new *type* of, subject (Breslin, 2004) is maintained.

Building a Citizenship-rich ethos: leadership, management and coordination

As Graham Morris makes clear in Chapter 6.1, strong clear leadership – from the top and throughout the school's organisational structure – is vital if a Citizenship-rich ethos is to be established.

Here, it is useful to think of leadership as involving those individuals and activities that are concerned with policy development and strategic direction: the Head or Principal, the senior leadership team, 'middle leaders' (NCSL, 2003; Breslin and Hammond, 2002) or heads of Key Stage, faculty, department, year or unit and, of course, designated Citizenship Coordinators. All of these post holders have or should have leadership roles: setting the tone, developing and promoting policy, motivating and encouraging colleagues, opening up opportunities for and supporting those at the chalk-face or in the community.

Management, by comparison is about the ongoing implementation of policy. In this context it might be about facilitating the successful delivery of a module in a 'carrier' course such as English or Science, overseeing resource or staffing provision for discrete Citizenship units or programmes such as a GCSE Short Course, taking responsibility for Citizenship events or activities, for instance the management of a mock election or the Student Council or taking care of the practical organisation of the Citizenship team. The principles of managing, that is being responsible for a particular aspect of the organisation's Citizenship 'offer', are no different to any other area. Clear planning, appropriate documentation, a clear understanding of policy or strategic direction, and an ability to work as part of an often dispersed team are needed and as necessary as in any other area of the curriculum or school life.

There is, though, a key distinction between managing, say, an AS course in the English department and managing a Citizenship module within the GCSE English course. The distinction is twofold: the colleague managing the Citizenship module, as set out above, is serving two sets of objectives (those for English and those for Citizenship) and he or she is working both with colleagues within the department (as their manager) and with those outside the department who also have Citizenship responsibilities (as a colleague in the Citizenship team). Here, their relationship with the Citizenship Coordinator is vital.

And by coordination, we are talking about supporting the relationship between discrete and dispersed Citizenship provision and between 'classroom' and non-classroom components of the Citizenship programme. Here, the typology developed by David Kerr and the NFER team (Kerr et. al, 2004) is very useful in judging where a school might be 'at' in the development of its Citizenship provision. Kerr and his colleagues refer to schools as 'progressing', 'focused', 'implicit' or 'minimalist'. The progressing school delivers strong curriculum provision and a range of opportunities for active student and community engagement – it both *teaches* and *lives* Citizenship. The focused school has strong curricular provision but the active, experiential learning opportunities provided by strong student participation and community links are largely absent. The implicit school *does* much Citizenship but does not offer a clear taught programme or pull this active citizenship activity into an explicitly branded Citizenship frame. Finally, the minimalist school has poor (or no) curriculum provision and offers insufficient experiences for students to learn and develop as active citizens. It is a mark of progress that only a quarter of schools remain in this final group as we go to press in spring 2006. But it is also a mark of how much there is still to do. Indeed, this variation in the quality of provision from 'progressing' to 'minimalist' (or more bluntly from exceptional to poor) underlines the need for a National Strategy for Teaching and Learning in Citizenship (Citizenship Foundation, 2006) if we are to address the areas of deficit and make current 'best practice' the norm. If school leaders and managers are to give Citizenship the support it needs, they must be clear about just how strong a political priority Citizenship Education remains, about the needs of Citizenship practitioners on the ground, about the value of investing in Citizenship in their schools for the long term and about where the starting points for improving practice might be.

In this context, there is a particular need to ensure a clear fit between Citizenship and that for other aspects of the social and values curriculum – notably PSHE and RE – and integrating the curricular and non- or extra-curricular dimensions of Citizenship – those aspects that are more about the school or college as a community and in the community and which do not necessarily take the form of conventional classroom delivery. The role of, and the level of support for, the Citizenship Coordinator is, therefore, vital. The Coordinator needs to have a direct line to the senior leadership team (if, indeed, they are not a member of it), status among other 'middle leaders' and the potential to develop a range of skills such that, to draw on an authoritative source (Huddleston and Kerr, 2006), they are able to:

- work across different departments and faculties, often coordinating colleagues who might be formally 'above' them in the structure of the organisation
- work with a range of non-teaching colleagues who might input to the Citizenship programme, some based beyond the organisation's boundaries
- understand the way in which the priorities, themes and objectives of 'carrier' subjects might fit with the priorities, themes and objectives of Citizenship
- pull together and render coherent the range of Citizenship activities, events and lessons that make up the organisation's overall Citizenship offer.

Against this background, other senior or middle leaders will need to support the efforts of the Citizenship Coordinator by, for instance:

- making a tangible contribution to the organisation's Citizenship effort, offering 'carrier' subjects or modules and other forms of 'departmental space', opening broader organisational spaces for Citizenship activities (be these mock trials or student councils)
- celebrating Citizenship successes

- giving time on departmental or organisational agendas for the exploration of Citizenship issues and CPD
- creating spaces and time slots where Citizenship teams can be based (many Citizenship team members will be 'on-loan' from other departments)
- creating designated timetable space for specialist Citizenship provision around which cross-curricular work, carrier modules, events and activities can be hung.

And the school's planning processes must underline this support. If the curriculum and timetable is a statement of societal values – of what we value as sufficiently important to want to pass on to the next generation – the organisation's development or 'improvement' plan and the associated budget are statements of that organisation's priorities. In short, leadership enables good management and effective coordination and, in its visibility, enhances the value that is given to an ethos that is genuinely 'Citizenship-rich'. Here, then, our recommendations are that:

1 a clear conceptual distinction is made between leadership, management and coordination and that these three processes support each other in respect of the delivery of Citizenship
2 the Citizenship Coordinator has a clear line to the senior leadership team (evidenced by public support and recognition within the school's strategic planning processes and documentation) and status among middle leaders
3 an audit of staff skills is carried out prior to the appointment of the Citizenship Coordinator and the assembling of the Citizenship team in terms of the attributes set out above and that appropriate CPD interventions are made or facilitated
4 *as* a community and *in* the community the school's ethos reflects Citizenship values and curriculum objectives and that as an organisation it enables students to not simply *learn* but to *do* Citizenship.

Support for Citizenship: resources and resourcefulness

Our intention is that this text will have inspired thinking about how Citizenship Education might best be resourced and that the book itself will prove a useful resource for school leaders, Citizenship coordinators and other departmental heads. A number of other sources of support should also be considered. The following are of particular note:

- The Association for Citizenship Teaching (ACT), the subject association for Citizenship practitioners, and other subject associations in related fields such as the Association for the Teaching of the Social Sciences (ATSS) and the Politics Association (PA). The ACT journal, *Teaching Citizenship*, until recently edited by one of our contributors, Graham Morris, is a particularly rich source for all, grappling with the introduction of this new – and, again, new *type* of – subject. Annual membership of any one of these organisations amounts to the price of a couple of classroom textbooks.

- The DfES-commissioned CPD handbook, *Making Sense of Citizenship*, conceived by David Kerr at NFER and edited by Ted Huddleston at the Citizenship Foundation (Huddleston and Kerr, 2006), all of whom are contributors to this text: if our book outlines the thinking behind Citizenship and the perspectives that different practitioners bring to it – knowledge that is vital for the leader, manager and coordinator – *Making Sense of Citizenship* provides an excellent toolkit for daily practice, especially for the less confident teacher or the teacher new to the area.
- The growing network of PGCE programme providers in Citizenship, now formalised through CitizED: the CitizED website (www.citized.info), supported by the Teacher Development Agency and ACT, is an excellent source of practical assistance on many of the issues raised in these pages. (Those seeking to recruit newly qualified Citizenship specialists should note that 18 schools of education now train approximately 175 Citizenship teachers every year.)
- Ofsted: perhaps under its initial Chief Inspector, the terms 'inspection' and 'support' did not sit easily together but times have changed and Ofsted's published guidance and website (www.ofsted.gov.uk) now offers a better balance between 'stick and carrot' across subjects, including Citizenship, especially given the post-September 2005 regime which is likely to see Citizenship as not just another subject but as a statutory requirement and a vital driver at the heart of the school as an institution.
- LEA and AST support: while many LEAs have moved away from advisory support towards a narrower, more generic 'school improvement' remit (a move that we regret), a number of LEAs continue to have inspectors or advisers with a Citizenship brief. In addition, nationally there are about 60 Advanced Skills Teachers (ASTs) specialising in Citizenship. These advisers and teachers can, and do, play a key role in informing local practitioners about the latest developments and in offering guidance on good practice. Critically, they can be the conduit to the local networks that are so vital in sharing Citizenship experience expertise between schools, locally and nationally.
- Community organisations: community involvement is a key component of the Citizenship Curriculum and community activity often provides the means by which students can develop the skills central to effective Citizenship and the source for visiting speakers and so forth. Here, the school's starting point should be the myriad of relationships that are already in place – with the local police, the community relations council, the local council, the health authority, work experience providers, the business-education partnership and so forth. The Citizenship Curriculum offers a space where these bodies can get their message across and is enhanced by their (carefully planned) contribution.
- The dedicated Citizenship NGOs (non-government organisations): these bodies – such as the Citizenship Foundation, the Hansard Society, CSV Education, School Councils UK and the recently formed English School Students Association – have played a vital role in campaigning for the introduction of Citizenship to the National Curriculum and/or for a range of complementary initiatives, for instance around volunteering and student

participation. They are a rich source of expertise and publications and their websites are a good starting point.
- NGOs and corporations: the issues that confront societies, countries and the world – and the issues that bring to life the 'knowledge, skills and understanding' of National Curriculum Citizenship – are usually addressed (and contested) by local and national NGOs and, in many cases, business interests, not least the global corporations. As with the dedicated Citizenship NGOs, they offer websites and publish resources, some designed specifically to enable the teaching of the Citizenship Curriculum. For example, the areas addressed in the chapters in this book on education for a green, just and safe world (Chapters 5.2–5.4) are contested by NGOs, all of which are active as pressure groups. As such, these NGOs, and the corporate and statutory bodies that they seek to influence, see education (and educationalists) as an important constituency as they struggle to raise awareness, effect change and influence current and future generations, or as we put it in the title of this text, as a conduit for *developing* citizens. Such materials need to be used critically but they are a vital resource.

Support, then, is available, almost too much of it, one might argue, for the Citizenship Coordinator and team to manage. In the absence of the kind of National Strategy that might pull these elements together, how might this support be consolidated and turned into practical assistance? Here, we offer not a set of recommendations but a set of questions:

1. Is the Coordinator engaged with the national Citizenship networks such as the Association for Citizenship Teaching and itCitized; associated with a project of at least one of the Citizenship NGOs, for instance the Citizenship Foundation's mock trial competitions; and aware of any DfES support, notably the *Making Sense of Citizenship* handbook?
2. Is the Coordinator supported by any LEA activity and any local Citizenship ASTs and, if not, can pressure be brought, perhaps by the local headteachers' forum, on the LEA to deliver such support?
3. Is the wider school aware of the growing status of Citizenship with Ofsted, notably through the latest framework introduced in September 2005?
4. Is the school well connected with community organisations and local service providers – for instance in the business, charitable and volunteering fields – and if not how might it become so? (This is not the Citizenship Coordinator's responsibility but he or she, and the Citizenship Curriculum, can be the major beneficiary.)
5. Is the school linked with any national NGOs or charities – for example through the Giving Nation programme or other charitable projects – or with any corporate partners that might have a role to play in Citizenship provision?

No school should seek to give quick and thoughtless 'yes's' to each of these questions but ought to address them more thoughtfully and in an evaluative spirit. They offer a key route to enhanced Citizenship learning and to a position that all – students, teachers, parents, the wider community – can recognise as 'Citizenship-rich'.

Moving forward: from Citizenship manifesto to school transformation

Throughout this book our co-authors have emphasised that effective Citizenship learning is delivered through a range of channels – indeed, this is why leadership, management, curriculum coordination and resourcing is so challenging and why we argue at various points for some kind of Citizenship Manifesto (Breslin, 2002; Watchorn, 2005). As well as bringing coherence to the Citizenship offer across the domains of curriculum, community and culture (Pattison, 2005), the manifesto also provides identity, profile and a public commitment to the school's Citizenship work. The manifesto is the school's promise on Citizenship. As one of us has remarked elsewhere '. . . an organisation that does not have a strong and very public commitment to Citizenship Education is unlikely to ever achieve the description "Citizenship-rich"' (Breslin, 2005). As a concise, public-, student- and parent-friendly document, the manifesto is, in the literal sense, a framework for accountability. Thus, it is much more than the traditional (and often internal) school policy document – it both defines the school's approach to Citizenship and sets out what students will do as they progress through the Key Stages and engage with the life of the school and the wider community.

It is in this role, in contributing to how the school is structured and operates as a community and how it engages with the broader community, that Citizenship is really radical. Citizenship is not simply, as Denis Lawton notes in his preface at the start of this book and elsewhere, probably the most important educational legacy of Blairism (Lawton, 2005); it signals how the schools of tomorrow might be shaped and what their purpose might be. To return to the title of Professor Sir Bernard Crick's seminal report, 'Education *for* Citizenship and the teaching of *democracy* in schools' (DfEE/QCA, 1998), if education is not *for* Citizenship, if it is not about how to function effectively in a modern (or even rather tired) democracy, then what is it for? Citizenship is *not* simply a repetition of the 'new civics' as our colleague Don Rowe has frequently remarked; it *is* the new literacy and, as such, it provides one of the key foundations for the school of tomorrow.

REFERENCES

Alexander, T. (2000) *Citizenship Schools*. London: Campaign for Learning.

Breslin, T. (2002) 'A citizenship manifesto for every school', *Teaching Citizenship,* (Issue 2), Spring 2002. London: Association for Citizenship Teaching.

Breslin, T. and Hammond P. (2002) 'Subject manager or strategy coordinator', *Managing Schools Today*. April 2002. London: The Questions Publishing Company.

Breslin, T. (2003) 'In pursuit of coherence and identity: the concept of the citizenship manifesto', *Citizenship News* (Vol.1, No.3), Spring 2003. London: Learning and Skills Development Agency.

Breslin, T. (2003) 'Calling citizenship to account: assessment, inspection and the quest for quality', *Teaching Citizenship,* (Issue 6), Summer 2003. London: Association for Citizenship Teaching.

Breslin, T. (2004) 'Curriculum, Schooling and the Purpose of Learning: Towards a conception of schooling in an age of lifelong learning,' *Citizenship Education – A Discussion Paper*. London: New Politics Network.

Breslin, T. (2004) 'New Subject: New Type of Subject', *Teaching Citizenship,* (Issue 8), Spring 2004. London: Association for Citizenship Teaching.

Breslin, T. (2004) 'Citizenship, "Subject Building" and the Rethinking of "Subject"', *Careers Education and Citizenship: an inclusive agenda,* Occasional Paper, Canterbury Christ Church University College, Lent Term 2004. Canterbury: VT Careers Management.

Breslin, T. (2005) 'Education for citizenship: towards a new literacy for all?, *Reflect,* Volume 1, Number 2, Summer 2005. London: Institute of Education University of London.

Citizenship Foundation (2006) *Citizenship Education: current state of play and recommendations*. Memorandum of submission to the Education Select Committee. London: Citizenship Foundation.

CSV (2003) *CSV Reports On 12: Citizenship in the Curriculum One Year On*. London: Community Service Volunteers.

CSV (2004) *CSV Reports On 16: Citizenship in the Curriculum Two Years On*. London: Community Service Volunteers.

DfEE/QCA (1998) *Education for Citizenship and the Teaching of Democracy in Schools*. London: QCA.

Dufour, B. (ed.) (1982) *New Movements in the Social Sciences and Humanities*. London: Maurice Temple Smith/Gower.

Dufour, B. (ed.) (1990) *The New Social Curriculum: a guide to cross-curricular issues*. Cambridge: Cambridge University Press.

Hannam, D. (2001) *A Pilot Study to Evaluate the Impact of the Student Participation Aspects of the Citizenship Order on Standards of Education in Secondary Schools*. London: CSV (online at www.csv.org.uk/csv/hannamreport.pdf).

Huddleston, T. and Kerr, D. (2006) *Making Sense of Citizenship: a continuing professional development handbook*. London: Hodder Murray / Citizenship Foundation.

Kerr, D., Ireland, E., Lopes, J., Craig, R. with Cleaver, E. (2004) *Citizenship Education Longitudinal Study, Second Annual Report: First Longitudinal Survey – Making Citizenship Education Real*. Nottingham: DfES Publications.

Lawton, D. (2005) *Education and Labour Party Ideologies: 1900–2001 and Beyond*. London: Taylor and Francis.

NCSL (2003) *Leading from the Middle: a cross-curricular perspective*, internal briefing paper. Nottingham: National College of School Leadership.

Ofsted (2005) *Citizenship in secondary schools: evidence from Ofsted inspections (2003/04)*. London: Ofsted.

Pattison, P. and Barnett, A. (2005) 'A School for Citizenship', *Teaching Citizenship* (Issue 10). London: Association for Citizenship Teaching.

Watchorn, E. (2005) *Citizenship Manifesto Project Briefing Papers*. London: Citizenship Foundation.

Whitty, G., Rowe, D. and Aggleton, P. (1994) 'Subjects and themes in the secondary school curriculum', *Research Papers in Education*, Volume 9; Number 2.

ORGANISATIONS AND WEBSITES

General Citizenship organisations and websites:
Association for Citizenship Teaching (ACT):
www.teachingcitizenship.org.uk
The Association for the Teaching of the Social Sciences (ATSS):
www.atss.org.uk
Citizenship and Teacher Education (citizED): www.citized.info
Citizenship Foundation: www.citizenshipfoundation.org.uk
Department for Education and Skills Citizenship Team (DfES):
www.dfes.gov.uk/citizenship
Qualifications and Curriculum Authority (QCA): Citizenship:
www.qca.org.uk/citizenship

Chapter 1.1
Association for the Teaching of Psychology: www.theatp.org
Economics and Business Education Association: www.ebea.org.uk
The Geographical Association: www.geography.org.uk
The Historical Association: www.history.org.uk
The National PSE Association for Advisers, Inspectors and Consultants: www.nscopse.org.uk
Politics Association: www.politicsassociation.com
PSHE Home Page: www.teachernet.gov.uk/pshe
The Royal Anthropological Institute: www.therai.org.uk
The Scottish Association for Education in Personal, Social and Vocational Skills: www.saepsvs.org/mag.html

Chapter 1.2
National Foundation for Educational Research (NFER):
http://www.nfer.ac.uk/research-areas/citizenship/

Chapter 1.3
There are no specific organisations and websites relevant to this chapter. See general list above.

Chapter 2.1
Architecture Centre Network: 70 Cowcross Street, London EC1M 6EJ, 020 7336 7378, www.architecturecentre.net

CABE Education Foundation: The Tower Building, York Road, London SE1 7NX, 0207 960 2400, www.cabe-education.org.uk
Institute of Education: University of London, 20 Bedford Way, London, WC1H OAL, 020 7612 6000
Platform: www.platform.org.uk
The Prince's Foundation: 19-22 Charlotte Road, London EC2A 3SG, 020 7960 2400, www.princes-foundation.org
Socially Engaged Art Practice – Interrupt 2003/4: www. Interrupt-symposium.org

Chapter 2.2
There are no specific organisations and websites relevant to this chapter. See general list on page 352.

Chapter 2.3
National Association for the Teaching of English (NATE): www.nate.org.uk
Teachit resources: www.teachit.co.uk

Chapter 2.4
Geographical Association: www.geography.org.uk
United Nations: www.un.org (This site will lead to all other sites within the UN system including the Specialised Agencies. The Cyberschoolbus is that part of the UN site aimed specifically at schools and young people.)
United Nations Environment Programme: www.unep.org (The lead UN agency on sustainable development.)

Chapter 2.5
The Building Exploratory: www.buildingexploratory.org.uk
Enfield Museum Service: education@enfield-museum-service.fsnet.co.uk
Guardian Education: www.learn.co.uk/citizenship
The Historical Association: 59a Kennington Park Road, London SE11 4JH
020 7735 3901
The National Curriculum and related resources: www.nc.uk.net and www.qca.org.uk
Schools History Project: Brownberrie Lane, Horsforth, Leeds LS18 5HD
0113 283 7100, www.tasc.ac.uk/shp

Chapter 2.6
National Association of Advisers in History (NAAH): Secretary: Bruce Hardman, Email: b.hardman@bury.gov.uk
National Association of Humanities Advisers (NAHA): Secretary: Colin Adams, Email: colin.adams@camden.gov.uk

Geography Advisers and Inspectors' Network, Secretary:
Kate Russell, Email: kate.russell@staffordshire.gov.uk
Humanities Association: www.hums.org.uk
TeacherNet: www.teachernet.gov.uk

Chapter 2.7
SAPERE: www.sapere.org.uk

Chapter 3.1
Economics and Business Education Association: www.ebea.org.uk
Just Business: 38 Exchange Street, Norwich, NR2 1AX,
Telephone: 01603 610993, E-mail: *jusbiz@nead.org.uk*
Young Enterprise: www.young-enterprise.org.uk

Chapter 3.2
Galleries of Justice: www.galleriesofjustice.org.uk
Magistrates Association: www.magistratessociation.org.uk
Rizer: www.rizer.co.uk

Chapter 3.3
Centre for Citizenship Studies in Education (based at the University of Leicester School of Education):
www.le.ac.uk/education/centres/citizenship.
Media, Communications and Cultural Studies Association:
www.meccsa.org.uk

Chapter 3.4
Consumer Education: www.consumereducation.org.uk/
DfES: Personal Finance:
www.dfes.gov.uk/publications/guidanceonthelaw/fcg/
Financial Services Authority:
www.fsa.gov.uk/consumer/teaching/index.html
National Consumer Council: 20 Grosvenor Gardens,
London SW1W 0DH, 020 7730 3469,
www.ncc.org.uk/policy/education.htm
National Grid for Learning: www.ngfl.gov.uk/
Personal Finance Education Group (pfeg): Third Floor South,
Lector Court, 151 - 153 Farringdon Road, London, EC1R 3AF,
020 7833 2184, www.pfeg.org

Chapter 3.5
There are no specific organisations and websites relevant to this chapter. See general list on page 352.

Chapter 3.6
British Sociological Association (BSA): www.bsa.org.uk

Chapter 4.1
The British Educational Communications and Technology Agency (Becta) is the prime site for information on development sin ICT.
The Virtual Teacher Centre: has specific advice on ICT and Citizenship, with ideas for integrating them.

Chapter 4.2
Association for Science Education: www.ase.org.uk
DfES: Science: www.nc.uk.net/esd/teaching/science/index.htm (especially useful for exploring Education for Sustainable Development issues)
Science Across the World: www.scienceacross.org
Science Learning Centres: www.sciencelearningcentres.org.uk
Wellcome Trust: www.wellcome.ac.uk

Chapter 4.3
There are no specific organisations and websites relevant to this chapter. See general list on page 352.

Chapter 4.4
Carel Press: www.carelpress.com
Charis Centre: http://www.e-stapleford.co.uk/Charis/charis.html
Electoral Reform Society: www.electoral-reform.org.uk
Fairtrade Foundation: www.fairtrade.org.uk
New Internationalist: www.newint.org
United Nations Children's Fund: www.unicef.org
United Nations Development Programme: www.undp.org
United Nations Educational, Scientific & Cultural Org - Institute of Statistics: www.uis.unesco.org
United Nations High Commission for Refugees: www.unhcr.ch
United Nations Population Fund: www.unfpa.org

Chapter 5.1
Commission for Racial Equality: www.cre.gov.uk
Disability Rights Commission: www.drc-gb.org
Equal Opportunities Commission: www.eoc.org.uk
European Commission Against Racism and Intolerance: www.coe.int/t/E/human_rights/ecri
Runnymede Trust: www.runnymedetrust.org
Respect for All: www.qca.org.uk/ages3-14/inclusion/301.html

Chapter 5.2
Greenpeace: www.greenpeace.org
The Food Commission: www.foodcomm.org.uk
Friends of the Earth: www.foe.co.uk

National Association for Environmental Education: www.naeeuk.plus.com
Worldwide Fund for Nature: www.panda.org

Chapter 5.3
The British Museum (which has a wide range of displays on different cultures including indigenous cultures): www.thebritishmuseum.ac.uk
Development Education Association: www.dea.org.uk
The Ecologist: www.theecologist.org
Global Dimension: www.globaldimension.org.uk (This site, developed at the University of Leicester School of Education's Centre for Citizenship Studies in Education with DfES and DFID support, provides teaching resources on all aspects of global education. It is now operated by the DEA.)
The New Internationalist: www.newint.org
Oxfam: www.oxfam.org.uk
The Royal Anthropological Institute: www.therai.org.uk
Survival International: www.survival-international.org

Chapter 5.4
Amnesty International: www.amnesty.org
Beth Shalom Holocaust Memorial Centre: www.holocaustcentre.net
Campaign Against Arms Trade: www.caat.org.uk
Campaign for Nuclear Disarmament: www.cnduk.org
Centre for Peace Studies: www.brad.ac.uk/acad/peace (contains a wide range of information including video clips)
Control Arms: www.controlarms.org
Giving Nation: g-nation.co.uk
Halo Trust: www.halotrust.org
Hiroshima Peace Memorial Museum: www.pcf.city.hiroshima.jp/peacesite
Home Office website (refugees/asylum seekers): www.homeoffice.gov.uk
Human Rights Watch: www.hrw.org
Landmine Action: www.landmineaction.org
Medicins Sans Frontieres: www.msf.org
Mines Advisory Group: www.mag.org.uk
NATO: www.nato.int
Oxfam: www.oxfam.org.uk (Oxfam's new conflict resource book for teachers working with 13-16 year olds was published in 2005. It is called *Making Sense of World Conflicts* and was written by Cathy Midwinter. It provides activities and source materials for teaching within English, Citizenship and PSE and suggests teaching ideas around explorations of the origin and nature of conflict as well as strategies for conflict resolution. Oxfam also produces a major resources guide: *The Oxfam Catalogue for Schools 2006: Resources for Global Citizenship*.)
Peace Pledge Union: www.ppu.org.uk
Quaker Bookshop: www.quaker.org.uk/bookshop

The Refugee Council: www.refugeecouncil.org.uk
Save the Children: www.savethechildren.org.uk
The United Nations: www.un.org

Chapter 5.5
National Education Business Partnership Network: www.nebpn.org

Chapter 5.6
Basic Skills Team: Qualifications and Curriculum Authority, 83 Piccadilly, London, W1J 8QA, 0207 509 5555, www.qca.org.uk/keyskills
Key Skills Policy Team: Department for Education and Skills, Room E3c, Moorfoot, Sheffield, S1 4PQ, 0114 259 3542, www.dfes.gov.uk/keyskills
Key Skills Support Programme: Learning and Skills Development Agency, Regent Arcade House, 19-25 Argyll Street, London W1F 7LS, Helpline 0870 872 8081, *www.keyskillssupoort.net*

Chapter 5.7
English Secondary Students Association (ESSA): www.studentvoice.co.uk
Organising Bureau of European School Student Unions (OBESSU): www.obessu.org
School Councils UK: www.schoolcouncilsuk.org.uk

Chapter 5.8
Changemakers: www.changemakers.org.uk
CSV Education: www.csv.org.uk
Giving Nation: www.g-nation.co.uk
National Youth Agency: nya.org.uk

Chapter 5.9
Community Partners: www.communitypartners.org.uk
CSV Education: www.csv.org
DfES: The Standards Site: www.standards.dfes.gov.uk/schemes
Every Child Matters – Change for Children: www.everychildmatters.gov.uk
National Children's Bureau: www.ncb.org.uk
National Curriculum in Action (QCA): www.ncaction.org.uk
School Councils UK: www.schoolcouncilsuk.org.uk
TeacherNet: PSHE: www.teachernet.gov.uk/pshe
Wired for Health: www.wiredforhealth.gov.uk

Chapter 6.1
There are no specific organisations and websites relevant to this chapter. See general list on page 352.

Chapter 6.2

QCA: PSHE: www.qca.org.uk/pshe has information about the national frameworks for Personal, Social and Health (PSHE) Education as well as news on the latest developments for PSHE.

Chapter 6.3

Christian Aid: www.christian–aid.org.uk
Council of Europe: www.coe.int
Islamic Relief: www.islamic–relief.co.uk
Professional Council for Religious Education: www.pcfre.org.uk
RE Online: www.REonline.org.uk
RE Today: www.retoday.org.uk

Chapter 6.4–6.6

There are no specific organisations and websites relevant to these chapters. See page 352.

CONTRIBUTOR BIOGRAPHIES

John Annette is Professor of Citizenship and Lifelong Learning and Pro Vice Master for Widening Participation and Community Partnerships at Birkbeck College, University of London. He has published articles on Citizenship and service learning, community development and community leadership. A recent publication includes *Education for Democratic Citizenship* co-edited with Sir Bernard Crick and Professor Andrew Lockyer, published by Ashgate in December 2003. He is on the advisory board of the DfES *Young Volunteer Challenge* and is advising the Civil Renewal Unit of the Home Office on their *Active Citizenship and Community Leadership* adult education programme.

Tony Breslin is Chief Executive at the Citizenship Foundation, a member of the Council of the Association for Citizenship Teaching (ACT) and a Vice President and former Chair of the Association for the Teaching of the Social Sciences (ATSS). A qualified Ofsted inspector and former Chief Examiner at GCSE (Social Sciences) and Principal Examiner at A level (Sociology), he has written widely on Social Science teaching, Citizenship Education, the future of schooling and lifelong learning. Tony has taught and held middle and senior management positions at state schools in Hertfordshire and Haringey and was formerly General Adviser 14–19 and Vocational Education in the London Borough of Enfield.

Lesley Burgess is a lecturer in Art, Design and Museology in the School of Arts and Humanities at the Institute of Education, University of London. She is Subject Leader for the PGCE course in Art and Design and teaches on the MA courses and the professional development courses for gallery educators. Before moving to the Institute she taught for 15 years in London comprehensive schools. She co-edited *Learning to Teach Art & Design in the Secondary School* (2000) and *Issues in Art and Design Education* (2003), both published by Routledge Falmer.

Michael Callanan teaches English at Rickmansworth School in Hertfordshire where he is also a governor. Head of English at an Enfield school for three years, he is now attempting to write a novel very slowly. Throughout his career he has combined a love for literature with an enthusiasm for cross-curricular innovation: his MA from Goldsmith's College derives jointly from Media and Sociology as well as English; his workshops at the ATSS have focused on the use of TV fictions in the humanities classroom; he is introducing Film Studies A Level to his school this year.

Jan Campbell is Head of the Humanities and Inclusion Team at the Qualifications and Curriculum Authority (QCA). The team has responsibility for Citizenship, Personal, Social and Health Education (PSHE), Religious Education (RE), History, Geography and Physical Education (PE) as well as the areas of diversity and inclusion. After a career in teaching and LEA advisory work, she joined QCA in 2000 as Principal Officer for Citizenship and PSHE. She is a regular contributor to conferences and seminars and has published articles on PSHE, Citizenship and inclusion in a range of educational publications.

Elizabeth Cleaver is a Senior Research Officer and the Study's Project Manager. Prior to joining NFER, she worked at Portsmouth University as a Senior Lecturer in Sociology, and at Southampton University as a Research Fellow. Her current recent research and writing (with Dr Sue Heath at Southampton University) debates the interface of career choices, intimate relationships and household formation practices amongst professional young adults as they navigate the increasingly *individualised* society of the twenty-first century.

Liz Craft is Adviser for Citizenship at the Qualifications and Curriculum Authority. She leads the national development of Citizenship Education in England for curriculum, assessment and qualifications. She has developed the curriculum and qualifications for Citizenship and produced materials to support Citizenship in schools at Key Stages 1–4 including the Schemes of Work for Citizenship, guidance on assessment, and the 'Play your part' guidelines for developing post-16 Citizenship. She was previously a manager for National Curriculum review and the Project Manager for the *Advisory group on Citizenship Education and the teaching of democracy in schools* and the publication of the Crick report. She is a member of the *Ministerial Working Party for Citizenship* at the DfES and regularly contributes to conferences on Citizenship Education.

Ian Davies is based at the University of York. His previous experience includes ten years as a teacher in comprehensive schools in England. His publications include *Developing European Citizens* (1997), *Good Citizenship and Educational Provision* (1999), *Teaching the Holocaust* (2000), *Citizenship Through Secondary History* (2001) and *Key Debates in Education* (2002). He is the editor of the *International Journal of Citizenship and Teacher Education.* He has worked on Citizenship Education projects in various countries including parts of Europe, Russia, Canada and Japan.

Barry Dufour teaches a wide range of education courses at the University of Leicester School of Education, De Montfort University and Loughborough University. He is one of the UK's leading authorities on the social curriculum in schools. His main publications include *The New Social Studies* (1973) with Professor Denis Lawton, *New Movements in the Social Sciences and Humanities* (1982) and *The New Social Curriculum* (1990). He also has extensive experience in LEA advisory and inspection work and as an independent consultant to inner city schools. His other specialisms include disruptive behaviour in schools and school management. A founder member of the Association for the Teaching of the Social Sciences (ATSS), he holds several fellowships and vice presidencies with national education organisations and serves on their committees.

Jennifer Foreman is an Assistant Headteacher at Newland School for Girls, an inner-city school in Hull. She has responsibility for Citizenship across the school and is also Head of the Department of Creative and Performing Arts. She has written a book on creative arts activities for use by teachers and arts practitioners entitled *Maskwork*, published by Lutterworth Press, Cambridge, 2000.

Derry Hannam is a Visiting Fellow at the University of Sussex Centre for Educational Innovation. He was a teacher practitioner of student participation in all aspects of secondary school life for 21 years. He has advised DfES, QCA, Council of Europe, Organising Bureau of European School Student Unions, LEAs, and UK NGOs (such as the Citizenship Foundation, CSV, School Councils UK and the NSPCC) on school student participation issues. Recent work includes a pilot study for the DfES to explore associations between student participation in secondary schools and achievement, exclusion and attendance, as well as a study for QCA on ways in which students' perceptions of the curriculum can be communicated to government. He is currently leading the Citizenship Foundation/IPPR *I Was A Teenage Governor* project to develop school student participation in school governance. He has written widely and spoken in this field both in the UK and internationally.

Eleanor Ireland is a Research Officer and one of the lead researchers on the Study. She joined NFER after completing a post-graduate diploma in Social and Cultural Geography at the University of Sheffield. Prior to this she attained a degree in Sociology and Psychology, also from the University of Sheffield. She has experience of a variety of areas of research including citizenship-education, work-related learning, new applications of ICT and specialist schools. She is currently working on an evaluation of the Excellence Challenge initiative.

John Keast taught at all levels in secondary schools in England for 15 years, before going on to become adviser and inspector of RE and PSE for Cornwall LEA. He then worked for the Qualifications and Curriculum Authority (QCA) in London to advise on Religious Education and Citizenship Education in England. John is currently employed by the Department for Education and Skills, the QCA and others, as a consultant for RE, Citizenship and Intercultural Education. He also leads training sessions and is studying for a Masters degree in Christianity and Inter Religious Dialogue at the University of London.

David Kerr is a Principal Research Officer and the Study's Director. He was Professional Officer to the *Citizenship Advisory Group* chaired by Professor (now Sir) Bernard Crick. David is also leading the national evaluation of the Post-16 Citizenship pilot development projects. Previously, David was national research coordinator (England) for the 28 country IEA Civic Education Study. Currently he is a committee member of the Association for Citizenship Teaching (ACT) and on the Steering Group of the Council of Europe's Education for Democratic Citizenship (EDC) project. He has led a number of international seminars for the British Council on citizenship and human rights education.

Tony Lawson is Senior Lecturer in Education at the School of Education, University of Leicester, where he trains Sociology and Psychology teachers. He has published material on Citizenship and the Social Sciences and was a member of the Crick Committee on Post-16 Citizenship Education. He is National President of the Association for the Teaching of the Social Sciences, in which capacity he has supported various Citizenship initiatives. He has a particular interest in the impact of ICT on education, being involved in six national evaluations of ICT funded by Becta and the DfES.

Pat McNeill taught Sociology, Social Care, General Studies and access courses in further education colleges for over 20 years, during which time he was heavily involved in curriculum development, examining, and writing and publishing textbooks and other learning materials. He left teaching in 1990 to become a publisher at Collins Educational with responsibility for A level, GNVQ and key skills materials. He has been working as a freelance education, training and publishing consultant since 1995. His work covers the full range of 14–19 curriculum and qualifications in both educational and work-based settings.

Mike Moores currently teaches Sociology and Government and Politics at St Albans Girls School. Previously he taught for over 20 years in mixed schools and colleges. He is a former Principal Examiner in A-level Sociology and has written a range of materials for students of Sociology, including study guides and articles on exam skills. Mike has extensive experience of delivering INSET with teachers and lecturers and has specific interests in equal opportunity and Citizenship issues.

Kate Moorse was a History and Humanities teacher, LEA adviser and inspector, prior to moving to the Qualifications and Curriculum Authority where she now works as a member of the Curriculum Division, focusing mainly on Key Stage 3. Throughout her career, she has taken a close interest in Citizenship Education and inclusion and diversity issues. During her time as Warden of ILEA's History and Social Sciences Teachers' Centre, she oversaw the development of Political Education and in 1998 she co-initiated a national primary project linking Citizenship with History and Geography. She is currently a trustee of the Building Exploratory based in the London Borough of Hackney. She has co-authored works on curriculum planning in History and Cross-Curricular Themes in the first phase of the National Curriculum as well as a Key Stage 3 History textbook, *The Changing Role of Women*.

Graham Morris is an Associate Consultant and was formerly the Training and Advisory Support Manager at The Citizenship Foundation, where he runs and contributes to in-house and commissioned training and professional development courses and seminars, including policy development work in European new democracies and the Middle East. He was previously the headteacher of two comprehensive schools and was seconded as sometime Visiting Senior Research Fellow at the University of Sussex, devising and running leadership courses and support and mentoring activities for heads and deputy heads. He was also Founding Editor of *Teaching Citizenship*, the journal of The Association for Citizenship Teaching.

Will Ord has been a Head of RE, Deputy Head of Sixth Form, and a school governor. Until March 2004, Will is now Chair of SAPERE (the UK charity that promotes the Philosophy for Children approach to teaching and learning), and also works as an education consultant. Will is a regular speaker on the conference circuit, and has provided training to schools and institutions throughout the UK, as well as in Colombia, America and Bahrain. He is also an education author, focusing on Thinking Skills, RE, and Citizenship Education, and writes for the *TES* and other journals.

Stuart Price is Senior Lecturer in Media and Cultural Production at De Montfort University, Leicester. In 1993, he produced the first comprehensive academic textbook on Media Studies, followed by companion volumes in related fields. He writes and presents lectures and papers on realist discourse analysis, public relations and politics, representations of masculinity in film, visual sociology and studies of rhetoric and the 'war on terror'.

Linda Prince is the Interim Schools Standards Service Director in Ealing. She began life as a Geography teacher but soon moved into teaching and assessing courses with a more vocational flavour. She was a SCIP co-ordinator for Haringey EBP in the 1980s and organised the whole of the Borough's work experience for several years before becoming an LEA TVEI curriculum leader for Work-Related Activities. Linda was one of the first Ofsted inspectors to be able to inspect Vocational and Work-Related Activities. She has written several articles and given many training sessions, both for national and international colleagues on work experience and associated activities.

Mary Ratcliffe is a professor in the School of Education at the University of Southampton, where she is also Director of the Science Learning Centre South East. Her prior experience included 16 years teaching Science in comprehensive schools. She has researched and written widely about students' engagement with socio-scientific issues. Recent research projects funded by ESRC, QCA, and Wellcome Trust have focused on effective teaching and assessment of the nature, processes and practices of science.

Don Rowe is Director of Curriculum Resources at the Citizenship Foundation. Since November 2003 he has been Coordinator of the DfES National Citizenship CPD team. He has written a wide range of teaching and training materials for Citizenship in both primary and secondary schools. In particular, he has conducted research and development in the areas of moral education, law-related education, race equality and education for democracy. He has acted as international consultant to a number of projects in central Europe and is currently part of an international team developing the Citizenship curriculum in Bosnia and Herzegovina for the Council of Europe.

Deirdre Smith has served on The Humanities Association's Executive Committee since its inception, was the inaugural Chair, and is currently Secretary of the association. She has represented The Humanities Association on the Specialist

Schools Trust Humanities Expert Panel, AQA's Humanities panel, QCA subject committees for History, Geography and Citizenship, and has led QCA scrutiny exercises of Humanities and History specifications and participated in a range of syllabus reviews. She has been conference organiser for the Humanities Association for five of the 19 annual conferences and has contributed to a wide range of curriculum development and INSET across the Humanities. She was formerly Humanities Advisory Teacher in Clwyd and a member of the Executive Committee of the Association of History Teachers in Wales. She is General Inspector for Humanities for Wirral LEA and has responsibility for curriculum advice and support and monitoring of standards across the broad Humanities curriculum area including History, Geography, RE, Sociology, Social Sciences, Politics, Economics, ESD and Citizenship. She is also Key Stage 3 Strategy Manager for Wirral.

Geoff Tennant is the Secondary Mathematics PGCE tutor at the School of Education, University of Leicester. He previously taught Mathematics in comprehensive schools in Berkshire and London. He has published articles on differential classroom interactions by ethnicity and gender, and the role of the classroom assistant. He is an active member of the Mathematical Association, acting as secretary to both the Teaching Committee and also the East Midlands local branch. He is coordinating the *Beyond the Bar Chart* project on behalf of the Mathematical Association and the Association for Citizenship Teaching, which is writing, evaluating and disseminating materials on the Mathematics–Citizenship interface.

Linda Thomas is Professor of Education, Head of the School of Sport and Education and Pro-Vice-Chancellor at Brunel University. During her career as a teacher in schools and at the Institute of Education she published articles and resources on Economics and Economic Awareness. From 2001–03 she led the team that evaluated the Personal Finance Education Group's *Excellence and Access* project and her evaluation report was published in 2004.

Tony Thorpe was a teacher for fourteen years and has worked for the Citizenship Foundation since its inception. He has written a wide range of teaching materials, including the *Young Citizen's Passport*, the *Understanding Citizenship* series and *Citizenship Studies for OCR GCSE*. He has just finished working on *Inside Britain: A Guide to the British Constitution* (Hodder Murray, 2006). Tony has worked as a trainer with many organisations in the Citizenship field, including several in Eastern Europe and the former Soviet Union.

Catherine Williamson is an independent consultant involved in research and curriculum development in Art, Design and Built Environment Education. She is an Associate Tutor for the Art and Design PGCE at The Institute of Education, University of London and collaborated on Place Making. She is part-time Education Coordinator for the Architecture Centre Network and advises on Architecture Week for Arts Council England. Her recent publication *Neighbourhood Journeys*, commissioned by CABE Education, is a Key Stage 2 learning resource that introduces primary teachers to using their built environment.

Jenny Wales is Director of Education for Citizenship at the Nuffield Foundation and Chair of Examiners for Edexcel. Her publications include *Citizenship Today for GCSE*, *A Citizen's Guide to the Economy* and *Learning Citizenship: a handbook on teaching strategies*. As a consultant, she has assisted in the development of the BBC's web based secondary resources for Citizenship and written programmes of study for QCA. Her background in education includes teaching experience in schools, colleges and higher education, assessment and training.

Jayne Wright is currently working as a Regional Certification Adviser and National Assessor for the Department of Health on the PSHE Certification Programme. She also holds a part-time post as a Healthy Schools and Citizenship Consultant for Buckinghamshire County Council. As an independent consultant she provides training, writing and consultancy for schools and organisations including the Citizenship Foundation. She has also held the position of PSHE & Citizenship Adviser and Healthy Schools Programme Line Manager for Hertfordshire. She began her teaching career in Ealing, London and has since taught and coordinated the delivery of PSHCE, English, Media and Psychology, holding posts at schools in Buckinghamshire and Hillingdon. Recently she trained and qualified as an Ofsted inspector and she now also holds an MA in Education.

Nigel Zanker is Design and Technology Programme Leader for Initial Teacher Training at Loughborough University, an Ofsted Inspector for Design and Technology, ICT and Citizenship and an accredited trainer for the Marconi Electronics in School Project. Principal areas of research are pupils' technology capability in general education and new and emergent technologies in teaching and learning in design education. He has published in ICT education, Design education, and curriculum auditing. He is former editor of the Journal of the National Association for Design Education. His professional experience includes posts of responsibility in secondary schools for Science, Technology and TVEI Curriculum development, Open University PGCE Tutor; Design and Technology Subject Leader for New Opportunities Funded ICT Training Consortium.

INDEX